Teaching Korean as a F

Teaching Korean as a Foreign Language: Theories and Practices is designed for prospective and in-service Korean as a Foreign Language (KFL) teachers.

With contributions from leading experts in the field, readers will gain an understanding of the theoretical framework and practical applications of KFL education in the context of Second Language Acquisition (SLA). The eight chapters explore the history of and current issues in language education, the practicalities of being a classroom teacher, and teaching and evaluation techniques for developing language and cultural proficiency.

This comprehensive volume also includes an annotated bibliography which lists over 500 of the most recent and pertinent research articles and doctoral dissertations in the area. This bibliography will be of great service to students, teachers, and researchers in applied linguistics and second language acquisition interested in Korean language education.

Young-mee Yu Cho is Associate Professor of the Korean Language in the Department of Asian Languages and Cultures at Rutgers, The State University of New Jersey in the USA. While regularly supervising the four-level Korean program that offers Korean Major and Minor, she initiated the K-12 New Jersey Korean Teacher Certification in 2008 and developed "The Korean–English Translation/Interpreting Certificate Program" to start in Fall 2020. She is one of the five authors of the first four volumes of the definitive Korean language textbook series, *Integrated Korean* (2000–2019) adopted by more than 70 universities in North America and Oceania. A new co-authored series for heritage learners, *Integrated Korean: Accelerated 1 & Accelerated 2* will be published in 2020. As the 5th President of the American Association of Teachers of Korean (AATK) (2006–2009), she spearheaded the publication of the *National Standards for Korean Language Learning* (2012, with Korean as the 12th language in the new edition of the *National Standards for Foreign Language Education in the 21st Century*, ACTFL Publications). Her interest in curriculum development and instructional strategies resulted in the *College Korean Curriculum Inspired by National Standards for Korean* (CKC) as a special edited issue of the journal, *Korean Language in America* (2015). Besides her engagement as foreign language educator, she continues to do research on Korean phonology, morphology, and pragmatics.

Teaching Korean as a Foreign Language

Theories and Practices

Edited by Young-mee Yu Cho

Routledge
Taylor & Francis Group

LONDON AND NEW YORK

First published 2021
by Routledge
2 Park Square, Milton Park, Abingdon, Oxon OX14 4RN

and by Routledge
52 Vanderbilt Avenue, New York, NY 10017

Routledge is an imprint of the Taylor & Francis Group, an informa business

British Library Cataloguing-in-Publication Data
A catalogue record for this book is available from the British Library

Library of Congress Cataloging-in-Publication Data
Names: Cho, Young-mee Yu, editor.
Title: Teaching Korean as a foreign language: theories and practices/
edited by Young-mee Yu Cho.
Description: London; New York: Routledge, 2020. |
Includes bibliographical references and index.
Identifiers: LCCN 2020017665 (print) | LCCN 2020017666 (ebook) |
ISBN 9780367199616 (hardback) | ISBN 9780367199630 (paperback) |
ISBN 9780429244384 (ebook)
Subjects: LCSH: Korean language–Study and teaching–Foreign speakers. |
Second language acquisition–Methodology.
Classification: LCC PL907 .T44 2020 (print) | LCC PL907 (ebook) |
DDC 495.7/071–dc23
LC record available at https://lccn.loc.gov/2020017665
LC ebook record available at https://lccn.loc.gov/2020017666

ISBN: 978-0-367-19961-6 (hbk)
ISBN: 978-0-367-19963-0 (pbk)
ISBN: 978-0-429-24438-4 (ebk)

Typeset in Times New Roman
by Deanta Global Publishing Services, Chennai, India

Contents

PART II
Annotated bibliography on KFL pedagogy 195

Contributors

Lucien Brown is Senior Lecturer in Korean Studies at Monash University.

Young-mee Yu Cho is Associate Professor in the Department of Asian Languages and Cultures at Rutgers, The State University of New Jersey.

Bumyong Choi is Senior Lecturer and Director of the Korean Language Program in the Department of Russian and East Asian Languages and Cultures at Emory University.

Ho Jung Choi is Senior Lecturer and Director of the Korean Language Program in the Department of East Asian Studies at Princeton University.

Hee Chung Chun is Assistant Teaching Professor in the Department of Asian Languages and Cultures at Rutgers, The State University of New Jersey.

Ji-Young Jung is Lecturer in the Department of East Asian Languages and Cultures at Columbia University.

Hae-Young Kim is Professor of the Practice of Asian and Middle Eastern Studies at Duke University.

Hi-Sun Kim is Senior Preceptor and Director of the Korean Language Program in the Department of East Asian Languages and Civilizations at Harvard University.

Mary Shin Kim is Associate Professor in the Department of East Asian Languages and Literatures at University of Hawai'i at Manoa.

Seongyeon Ko is Assistant Professor in the Department of Classical, Middle Eastern, and Asian Languages & Cultures at Queens College, CUNY.

Ahrong Lee is Assistant Professor of Teaching Stream in the Department of Languages, Literatures and Linguistics at York University.

Hyo Sang Lee is Associate Professor in the Department of East Asian Languages and Cultures at Indiana University Bloomington.

Mee-Jeong Park is Associate Professor in the Department of East Asian Languages and Literatures at University of Hawai'i at Manoa.

Mi Yung Park is Senior Lecturer in Korean at the University of Auckland.

Sun-Young Shin is Associate Professor in the Department of Second Language Studies at Indiana University Bloomington.

Joowon Suh is Senior Lecturer and Director of the Korean Language Program in the Department of East Asian Languages and Cultures at Columbia University.

Hye-Sook Wang is Associate Professor in the Department of East Asian Studies at Brown University.

Kyung-Eun Yoon is Senior Lecturer and Coordinator of the Korean Program in the Department of Modern Languages, Linguistics, and Intercultural Communication at the University of Maryland, Baltimore County.

Preface

The past 30 years witnessed the evolution of Korean as a Foreign Language (KFL) education from a newly emerging subject to a rigorous academic discipline within foreign language learning in North America. Currently a dozen universities in North America offer KFL-specific pedagogy courses, either as upper-level undergraduate or graduate courses, and a growing number of Second Language Acquisition (SLA) courses include KFL pedagogy as part of East Asian language education or world language education. According to the MLA report, the Korean language has emerged as the fastest growing foreign language in university enrollment for the past decade. Consequently, there are over a thousand current, prospective, and in-service teachers, as well as teaching assistants, who are involved in KFL education in 114 primary/secondary schools and over 120 tertiary institutions.

In this exciting time in KFL history, the American Association of Teachers of Korean (AATK) is playing the key role of initiating collaborative projects whose results impact the whole field in positive ways. Two projects deserve special mention: the publication of the *National Standards for Korean Language Learning* (2012, 2015) and *College Korean Curriculum Inspired by National Standards for Korean* (2015). Both documents laid solid foundations by articulating a set of common KFL goals and implementing a systematic curriculum. Against this backdrop, it is apparent that the next step is to address the lack of KFL teacher training resources. In the true spirit of collaboration, 19 experts from 14 institutions in the US, Canada, and Oceania gathered at the first pedagogical workshop at Rutgers University in 2017. The participants unanimously agreed that there is an urgent need for a standard comprehensive textbook that will also serve as a reference guidebook beyond the scopes of previous studies such as Byon & Pyun (2012) and Wang (2015). This book is the result of the active two-year discussion and collaboration across the continental and oceanic divides. I am honored to be the editor of *Teaching Korean as a Foreign Language: Theories and Practices*. I hope that it will meet the needs of anyone who has an interest in acquiring knowledge, skills, and experience in teaching KFL and will be useful for curriculum developers, researchers, and school administrators involved in foreign language education and applied linguistics. The main goal of our project is to introduce the reader to the development of KFL as an independent discipline and guide through theories and applications of KFL in the proper context of second language theories and practices. In the process, we have benefited greatly from research findings in foreign language education and practices in other languages (Hadley, 2001; Long & Doughty, 2009; Everson & Xiao, 2011; Sohn, 2013; Brown & Yeon, 2015, among others).

In consideration that the volume is a textbook mainly intended for courses for prospective and in-service KFL teachers, we have determined that each chapter should articulate the scope and the focus appropriate to our readers. Our emphasis is in contextualizing KFL theories and applications and offering concrete data and examples specific to KFL. I hope that the result will be a well-balanced pedagogical reference where each chapter connects with others seamlessly to project the comprehensive landscape of our field for K–16 teachers, prospective teachers, and students who aspire to acquire knowledge, skills, and experience in teaching KFL. We hope that examination of the current status of KFL pedagogy will point to the directions in which we would like to move forward.

The book consists of two parts: the first that presents the "state of the art" treatment of key issues in eight chapters in KFL pedagogy, and the second part, the annotated bibliography (AB). We have identified the following eight key areas: (1) Second language acquisition; (2) Pedagogical approaches and practices; (3) Language in use; (4) Culture in language learning; (5) Korean as a heritage language (KHL); (6) Literacies and multiliteracies; (7) Assessment; and (8) Program building. Each chapter contextualizes the theme within foreign language research and offers concrete data and examples specific to KFL. Each chapter is written by authors who have been actively engaged in understanding theory in the field and have ample experience applying the theory in a collegiate FL setting.

We start the book with Chapter 1 which lays out a theoretical coverage of SLA theories as reflected in KFL research. It brings to the readers many important questions with regard to L2 acquisition so that they can understand the complexities of teaching and learning. Chapter 2 introduces the most widely practiced and researched topics within Communicative Language Teaching such as content-based instruction, task-based language teaching, and technology-mediated language teaching. Chapter 3 offers an overview of the interactional linguistic organizations of L1 Korean and provides pedagogical strategies for developing KFL learners' interactional competence, while Chapter 4 demonstrates the importance of integrating culture and sociolinguistic competence into the KFL classroom. Chapter 5 characterizes the linguistic characteristics, language processing issues, and the heritage language (HL) identity to facilitate HL curriculum development and classroom teaching. Chapter 6 reviews literacy research in foreign language education and introduces newly emerging applications of multiliteracies and multimodalities in KFL. Chapter 7 reviews vital issues in language assessment and provides concrete examples of test development and validation for different types of Korean language assessment. Finally, Chapter 8 provides a history of KFL as an academic discipline in the context of program building, curricular development, and professional training. Moreover, each chapter seamlessly connects with the others to serve as a well-balanced teaching tool.

The Annotated Bibliography (AB) is a synthesis of both quantitative and qualitative methods based on a database of 500 entries from 31 peer-reviewed journals published in North America and South Korea between 1995 and 2019. AB is organically related to the first part of the book in the identification of research references and select annotations. It is of special importance to KFL education now that the field has reached a point of serious disciplinary assessment for future development. However, the relationship between the chapters and the corresponding AB references is not one-to-one. AB is not a mere extended list of references on the content of the chapter. Rather, the list of references under each category and the annotations on a number of studies are constructed to illustrate actual publications on that topic and, as such, are not meant merely to augment the contents of each chapter. When what the author(s) deem important to the topic diverges from the reality of research, the correspondence between the chapter and the AB is much looser. The result is a topography of the current landscape of the entire field that reveals a number of significant trends in the types of research. For instance, one of the most pronounced developments is a shift of emphasis from top-down teacher-oriented research on pedagogical practices to learner language, processing, and bilingualism, including ever-increasing interests in KHL. In addition, an in-depth qualitative analysis within each category reveals interesting patterns. Earlier KHL research centers on unique psycholinguistic processes of KHL learners, distinct from KFL acquisition by non-heritage learners. On the other hand, an increasing number of studies in later periods tend to integrate KHL learners as part of the FL/SL teaching community. In addition, KFL studies have begun to see the usefulness and validity of digital tools of communication and to address the needs of students known as digital natives with pedagogical interventions. Standards-based teaching and proficiency-based assessment are also emerging topics.

In closing, I owe special thanks and appreciation to every one of the participants who, from the first two workshops at Rutgers in 2017 and 2018 to the final meeting at Harvard in March 2019, shared their broad and diverse experiences in KFL pedagogy and identified eight essential areas in KFL instruction upon careful examination of the current status. In the true spirit of collaboration, each author volunteered to write or co-write a chapter in which they believe they will be contributing most. In designing this textbook, I was also able to draw from my own experiences of teaching KFL pedagogy over the past 12 years. At Rutgers University, we offer two KFL-specific pedagogy courses for upper-level undergraduates, MA students, and New Jersey State Korean teacher certification candidates: (1) "Teaching Korean as a Foreign Language: Theories and Applications" and (2) "Advanced Topics in the Korean Language and Linguistics." I get constantly reminded of the Confucian adage that says the best way to learn is by teaching others. Lastly, I would like to acknowledge the contributions my students have unwittingly made in my conception of KFL theories and practices. Lastly, I would like to express my sincere thanks to the Seoul Metropolitan Library for giving permission to use the photo of Seoul Treasure Den for Books on the cover of this book.

Young-mee Yu Cho

References

Brown, Lucien, & Yeon, Jaehoon. (2015). *The handbook of Korean linguistics*. Chichester, UK: Wiley-Blackwell.

Byon, Andrew, & Pyun, Danielle. (2012). *Teaching and learning Korean as a foreign language*. Columbus, OH: National East Asian Languages Resource Center, The Ohio State University.

College Korean Curriculum Inspired by National Standards for Korean. (2015). *Korean Language in America*, *19*(2), 149–460.

Everson, Michael, & Xiao, Yun. (2011). *Teaching Chinese as a foreign language*. Boston, MA: Cheng & Tsui.

Hadley, Alice Omaggio. (2001). *Teaching language in context*. Boston, MA: Heinle & Heinle.

Long, Michael, & Doughty, Catherine. (2009). *The handbook of language teaching*. Malden, MA: Wiley-Blackwell.

Sohn, Ho-min. (2013). *Topics in Korean language and linguistics*. Seoul: Korea University Press.

The American Association of Teachers of Korea. *Standards for Korean language learning*. (2012). [Revised as *World-Readiness Standards for Learning Languages* (2015).] National Standards Collaborative Board. ACTFL. (2015). *World-readiness standards for learning languages*. ACTFL. Retrieved from https://www.actfl.org/publications/all/world-readiness-standards-learning-languages on July 18, 2018.

Wang, H.-S. (2015). *The history and evolution of Korean language education in U.S. colleges and universities*. Seoul: Korea University Press.

Part I
Key issues in KFL pedagogy

1 Second language acquisition and its implications for teaching Korean

Hae-Young Kim

1.1 Introduction

Language teachers are faced with making complex and consequential decisions at various phases in teaching, from lesson planning to classroom teaching, homework grading, assessments, and so on. For example, should a particular grammatical feature be introduced? If so, when, and how? How could the texts be adjusted to the students' level of knowledge? Should the original text be simplified or left intact and supplemented with a glossary and a grammatical explanation? Should the contextual or background information be provided rather than helping with difficult language structure and vocabulary? How could students be incentivized to talk more or produce more spoken language? Does a mixed-level class or grouping have an advantage over a homogeneous one? At what point should accuracy be prioritized over fluency? Which or what kinds of errors should be taken seriously and corrected, and how?

A language teacher displays professionalism through their awareness, knowledge, and rationale for each choice described above. It is imperative that the field of language education and the teacher preparation program equip the teacher with conceptual frameworks and guidelines for discovering and navigating a variety of possibilities of language pedagogies. The history of foreign language teaching has seen different schools and approaches become prominent and dominant and then recede, from grammar translation to audio-lingual methods to the current communicative approaches. With the rise of second language acquisition (SLA) as a field of inquiry, more systematic and rigorous research has been conducted to evaluate the effectiveness of specific approaches to and techniques for foreign language teaching.

This chapter concerns what SLA, with its theoretical frameworks and empirical evidence, could offer to language pedagogy in general and the specifics of instruction in the classroom and beyond. Let us start by clarifying what is meant by "second language" or L2. Second language comprises "any language" which is learned "sometime later than the acquisition of the first language" (Mitchell et al., 2013: p. 1). First language or languages (L1) are typically learned "from the womb up to about four years of age," and second language (L2) refers to any language learned after the L1, hence often called additional languages (Ortega, 2013: p. 5).[1] Given that L2 is a construct for distinction with L1, it should not be surprising that, in SLA literature, L2 refers to both second language and foreign language instead of making the distinction customary in discussion of language pedagogy. Different contexts of learning denoted by SL and FL, namely, whether the linguistic environment outside of the classroom is in the target language or not, are not always central in SLA research.

1.2 First and second language acquisition

SLA has drawn on the insights and methodology of Child First Language Acquisition research, as well as being broadly influenced by linguistics and psychology. In particular, early conceptualizations of second language acquisition were inspired by L1 acquisition research, such as Roger Brown's findings of the order of acquisition of English morphemes by L1 children. L2 English morpheme studies followed the suit to analyze cross-sectional data of different language groups and learners of different ages. Surprisingly, a similar, though not identical, order of morpheme acquisition was observed across the learner groups, regardless of L1 background, age, and learning environment. For one, "be" is used first as a copula ("it is cold") and then as an auxiliary in the progressive construction ("it is raining"). For another, irregular past ("went") is marked before regular past ("played") (Krashen, 1982: p. 13). These observations constituted a watershed moment in the development of SLA research.

1.2.1 Age

The introduction of L2 morpheme studies revealed an unforeseen similarity between L1 and L2 acquisition. However, differences between L1 and L2 acquisition processes, including the age of the learner, call for serious attention. L2 learning occurs later in life, whereas L1 learning begins with, or even before, birth. The conventional wisdom is that the earlier L2 learning takes place, the better. We should ask, if so, why the younger learner has the advantage? Is it a biological clock, as is commonly believed? Is an older learner's brain not as plastic as a younger learner's? Or is the issue of age a social one rather than a biological one? That is, is it because the older learner likely has lower access to target language speakers or higher anxiety about speaking and communicating in L2? Or is it not at all an issue of age? Could it instead be that L1 is so entrenched in an older learner's linguistic system that L2 development is inevitably "tainted" by L1?

Age as a biological property is a hotly debated factor in SLA in relation to the nature and level of linguistic knowledge attained and the mechanism of learning. Earlier research looking into the relationship between increasing age and knowledge of L2 found that younger learners have an advantage in phonology and morphology, but not necessarily in all levels of language such as syntax and vocabulary. More recent studies attempting to identify locations and patterns of brain activities in language processing have not yielded a definitive answer about whether the brain functions fundamentally differently for language learning in older age (Ortega, 2013).

Other environmental issues are critically associated with age. For example, children learning L1 are exposed to millions of utterances directed to them until they master the language, whereas L2 learners starting at later ages are not. It is not only a matter of quantity of exposure or amount of language input, but also of quality of exposure. It is crucial for input to be useful. That is, it is not enough to be surrounded with a vast amount of input. Novel language forms must be noticed and comprehended. L1 learning children receive input that is tailored to their needs, whereas older L2 learners are not accommodated to the same extent. Motivation for making efforts to make sense of new language also differs between L1 learning children and older L2 learners, as the necessity of learning L2 varies greatly depending on individual life circumstances for the latter group.

Age is also entangled with whether the language being learned is L1 or L2. Unlike L1 learning children, older L2 learners have a well-established knowledge of a language (i.e., their L1). Should knowledge of a language not help acquiring another language? Would it interfere with forming a correct representation of a different language? In the view of the earlier structuralist/behaviorist approach which characterized language learning as the acquisition of new habits, L1 knowledge is a set of old habits that interfere with forming new L2 habits. Later approaches have shown that L1 plays more a complex role, facilitative as well as obstructive, mediating L2 learning in different ways depending on specific linguistic features and perceived difference or similarity. While views about the exact role of L1 vary, L2 development clearly does not take place on blank slate, but in the interstice with L1. This will be discussed further in Section 1.3.2.

1.2.2 Commonality of first and second language acquisition

While admitting L2 acquisition is distinct from L1 acquisition in various ways, the commonality between L1 and L2 acquisition has received attention with respect to developmental trajectories. Based on the L2 English morpheme studies described above, Krashen (1981) proposed an influential model of second language acquisition which comprises five hypotheses: (i) the acquisition–learning distinction, (ii) the natural order, (iii) the monitor, (iv) the input, and (v) the affective filter. Acquisition, which is a subconscious process of language development through using language for communication, is distinguished from learning, which is gaining a conscious knowledge of a language. Acquisition is supposed to result in internal grammar represented in the brain which is unconsciously and automatically tapped into for real-time language use. On the other hand, explicit knowledge from conscious learning is not accessed for processing and generating utterances in real time. For example, learners often produce inaccurate forms such as 그 영화를 싫습니다, despite having "learned" the case marking and grammatical structure of emotive verbs (i.e., -가 좋다/-를 좋아하다, -가 싫다/-를 싫어하다). The second hypothesis is that acquisition of grammatical structures proceeds in a predictable order. In addition to L2 English morpheme studies demonstrating striking similarities among different groups of learners as mentioned above, developmental sequences have been identified for syntactic structures such as negation, question formation, and relative clauses in English and other languages. Korean learners, for example, produce short-form negation (e.g., 같이 안 갔다) before long-form negation (e.g., 같이 가지 않았다). They produce subject relative pronouns (e.g., 버스를 기다리는 남자) before object relative pronouns (e.g., 남자가 기다리는 버스) (Jeon and Kim, 2007). In this process, learning and conscious grammatical knowledge is seen to play only a limited role. It cannot change the natural order and can only be put to use when there is room for conscious and deliberate attention to forms, such as when editing writing or taking a written test. Hence, the third hypothesis about the monitor as the appellation and characterization of the consciously learned knowledge of grammatical rules.

Given the advantage of acquisition (of a generative linguistic system, or implicit grammatical knowledge) and the limitation of learning (of explicit grammatical knowledge) and the natural order, the process of acquiring a second language should logically simulate the process of a child's first language acquisition. The fourth hypothesis about input concerns exposure to and understanding of necessary language data: "comprehensible input" that will move the learner's internal grammar to the next stage. Comprehensible input contains both familiar and new forms, the meaning of which the learner can figure out from contextual cues and which then get incorporated into their developing internal grammar. In this conceptualization, error correction or grammar instruction has no effect on acquisition, though it might alter conscious knowledge. The fifth hypothesis, affective filter, concerns the learner's motivation, confidence, and anxiety that affect the pace and the endpoint of acquisition. By invoking psychological variables, Krashen's model attempts to explain individual differences in the outcome of L2 development, which is rarely an issue in L1 development.

Emphasizing the commonality between L1 and L2 acquisition in early SLA research has meant that the L2 instruction should provide rich language input and simulations of naturalistic language use as much as possible so that the learner can develop the system of language internally. This has lent a strong conceptual foundation to the communicative approach to language teaching that prioritizes successful use of language in real-life situations over the mastering of grammatical forms and rules for future use and application. Language immersion programs pioneered in Canada implemented this philosophy most comprehensively and consistently. In French immersion, the students are taught all school subjects in the second language, whereby the input is maximized and the interaction in the language is purposeful and authentic. With its outcome of high-level French proficiency, as well as successful learning of content subjects, the immersion program is seen as evidence of the success of, and held as a model of, communicative language teaching. At the same time, however, it was also observed that the students' French-speaking was lacking particularly in terms of grammatical accuracy.

Seen together with the rarity of "native-like" L2 speakers even after a prolonged period of L2 learning and use, the outcome of the French immersion program brings out the question of whether L2 acquisition proceeds in the same manner as L1 acquisition, and whether the premise of L2 teaching focusing on "naturalistic" acquisition is viable. More fundamental questions arise as to whether L2 acquisition follows the same trajectory of L1 acquisition and whether a different learning mechanism should be envisioned for L2 development.

1.2.3 Theoretical perspectives on second language acquisition

Since Krashen's model, diverse views about the nature of language cognition based on more extensive theoretical work and empirical grounds have been proposed (Mitchell et al., 2013; Ortega, 2013). Broadly, three main groups could be identified in contemporary theories of second language acquisition; generative linguists including proponents of Universal Grammar, cognitive psychologists subscribing to probabilistic and statistical learning, and other cognitive psychologists arguing for conscious skill acquisition (Ortega, 2007; Mitchell et al., 2013). Generative linguists put forward a modular view of language acquisition, theorizing the existence of language-specific knowledge, often called Universal Grammar, separate from other cognitive functions. The module of language-specific knowledge is highly abstract, formal, and tacit, as exemplified by grammatical principles and parameters that generativists are interested in such as wh-movements, as in "What does John think that Mary bought?" (White, 2007), and functional projections such as CP (Complementizer Phrase), IP (Inflection Phrase), and TP (Tense Phrase). Another example would be binding, that is, rules governing the interpretation of pronouns and reflexive pronouns, as in "존은 메리가 자기를/자신을 싫어한다고 생각한다" (J. Kim et al., 2009). Abstract grammatical rules like these are deemed to be inaccessible to conscious and deliberate learning but instead to be existent in the learner's cognition as an innate program, just in need of being fleshed out with a trigger from input containing an appropriate set of examples. Generativists disagree with each other, however, on the question of whether the innate linguistic knowledge is available for L2 acquisition. Some scholars believe that Universal Grammar is only available for L1, while others maintain that it is available for additional languages as well.

In contrast to this modular view of language cognition held by generative linguists, psychologists arguing for probabilistic learning maintain a view of language cognition as an integral part of general cognition, and a view of grammar as constructed from usage data, rather than innate grammar. In this view, language knowledge is constructed as a result of recognition of patterns and regularities in the input the learner frequently processes and remembers (Ellis, 2007). Frequency and repeated usage lead to the formation of neural pathways in the learner's brain. With repetition, the pathways become strengthened and will thus activate faster. At the same time, the pathways expand and become more complex with exposure to new and more varied usage. Connections between forms and meanings are also made and strengthened through frequent usage and activation. For example, the verbal suffix 어서 signals two distinct meanings, sequence (e.g., 집에 가서) and cause (e.g., 날씨가 좋아서). Through frequent usage in the input, the learner is likely to associate 어서 with the meaning of sequence first, and then after encountering usage with a different meaning, will make an additional association with the second meaning. According to this conceptualization, the L2 developmental sequence is determined by frequency, the reliability of form-meaning mapping, and salience of forms. Indeed, a meta-analysis of L2 English morpheme studies showed that these factors jointly accounted for 71% of the variance in the acquisition order (Ellis, 2007: p. 87).

Interestingly, while axiomatically diverging on the issue of modularity of language knowledge, the generativist and connectionist frameworks converge in viewing it primarily as unconscious and implicit knowledge to be either switched on by the relevant input or mapped out as a byproduct of input processing. The two conceptual frameworks do align with Krashen's distinction of acquisition and learning and downplaying of learning. In contrast, skill acquisition theorists put forward a drastically different view on this matter. Refuting the acquisition–learning distinction, they instead posit progression from learning to acquisition. Explicit knowledge is seen to interface with implicit knowledge such that through practice, conscious and deliberate learning can be converted into behaviors resembling performances putatively deriving from implicit knowledge. As the name suggests, the skill acquisition theory views language development like any other cognitive and psychomotor skills. Like other skills, language development follows progression from initial effortful behavior to eventual fluent, spontaneous, and effortless behavior (DeKeyser, 2007). Underlying the development is change of knowledge from declarative (i.e., knowledge about) to procedural (i.e., knowledge how), followed by the automatization of procedural knowledge. For example, L2 Korean learners are usually taught, and thus are aware of, grammatical case marking (topic, subject, object, and the like). However, they do not necessarily use the case markers accurately in speech until it is proceduralized and automatized. Indeed, learners' case-marking errors are more pronounced in speaking than in writing (Ahn, 2015), as speaking involves spontaneous use under time pressure, whereas writing allows for taking time for conscious rule application. According to the skill acquisition framework, "the combination of abstract rules and concrete examples is necessary to get learners past the declarative threshold into proceduralization" (DeKeyser, 2007: p. 100). That is, the explicit instruction of grammar and usage takes on an important role in language pedagogy here, unlike other perspectives.

These theoretical positions and foci have been resorted to in more recent proposals and formulations of second language pedagogy. As mentioned above, various iterations of the communicative approach prioritizing exchange of meaning and social interaction find theoretical grounds in the generativist and the probabilistic perspectives focusing on cultivating implicit knowledge in general. However, concerns over the stalling of L2 development and lack of accuracy in L2 production have led to increasing attention to the role of explicit knowledge. The following section discusses the "natural order" of acquisition or developmental sequence, which is the basis of the argument for implicit instruction. The section will then discuss the role of L1 influence that is seen as being responsible for variations in pace, and sometimes even route, of the development, which suggests room for the role of explicit instruction.

1.3 Developmental sequence and L1 influence

1.3.1 Developmental sequence

Going beyond the morpheme acquisition order, predictable paths of development have been identified for other morpho-syntactic features in second language acquisition. What is remarkable is that they are nearly identical to the paths documented in L1 acquisition and are similar across various first language backgrounds, while learners from different language backgrounds behave slightly differently within each developmental stage (see the summary in Lightbown and Spada, 2006). Well-documented examples include developmental stages of negation: (i) "no" fronting at stage 1, (ii) pre-verbal placement of uninflected "no," "not," "don't" at stage 2, (iii) use of auxiliary with "not" at stage 3, and (iv) inflection of "do" for tense and number at stage 4. Another example is accessibility hierarchy of relative clauses: (i) subject ("the girl who was sick"), (ii) direct object ("the story that I read"), (iii) indirect object ("the man who Susan gave the present to"), (iv) object of preposition ("the book that John was talking about"), (v) possessive ("the woman whose father is visiting"), and (vi) object of comparison ("the person that Susan is taller than").

Let us take a look at findings about developmental sequences in L2 Korean, focusing on confluences between L1 and L2 acquisition irrespective of the learner's language backgrounds. H. Park's (2010) study of naturalistic L1 Chinese learners found the order of the appearance of sentence-enders went from all purpose어/어요, to 지/지요 and 잖아/잖아요, and then to 는데/는데요 and finally to 거든/거든요. Not only do L1 Korean children acquire all purpose 어 first, and then use 지 (Choi, 2015), this sequence reflects the progress from the more straightforward to the more subtle modal meanings. The same order is likely to be observed in learners of other L1 backgrounds, although the sequence and speed of learning could also be influenced by the modal meanings available in the learner's L1.

En route to the final stage of development, L2 learners produce transitional forms or interlanguage forms that have internal consistency and systematicity. A longitudinal study of case marking (Brown and Iwasaki, 2013) showed developmental patterns common among the learners of different L1 backgrounds in English and Japanese. Regardless of their L1, the learners produced overgeneralization of 을/를in replacement of other postpositions (e.g., 어제 미나가 앤디를 영화를 봤어요. 누구를 (누구와) 먹어요?). Also, both groups of learners merged stative locative 에 with dynamic locative에서 (e.g., 집에서 학생이 있어요 or 커피집에 홍차를 마셔요). It is noticeable that L1 Japanese learners produced the same errors as L1 English learners, despite that Japanese makes a similar distinction of stative and dynamic locations (*ni* versus *de*).

With regard to morphemes for adverbial subordination, slightly divergent, but largely overlapping sequences are found between a group of naturalistic L1 Chinese learners (H. Park, 2010) and a group of bilingual Korean-English speakers (H. Kim, 2018), as can be seen in Figure 1.1. In H. Park's cross-sectional data of oral production, the morphemes seemed to develop from Group 1 (condition 면, sequence 어서) to Group 2 (circumstance 는데, cause 니까, cause 어서) to Group 3 (interruption 다가, simultaneous 면서, purpose 려고, concession 어도). In Kim's cross-sectional data of written narratives, the same forms appear in the order of Group 1 (condition 면 , sequence 어서, cause 어서), to Group 2 (circumstance 는데 , simultaneous 면서, interruption 다가, cause 니까) and to Group 3 (concession 어도, purpose 려고)[2]. In both learner corpuses, the marking of condition and sequence emerges very early, whereas the morphemes to mark concession and purpose appear quite late.

1.3.2 *L1 influence*

The universal acquisition order for L2 English morphemes across learners' language backgrounds proclaimed by Krashen and his associates has been challenged with mounting evidence of L1 influence (Murakami and Alexopoulou, 2016). Nonetheless, a common acquisition order is still identifiable and observed within L1 groups. For example, L1 French and English learners acquire articles first, then progressive *–ing*, and finally possessive *'s*, while L1 Korean or Japanese learners acquire progressive *–ing* first, then possessive *'s*, and finally articles, if ever. At the same time, L1 influence is not always straightforward but depends on the nature of the morpheme, whether it marks an evident (e.g., past tense) or

	L1 Chinese learners (Park, 2010)	English dominant heritage learners (H.Kim, 2018)
Group 1	condition 면, sequence 어서	condition 면 , sequence 어서, cause 어서
Group 2	circumstance 는데, cause 니까, cause 어서	circumstance 는데 , simultaneous 면서, interruption 다가, cause 니까
Group 3	interruption 다가, simultaneous 면서, purpose 려고, concession 어도	concession 어도, purpose 려고

Figure 1.1 Developmental order of verbal suffixes (H. Park, 2010; H. Kim, 2018).

opaque (e.g., articles) concept. Also, whether the marking of a grammatical concept is obligatory or not in L1 (e.g., plurality marking is optional in Korean and Japanese) is likely to influence acquisition of the L2 form.

Slobin (1996; cited in Murakami and Alexopoulou, 2016) distinguished between language-independent concepts (e.g., plurality) and language-specific categories of thinking for speaking (e.g., definiteness, aspect, and voice), and predicted that acquisition of the latter will be more vulnerable to L1 influence. One piece of evidence is that English articles are acquired relatively early by speakers of languages such as French and Spanish which make similar distinctions of definiteness, whereas they are acquired slowly or hardly at all by speakers of languages such as Japanese and Korean that do not have a grammatical concept of definiteness. Conversely, the grammatical concept of topic and focus in topic prominent languages like Korean (i.e., 영희는 도서관에 갔어요 and 영희가 도서관에 갔어요) will be opaque to speakers of a subject-prominent language such as English. In the study of L2 Korean case marking introduced above (Brown and Iwasaki, 2013), L1 Japanese learners were observed to have a head start with delimiters, producing 은/는, 이/가, 을/를 more accurately than learners of L1 English. Japanese has delimiters (i.e., topic, subject, and object markers), whereas English does not, which suggests the influence of the learner's L1 on L2 Korean. On the other hand, little difference was observed between the two groups in accuracy of postpositions, which was expected given that English has similar grammatical markers (i.e., *to, at, with*), although as prepositions they are in a different position in relation to nouns.

In L2 acquisition of Korean case marking, it would be expected that Japanese speakers would outperform English and Chinese speakers, given that Japanese has a mostly similar morphological case marking to Korean. This hypothesis was partially supported in Ahn's (2015) study, which showed that Chinese learners demonstrated the most difficulty with accurate use of case markers, but did not find a robust statistical difference between English and Japanese learners. Other interesting observations were provided: Chinese learners tended to make errors of dropping case marking (e.g., 남자∅ 여기 살고 있어요), while English learners frequently made errors of replacement (e.g., 저는 이것이 썼어요). Meanwhile, errors almost unique to Japanese learners concerned 이/가 alternation (e.g., 1년가 다 갔어요).

Studies on the acquisition of Korean verbal suffixes (H. Park, 2010; H. Kim, 2018) also show how L1 influence might interact with L2 developmental sequence. We have seen above in Section 1.3.1 that the marking of condition (면) and sequence (어서) emerges very early, whereas the forms to mark concession (어도) and purpose (려고) appear quite late both Chinese L1 and Korean heritage English speakers. At the same time, the two groups showed some differences; temporal relations of simultaneity (면서) and interruption (다가) appear later in the L1 Chinese group than in the English group. In accounting for why Chinese speakers seemed to be slower in learning 다가 and 면서 than English speakers, it would be helpful to find out whether Chinese language marks these particular grammatical concepts, or even more importantly how it encodes temporal relations between events, grammatically or lexically.

L2 phonology may appear to be where L1 influence is most pronounced, but L1 background interacts with hierarchies of the difficulty of sounds (in terms of perception and articulation) in complex ways. Korean three-way distinctions within stops and affricates (e.g., ㄱ/ㅋ/ㄲ, ㄷ/ㅌ/ㄸ, ㅂ/ㅍ/ㅃ, ㅈ/ㅊ/ㅉ) are typologically quite unique and difficult. In comparison with a majority of languages which make a distinction in terms of voice (i.e., /k/ versus /g/), Korean makes the less common distinction of aspiration (i.e., k ㄱ versus kʰ ㅋ) and the even rarer distinction of laryngeal constriction (i.e., k ㄱ versus k' ㄲ). The common voiced/ voiceless distinction across languages is based on VOT (voice onset time: the interval between the release of closure of the articulators and the start of the vibration of the vocal tract); typically, zero or minus VOT for voiced consonants and some duration of VOT for voiceless consonants. Meanwhile, there are variations in relative lengths of VOT for voiceless consonants, in that some languages (e.g., Swedish) have "long lag" (60–100 ms) while others (e.g., French) have "short lag" (0–40 ms).

Three consonant types in Korean are supposed to have distinctive VOT ranges: shortest for tense stops (7–20 ms), medium for plain stops (51–71 ms), and longest for aspirated stops (89–125 ms) (Silva, 1992, cited in J.Y. Kim, 2005). However, it has been observed that the VOT difference between plain and aspirated stops is disappearing, particularly among speakers from the Seoul and Kyonggi areas (Silva, 2006; M.-J. Park, 2009; 권성미, 2019). Simultaneously, it is the width and tension of the glottis, not specifically VOT, that distinguishes plain and tense stops in Korean; higher tension of muscles in the vocal folds and pharynx walls and higher pressure is accompanied with making tense sounds (Cho, 2011). Furthermore, both tense and aspirated consonants induce a higher F0 in the following vowel than plain counterparts (Cho, 2011). Consequently, the consonants interact with the prosodic structure so that plain stops trigger a low initial tone for the intonation at the sentence level, whereas aspirated stops trigger a higher initial tone (Jun, 1998, cited in M.-J. Park, 2009).

The unusual tripartite consonant system involving aspiration and tenseness poses great difficulty for L2 Korean learners, as has been observed by teachers and documented in studies of learners of various L1 backgrounds (M. Kim, 2007; Lee, 2012 on L1 English; J.Y. Kim, 2005 on L1 Finnish; 권성미, 2019, review of L1 Chinese and Japanese learners). Apart from universal difficulty across the board, comparisons of English, Japanese, and Chinese learners show complex L1 phonology influence on the learning of three-way distinction of Korean consonants. English and Japanese make the usual voiced and voiceless distinction, albeit with some phonetic differences. Japanese has short lag VOT for voiceless consonants, while English has long lag VOT for voiceless consonants; rather peculiarly, even voiced consonants in English have short lag VOT. In comparison, Chinese does not distinguish voiced and voiceless consonants at all, but distinguishes plain and aspirated consonants. The Chinese distinction of aspiration is marked by short lag and long lag VOT (권성미, 2019). In short, Japanese and English share the phonemic distinction of voiced and voiceless, but phonetic qualities, VOT's, differ.

On the other hand, Chinese and English share phonetic characteristics, short and long lag VOT, for different phonemic distinctions.

On surface, Chinese phonology seems the closest to Korean, sharing a phonemic distinction of aspiration. However, Chinese speakers have not shown any noticeable advantage over English or Japanese speakers in learning the three-way distinction (see review of the research in 권성미, 2019). Rather, L1 Chinese learners showed similar patterns of learning to L1 English learners, both experiencing the most difficulty with the plain-aspirated distinction, compared to plain-tense and aspirated-tense distinctions. L1 Japanese learners, on the other hand, had the most difficulty with the plain-tense distinction, while doing better with plain-aspirated and aspirated-tense distinctions. The intrinsic difficulty of acquiring the Korean tripartite consonant system seems to preclude transfer of any partial similarity with an L1 binary consonant system.

1.3.3 Learner's perception of transferability

We have seen so far how opaqueness, intrinsic difficulty, or markedness of the structure would affect the developmental sequence, while at the same time the availability of the form and concept in L1 plays a role in the development of the L2 forms. In this process, the learner's own conscious or subconscious intuition can facilitate or abate the L1 influence. That is, the learner might think that certain L1 features can or cannot be transferred to L2. Eric Kellerman (1979) documented that the learner's willingness to apply L1 grammatical intuition to L2 showed a U-shaped pattern. In his observation of L1 Dutch learners' grammaticality judgment of L2 English transitive and intransitive verbs, elementary learners were very keen to transfer L1 patterns, intermediate learners were more conservative, and advanced learners were more willing, but not to the same extent as inexperienced learners (cited in Ortega, 2007: pp. 38–39). This phenomenon of the learner's "psychotypology," which becomes more refined as the learner's proficiency increases, seems to be particularly in evidence in the development of L2 Korean phonology with regard to ㄹ /L/.

The Korean liquid /L/ (represented as ㄹ in orthography) has two allophones, the flap [ɾ] in the syllable-initial position (e.g., 거리) and the light [l] in the syllable-final position (돌). L1 English learners seem to understand the complementary distribution of the allophones quite well, but still show difficulty producing [ɾ] and [l] in the target-like manner. They tend to replace the tap with the approximant [ɹ] and the light [l] with the dark [ɫ], indicating transfer of the English [r] and [l] sounds and mis-analysis of [ɾ] as an allophone of /t/ as in English (M.Kim, 2007). A more advanced group of L1 English learners, however, show much better performance with /ɾ/ in the syllable-initial position, while they had continued difficulty with [l] in the syllable-final position (S. Lee 2012). This suggests that once [ɾ] is reanalyzed as an allophone of /L/ in L2 Korean, L1 English learners would not experience difficulty pronouncing it any longer, while it takes a longer time to learn to pronounce light [l] in syllable-final position.

The acquisition of Korean /L/ by Chinese L1 learners shows a different trajectory. Chinese has two phonemes, /r/ and /l/ (pronounced as [ʐ] and [l] respectively), which do not occur in the syllable-final position, but only in the syllable-initial position, with the further restriction for [ʐ] with no occurrence with /i/ or /y/. A study (김부영·권성미, 2013) observed that L1 Chinese learners at high-intermediate level (who had received more than 500 hours of instruction) had great difficulty perceiving the phonetic realizations of /L/ in utterance-initial as well as utterance-final positions, with accuracy rates of 9% and 7% respectively. For pronunciation, they received the average rating of around 3 (out of 5-point scale) in both positions. Typical pronunciation errors included substitution of [ɾ] with [n] in the initial position (83%), omission of [l] (72%), or substitution with [ər] (28%) in the final position. In another study examining L1 Chinese learners' perception and production of syllable-final consonants (후지아루, 2014), pronunciation of /L/ turned out to be the most difficult of all consonants considered. In a production task with a high level of focus and monitoring, the accuracy rate of pronouncing /L/ was 69%, whereas the accuracy rates for nasals (/ŋ/, /n/, and /m/) were 70–78%, and those for stops (/t/, /k/, /p/) were 72–84%. Combining the results of these two studies, for L1 Chinese students, the syllable-initial [ɾ] tends to be perceived as /n/ rather than [ʐ], because the acoustic quality of [ɾ], being a dental obstruent, is likely to be perceived more like /n/ which shares the position and manner of articulation. Syllable-final /l/ seems to be the harder of the two, as it involves the new syllable structure (i.e., producing a syllable coda) for Chinese speakers.

A final note is that, for a better understanding of the acquisition of L2 phonemes, not only do the allophonic variations need to be considered, but also the phonological processes. For example, intervocalic voicing (e.g., 고기 [kogi], 달다 [talda], 부부 [pubu]) could cause confusion both in perception and production of the consonants. Lack of awareness or knowledge of resyllabification (e.g., 남이 [나미]) and tensification (e.g., 학교[학꾜]) pose difficulties for naturalistic learners as well as for classroom learners, leading to persistent spelling errors in one group and halting and unintelligible pronunciations in the other group. L2 pronunciation accuracy involves both segmental and suprasegmental phonology development, as individual phonemes interact with higher level phonological units, such as syllable, foot, accentual phrase, and intonational phrase (see J.Y. Kim 2005, for a more detailed discussion on this). On the other hand, comprehensibility of L2 pronunciation varies with contexts and listener backgrounds, as manifested in variability of subjective measures of pronunciation tests (Saito and Polinsky, 2019).

Extending the final observation about L2 phonology to other areas of L2 development, accuracy of a particular form, be it a tense marker or a relative pronoun, is interlocked with various other parts of lexis, morphology, and syntax. Whether isolating a particular form for instruction would have an effect on improving its accuracy is among the issues addressed in instructed SLA, which we discuss below (Section 1.4).

1.4 Instructed second language acquisition

SLA research has demonstrated what could be called an "internal syllabus," a development trajectory that is shaped by the inherent difficulty and complexity of the L2 linguistic system. At the same time, it has also been shown that L1 plays a significant role, influencing how fast and how far the learner makes progress along what appear to be pre-determined developmental stages. Questions then arise as to the role and contribution of classroom instruction in the attainment of L2 knowledge, whether it increases effectiveness and the end state. Two broad approaches exist, implicit and explicit instruction, each informed by different theoretical perspectives on SLA. Implicit instruction aims to replicate and augment the naturalistic environment in the classroom, typically in the form of input flood, interaction, and recast (Spada and Tomita, 2010). Explicit instruction, on the other hand, comprises rule explanation or guiding learners "to attend to particular forms and to try to arrive at metalinguistic generalizations on their own" (Norris & Ortega, 2000: p. 437). Theoretical bases of implicit instruction include the generativist framework that presupposes Universal Grammar for L2 and the psycholinguistic framework that espouses the model of probability-driven learning. Meanwhile, explicit instruction is espoused most notably by the skill acquisition framework that posits that linguistic knowledge or competence is developed as a result of conscious efforts and repetition of the rules and forms through proceduralization and automatization. As discussed below, however, not only skill acquisition theorists, but also proponents of the other perspectives acknowledge the benefits of, and even the need for, some degree of explicit instruction, particularly for areas of grammar where L1 creates blind spots or distortions in the process of figuring out an L2 rule or pattern.

1.4.1 Implicit instruction

Early SLA researchers who discovered remarkable similarities between L1 and L2 acquisition underlined "input" (i.e., usage instances in naturally occurring communication) as the most important and critical in the process of acquisition. The logical corollary and implication for L2 teaching therefore was to maximize the amount of exposure to, and engagement with, meaningful L2 use, in the manner it in which it happens in first language acquisition. In other words, the ideal was to make the L2 learning environment as close as possible to that of naturalistic L1 acquisition. It was believed that this would engage the learner in understanding the meaning of input and figuring out the form-meaning mapping of new usage. Abundant input would provide learners with data to work with and help them absorb the form into their developing L2 system. Based on this theory, "input flooding" was recommended for the language classroom, and priority was given to comprehension (i.e., listening and reading) over production (i.e., speaking and writing). It was assumed that production would naturally follow comprehension.

The condition for input for acquisition was that input should be "comprehensible." The challenge for instruction is then how to ensure that input is suitable for the learner (viz., not too difficult, not too easy, but just challenging enough). This question was largely left at the level of an intuitive principle in the early conceptualization. The teacher is responsible for providing the learner with a sufficient amount of comprehensible input, just above the current level of their knowledge (i.e., i + 1, in Krashen's model) to enable the acquisition of more novel language forms, or to stretch the interlanguage to the next level. The vagueness of this concept was much criticized, but it could be said that the inchoate concept was further developed and elaborated in later formulations such as "developmentally ready" based on the linguistic theory of processability (Pienemann, 2007) or "Zone of Proximal Development" following the Vygotsky's model of socio-cognitive development (Lantolf & Thorne, 2007).

The next generation of SLA scholars succeeding Krashen's Input Hypothesis put forward an Interaction Hypothesis which sees interaction as the key mechanism of how input can be made into intake or uptake for acquisition (Long, 1981; Pica et al., 1987; Gass and Varonis, 1994, cited in Mitchell et al., 2013). It is hypothesized that through the negotiation of meaning, interaction makes it possible for input to be tailored and adjusted for comprehension. That is, the L2 learner would indicate incomprehension or lack of understanding to the interlocutor, who would then modify and repeat the message for the learner to understand it better. Through a series of checking and confirming mutual understanding, the L2 learner gets comprehensible input customized to his or her level and needs as well as corrective feedback on their output from the expert interlocutor. The primary role of the L2 classroom should thus be providing learners with opportunities to practice L2 interaction which would generate a feedback loop for comprehensibility of input and grammaticality of the learner's output. The most effective way to achieve this is not teacher-led practice with the entire class, but to organize pair or small group work between students with information or opinion gap tasks which promote communication between the students in L2. Research shows that this provides maximum time for students to use L2 in classroom, as well as evidence of acquisition.

Effects of implicit instruction focusing on interaction have been investigated in research on L2 Korean development. Jeon (2004; 2007) investigated the effect of interaction on lexical learning (i.e., concrete nouns, such as 경기장 and 소방관, and action verbs, 속삭이다 and 훔치다) and morpho-syntactic learning (i.e., object relative clauses like [남자가 t먹는] 사과[3] and honorific agreement such as 할아버지께서 책을 읽으세요). Participants in the experiments performed communicative tasks such as information gap and story-telling with the experimenter. The tasks were designed to elicit the target forms, but the learner had to pay attention to meaning in order to do the tasks, such as locating or describing objects, people, or places in a picture and giving a narrative account of events. Before and after these instructional treatments of 45 minutes for each target form, the participants were tested with similar oral elicitation tasks about their knowledge of the target form three times: pre-test, immediately post-test, and delayed post-test.

The experimental groups who received the instruction made significant gains from pre- to post-tests, compared to the control group who simply took the tests without receiving any instruction. According to delayed post-tests, the gains from instructional treatments seemed to be sustained longer for morpho-syntax than for vocabulary. The study overall demonstrated that students made solid progress in L2 morpho-syntax just by engaging in interaction, without being explicitly taught about them. The conclusion to be drawn is that L2 forms are learned incidentally while the focus is on meaning. This incidental learning is the cornerstone of the implicit approach to L2 instruction.

In addition to input flood and interaction, implicit instruction includes recasts (Spada and Tomita, 2010). Recasts are corrective feedback given in the course of interaction without disruption of the flow of the talk or diversion to discussion of grammar. Recasts sound like checking or confirming the message pragmatically, rather than correction of the form. When a speaker produces an erroneous form (e.g., *Why he get divorced?*), the interlocutor repeats the utterance, but in the grammatically accurate form in rising intonation (e.g., *Why did he get divorced?*) as if checking the receipt of the message as intended. Noting the natural occurrence of this as corrective feedback, SLA researchers have been interested in whether recasts could be replicated as effective instructional treatment. The information gap tasks designed to elicit objective relative clauses in Jeon (2004) described above were adopted in Huh's (2013) study to investigate the effects of recast. It investigated two modalities of recast, interrogative and declarative. In response to errors, such as "여자 책 읽는 책에 동그라미 있어요," corrective feedback could be given in the question form, "여자가 읽는 책에요?" or in the statement form "여자가 읽는 책에" (see English glossary in the endnote).[4] Huh assumed that the interrogative form would probably be interpreted as a clarification request, not a correction, and was thus more implicit. The declarative form in a falling intonation, on the other hand, was more likely assumed to be interpreted as a correction. The hypothesis was that the more explicit declarative recast would be more effective. During the instructional treatment tasks, the learners in the declarative condition tended to follow the recast with a corrected repetition. In comparison, those in the interrogative condition were likely to just acknowledge the recast (e.g., with a "yes"). However, no significant difference in gain was found between the two conditions in the post-test. Also, both groups that received recasts did not show an advantage over the learners in the control group who just participated in the interaction without receiving any recast in either form. Performing the information gap task designed to elicit the target structure itself seemed to be beneficial for the development of the target form, the object relative clause.

1.4.2 Explicit instruction

In contrast to implicit instruction that aims for incidental learning of language through a focus on meaning and communication, explicit instruction promotes deliberate learning of the L2 system. Explicit instruction includes grammar rule explanation, L1/L2 contrasts, and metalinguistic feedback, while implicit instruction includes "neither rule presentation nor directions to attend to particular forms" (Norris & Ortega, 2000, p. 437). The theoretical perspective that is most consistent with explicit instruction is the skill acquisition theory, which assumes conscious learning and repeated practice of grammatical rules to be responsible for fluent performance in L2. The approach is essentially deductive: the rule should be taught first, followed by exemplars to be practiced in different contexts for automatization. From the perspective of the probabilistic and statistic learning theory, explicit instruction, though not primary, could be used as a supplement. Explicit feedback, grammar explanations, and practices that illuminate L2 patterns for learners with a view to "offset[ing] the effects of L1-learned attention" (Ortega, 2007: p. 242) would complement abundant, rich, and authentic input provided by implicit instruction. The generativist theory that postulates L2 acquisition as an unconscious setting of abstract principles and parameters would be least favorable toward explicit instruction. Instead, the contribution of classroom teaching should be in "recreating natural language use" while providing specific language data that conflict with the L1 parser and reveal the "relevant L2 cues" (Ortega, 2007: p. 240).

How would implicit and explicit instruction treat difficult grammatical patterns in Korean, such as the pronoun system? Korean has zero pronouns, whereas many European languages, including English, have overt pronouns. Zero pronouns refer to omission of a subject or object when the referent is retrievable from context. For example, the question, "어디 가세요?" does not specify the addressee 너 when it is obvious. Furthermore, the answer would not specify the first person either, "집에 가요." In languages such as English without zero pronouns, dropping of the contextually obvious addressee "you" would make the utterance "Where are going?" ungrammatical. Research has shown that beginning and intermediate Korean learners under-use zero pronouns and provide the overt nouns unnecessarily, thereby stripping the relatedness of utterances (Jun 2004; 2006; H-Y Kim, 2012). Proponents of implicit instruction would assume that learners would figure out Korean zero pronouns on their own eventually, as long as sufficient input and interaction is provided. Generativists who believe Universal Grammar is available for L2 would support this on the grounds of their model of the parameter resetting in the learner's mental grammar in accordance with the Korean pro-drop data. Psycholinguists subscribing to probabilistic learning are also likely to support the implicit approach. In comparison, those who advocate explicit instruction would argue that input and interaction in an instructional setting might not be adequate for the learner to figure out zero pronouns. Instead, with explicit explanation and through focused practice, the learners should be guided to become aware that an explicit noun or pronoun in every utterance may not only be redundant and awkward, but could impede communication. Skill acquisition theorists would call for such explicit instruction with a view to bringing learners' attention to the different pronoun system in Korean. Empirical studies have yet to be undertaken to test implicit or explicit instruction of zero pronouns in L2 Korean.

The theoretical debate on implicit and explicit instruction has generated a number of empirical studies to look at the effects of implicit or explicit instruction or both on development of other L2's. These studies have offered divergent results and conclusions, with some finding no effects of either an implicit or an explicit approach, while others find positive effects of one or the other. It is difficult or impossible to draw a conclusion on the issue from an individual study, as each study is limited in a variety of ways (i.e., target form, the L1–L2 distance, the learner's proficiency level, length of instruction, and so on). Norris and Ortega's (2000) study was an attempt to overcome the limitation by examining a broad range of published data with different outcomes and observations. On the basis of a meta-analysis of 45 studies published between 1980 and 1998 meeting their selection criteria, they offered a conclusion that explicit instruction was more effective than implicit instruction. This conclusion was greeted with criticisms that the observation was the artifact of the selected studies that were oriented to explicit knowledge in measurement: "overall benefits they observed for explicit instruction were a result of the fact that most of the language measures were measuring explicit knowledge" (Spada and Tomita, 2010: p. 288). Spada and Tomita (2010) conducted a new meta-analysis of 41 published studies, which included more recent ones using measures of implicit knowledge (i.e., open oral production tasks as opposed to controlled, form-focused tasks). The new meta-analysis confirmed the advantages of explicit instruction over implicit one. The effect sizes for explicit instruction were found to be consistently larger than for implicit instruction for both complex (0.84 versus 0.29) and simple (0.88 versus 0.66) grammatical features (2010: p. 282). In the meantime, it was noted that implicit instruction, even if the effect sizes were small (d = 0.29) or medium (d = 0.66), had reliably positive effects.

If we take stock of empirical studies, while both implicit and explicit instruction is beneficial for L2 development, explicit instruction has been shown to be more effective, particularly for complex grammatical features. At the same time, even if different positions are taken as to whether explicit instruction is necessary, L2 researchers share the view of language development as a process of form-meaning mapping in which intention and desire to understand and express meaning is primary and central. Regardless of theoretical orientations, the ultimate goal of L2 development is implicit knowledge that is usable in rapid and spontaneous productions, not explicit knowledge that is typically manifested as ability to describe or articulate the rules and does not necessarily lead to correct use in real-time performance. Even the most deductive approach advocating explicit instruction is still meaning- and communication-oriented in presenting grammatical rules.

1.5 Conclusion

Second language acquisition research has shown important insights into the process of L2 development, which have significant implications for L2 teaching. However, the scope of research has been largely limited to specific linguistic features, phonology, or morpho-syntax, due to the research goals being driven by theoretical models and research methodology that conform with psychometric frameworks. Consequently, the connection to, and direct relevance for, language teaching has been rather weak (Byrnes, 2019), and the concerns with the social value and educational relevance have been lacking (Ortega, 2012). Byrnes (2019) proposes that L2 development over a long span of time and reconceptualization of L2 learning in terms of the "real" educational context should be the mandate of research on instructed second language acquisition. In her proposal, curriculum emerges as the main construct, which envisions a "longitudinal" inquiry "in the sense of deliberately seeking to enhance, over long stretches, learners' meaning-making capacity" (2019: p. 526). Language teaching practitioners too would have to be mindful of the long-term goals of their learners in applying the insights of SLA research findings to their teaching.

Discussion questions

1. Review and discuss where L2 development converges with L1 development and where it diverges. Consider similarities and differences in terms of the processes of acquisition of phonology, grammar, and lexis, and the environments in which they take place.
2. In your own experience or observation of others, do you agree that younger learners have an advantage over older learners in L2 development? What are the factors that facilitate successful L2 development for older learners? What are the factors that result in lack of success for younger learners?
3. Think of a set of transitional forms (or interlanguage forms) produced by L2 Korean learners, and infer and discuss what might cause the usage that does not conform to the target norm (e.g., developmental overgeneralization, simplification, L1 influence, and so on).
   - e.g., 꽃을 예뻐요/차를 있어요/날씨를 추워요,
   - 신문 읽으는 여자/여자가 먹으는 핫독/여자가 밀어는 자전거
4. Describe the major theoretical perspectives of L2 acquisition introduced in the chapter. Which perspective are you most interested in and would like to research more, and why? Go to the source or related reading or provide more information about it.
5. Input flooding and recasts were introduced as examples of implicit instruction. Can you think of any other examples of implicit instruction (e.g., input enhancement)? Find out and describe what it does for the learner.
6. In a small group, brainstorm strategies for implicit and explicit instruction for a challenging grammatical feature for your students. Present strategies including at least one implicit and one explicit one, and provide rationale and justifications.
   - e.g., Geminate: 식우 (식구), 부렀습니다 (불렀습니다), 아주마 (아줌마), 만았어 (만났어)
   - Classifier: 몇 백 일본 비행기, 만 팔천 건물들, 백개 조그만 장소들
   - Active/passive: 내 생각이 바꼈다, 바깥에 보니 큰 건물 많이 봤다, 그 냄새하고 더러운 바닥이 안 잊어버렸습니다.

Notes

1 The L1–L2 distinction could be more complicated; for example, children in multi-lingual environments are exposed to two or three languages which might be learned simultaneously or sequentially, and the language(s) they acquire to the highest level may not necessarily be the language they were exposed to first.
2 This is a reanalysis of the data presented in Table 7 (H. Kim, 2018: p.201).
3 t stands for "trace" or a gap in the surface structure as a result of the movement of a sentence element.

4

Learner	여자 책 읽는 책에 동그라미 있어요.
Utterance	(*The circle is on the book that the woman is reading the book*)
Interrogative	여자가 읽는 책에요?
Recast	(*Is it on the book that the woman is reading?*)
Declarative Recast	여자가 읽는 책에.
	(*On the book that the woman is reading*)

Bibliography

Ahn, H. (2015). *Second language acquisition of Korean case by learners with different first languages* [PhD Dissertation]. University of Washington.

Brown, L., & Iwasaki, N. (2013). Cross-linguistic influence in the L2 acquisition of Korean case particles by Japanese-speaking and English-speaking learners: L1-L2 proximity and learner perceptions. *Electronic Journal of Foreign Language Teaching*, *10*(2), 176–195.

Byrnes, H. (2019). Affirming the context of instructed SLA: The potential of curricular thinking. *Language Teaching Research*, *23*(4), 514–532.

Cho, Y. (2011). Laryngeal contrast in Korean. In M. van Oostendorp, C.J. Ewen, E. Hume, & K. Rice (Eds.), *The Blackwell companion to phonology* (pp. 2662–2684). Malden, MA/Oxford: Wiley-Blackwell.

Choi, S. (2015). First language acquisition. In L. Brown & J. Yeon (Eds.), *The handbook of Korean linguistics* (pp. 339–354). Malden, MA: Wiley-Blackwell.

DeKeyser, R.M. (2007). Skill acquisition theory. In B. VanPatten & J. Williams (Eds.), *Theories in second language acquisition: An introduction* (pp. 97–114). Mahwah, NJ: Lawrence Erlbaum.

Ellis, N.C. (2007). The associative-cognitive CREED. In B. VanPatten & J. Williams (Eds.), *Theories in second language acquisition: An introduction* (pp. 77–96). Mahwah, NJ: Lawrence Erlbaum.

Huh, S. (2013). *Explicitness of recasts, learner responses, and L2 development of Korean relative clauses: An experimental study* [PhD Dissertation]. University of Hawaii at Manoa.

Jeon, K.S. (2004). *Interaction-driven learning: Characterizing linguistic development* [PhD Dissertation]. Washington, DC: Georgetown University Press.

Jeon, K.S. (2007). Interaction-driven L2 learning: Characterizing linguistic development. In A. Mackey (Ed.), *Conversational interaction and second language acquisition: A series of empirical studies* (pp. 379–403). Oxford: Oxford University Press.

Jeon, K.S., & Kim, H.-Y. (2007). Noun phrase accessibility hierarchy in head-internal and head-external relativization in L2 Korean. Yasuhiro Shirai (Guest Editor). *Studies in Second Language Acquisition*, *29*(2), 253–276.

Jung, Eun Hyuk. (2004). Topic and subject prominence in interlanguage development. *Language Learning, 54*(4), 713–738.

Jung, Eun Hyuk. (2006). The acquisition of spoken features in Korean as a second language. In J.J. Song (Ed.), *Frontiers of Korean language acquisition* (pp. 37–48). London: Saffron Books.

Kellerman, E. (1979). Transfer and non-transfer: Where we are now. *Studies in Second Language Acquisition, 2*(1), 37–57.

Kim, H. (2018). 재미 한국어 계승어 학습자 작문에 나타난 통사 복잡성: Syntactic complexity in the writing of Korean heritage learners in the United States. *Korean Language in America, 21*(2), 186–217.

Kim, H.-Y. (2012). Development of NP forms and discourse reference in L2 Korean. In Ho-min Sohn et al. (Guest Eds.), *Innovations in Teaching Korean: 2012 Special issue of the Korean Language in America, 17*, 211–235. The American Association of Teachers of Korean.

Kim, J., Montrul, S., & Yoon, J. (2009). Binding interpretations of anaphors by Korean heritage speakers. *Language Acquisition, 16*(1), 3–35.

Kim, J.Y. (2005). *L2 Korean phonology: The acquisition of stops by English-and Finnish-speaking adults* [PhD Dissertation]. Durham University.

Kim, M. (2007). *Aspects of Korean second language phonology* [PhD Dissertation]. The University of Wisconsin-Milwaukee.

Krashen, S.D. (1982). *Principles and practice in second language acquisition*. http://www .sdkrashen.com/content/books/principles_and_practice.pdf

Lantolf, J.P., & Thorne, S.L. (2007). Sociocultural theory and second language learning. In B. VanPatten & J. Williams (Eds.), *Theories in second language acquisition: An introduction* (pp. 201–224). Mahwah, NJ: Lawrence Erlbaum.

Lee, S. (2012). *Orthographic influence on the phonological development of L2 learners of Korean* [PhD Dissertation]. The University of Wisconsin-Milwaukee.

Lightbown, P.M., & Spada, N. (2006). *How languages are learned*, 4th ed. *Oxford handbooks for language teachers (Kindle Location 1164)*. Oxford University Press. Kindle Edition.

Mitchell, R., Marsden, E., & Myles, F. (2013). *Second language learning theories*. New York: Routledge.

Murakami, A., & Alexopoulou, T. (2016). L1 influence on the acquisition order of English grammatical morphemes: A Learner Corpus Study. *Studies in Second Language Acquisition, 38*(3), 365–401.

Norris, J., & Ortega, L. (2000). Effectiveness of L2 instruction: A research synthesis and quantitative meta-analysis. *Language Learning, 50*(3), 417–528.

O'Grady, W., & Choi, M.H. (2015). Second language acquisition: Syntax. In L. Brown & J. Yeon (Eds.), *The handbook of Korean linguistics* (pp. 355–372). Malden, MA: Wiley-Blackwell.

Ortega, L. (2007). Second language learning explained? SLA across nine contemporary theories. In B. VanPatten & J. Williams (Eds.), *Theories in second language acquisition: An introduction* (pp. 225–250). Mahwah, NJ: Lawrence Erlbaum.

Ortega, L. (2009/2013). *Understanding second language acquisition*. London and New York: Routledge.

Ortega, L. (2012). Epistemological diversity and moral ends of research in instructed SLA. *Language Teaching Research, 16*(2), 206–226.

Park, H. (2010). Acquisition of final endings by Chinese learners of L2 Korean. *언어와 문화, 6*(2), 165–193.

Park, M.-J. (2009). Perception and production of Korean obstruents through prosody. *국어교육연구*, *24*, 143–163.

Pienemann, M. (2007). Processability theory. In B. VanPatten & J. Williams (Eds.), *Theories in second language acquisition: An introduction* (pp. 137–154). Mahwah, NJ: Lawrence Erlbaum.

Saito, K., & Plonsky, L. (2019). Effects of second language pronunciation teaching revisited: A proposed measurement framework and meta-analysis. *Language Learning*, *69*(3), 652–708.

Silva, D.J. (2006). Acoustic evidence for the emergence of tonal contrast in contemporary Korean. *Phonology*, *23*(2), 287–308.

Spada, N., & Tomita, Y. (2010). Interactions between type of instruction and type of language feature: A meta-analysis. *Language Learning: A Journal of Research in Language Studies*, *60*(2), 263–308.

White, L. (2007). Linguistic theory, universal grammar, and second language acquisition. In B. VanPatten & J. Williams (Eds.), *Theories in second language acquisition: An introduction* (pp. 37–56). Mahwah, NJ: Lawrence Erlbaum.

권성미. (2019). 음운론적 대립 유형과 음성학적 유형에 따른 한국어 파열음 인식 양상 연구. *Korean Education*, *118*, 223–255.

김부영·권성미. (2013). 중국인 학습자의 한국어 유음 습득 양상 연구. *우리어문연구*, *45*, 57–77.

후지아루. (2014). 중국 사천방언권 학습자의 한국어 종성 발음 교육 연구. [석사논문]. 서울대학교.

2 Pedagogical approaches and practices in teaching Korean

*Mee-Jeong Park, Bumyong Choi,
and Seongyeon Ko*

2.1 Introduction

2.1.1 A brief history of language teaching methods

The history of language teaching goes far back to the ancient world when the Sumerians used the first writing system. Actual language teaching, however, started about 2,000 years ago with the Greeks studying their own language and teaching Greek and Latin in ancient Rome (Wheeler, 2013). Since then, the teaching of language, whether one's own or a foreign one, has changed in method and approach. The changes in language teaching practices can be divided into two main stages: (1) modern language teaching in Europe; and (2) English language and foreign language teaching in Europe and beyond. During these two stages, the way a language was taught went through several transitions, and each time, teachers chose the most effective and innovative approaches.

(1) The first stage includes the teaching of classical languages, such as Greek and Latin, in Europe beginning in the 15th century. Since the teaching of these classical languages did not involve any spoken form, the Grammar-Translation Method was developed. This method further evolved into a more formalized system that gained popularity in the 18th century, with little to no emphasis on speaking. Language teaching during this period emphasized the grammar of the target language, often taken from literary works, leading to highly structured lessons. In the late 19th century, the Direct Method (or Natural Method, the Berlitz Method) emerged as a response to the Grammar-Translation Method in order to place more emphasis on teaching the spoken language. Influenced by new theories of linguistics, listening and speaking skills were prioritized and grammar was taught using a deductive approach.

(2) The second stage encompasses the teaching of the English language in Europe and beyond in the 20th century. This is also known as the scientific period, when scientific theories from different disciplines influenced language teaching. The most representative language teaching method at the beginning of this stage was the Audio-lingual Method, which started in the US military during World War II. This method was deeply rooted in behavioral psychology and emphasized mechanical habit formation through repetitive oral

pattern-drills and memorization. Grammar was introduced in an inductive way using dialogs with key structures. Since listening and speaking skills played an important role, teachers used audio-tapes, visual aids, and even language labs. Although not as popular as the Audio-lingual Method, several other teaching methods emerged during this scientific period. Total Physical Response emphasized learners' physical responses elicited by the teacher's commands. Through the Silent Way, students learned language through discovery rather than active teaching. In Community Language Learning, the teachers took a counseling role, providing a supportive community atmosphere to the learners.

In the late 20th century, Communicative Language Teaching gained attention. In this approach, all four language skills (speaking, listening, reading, and writing) were pertinent to achieve "real-life" communication. Language educators started to place priority on "communicative competence" over "linguistic competence," and as a result, fluency gained priority over accuracy, and language function over language structure. Language teaching was no longer based on methods, but rather on philosophy. Therefore, the term *approach* was used rather than *method*. In the field of foreign or second language teaching, we often hear terms like *teaching method*, *approach*, and *technique*. It is generally understood that *approach* is a broad term that reflects a research philosophy, model, or paradigm (e.g., Communicative Approach). A *method*, on the other hand, is more specific than an approach, but less specific than a technique, and it provides more precise procedures related to language teaching (e.g., the Audio-lingual Method). A *technique* is the narrowest term of the three, and it provides specific details related to classroom activities (e.g., repetition).

Although the history of language teaching started with the Grammar-Translation Method over 500 years ago, this very method was used in American language classrooms until about 50 years ago. The fast-paced transition of language teaching methods and approaches in the past half-century reflects the expansion of the way English is specifically used in global communities. In addition, the increase in research in language learning and teaching has influenced the ways we teach one's native language, and foreign languages. As a result, some philosophies from prior methods and approaches have been reconceptualized and integrated into contemporary language classrooms, following the latest theories in language learning and teaching.

2.1.2   Communicative language teaching and beyond

Since the appearance of Communicative Language Teaching (CLT) in the 1970s, several teaching approaches have been developed with communicative competence as the central goal. According to Howatt (1984), there are two versions of the Communicative Approach: (1) the weak version, where learners learn to speak the target language, and (2) the strong version, where learners use the target language to learn the target language. The strong version gained more popularity, resulting in the development of more refined versions of Communicative Language Teaching, such as Content-based Instruction and Task-based Language Teaching.

Although CLT does not rely on a particular teaching methodology or curricular design, Richards and Rodgers (2001) include the following theoretical premises deduced from this approach: (1) the communicative principle; (2) the task principle; and (3) the meaningfulness principle. This chapter introduces the most widely practiced and researched language teaching approaches that are based on these principles: (1) Task-based Language Teaching; (2) Content-based Instruction; and (3) Technology-enhanced Language Instruction.

2.2 Task-based language teaching

2.2.1 Introduction

Over the last three decades, there has been a great deal of interest in Task-based Language Teaching (TBLT) as a new teaching approach among researchers and educators of foreign and second language education. The second language (L2) literature on TBLT has been consistently discussed in symposiums, seminars, workshops, colloquiums, and conferences that are specifically dedicated to TBLT (e.g., Ellis, 2003; Long, 2015; Samuda & Bygate, 2008; Van den Branden et al., 2009). As a result, TBLT research and its applications have expanded. However, TBLT in the Korean language education setting has received scant attention from TBLT researchers. In this chapter, we will first introduce the rationale of TBLT, the guiding principles in designing both tasks and a TBLT curriculum in a language class, and two examples of a TBLT curriculum in Korean language education.

2.2.2 The rationale for TBLT

TBLT is an attempt to develop a new language teaching approach by addressing fundamental problems with existing language teaching approaches. In the discussion of the existing language teaching approaches or syllabus types, Long and Crookes (1993) adopt Wilkins' (1976) distinction between two superordinate categories: analytic and synthetic syllabi.

The term "synthetic" refers to the learner's role as a synthesizer of various elements of linguistic features when presented explicitly one at a time in the language classroom. In this syllabus, acquisition is a process of gradual accumulation of separately taught parts building up to the whole structure of the language. The learner is exposed to a deliberately limited sample of language at any time and has to "re-synthesize the language that has been broken down into a large number of small pieces with the aim of making this learning task easier" (Wilkins, 1976: p. 2). The synthetic syllabus is based on the belief that the learner can reach a certain proficiency level or learning outcomes by adding up the elements of a linguistic system, such as words, grammatical structure, notion, function, situation, and topic (Long & Crookes, 1993). A vast number of language teaching methods (e.g., Grammar Translation Method, Audio-lingual Method, the Silent Way, Total Physical Response, Notional and Functional Approach, and

Communicative Language Teaching, etc.) take this position. In this approach, the syllabus is designed to organize each element and present each form to learners, since synthetizing these elements to achieve a certain level of proficiency depends on the learners' internalized process (Wilkins, 1976). A teacher decides the syllabus content and chooses to segment the target language into discrete linguistic items and presents them to the learners one at a time. Therefore, the instructions in the synthetic syllabus "focus on forms" of the language (Long, 1991; Long & Robins, 1998). Due to its effectiveness and the simple processes of developing teaching materials and assessment plans, the majority of language education institutes and textbook developers adopt these approaches (Long, 2016). This kind of structural focus found in a synthetic syllabus provides learners with reasonably good knowledge of simplified grammar rules; however, in most cases, it fails to develop fluent speaking skills because the conscious form of knowledge is not readily available. These approaches have received criticism over time due to limited analysis of learners' needs, ignorance of interlanguage development, and weak support from second language acquisition (SLA) research findings (Long, 2015; Long & Norris, 2000).

On the other hand, the analytic syllabus takes the stance that the learner acquires the language as a whole. The term "analytic" emphasizes the student's natural internal process of language learning by identifying the relevant linguistic structure through analyzing the whole breadth of performance or communication sequence. According to Wilkins (1976: p. 13), in analytic syllabi, "analytic approaches … are organized in terms of the purposes for which people are learning languages and the kinds of language performance that are necessary to meet those purposes." This syllabus focuses on how the language is learned, rather than what is learned. In other words, it is more concerned with the learning process than the content. In the synthetic syllabus, the content is pre-selected by the expert and becomes a goal of instruction, whereas the content in the analytic syllabus is the byproduct of what the learner brings to the authentic and meaningful communication process. The role of the instructor is to provide enough input comprehensible to the learners to facilitate their target language use and production. Since it is assumed that students will incidentally learn through meaningful target language use, the explicit instruction of linguistic features is unnecessary. Examples of analytic syllabus includes immersion programs, the natural approach, sheltered subject matter instructions, and some content-based approaches. Since the content and focus of the lessons are not the forms of the linguistic features but the message, subject matter, and communication, it is considered a "focus on meaning" (Long, 1991). Although the analytic approach is more relevant to the natural language learning process because it can motivate students, draw more attention to the learning process, and focus on communication, it has also been criticized due to its ineffective treatment of learners' persistent grammatical errors (Long, 2016). Long (2015) also claims that analytic approaches are inadequate for adult learners whose capacity for purely incidental learning is reduced and for whom intentional learning becomes more necessary.

The TBLT syllabus resembles the analytic syllabus in that it focuses on learning strategies and processes rather than linguistic features by setting a task as the unit of analysis and teaching. It also takes a holistic view of language, with a focus on the whole use of language performance during communication (Long, 2015). However, it is distinguished from analytic approaches in which form-focused activities such as error correction are often disregarded or intentionally avoided, since TBLT also pays attention to form in certain conditions. Therefore, TBLT is considered an analytic approach with "Focus on Form" (Doughty & Williams, 1998; Long, 1991; Long & Robinson, 1998). TBLT is based on meaningful tasks with the notion that meaning is primary and learning is accomplished through doing. Through its methodological principles, TBLT tries to integrate form and meaning in one syllabus (Long, 2016).

2.2.3 Designing a TBLT curriculum

TBLT provides students with opportunities to practice both spoken and written language through tasks that are designed to engage learners in an authentic, practical, and functional use of the target language (Ellis, 2003). In TBLT, tasks can be classified as pedagogic, target, and real-world tasks. The goal for a TBLT curriculum is to enable students to reach the target tasks by completing a series of pedagogic tasks that lead students to become proficient in the real-world tasks in the target language. Thus, the curriculum development in TBLT is the process of developing the series of pedagogic tasks and organizing them into a syllabus to help the student accomplish the target task. The pedagogic tasks in the syllabus are implemented in the class based on TBLT methodological principles and are assessed by task-based assessments (Norris, 2009).

2.2.3.1 Needs analysis

In the TBLT syllabus, the target tasks are directly related to students' learning outcomes and it is crucial to identify the target tasks in each lesson. To identify the target tasks, it is important to find the students' needs for learning the target language (i.e., needs analysis). After identifying and analyzing the students' needs, the instructors will be able to find out what kinds of tasks learners want and need to engage with the target language in real life. The researchers and language professionals in TBLT put a strong emphasis on the needs analysis. As Long and Norris (2000) highlighted, the lack of learners' needs analysis results in curriculum goals and students' learning outcomes that are irrelevant to learners' genuine needs. This leads to learners' demotivation. Therefore, needs analysis is the first step in developing a TBLT curriculum by identifying communicative tasks using input that is gathered from multiple sources of information and methods (Long, 2005). According to Long, these multiple sources include information from published and unpublished literature, students, applied linguists, domain experts such as licensed certified public accountants, in-service practitioners such as travel agents or small business owners, and pre-experience learners, such as college interns. In addition to gathering various sources of information, a needs analysis also should employ multiple data collection methods, including both qualitative (e.g., interviews) and quantitative (e.g., Likert-style surveys). Long (2005) emphasizes the triangulation of the multiple sources of information and methods in the process of doing a needs analysis to validate the data and ultimately to increase the credibility of the data interpretation.

2.2.3.2 Identifying a target task

To date, L2 researchers and practitioners alike have offered a variety of definitions of a "task," and debates still occur on how to define the task and distinguish it from communicative activities. Taken broadly, all of the learner-centered communicative activities in the classroom can be called tasks. In both CLT and TBLT curricula, learning is centered on tasks. However, while CLT curricula tasks introduce communicative functions through learning activities to create predictable situations, TBLT curricula tasks do not aim to create a specific function or a specific language form. The CLT focuses on the language used in the course to perform the task, while the TBLT emphasizes the completion of the task itself (Long & Crookes, 1993). In this vein, Long defines the task as what "people do in everyday life, at work, at play, and in between" (Long, 1985: p. 85). He further argues that only "the real world communicative activity that learners will engage in L2 beyond the classroom is qualified to be the task in the TBLT approach" (Long, 2016: p. 6). This concept is not limited to the language that is required to perform the particular task, but also focuses on the task itself to encourage the use of the L2. On the other hand, Ellis (1997, 2003, & 2009) holds a more flexible view as he conceptualizes a communicative activity with specific linguistic goals and interactional authenticity in mind. Ellis states,

> A pedagogic activity where the learners are provided with L2 data in some form and required to perform some operation on or with it, the purpose of which is to arrive at an explicit understanding of some linguistic property or properties of the target language.
>
> (Ellis, 1997: p. 160)

Ellis defines the concept of a task as a workplan that aims to develop "language use that bears resemblance, direct or indirect, to the way language is used in the real world. Like other language activities, a task can engage productive or receptive, and oral or written skills, and also various cognitive processes" (Ellis, 2003: p. 16). Whether it is real life, or communicative tasks in the classroom context, the first fundamental step in developing TBLT curricula is identifying target tasks using the various information from students' needs analysis (Long, 2005).

2.2.3.3 Pedagogic task

The types of real-life tasks vary by the required proficiency level and task complexities. Thus, depending on the task types, some can become a target task for a short-term learning objective for one lesson, while others can become long-term goals. The long-term plan can include a series of short-term tasks, and some of these can be broken down to smaller tasks. Tasks that enable students to reach learning goals are called pedagogic tasks. In designing the TBLT curriculum, some tasks can be grouped by their general functions or major characteristics. For example, writing bank applications, applying for a sports center membership, and joining a fan club of a K-pop group are all related to the same type of task: "filling in information on an application." Long (1993) calls these examples task types. The task types show how students can extend their learning experience from one specific task to another. By mastering one task, students are ready to apply what they have learned. The pedagogic tasks are developed from the identified target task types and what learners and instructors actually do in the classroom.

2.2.3.4 Developing a task syllabus

After target tasks and pedagogic tasks are identified by the needs analysis, the curriculum designer needs to organize these tasks to form a task syllabus (Long, 2015; Long & Norris, 2000). The pedagogic tasks must be sequenced according to their task complexity, not linguistic complexity, to match the learner's developmental stage and facilitate optimal L2 learning (Long, 2015; Robinson, 2011). Therefore, determining the complexity of the tasks is a crucial component of designing the TBLT curriculum. There have been two main approaches in task complexities (Robinson, 2001, 2011; Skehan, 2009; Skehan & Foster, 2001). Defining task complexities requires predicting how various features of the tasks will affect task-generated cognitive demands and the allocation of students' attention. In Skehan's Limited Capacity Model, the level of task demands depends on three task-related factors: (1) code complexity, which pertains to linguistic complexity; (2) cognitive complexity, which entails processing and computational requirements; and (3) communicative stress, which includes time pressure, number of participants, and opportunity to control (Skehan, 2009; Skehan & Foster, 2001). Based on a single resource view, Skehan claims competition between linguistic complexity and accuracy is triggered by the natural limitation of attention. On the other hand, Robinson defines task complexity as "the result of the attentional memory, reasoning and other information-processing demands imposed by the structure of the task on the language learner" (Robinson, 2001: p. 28). Based on the Multiple Attentional Resources Model, Robinson claims that increasing the task complexity can result in increased linguistic complexity without reducing accuracy. From the two major models of task complexities, numerous studies that explore the relationship between the task complexity and the language learning process exist. However, these studies mainly sequence pedagogic tasks and still do not give strong insight into arranging target tasks, because of limitations in task variation and implementation (Ellis, 2017; Long, 2016).

2.2.3.5 Implementing pedagogic tasks in class

After organizing a series of pedagogic tasks into the syllabus, each task requires in-class implementation. Task-based lessons consist of three stages: pre-task, during-task, and post-task periods (Bygate et al., 2015). In the pre-task period, the teacher introduces the topic and activates the students' prior knowledge relevant to the task. The task-essential vocabulary and grammatical structures are introduced at this stage to help students complete the task adequately. The instructor presents students with a clear model of what will be expected of them through detailed instructions pertaining to the task procedure or an example of the completed tasks. In the during-task period, the students engage in a task individually, in pairs, or in groups using the language resources available to them. The teacher typically monitors the students' progress and supports the students with various strategies such as recasting, prompting, correcting errors, providing feedback on useful language, scaffolding, giving metalinguistic feedback, focusing on form, and asking open and closed questions (Bygate et al., 2015). In the post-task period, the students reflect on their task process and share outcomes. In this process, teachers can address linguistic and other obstacles that students encountered and use this period as an opportunity to provide additional practice on task-essential lexis, pragmatics, and grammar or give metalinguistic instruction on particular structures. The use of similar types of tasks or materials can improve students' fluency and accuracy in applying target linguistic features. Also, the teacher can provide the students with more real-life tasks to help them extend their language competencies to the target tasks or real-world context.

2.2.3.6 Task-based assessment

Since TBLT is a framework that takes the task as the central unit of analysis and teaching, the task should also be the fundamental unit for assessment and testing. Long and Norris (2000: p. 600) state that "genuinely task-based language assessment takes the task itself as the fundamental unit of analysis, motivating item selection, test instrument construction and the rating of task performance." The purpose for task-based assessment is not to measure the learners' linguistic knowledge, but to determine whether the students can achieve the target task using the target language (Long & Crookes, 1992). In a TBLT program, students should be assessed on their ability to perform the selected exit tasks using task-based, criterion-reference performance tests that focus on the students' task performance (Norris, 2009). Ellis states that

> task-based testing is seen as a way of achieving a close correlation between the test performance i.e., what the testee does during the test, and the criterion of performance i.e., what the testee has to do in the real world.
>
> (2003: p. 279)

Assessment tasks are thus viewed as "devices for eliciting and evaluating communicative performances from learners in the context of language use that is meaning-focused and directed towards some specific goal" (Ellis, 2003: p. 279).

2.2.4 TBLT in a Korean language classroom

2.2.4.1 TBLT versus TSLT

In the TBLT curriculum in which tasks are the central unit of instruction, tasks define the curriculum and the syllabi, as well as the modes of assessment (Samuda & Bygate, 2008). Samuda and Bygate (2008: p. 58) describe TBLT as follows:

- tasks define the language syllabus, with language being taught in response to the operational needs of specific learners
- tasks are seen as essential in engaging the key processes of language acquisition
- tasks are selected on the basis that they replicate or simulate relevant real-world activities
- assessment is in terms of task performance.

From the viewpoint of TBLT approaches, traditional structural teaching is theoretically indefensible and incompatible with TBLT approaches. The TBLT approach is difficult to adopt in a regular institutional language program, due to fewer classroom hours and a lack of resources (Swan, 2005).

On the other hand, tasks are used to actualize parts of the curriculum, to enrich the syllabus, or to provide additional learning opportunities in the Task Supported Language Teaching (TSLT) approach (Ellis, 2003, 2009). Samuda and Bygate (2008: p. 60) describe TSLT in the following ways:

- tasks are an important element, but not the sole element, in a pedagogic cycle
- tasks are used in conjunction with different types of activity
- tasks are one element in the syllabus, but not necessarily the defining element
- tasks may be used as an element of assessment, but not necessarily as the defining element.

In the TSLT approach, tasks serve as a supplement to enhance learning target features such as grammar and vocabulary. In the following section, we will discuss two cases of TBLT and TSLT curriculum in Korean language education.

2.2.4.2 TBLT curriculum: University of Hawaii Korean Flagship program

The Korean Language Flagship Center (KLFC) two-year Master's program consists of a one-year domestic program and a one-year overseas program, aiming to produce a Korean specialist with professional working proficiency. The program originally started as a non-degree post-Bachelor's program with the Flagship grant awarded by the US Department of Defense's National Security Education Program (NSEP). Later the program transitioned into a MA program at the University of Hawaii at Manoa (Kong, 2012). When the Korean Flagship program was established, the University of Hawaii was the heart of TBLT approaches and the institute enthusiastically applied this new language teaching theory to its robust Korean language program.[1] The substantial fund from NSEP provided the opportunity to hire enough program staff including curriculum experts, language instructors, domain experts, tutors, and administrators. Since the program began as a non-degree program, it had more flexibility to adopt new curriculum design.

Kong (2012) shows how the KLFC MA program was developed based on TBLT principles. At the beginning, Task-based needs analysis was conducted with multiple sources (e.g., students, instructors, language experts, domain experts, internship supervisors, alumni, and future employers) and with multiple methods (e.g., survey or questionnaire, interview, conference, observation, journals, discourse analyses, content analyses, expert intuitions, etc.) to develop and revise the curriculum. The needs analysis identified and classified target tasks into types such as translating, interpreting, transcribing, and summarizing of media materials. To teach the target task types, relevant courses were developed, such as a media research course, interdisciplinary research, and research seminars. Table 2.1 shows the target task types and the flagship courses covering the tasks.

The needs analysis also identified content areas that students needed to master, and the curriculum developer selected the most appropriate target task for each area. Thus, the unit of analysis of the flagship curriculum became a "task." To help students complete the target task, flagship courses, tutors, and domain experts provided the relevant pedagogic tasks. For example, for the target task of the content topic FTA (Free Trade Agreement), the instructor set a debate between two student groups. The pedagogic tasks included:

- understanding issues through interdisciplinary research
- identifying arguments through extended media research
- deepening the understanding of the issue and task through domain experts' lectures
- task preparation through individual research and meeting with domain experts and language instructors (Kong, 2012: pp. 38–39).

Table 2.1 Target Task Types and the Flagship Courses Covering the Task (Kong, 2012: p. 36)

Target task types	Flagship courses covering the tasks
Translating and interpreting Transcribing Summarizing of media materials	Media research
Analyzing and synthesizing information Gathering information and library research Discussing Reporting and presentation Critical writing Conducting interviews and surveys	Interdisciplinary research, research seminar, Directed research, and content lectures
Attending international meetings and lectures (e.g., academic conferences and meetings) Arranging meeting and or conferences	Content lectures and extra-curricular activities Internship in Korea

After completing the pedagogic tasks, students performed the target tasks and got feedback from their peers, audience, and instructors. The instructor videotaped the task performance and assessed the language and content appropriateness. In this way, the Korean Flagship program assessed the students' task performance weekly. Also, general proficiency tests assessed students' achievements and program evaluation: ACTFL OPI for speaking and the KLFC Proficiency Test (ILR-based test developed by KLFC) for reading, listening, and writing. TOPIK (Test of Proficiency in Korean) was also used to cross-check the results of the tests.

The KLFC MA program has presented its successful implementation and the outcome of its TBLT curriculum at several conferences and in several publications by showing the curriculum's achievement of its original goal to produce global professionals commanding a superior level of fluency in Korean (Kong, 2012). This achievement was possible with substantial support from the NSEP fund and available resources such as TBLT researchers' group, the well-established Korean language program, and experienced Korean teachers. Therefore, there have been ongoing criticisms that most programs in other institutes lack the available resources to build similar successful programs. In fact, this is a long-term criticism of TBLT itself, and one response to this criticism is the Task-Supported Language Teaching approach (Ellis, 2009).

2.2.4.3 TSLT curriculum: Emory University Korean program elementary level course

The Emory Elementary Korean language course is the first part of the four-year Korean curriculum, which is a proficiency-based curriculum with communicative language teaching approaches. It consists of two introductory courses for two semesters, which each meet four times a week for one hour over a 15-week semester. The proficiency goals are "novice high" according to the ACTFL proficiency guideline. The course curriculum consists of 16 units, based on situational textbooks which present key expressions, grammar points, and appropriate functions in each setting (Cho et al., 2010).

The original curriculum consisted of lecture, practice, and performance, which resembled the traditional PPP (Presentation–Practice–Production) model. Performance sessions are designed for the students to handle various realistic situations using language based on what they have learned from lecture and practice sessions. While the performance session was manageable and effective for both instructor and students in the first half of the elementary level, in the second half, students felt stress and the instructor had difficulty eliciting students to produce the target forms with the given textbook because of the increased complexity of the content and target features. To bring more communicative and meaningful approaches to this level, a Task-Supported Curriculum was adopted to overcome this limitation.

Most university language programs do not have the flexibility as the case of the KLFC MA program since they have limited resources such as budget, instructors, and teacher training opportunities. Also, the curriculum innovation takes place in relation to the existing curriculum. This is why many college-level language programs have a hard time adopting TBLT into their curriculum. Under these similar conditions, the Emory Korean program decided to innovate its curriculum based on a TSLT approach by substituting the performance session from the second half of the elementary Korean curriculum's task session. In this curriculum, each unit consisted of lecture, practice, and task sessions. The tasks were developed after identifying the proper themes and the equivalent task genres according to the situation in each unit. In the new curriculum, the lecture and practice sessions were categorized as general pedagogical task sessions since they were designed to help students get ready for the following task sessions. The task session focused on using target expressions in each unit in a culturally appropriate manner. After two task sessions, students had the chance to review their task performances and/or apply what they learned to their personalized situations in the post-task session. Students' performances in the task and post-task sessions were assessed based on the task evaluation rubrics and applied to their final grade. Table 2.2 shows the setting of each textbook unit and theme, and the task genres we developed for this course (Kim et al., 2020).

The newly developed tasks were piloted for four semesters, and the researchers and instructors conducted a series of classroom-based studies to examine the effects of tasks on students' ability and perception of Korean language learning. These studies proved that tasks can help students achieve the same level of language learning in terms of accuracy and fluency in speaking, writing, and grammar in the elementary Korean course with less pressure and anxiety about preparing for class (Kim at al., 2020). TSLT is more flexible than TBLT when applied to a college-level curriculum, since it is compatible with most of the synthetic syllabi, including the traditional PPP model (Ellis, 2009). However, it still requires more effort to apply it to the existing college curricula. Instructors require adequate training to develop tasks and implement them in their classroom. Developing relevant tasks is a difficult and time-consuming project.

However, the current trend in language pedagogy emphasizes the importance of language use in real-life tasks by promoting the 5 Cs (Communication, Culture, Comparison, Connection, and Community) in all levels of language curriculum

Table 2.2 Overall Course Curriculum

Textbook	Themes	Task genres
Unit 9: Birthday	Family events	Online journal writing
Unit 10: At a Professor's Office	University life I	Email/Voicemail
Unit 11: Living in a Dormitory	Spring break	Text messaging
Unit 12: Family	Social gathering	Posting on social media
Unit 13: On the Telephone	University life II	Phone conversation/Voice message
Unit 14: At the Airport	Traveling	Postcard/Voice message
Unit 15: Shopping	Shopping	Blog posting
Unit 16: At a Restaurant	Dining out	Vlog

(The National Standards Collaborative Board, 2015). The Standards-Based College Curriculum for Korean Language Education provides clear guidelines for using meaningful tasks even in the elementary-level curriculum (AATK, 2015). By adopting TSLT, lower-level classes can introduce the task as a unit of instruction without major changes to the existing curriculum in the college level Korean programs.

2.3 Content-based instruction

2.3.1 Overview

Content-based Instruction (CBI) is often associated with the Canadian immersion programs that started in the 1960s. In the 1970s CBI was developed through bilingual education in the United States and Canada. CBI expanded further when it was applied to ESL (English as a Second Language) programs with the purpose of assisting children in elementary and secondary schools with their English proficiency. Along with the rise of the Communicative Approach in language instruction in the 1980s, CBI was introduced into foreign language classrooms, aiming to integrate the study of content and language. In this approach, the classroom goal is not second language skills, per se, but mostly acquisition of academic content or information (Brinton, 2003; Brinton et al., 2003; Grabe & Stoller, 1997; Leaver & Stryker, 1989; Mohan, 1986; Snow, 2001). CBI is "the teaching of language through exposure to content that is interesting and relevant to learners" (Brinton, 2003: p. 201). In other words, students are required to acquire content using the target language, where the target language is simultaneously the goal and the means.

CBI offers many benefits, since the integration of subject matter and language not only helps students acquire both their target language and content, but also creates a natural and comprehensive, and thus more motivational, learning environment (Grabe, 2009; Lightbown, 2014; Mohan, 1986; Wesche & Skehan, 2002). At the postsecondary level in particular, the integration of language and academic content across disciplines has elevated the value of language education in academia. In recent years, the importance of performance-based evidence in language teaching has been well-supported by integrated language instruction. Empirical research in Second Language Acquisition has found that: (1) high frequency of repeated input through content facilitates the acquisition of language; (2) pushed output (e.g., class presentation) reinforces learners' productive skills; and (3) interactional skills (e.g., class discussion) facilitate learning through negotiation of meaning (Snow & Brinton, 2017).

On the other hand, CBI also poses limitations, as very little emphasis is placed on language, resulting in learners' deficiency in grammatical accuracy and sociolinguistic appropriateness. In addition, in language curricula with CBI, instructors are required to have knowledge of various subject matters such as history, politics, science, and culture.

Below is a summary of some major characteristics of CBI provided in Snow & Brinton (2017):

- focus on content instead of language
  Although CBI is implemented in a language learning curriculum, the main focus must be placed on content of the subject matter instead of the language lessons. Students learn language through content.
- choose content that is relevant and/or of interest to students
  The objective of learning is based on students' real-life experience, whether they are high school or college students. In other words, the learning objective should be appropriate, to reflect students' academic goals or interests.
- use of authentic texts and activities
  Since content is the focus of the instruction, use of authentic materials and activities are essential.
- integrated or multiple skills
  A curriculum based on CBI advocates for an integrated or multiple skills teaching approach to develop lessons based on authentic texts and real-life situations.
- student participation
  Under CBI, students play a very active role in the entire learning process. Instructors facilitate learning rather than controlling the class.

2.3.2 Models of CBI

Depending on the range of content and language integration and the purpose of instruction, CBI has been implemented in various ways. A curriculum can be total immersion with more emphasis on content compared to partial immersion. Brinton et al. (2003) identify three prototype models of CBI: theme-based, sheltered, and adjunct instruction. In theme-based instruction, more emphasis is placed on language, and class materials are organized around topics or themes. Sheltered instruction includes a subject matter course taught to a segregated or separated class of target language learners taught by a content area specialist. Finally, in adjunct instruction, language instruction provides two linked courses—a language course to consolidate the linguistic points, and a content course for students to focus on the subject matter.

2.3.2.1 Theme-based model

In a theme-based model, the curriculum is centered on specific themes of student interest and/or relevance. Themes or topics can include family, school life, saving the environment, and marriage. Students spend a week or more learning about these topics and acquire different language skills. The theme-based model is commonly found in EFL (English as a Foreign Language) of any foreign language teaching context. A language teacher or co-teaching team including a content specialist can teach these courses. This model is suitable for all levels, but most appropriate for intermediate- and advanced-level students. In fact, many advanced-level foreign language textbooks take this model in providing several units on different themes and topics, followed by interactive activities to strengthen reading, listening, speaking, and writing. These types of lessons include authentic texts followed by interactive activities, which promote critical thinking and autonomous learning.

2.3.2.2 Sheltered model

The sheltered model of CBI is more common in elementary and secondary schools with students whose first language is not English. Schools provide English assistance to the students outside the classes they are taking. For instance, students with English as an L2 taking a psychology class will have a sheltered ESL instruction to go over their psychology textbook to assist them in using charts, visual aids, pre-reading tasks, and vocabulary activities. The sheltered model was originally designed and successfully used at bilingual programs at the University of Ottawa (Briton et al., 2003).

2.3.2.3 Adjunct model

In this model, one class covering course content and another addressing language are paired to complement each other. Students have two teachers, one who is an expert on the subject matter, and one who is an ESL teacher. These two teachers work closely to design lesson plans and assess students. For instance, L2 English students take a psychology class with all students, but they separate to take the ESL adjunct class. In this adjunct class, students acquire target vocabulary, key linguistics features, and language skills, which help them learn the course content. Some adjunct classes are offered during summer breaks before the regular term starts, while others are offered concurrently.

As shown in the chart below, these three models place different weight on either content or language (Snow, 2001). Among the three models, the theme-based model focuses more on language instruction, the sheltered model emphasizes content, and the adjunct model places similar weight on both content and language. These models can accommodate various programs, classes, and/or instructors with different expectations or instructional goals and settings.

2.3.3 Hybrid models of CBI

Since the 1980s, with the emergence of the newly added content, a variety of altered or hybrid versions of CBI have appeared in the field. The three main models remain, but some of them have evolved further to accommodate different

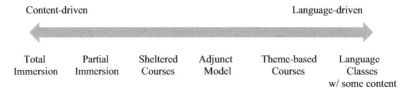

Figure 2.1 Modified from Snow (2001).

Table 2.3 Modified from Snow and Brinton (2017)

CBI						
Immersion Education	*Theme-based*	*Sheltered*	*Adjunct*		*CLIL*	*Other Hybrids*
–	Sustained Content	EMI	Modified Adjunct	Simulated Adjunct	–	–

student populations, instructional goals, and teaching settings. Snow and Brinton (2017) provide a list of hybrid models of CBI.

Some of the modified or evolved models are introduced below.

2.3.3.1 Sustained Content Language Teaching (SCLT)

Deriving from the theme-based model, a language instructor teaches the class. This model is different from the theme-based model in that the curriculum is based on a single content or topic for the entire term. This model's advantage over the theme-based model is the depth in which topics are covered during the whole term. As a result, students are exposed to extended levels of relevant vocabulary and acquire in-depth knowledge in a specific area leading to improved critical thinking and cognitive and meta-cognitive strategies.

2.3.3.2 Content and Language Integrated Learning (CLIL)

In Europe in particular, this model has gained special attention and rapid adaptation. This is a dual language model where the target language is used in the delivery of course content. Students simultaneously acquire both content and language through this model, and therefore successful students will be able to learn academic subjects like physics, history, and biology, in addition to a language that is not their first language.

2.3.3.3 English-Medium Instruction (EMI)

This is a variation of CLIL where a content course is taught in English to students whose first language is not English. This model is popular in non-English-speaking countries where course content is taught in English only. The details vary across countries, schools, and programs. The weak version of this model does not focus on language skills, but content only, whereas in language-enhanced versions, language skills are also part of the curriculum.

2.3.4 Advantages and challenges

As in all teaching approaches, CBI has merits and potential problems as well.

2.3.4.1 Advantages

- Instruction content can make learning a language more interesting. Students use authentic material to perform real-life and interactive activities which can make the learning process more fulfilling and meaningful.
- Students exposed to a variety of content can deepen their knowledge and improve their performance in general education.
- CBI is very popular among EAP (English for Academic Purposes) instructors as students can develop the advanced skills that are commonly used in academic settings, such as extracting main ideas and key information from passages and organizing and summarizing ideas.
- The interactional activities and group work within this framework allow students to develop their collaborative skills and enhance their social competence.

2.3.4.2 Potential problems or issues

- various models of CBI weigh language and content differently, but students frequently believe they are not getting enough language lessons in their non-language courses
- since language is only used to deliver content, it is difficult to implement CBI in low-level language curricula
- for CBI models (e.g., sheltered and adjunct) that separate students who require additional language skills, students who share the same native language might communicate with each other in their own L1.

2.3.5 CBI in Korean language classrooms

There are numerous publications on CBI, yet only a few are related to the teaching and learning of Korean as a second or foreign language, both at college-level (Cheon, 2007; Kim, 2005; Noji et al., 2012; Shin & Kim, 2000) and primary and secondary education in dual-language immersion programs (Howard et al., 2007; Valdes, 1997). In this section, those studies that are relevant to college-level language classrooms will be introduced.

Shin and Kim (2000) developed a theme-based model of CBI based on a sample ten-week class curriculum for intermediate to advanced heritage learners studying Korean at the University of California at Los Angeles. The syllabus included topics on current issues in Korea, such as mass media, economy, gender, fashion, politics, social welfare, and education. Each of these weekly topics followed a similar lesson plan, starting with the introduction to the topic, grammar and vocabulary review, small group discussions, and listening activities using TV programs followed by discussion. Students engaged in a writing assignment that was used later in their oral presentation before the class came together for open comments and more discussions.

Although her research did not explicitly focus on CBI approaches, Kim (2005) observed a 15-week-long advanced-level language class using a CBI-based curriculum for heritage students at Duke University. The class emphasized Korean culture and covered a wide range of cultural aspects such as *kimchi*, the *Koguryo* wall paintings, poems, *pansori*, military culture, and academic ties. Every lesson consisted of discussions based on assigned readings, student oral presentations followed by Q&A, grammar instruction, and tests and quizzes. Kim's study included a discourse analysis of the instructor and students in a CBI classroom setting, and she argued that the CBI format increased student engagement and resulted in more dynamic discussions.

Cheon (2007) analyzed a theme-based advanced language class at the University of Hawaii at Manoa where students watched films as the core class content. The class was designed as a 16-week course to cover the four skills on oral presentations, group discussions, and the viewing of films assigned for each unit. In addition, students received supplementary reading materials relevant to the assigned films. The lesson cycle ended with short reaction papers as well as a final paper. The course covered only three to four films per term. As a result, students were able to conduct an in-depth analysis of each film including its historical, social, and political issues.

Noji et al. (2012) recommended a CBI curriculum for a one-year special program at the Kapiolani Community College in Hawaii. In this design, students spent one semester at their home college and then for their second semester went abroad to Korea where they completed a capstone project. This program's main objective was to push their advanced-level students up to the superior level of proficiency. The program chose CBI to enhance students' reading skills to the highest proficiency level. It also chose topics such as history, traditional and contemporary culture, customs, and geography. Each lesson was connected to interactive and relevant activities using the scaffolding strategy.

2.4 Technology-enhanced language instruction

Use of technology such as computers, mobile devices, and social media has become an integral part of teaching and learning language. The question now is not whether to use technology, but how to use it (Hubbard, 2009). Language teachers use technology to present linguistically and culturally authentic input, give students access to linguistic and cultural knowledge, and help students improve language skills with enhanced learning efficiency and effectiveness. Technology also enables students to interact with other language users and learners. Through the use of technology in classrooms, teachers can build a community, help students produce and publish their work, engage with and motivate students to develop agency, and offer inclusivity through the creation of a non-threatening and less restrictive learning environment. It also offers immediate and individualized feedback, computerized testing, alternative methods for assessment, effective tools to manage and organize teaching and learning, and ways to automate routine duties such as grading.[2] Technology even allows for various alternative modes of instruction including blended and distance learning. It is imperative for language teachers to utilize technological tools for educational purposes. In this section we will review widely used technologies[3] and discuss their applicability to the KFL context.

2.4.1 *Technology and language skill development*

The development of Computer Assisted Language Learning (CALL), which is now referred to as Technology-Enhanced Language Learning (TELL), has been significantly influenced by the traditional division of language skills such as speaking, listening, reading, and writing. The belief that language skills can be taught separately is outdated in contemporary practices of integrated language teaching under the communicative teaching paradigms. However, we follow the traditional taxonomy in reviewing current technologies used for discrete language skills as well as lexico-grammatical competence to reach practitioners who may be less familiar with the communicative teaching paradigms.[4]

Online flashcard programs (e.g., Quizlet) and online dictionaries are two main tools used for learning vocabulary. Teacher- or students-generated sets of online flashcards offer multiple modes of study and play that can be easily embedded into a course website. Online dictionaries, including those offered by Korean web portals such as Naver and Daum, are easier to navigate than paper dictionaries. They generally include audio recordings by native speakers along with a thesaurus. Naver Korean Dictionary[5] even offers a variety of additional features such as thematic search options (for proverbs, idioms, dialects including North Korean, loanwords), an online translation tool called Papago, Open Dictionary (i.e., a crowdsourced dictionary for slang and neologisms), and word quizzes. It also allows users to create their own vocabulary lists. The National Institute of Korean Language (NIKL) has recently launched learners' dictionaries for speakers of English and nine other languages,[6] which offer variable search options (e.g., search by the learner level and by themes and situations) and grammatical explanations for functional elements, such as verbal endings and suffixes. NIKL also operates web-based corpora, a general corpus[7] and a learner corpus,[8] which can be used as a data-driven learning tool for both vocabulary and grammar. Through these corpora, learners can access authentic language samples and infer usage rules, grammatical functions, and collocation or colligation patterns (i.e., lexical or syntactic relationships between words, respectively), with greater autonomy. Spelling and grammar checkers, whether integrated within word processors or available online, are useful for the development of lexico-grammatical accuracy. Pusan National University's web-based spelling and grammar checker for Korean[9] is useful as a spellchecker, although its performance as a grammar tool needs improvement.

For a more explicit grammar teaching tool, tutorial CALL has been used since the 1960s, in the form of multiple choice, fill-in-the-blank, matching, ordering, jumbled sentence, and short answers. Tutorial CALL has certain drawbacks. In general, it cannot accommodate answers deviating from predefined correct answers nor provide individualized feedback for various types of ill-formedness. Tutorial CALL-type questions are now integrated in authoring programs such as Hot Potatoes (Park, 2003) and other test-generating tools available in most virtual learning environments.

More recently, asynchronous text-based computer-mediated communication (CMC) tools (e.g., online chat) have also been explored as a new grammar learning tool. Although the basic purpose of using CMC tools is to promote inter-active and sociocultural aspects of language learning, online chatting, with its longer processing time, often helps students monitor and revise any spelling and grammatical errors.

Using websites provides learners with authentic and varied multimodal read-ing materials that combine texts with graphics, audio, or videos. Text-to-speech applications are often freely available to convert reading materials on the internet into audio formats, which are specifically useful to auditory learners. Online or electronic glossing applications such as Google Dictionary are useful for both reading comprehension and vocabulary learning. It helps learners understand the meaning of a word in a bottom-up approach and simultaneously frees up working memory and allows readers to focus on their top-down reading process.

Tech-savvy teachers with knowledge of HTML can create dedicated webpages to present pre-selected reading materials with tailored content at an appropriate level of difficulty. With these online reading materials, teachers can generate fol-low-up quizzes using the available authoring tools to test out reading comprehen-sion and offer immediate feedback.

L2 writing can be viewed as a product, process, or social practice (Walker & White, 2013). As a product, L2 writing means the actual piece of writing, and therefore the focus is the language and organization of the written texts. For this aspect of L2 writing, the same technology tools for vocabulary and grammar learning are useful.

L2 writing is also a complex process comprised of idea development, planning, drafting, composing, editing, and revising. It focuses more on writers and what they do to produce texts. Representative tools for writing as a process include mind-mapping, digital story-telling, and online encyclopedias for idea develop-ment; genre analysis from the internet and outlining tools for planning; word processors, collaborative writing tools, and spelling and grammar checkers for drafting, composing, and editing; and automated writing evaluation systems and plagiarism prevention services for revising (Walker & White, 2013: p. 64).

L2 writing as a social practice shifts focus to readers and the social contexts that writers engage with. Microblogging and instant messaging on social network-ing platforms easily turn cyberspace into real-life venues for L2 writing, despite the potential misuses (e.g., cyberbullying) or security breaches.[10] Some concrete ideas to use microblogging for short L2 writing include the five-sentence photo story activity for all levels (Stanley, 2013) and the news "tweetment" activity for more advanced levels (Walker & White, 2013). In the KFL/KSL context, 권정아 (2012), 박은선 (2012), and 안재린 and 심은진 (2018) have showcased their respective applications of Facebook, Twitter, and Instagram to writing practices. For longer pieces of writing in social contexts, blogs (for single-author writing) and wikis (for multi-author collaborative writing) are more suitable. These Web 2.0-based writing tools promote learners' attention to grammatical accuracy, lexi-cal diversity, and syntactic complexity.

As for listening skills, the current technologies can provide learners with expo-sure to authentic materials of personal relevance (e.g., songs of their favorite singers or video clips of preferred movie genres) with less spatio-temporal restriction and greater user controllability. While digital devices are still widely used for listening, network-based audio- and video-sharing platforms are gaining more popularity largely due to ever-increasing number of free, high-quality materials of all types, including those created by native speakers.

Videos are a rich source of both verbal and nonverbal (e.g., visual and contextual) input. Captioned videos such as movie clips with subtitles are even more useful and powerful in helping learners improve their L2 listening and comprehension skills with increased attention and reduced anxiety (Li, 2017). It has become easier to add subtitles, insert comprehension questions (e.g., EdPuzzle), and download and modify online videos. YouTube videos and other multimedia in general can be incorporated into virtual learning environments such as Blackboard (using their "mashup" tools) for an assignment, test, or other types of activities.

Podcasts are also a highly useful media format for L2 listening (Stanley, 2013). They generally increase the allocated time for listening outside the classroom and help learners gain autonomy. Learners can choose a subject of their choice, which gives them a more personalized listening experience and, as in the case of YouTube videos, allows them to repeat, slow down, and speed up playback according to their preference. One problem teachers and independent learners more frequently encounter nowadays is the excessive abundance rather than the paucity of materials. This situation calls for teachers to properly evaluate and curate authentic materials (Hubbard, 2017).

Speaking competency entails accuracy and fluency. To increase accuracy in speaking, self-directed speaking aloud has been a common practice, although it normally lacks human feedback. Automatic speech recognition systems such as Google Assistant can be repurposed as an L2 dictation tool with which L2 learners speak the target language and see if what they say converts well into the intended commands. Speech analysis software may also be useful for teaching L2 pronunciation and intonation (cf. Park, 2000). Speech shadowing can fine-tune accuracy in pronunciation and also increase speech rate, fluency, and comprehensibility (Martinsen et al., 2017).

Fluency-oriented technology tools for L2 speaking include synchronous CMC, asynchronous CALL story-telling, and podcasting. Synchronous voice- or video-based CMC tools such as Skype, Zoom, Adobe Connect, or Blackboard Collaborate (either for one-on-one communication or for multi-user conferencing) provide a real-time communication environment to improve fluency by having interlocutors communicate without pause or disrupted turn-taking unlike in text-based CMC. Asynchronous CALL story-telling (e.g., StoryKit and VoiceThread) allows students to work individually or collaboratively in producing rehearsed and recorded narratives in audio or video formats and to receive feedback in a more communicative environment. Its asynchronous nature allows learners to focus on form (accuracy) in a fluency-oriented real-life activity. For more advanced learners, creating podcasts (or vodcasts) might be a viable option (Smith, 2016). Similar to blogging for L2 writing, podcasting enables learners to create and publish on topics of their own interest for a real audience.

2.4.2 Technology and modes of instruction

Given the abundance of types and purposes of technology tools, it is quite natural for teachers to adopt multiple tools. The question, then, is how to incorporate them into a single course structure. Roh and Kim (2019) offer a reference point by presenting a coherent coursework design integrating four different technology-enhanced activities into an existing course structure. They utilized VoiceThread speaking assignments, Padlet-based collaborative writing assignments, spelling and grammar checking activities using Pusan National University's spelling and grammar checker, and a synchronous text-based CMC session using KakaoTalk Urimal 365, to develop language skills and foster learner autonomy and a sense of e-learning.

Technology also dramatically changes how we organize the entire course. With the increased availability of online technology tools, restructuring an existing course into a blended or fully online format is becoming easier and more effective than ever. Blended learning (or hybrid learning) is defined as an integration of face-to-face (f2f) and online activities in a planned, pedagogically valuable manner with a portion of the original f2f instruction replaced with online instruction (Picciano, 2009). It is easy to see the benefits of blended (and fully online) learning in terms of saving costs and spatio-temporal flexibility. It has been shown that blended courses seem to be as effective as, or better in certain respects than, traditional f2f-only courses in terms of students' performance and satisfaction (see Grgurović, 2017: pp. 151–162 and references therein), although our current understanding of this issue is still fairly limited. In addition, blended learning environments generally make students spend more time studying, which is desirable for foreign language learning.

The flipped classroom model (Bergmann & Sams, 2012; Muldrow, 2013) is often adopted in a blended course to compensate for the reduced classroom interactions. In a flipped classroom environment, students first study on their own, using the online instructional materials in the form of lecture videos, screencasts of lecture slides, or electronic reading materials uploaded onto a course repository. Then students come to f2f class and participate in various in-class communicative activities, applying what they have learned through pre-class online self-study. Conceivable pedagogical benefits of flipped instruction in foreign language education may include (but are not limited to) enhanced learner agency and motivation, increased speaking time, and focus on performance and problem-solving. Kim et al. (2017) report a positive effect of flipped instruction on L2 Korean learners' higher-order cognitive processing in a small-group discussion.

A common way to implement a flipped and/or blended learning approach while integrating technology is using a Virtual Learning Environment (VLE; also known as a Learning Management System) such as Moodle, Canvas, and Blackboard. One can start with the simplest but still highly useful technology features of a VLE such as sending an email, posting an announcement, sharing a course syllabus and lecture slides, using a discussion forum for Q&As, and posting exam grades. The teacher can then venture to use the more advanced features in order to create an online lesson quiz, have a synchronous speaking session, or mash up social media elements and web applications from external sources. A VLE is normally integrated with other IT systems of an institution, thus directly receiving student enrollment data. This makes a VLE offered by the institution still useful, although some teachers are instead turning to a Personal Learning Environment for its flexibility and manageability. Yong and Ko (2019) provide a concise illustration of how they built their flipped and blended elementary-level Korean courses using Blackboard and other technology tools.

Telecollaboration in foreign language learning is the application of synchronous or asynchronous online communication tools to bring together two groups of language learners in different geographical locations and from different lingua-cultural backgrounds. The aim is to develop foreign language skills and global cultural competence. Telecollaboration can be done in various formats from a loosely guided language exchange between paired partners to a more sophisticated collaborative research project. For instance, a weekly video-conferencing assignment between a Korean learner of English in Korea and an American learner of Korean in the US can be a great way to compensate for the lack of interactions with native speakers of similar ages in a conventional classroom setting. Also, students can experience an extended series of task- or project-based collaborative interactions, and receive more structured guidance and feedback from the instructors. For example, students in a pair or group may conduct in-depth research into the other's culture, society, or history in collaboration and publish their research on a class wiki. An implementation of telecollaborative projects in KFL contexts can be found in Lim and Lee (2015).

Technology has also been revolutionizing the way we make assessments of (and give feedback on) student learning (Walker & White, 2013). Not only do digital tools provide more efficient and cost-saving alternatives to traditional written and oral tests, but they also open up new possibilities. For example, it is much easier now to incorporate image, sound, and/or video with text into an online test, as well as for students to create a digital audio- and video-recording. Also, digitally written essays, when directly entered or uploaded as a digital file, are easier to comment on and check for originality (using Turnitin or SafeAssign for English and CopyKiller for Korean). E-portfolios are another example of an alternative assessment tool made available with the advancement of educational technology (Shin & Lee, Chapter 7, this volume). Yet, there are certain limitations in using technology for assessment that require caution. For instance, there is no good technological tool for automatic essay or speech scoring. Also, the use of computerized tests may incur new issues of academic integrity or the need for technical support for examinees.

2.4.3 *Effectiveness of technology use and effective use of technology*

Skepticism about the effectiveness of technology use in language instruction is justifiable. It is frequently the case that technology is adopted, not as a result of careful comparison studies between instructions carried out with and without technology, but for various other reasons put forward by program administrators and institutions (Chapelle, 2017). However, large-scale meta-analyses such as Grgurović et al. (2013) have found that technology-supported L2 instructions are as effective as those without technology support. Golonka et al. (2014), who reviewed over 350 empirical studies on various technology types and their effectiveness, also found moderate, albeit limited, support for technology use in foreign language learning. Empirical research projects focusing on individual skill areas also showed positive effects of technology use. For example, Yun (2011) reported that hypertext glosses had a moderately positive effect for L2 vocabulary acquisition, while Strobl (2014) discovered that computer-mediated collaborative writing was superior to individual writing in terms of appropriate content selection and organization, although there was no difference in complexity, accuracy, and fluency. (See Chun 2017 for an overview of other seminal works). Accepting the overall positive effects of technology in L2 learning cited in the studies above, we now turn to a more practical question of how to most effectively use technology in language teaching.

Teachers may well be captivated by a certain fancy feature of a new technology and be tempted to adopt it without much contemplation. However, it is beneficial for teachers to first ask themselves the five Ws and a H questions i.e., why, for whom, for what, where, when, and how the technology should be used (Stanley, 2013). For instance, one may ask the question "for whom should the technology be used" in order to determine the suitable age group, language level, and or required technical training for the target learners.

The SAMR model proposed by Puentedura (2013) also provides a practical insight into different levels of technology integration. SAMR stands for Substitution, Augmentation, Modification, and Redefinition. Substitution refers to when technology acts as a direct tool substitute with no functional change, as in the case of students using an online dictionary in place of a paper one to learn the definition and usage of new vocabulary items. Augmentation is the next level of integration, at which technology acts as a direct tool substitute with some functional improvement. For example, students use the online dictionary to listen to native speakers' pronunciation and build their own vocabulary lists. Modification is when technology allows for a significant task redesign. For instance, a teacher creates sets of online flashcards with integrated audio and images that are used by individual students in a study, test, or game mode on a mobile device. Redefinition is the highest level of integration, where technology enables teachers to create new tasks that were previously inconceivable. One example is when after studying online flashcards, students participate in collaborative live competition in classroom using an app like Quizlet Live.[11] Although Substitution and Augmentation may enhance teaching effectiveness, it is advised that teachers aim to achieve the transformative levels i.e., Modification and Redefinition, when designing a task using new technology (Puentedura, 2013).

A concerned teacher may ask whether technology can and will eventually replace classroom teachers. Reassuringly however, the American Council on the

Teaching of Foreign Languages asserts that "language instruction is best guided by language educators rather than solely delivered via a computer program or by a non-content specialist" (ACTFL, 2017). On the one hand, school administrators are advised "to place the responsibility for language instruction in the hands of *qualified* [emphasis added] language teachers rather than solely in technology programs" and, on the other hand, language educators should be able to "use content knowledge, research-informed teaching strategies, and effective technology applications to support language learning" (ACTFL, 2017).

However, as Clifford (1986) predicts, "while computers will not replace teachers, teachers who use computers will eventually replace teachers who don't" (p. 13). Admittedly, the reality is that recent job postings for a Korean instructor position often list some familiarity with instructional technology as a required or preferred qualification. Yet, it is unclear how much and what kind of technology proficiency a Korean language teacher should be equipped with. Given the lack of established technology standards in KFL, interested Korean instructors may refer instead to the *TESOL Technology Standards* (Healey et al., 2008). Its *Teacher Standards* consist of 14 standards under four overarching goals concerning teachers' knowledge and skills in technology (Goal 1), integration of pedagogy with technology (Goal 2), technology use in record-keeping, feedback, and assessment (Goal 3), and technology use for improved communication, collaboration, and efficiency (Goal 4). Each standard introduces several performance indicators and occasional vignettes, presenting more specific competencies and illustrative example situations.

In order to keep abreast of constantly evolving technologies and relevant teaching practices, it is important for CALL/TELL teachers to get training and support from various sources. Most higher education institutions offer their teaching staff education and training opportunities through an administrative unit such as a Center for Teaching and Learning. Webinars and online lecture materials hosted by a CTL unit are often made available for external members to remotely participate in real-time or for review afterwards. Membership-based professional development workshops, such as those organized by AATK (Cho et al., Chapter 8, this volume) and ACTFL, provide valuable opportunities to learn and exchange ideas about current practices in the field. ACTFL's Tech Watch page[12] periodically provides practical tips for the application of the newest technology tools to foreign language education. Finally, there are many resource websites such as Technology Is Learning.[13] Teachers can benefit from using various technology tools such as an E-portfolio or a VLE for the purpose of their own continuing professional development.

Discussion questions

1. How can the TBLT syllabus be distinguished from the Synthetic Syllabus and the Analytic Syllabus?
2. What are some of the problems of "Focus on Forms" and "Focus on Meaning"? Why is "Focus on Form" recommended? Are there any problems you perceive as a teacher using "Focus on Form"?

3. Imagine you are teaching an intermediate-level Korean course in a college setting and want to implement a TBLT curriculum. What would be the most challenging part among the six steps in the curriculum development in TBLT described in Section 2.2.3?
4. What is the major difference between TBLT and TSLT? Which approach do you prefer as a language teacher and why?
5. Why have so many different modified and hybrid models of CBI emerged over time?
6. What are the similarities and the differences between CBI and TBLT?
7. If you choose to adopt CBI in your language classroom, what would you feel to be the most effective ratio of content to language?
8. How is CBI similar to and/or different from CLIL?
9. What would be the potential advantages and disadvantages if you adopted CBI for beginning-level courses in comparison to advanced-level language classrooms?
10. Which of the technologies introduced in relation to language skill development do you think will work effectively for your current teaching situation? Why? What challenges, if any, do you expect to encounter and how would you be able to overcome them?
11. Navigate the VLE your institution provides. Spend some time in exploring different menus and functions (using the HELP menu or guidance website of the particular VLE, e.g., Blackboard Help, if necessary). What features do you think you will be able to start to use immediately? What will be the benefits of using them? What features do you think you would not use? Why not?
12. How would you set up a telecollaborative exchange for your Korean language course? Be as specific as possible about your ideal collaborative partner, the logistics of the partnership, and the collaborative assignment(s) your students will be working on.

Notes

1 Michael Long, Graham Crookes, John Norris, Catherine Doughty, and Ortega Lourdes were at the University of Hawaii and actively involved in the development of TBLT approaches at the time when Korean Flagship program was established.
2 See Hubbard (2009), Stanley (2013), and Li (2017) for further discussion on the affordances and benefits of technology in language teaching and learning.
3 For a concise overview, see Smith (2016). We also have consulted many chapters in Farr and Murray (2016) and Chapelle and Sauro (2017), most of which are not introduced individually in this chapter due to space limitations.
4 For detailed descriptions of sample activities, we refer to Stanley (2013), Walker and White (2013), and Li (2017), whose case studies from ESL are applicable to KFL. Teaching materials shared at AATK annual meetings (links available at http://aatk.org/) provide practical ideas on technology-enhanced activities for Korean language classrooms.
5 See https://ko.dict.naver.com/.
6 See https://krdict.korean.go.kr/.
7 See https://ithub.korean.go.kr/.

8 See https://kcorpus.korean.go.kr/.
9 See http://speller.cs.pusan.ac.kr/.
10 Private social media platforms such as Twiducate and Edmodo may be more suitable for L2 context.
11 A variety of sample activities and tasks for world language classes designed in relation to SAMR model are available at https://sites.google.com/a/ccpsnet.net/edtechhub/tech-services/samr/samr_high_school/world-language.
12 See https://www.actfl.org/publications/all/the-language-educator/tech-watch.
13 See https://sites.google.com/a/msad60.org/technology-is-learning/home.

References

ACTFL. (2017, May 20). The role of technology in language learning. Retrieved from https://www.actfl.org/news/position-statements/the-role-technology-language-learning.

Bergmann, J., & Sams, A. (2012). *Flip your classroom: Reach every student in every class every day*. Washington, DC: International Society for Technology in Education.

Brinton, D. (2003). Content-based instruction. In D. Nunan (Ed.), *Practical English language teaching* (pp. 199–224). New York: McGraw Hill.

Brinton, D., Snow, M. S., & Wesche, M. (2003). *Content-based second language instruction*. Ann Arbor, MI: The University of Michigan Press.

Bygate, M., Norris, J., & Van Den Branden, K. (2015). Task-based language teaching. In C. A. Chapelle (Ed.). *The encyclopedia of applied linguistics*. Hoboken, NJ: John Wiley & Sons, Ltd.

Chapelle, C. A. (2017). Evaluation of technology and language learning. In C. A. Chapelle & S. Sauro (Eds.), *The handbook of technology and second language teaching and learning* (pp. 378–392). Hoboken, NJ: John Wiley & Sons.

Chapelle, C. A., & Sauro, S. (Eds.) (2017). *The handbook of technology and second language teaching and learning*. Hoboken, NJ: John Wiley & Sons.

Cheon, S. Y. (2007). Content-based language instruction through Korean film. *Korean Language in America, 12*, 15–30.

Cho, Y.-M., Lee, H. S., Schulz, C., Sohn, H.-M., & Sohn, S.-O. (2010). *Integrated Korean: Beginning 2* (2nd edn.). Honolulu, HI: University of Hawaii Press.

Chun, D. M. (2017). Research methods for investigating technology for language and culture learning. In C. A. Chapelle & S. Sauro (Eds.), *The handbook of technology and second language teaching and learning* (pp. 393–408). Hoboken, NJ: John Wiley & Sons.

Clifford, R. (1986). The status of computer-assisted language instruction (Opening Keynote Address, CALICO'87 in Monterey). *CALICO Journal, 4*(4), 9–16.

Doughty, C. J., & Williams, J. L. (1998). *Focus on form in classroom second language acquisition*. New York: Cambridge University Press.

Ellis, R. (1997). Task-based language teaching: Sorting out the misunderstandings. *International Journal of Applied Linguistics, 19*(3), 221–246.

Ellis, R. (2003). *Task-based language learning and teaching*. Oxford, UK: Oxford University Press.

Ellis, R. (2009). Task-based language teaching: Sorting out the misunderstandings. *International Journal of Applied Linguistics, 19*(3), 221–246.

Ellis, R., & Shintani, N. (2014). *Exploring language pedagogy through second language acquisition research*. Milton Park, Abingdon: Routledge.

Ellis, R. (2017). Moving task-based language teaching forward. *Language Teaching, 50*(4), 507–526.

Farr, F., & Murray, L. (Eds.) (2016). *The Routledge handbook of language learning and technology*. London, UK/New York: Routledge.

Golonka, E. M., Bowles, A. R., Frank, V. M., Richardson, D. L., & Freynik, S. (2014). Technologies for foreign language learning: A review of technology types and their effectiveness. *Computer Assisted Language Learning, 27*(1), 70–105.

Grabe, W., & Stoller, F. L. (1997). A six-T's approach to content-based instruction. In M. A. Snow & D. M. Brinton (Eds.), The content-based classroom: Perspectives on integrating language and content (pp. 78–94). White Plains, NY: Longman.

Grabe, W. (2009). *Reading in a second language: Moving from theory to practice*. Cambridge: Cambridge University Press.

Grgurović, M., Chapelle, C. A., & Shelley, M. C. (2013). A meta-analysis of effectiveness studies on computer technology-supported language learning. *ReCALL, 25*(2), 165–198.

Grgurović, M. (2017). Blended language learning: Research and practice. In C. A. Chapelle & S. Sauro (Eds.), *The handbook of technology and second language teaching and learning* (pp. 149–168). Hoboken, NJ: John Wiley & Sons.

Healey, D., Hegelheimer, V., Hubbard, P., Ioannou-Georgiou, S., Kessler, G., & Ware, P. (2008). *TESOL technology standards framework*. Alexandria, VA: TESOL, Inc. Retrieved from https://www.tesol.org/docs/default-source/books/bk_technologystandards_framework_721.pdf.

Howard, E., Sugarman, J., Christian, D., Lindholm-Leary, K., & Rogers, D. (2007). *Guiding principles for dual language education* (2nd ed.). Washington, DC: Center for Applied Linguistics.

Howatt, A. (1984). *A history of English language teaching*. Oxford: Oxford University Press.

Hubbard, P. (2009). General introduction. In P. Hubbard (Ed.), *Computer assisted language learning* (Critical Concepts in Linguistics), *1* (pp. 1–20). London, UK: Routledge.

Hubbard, P. (2017). Technologies for teaching and learning L2 listening. In C. A. Chapelle & S. Sauro (Eds.), *The handbook of technology and second language teaching and learning* (pp. 93–106). Hoboken, NJ: John Wiley & Sons.

Kaufman, D., & Crandall, J. (2005). *Content-based instruction in primary and secondary school settings*. Alexandria, VA: TESOL.

Kim, H.-Y. (2005). Construction of language and culture in a content-based language class. *Korean Language in America, 10*, 50–70.

Kim, J.-E., Park, H., Jang, M., & Nam, H. (2017). Exploring flipped classroom effects on second language learners' cognitive processing. *Foreign Language Annals, 50*(2), 260–284.

Kim, Y., Choi, B., Kang, S., Kim, B., & Yun, H. (2020). Comparing the effects of direct and indirect synchronous written corrective feedback: Learning outcomes and students' perceptions. *Foreign Language Annals, 53*, 176–199.

Kim, Y., Choi, B., Yun, H., Kim, B., & Choi, S. (2020). Task repetition, synchronous written corrective feedback and the learning of Korean grammar: A classroom-based study. *Language Teaching Research*. https://doi.org/10.1177/1362168820912354.

Kong, D. (2012). Task-based language teaching in an advanced Korean language learning program. *Korean Language in America, 17*, 32–48.

Li, L. (2017). *New technologies and language learning*. London, UK: Palgrave.

Lightbown, P. (2014). *Focus on content-based language teaching*. Oxford: Oxford University Press.

Lim, B.-j., & Lee, H.-J. (2015). Videoconferencing for Korean language education: Synchronous online interactions between learners of Korean and English beyond the classroom. *Journal of Korean Language Education, 26*, 1–8.

Long, M. (1991). Focus on form: A design feature in language teaching methodology. In K. de Bot, R. Ginsberg & C. Kramsch (Eds.), *Foreign language research in cross-cultural perspective* (pp. 39–52). Amsterdam: John Benjamin.

Long, M., & Crookes, G. (1993). Units of analysis in syllabus design: The case for task. In G. Crookes & S. Gass (Eds.), *Tasks in language learning* (pp. 9–54). Clevedon: Multilingual Matters.

Long, M., & Robinson, P. (1998). Focus on form: Theory, research and practice. In C. Doughty & J. Williams (Eds.), *Focus on form in classroom second language acquisition.* Cambridge, UK: Cambridge University Press.

Long, M. (2005). Methodological issues in learner needs analysis. In M. Long (Ed.), *Second language needs analysis* (pp. 1–76). Cambridge: Cambridge University.

Long, M. (2005). *Second language needs analysis.* Cambridge: Cambridge University.

Long, M. (2015). *Second language acquisition and task-based language teaching.* Malden, MA: Wiley Blackwell.

Long, M. (2016). In defense of tasks and TBLT: Nonissues and real issues. *Annual Review of Applied Linguistics, 36,* 5–33.

Long, M. H., & Norris, J. M. (2000). Task-based language teaching and assessment. In M. Byram (Ed.), *Encyclopedia of language teaching* (pp. 597–603). London: Routledge.

Martinsen, R., Montgomery, C., & Willardson, V. (2017). The effectiveness of video-based shadowing and tracking pronunciation exercises for foreign language learners. *Foreign Language Annals, 50*(4), 661–680.

Met, M. (1998). Curriculum decision-making in content-based language teaching. In J. Cenoz & F. Genesee (Eds.), *Beyond bilingualism: Multilingualism and multilingual education* (pp. 35–63). Clevedon: Multilingual Matters.

Mohan, B. (1986). *Language and content.* Reading, MA: Addison-Wesley.

Muldrow, K. (2013, November). A new approach to language instruction—Flipping the classroom. *The language educator,* November 2013, *28–31.* Retrieved from https://www.actfl.org/sites/default/files/pdfs/TLE_pdf/TLE_Nov13_Article.pdf.

Noji, F., Yuen, S.-A., & Yuen, S.-A. K. (2012). Developing content based curriculum: Aimed toward superior level of proficiency. *Korean Language in America, 17,* 93–108.

Norris, J. M. (Ed.) (2002). Special issue: Task-based language assessment. *Language Testing, 19*(4).

Norris, J. M. (2009). Task-based teaching and testing. In M. Long & C. Doughty (Eds.), *Hand-book of language teaching* (pp. 578–594). Chichester, England: Wiley-Blackwell.

Park, B. Y. (2003). Using the hot potatoes program for improvement of grammar. *Korean Language in America, 8,* 141–142.

Park, M.-J. (2000). Incorporating intonation in Korean language instruction. *Korean Language in America, 5,* 373–384.

Picciano, A. (2009). Blending with purpose: The multimodal model. *Journal of Asynchronous Learning Networks, 13*(1), 7–18.

Puentedura, R. R. (2013, May 29). SAMR: Moving from enhancement to transformation [Web log post]. Retrieved from http://www.hippasus.com/rrpweblog/archives/000095.html.

Richards, J., & Rodgers, T. (2001). *Approaches and methods in language teaching.* New York: Cambridge University Press.

Robinson, P. (2001). Task complexity, task difficulty, and task production: Exploring interactions in a componential framework. *Applied Linguistics, 22*(1), 27–57.

Robinson, P. (2011). Second language task complexity, the cognition hypothesis, language learning, and performance. In P. Robinson (Ed.), *Second language task complexity.*

Researching the cognition hypothesis of language learning and performance (pp. 3–37). Amsterdam: John Benjamins.

Roh, J., & Kim, T. (2019). Fostering learner autonomy through CALL and MALL in a Korean class: A case study. *Journal of Interactive Learning Research, 30*(2), 215–254.

Samuda, V., & Bygate, M. (2008). *Tasks in second language learning.* Houndmills: Palgrave.

Shin, S., & Kim, S. (2000). The introduction of content-based language teaching to college-level Korean program for heritage learners. *Korean Language in America, 5,* 167–179.

Skehan, P., & Foster, P. (2001). Cognition and tasks. In P. Robinson (Ed.), *Cognition and second language instruction* (pp. 183–205). Cambridge, UK: Cambridge University Press.

Skehan, P. (2009). Modeling second language performance: Integrating complexity, accuracy, fluency, lexis. *Applied Linguistics, 30*(4), 1–23.

Smith, B. (2016). *Technology in language learning: An overview.* New York: Routledge.

Snow, M. A. (2001). Content-based and immersion models for second and foreign language teaching. In M. Celce-Murcia (Ed.), *Teaching English as a second or foreign language* (3rd ed.) (pp. 303–318). Boston, MA: Heinle & Heinle.

Stanley, G. (2013). *Language learning with technology: Ideas for integrating technology in the classroom.* Cambridge, UK: Cambridge University Press.

Strobl, C. (2014). Affordances of Web 2.0 technologies for collaborative advanced writing in a foreign language. *CALICO Journal, 31*(1), 1–18.

Valdes, G. (1997). Dual-language immersion programs: A cautionary note concerning the education of language-minority students. *Harvard Educational Review, 67*(3), 391–430.

Van den Branden, K., Bygate, M., & Norris, J. M. (Eds.) (2009). *Task-based language teaching: A reader.* Amsterdam: John Benjamins.

Walker, A., & White, G. (2013). *Technology enhanced language learning: Connecting theory and practice.* Oxford, UK: Oxford University Press.

Wesche, M., & Skehan, P. (2002). Communicative, task-based, and content-based language instruction. In R. Kaplan (Ed.), *The Oxford handbook of applied linguistics* (pp. 207–228). Oxford: Oxford University Press.

Wheeler, G. (2013). *Language teaching through the ages* (Routledge Research in Education; 93). New York: Routledge.

Wilkins, D. (1976). *Notional syllabuses.* London: Oxford University Press.

Yong, N., & Ko, S. (2019). The hybrid course for college-level elementary Korean: Its development and implementation. *Korean Language in America, 22*(2), 156–166.

Yun, J. (2011). The effects of hypertext glosses on L2 vocabulary acquisition: A meta-analysis. *Computer Assisted Language Learning, 24*(1), 39–58.

권정아 (2012). 페이스북을 이용한 한국어 초급 수업—쓰기 활동을 중심으로 [The application of Facebook to Korean elementary class]. *Journal of Korean Language Education, 23*(4), 1–29.

박은선 (2012). 한국어 교육에서 트위터 사용의 교육적 효과 [The educational effect of Twitter on Korean education]. *Journal of Korean Language Education, 23*(2), 115–141.

안재린 & 심윤진 (2018). 한국어 교육에서의 인스타그램 활용 가능성 탐색—미국 대학교의 사례를 중심으로 [Exploring the instructional use of Instagram for Korean language learning]. *Journal of Korean Language Education, 29*(4), 65–92.

3 Language in use

Mary Shin Kim and Kyung-Eun Yoon

3.1 Introduction

The concept of communicative competence, using language appropriately to communicate in authentic situations, has been widely incorporated in foreign language teaching and second language acquisition (Hymes, 1972; Celce-Murcia et al., 1995). The communicative approach was developed in line with the functional linguistic theory which started to consider grammar to originate in recurrent patterns in the actual uses of language (Givón, 1979). The functional linguistic perspective has been influential to the interactional linguistic approach, in which language structures and uses are formed through interaction (Ochs et al., 1996). In the field of language pedagogy as well, Kramsch (1986) suggested "an interactionally oriented curriculum" (p. 369) based on the concept of "interactional competence" (p. 367). This approach challenges a view which treats language learning as a static, cognitive process of individuals rather than a dynamic, interactive process. Interaction is a collaborative activity which involves a negotiating process of "anticipating the listener's response and possible misunderstandings, clarifying one's own and the other's intentions and arriving at the closest possible match between intended, perceived, and anticipated meanings" (p. 367). Therefore, it is important for an interactionally oriented curriculum to include "a critical and explicit reflection of the discourse parameters of language in use" (p. 369).

Inspired by Kramsch, many researchers have further developed the concept of interactional competence (Young, 2008; Hall & Pekarek Doehler, 2011) and investigated it pedagogically (Kasper, 2006; Galaczi, 2014). Within this approach, it is important to comprehend various types of linguistic, pragmatic, cultural, and interactional resources employed in interactions (i.e., the features of pronunciation, vocabulary, and grammar that typify a practice; speech acts and the selection of acts in a practice and their sequential organization; how participants select the next speaker, and how participants know when to end one turn and when to begin the next, etc. [Young, 2008]). It is also important to note that interactional competence involves all participants' mutual and reciprocal employment of these resources in social contexts. Following this view, we suggest that language educators make pedagogical attempts to develop learners' interactional competence in their teaching, so that the learners can use language in communicating with others in real contexts. This chapter will therefore review some specific aspects of linguistic, pragmatic, and interactional resources for developing interactional competence in Korean, and make suggestions for teaching. The following sections will discuss three aspects: (1) how we manage what we talk about; (2) how we structure language; and (3) what we do with language in Korean.

3.2 Managing topic and reference

This section will review linguistic, pragmatic, and interactional aspects of how we manage what we talk about, meaning the management of topic and reference in Korean discourse. Topic and reference management is important in establishing discourse coherence and communicating ideas in language use. Therefore, many studies from functional and interactional perspectives have investigated discourse-pragmatic characteristics of noun phrase (NP) forms and post-nominal markers in Korean (Chang, 1978; Lee, 1986; Kim, 1993; Oh, 2007). Before discussing explicit NP forms, this section will begin with the use of zero anaphora in Korean. Although it is an invisible linguistic construct, zero anaphora plays an important role in discourse as the most utilized resource for simple reference in Korean. After reviewing zero anaphora as the default form, this section will discuss functions of NPs or pronominal forms with post-nominal markers.

3.2.1 Zero anaphora

Zero anaphora is a morphologically unrealized form of reference and it is used when the referent can be understood from the context, as seen in Excerpt (1).

(1) [Phone call from Daughter to her family]

1 Daughter: 그래 준수는 갔어요?

   kulay Junsoo-nun ka-ss-eyo?

   "So, is *Junsoo* (Brother) gone?"

2 Mom: 준수 있어.

   Junsoo iss-e.

   "*Junsoo* is here."

3 Daughter: Ø 있어? Ø 자?

   Ø iss-e? Ø ca?

   'Is **(he)**? Is **(he)** sleeping?'

The referent, *Junsoo*, is clearly established in lines 1 and 2 by the two speakers, and then omitted in line 3, leaving gaps in the subject positions of the two interrogative sentences. Such a use of zero anaphora is "a referential strategy for presuppositionally background information established by context" (Lee, 1987: p. 23). That is, it is used for simple reference and functionally equivalent to lexical pronouns in English (Kim, 2012). It is a highly salient feature in Korean (Oh,

2007), and its extensive usage in Korean is for the function of maintaining discourse cohesion (Kim, 2012).

Recognizing the importance of the use of zero anaphora in Korean, Kim (2012) examines its use by L2 Korean learners at three different proficiency levels: the lowest group approximately at elementary-high to intermediate-low levels, the second group approximately at an intermediate-mid, and the third group approximately at intermediate-high or advanced. An important finding is that the lowest proficiency learners use zero pronouns extensively in short, single-clausal utterances. The learners in the second group also show a tendency to use zero anaphora limitedly. They use it only in utterances immediately following the prior mention, rather than moving the story forward. They prefer to use explicit NPs even when there was no switch in the main topic, which tends to punctuate narrative progression. On the other hand, the learners in the third group produce narratives more smoothly by taking advantage of the economy of zero anaphora when the referent was well-established and continuous. This study notes the crucial role of the appropriate use of zero anaphora, overt pronominal forms, and NPs for text cohesion and effective organization of talk, and therefore suggests that discourse functions and constraints of zero anaphora be included as important pedagogical elements in referential communication for Korean learners. See Section 3.3.1 and 3.3.2.1 for more discussion on the use of zero anaphora in written and oral discourse. The following activity is a sample exercise for students which can be used in class.

Student Activity 1: Compare the Korean and English versions of the same conversation and find the elements that are omitted in Korean.

[Modified from the Linguistics Data Consortium Korean Corpus of Telephone Speech, 5074]

1 W: 면허증 있어?	Do you have a driver's license?
2 M: 아, 지금 교육 받고 있어.	Oh, I am getting training now.
3 W: 받고 있어?	You're getting training?
4 M: 어, 이번에 따야지.	Yes, I need to get it this time.
5 M: 거긴 몇 살부터야?	From what age can you get a license there?
6 W: 열 일곱인가 열 여섯인가?	I think at 17 or 16?
7 M: 여긴 열 여섯.	You can get a license at 16 here.
8 M: 면허증 땄어?	Did you get your driver's license?
9 W: 아직.	Not yet.

3.2.2 NP with subject marker

As stated earlier, simple reference in Korean is typically done through zero anaphora, which is the unmarked referential choice (Chang, 1978). Therefore, overt reference term such as NPs or pronominal forms are used to accomplish something else in discourse. Overt reference terms are commonly expected to have postnominal markers for cases and functions, of which this section focuses on NPs with *i/ka* (이/가). *I/ka* has traditionally been considered to mark the grammatical category of subject in a sentence, but many studies have attempted to find their functions from discourse functional and interactional perspectives. Lee (1987) emphasizes the importance of investigating post-nominal markers such as *i/ka* and *un/nun* (은/는) from a discourse perspective, rather than relying on sentence-based analysis. He considers it to be highly important to comprehensively understand how discourse is organized and what roles the markers play in discourse organization. From this viewpoint, he explains that the use of *i/ka* is for "expressing happenings where the relation of participants and events is specific but not known to the addressee," meaning that the speaker uses it to specify the participants and individualize them as specific participants of the event (Lee, 1987: p. 23).

Inspired by such discourse pragmatic approaches, Oh (2007) conducts a conversation analytic study on interactional functions of overt reference forms including NPs with subject markers, focusing particularly on how the speaker makes reference to himself/herself and to the recipient. The findings demonstrate that the speaker employs overt self- (e.g., *nayka* 내가) or recipient-reference (e.g., *neyka* 네가) marked with *ka* in order to attribute credit or responsibility to the agent, whether it be the speaker or the recipient. It is noted that "the particle *ka* emphasizes the status of the NP that it follows (i.e., the speaker or the recipient) as an active participant in the state-of-affairs described by the predicate" (Oh, 2007, p. 478). Excerpt (2) is an example.

(2) [Modified from Oh, 2007: p. 478, (10)]

1   K: 그랬드니 아무 애기 못하구 그냥 가드라구: 근데 또

         kulayss-tu-ni amwu yayki mos ha-kwu kunyang ka-tu-lakwu: kuntey tto

2   되:게 미안하데 애기하니까 또¿ (0.2) 열변을 토하니까¿=

         toy:key mianhatey yaykiha-nikka tto¿ (0.2) yelpyen-ul thoha-nikka¿=

         "I said that, and he just went away, being able to say nothing. But then I felt

         really sorry, after I said it. (0.2) After I delivered a fervent speech."

3   N: =그래:: (1.8) **니가** 그런 식으루 뭐 영업부 직원들을 (1.2)

         =kulay:: (1.8) ni-ka kulen sik-ulwu mwe yengep-pwu cikwen-tul-ul (1.2)

4   죽이면 안 되는 거야::.

         cwuki-myen an toy-nun ke-ya::.

         "That's right. (1.8) **YOU** SHOULD NOT (1.2) SMASH the members of the business department like that:::.."

5   L: ((laugh))

This function of *ka* is found to be exploited especially in the context of praising or blaming the agent. For example, when the speaker seeks recognition or appreciation from the recipient for what s/he has done, a first-person pronoun marked with *ka* is used more often than is necessary for resolving the ambiguity. Also, when the speaker tries to attribute responsibility for a particular event to the recipient, or blame the recipient for the event's negative consequence, an overt recipient reference form marked with *ka* is frequently used. In sum, this study shows how the referential practices can be based on interactional motivations.

3.2.3 NP with topic marker

NPs marked with *un/nun* (은/는) have gained much attention in prior studies in semantic, functional linguistic, and interactional approaches. *Un/nun* is commonly called a topic marker in Korean, and its functions have been considered to be marking topical elements or contrastive elements. Lee (1986), however, argues that topicality and contrastiveness should be understood on a continuum rather than as distinct functions from each other. This study shows that marking of topical elements and marking of contrastive elements serve the same communicative function, since the topic marker signals a topic or thematic shift and contrastiveness is one subcase of thematic shift. In line with this account, Kim (1993) notes thematicity and contrastiveness as two essential properties of topicality and examines how they are interactionally managed in ordinary conversation. Kim's study finds utterances with NPs and *un/nun* to be frequently used in the contexts of disagreement and backing down before the person reasserts his/her point. In terms of discourse-organizational contexts, those utterances are observed to occur when the speaker initiates a story or provides a situational comment.

Another study from the interactional perspective (Oh, 2007), focusing on the usage of the self- and recipient-reference forms with *nun* (e.g., *nanun* (나는) and *nenun* (너는) respectively), also demonstrates that these forms are frequently utilized for signaling some sort of contrast and thereby showing disagreement. When the speaker needs to bring up a difference between himself/herself and the recipient or others, s/he recurrently uses *nanun* or *nenun*, as seen in Excerpt (3).

(3) [Modified from Oh, 2007: p. 482, (12)]

1   K: 에이 **너는** 얘 하나라 (.) 좋겠다 **나는** 둘이라

        eyi ne-nun <u>yay</u> hana-la (.) coh-keyss-ta na-nun twul-i-la

2   하나 <u>얘</u> 해주면 애두 똑같이 해줘야 되구

        hana <u>yay</u> haycwu-myen yay-twu <u>ttok</u>kathi haycweya toy-kwu

        "Well, hey, **you** must be happy that you have only one daughter-in-law. Because **I** have two, if I do something for this one, I have to do the same for the other and … ."

The function of *nun* in the speaker's presentation of a contrasting aspect is to make the contrast between the two parties more explicit. In the case of *nanun*, another function of *nun* is to limit the boundary of the contrasted opinion to himself/herself, meaning it is used to claim that what s/he is saying is only his/her opinion, not that of others.

3.2.4 NP and phrasal unit boundary in conversation

NP forms in Korean play a role in organizing the interactional structure of oral discourse as well. A speaker's turn in conversation commonly consists of sentential, phrasal, or lexical units (Sacks et al., 1974). On a possible completion of a turn based on these units, transition to the next speaker becomes relevant. While a transition to the next speaker often becomes relevant at a boundary between sentence units in English, Kim (1999) demonstrates that unit boundaries in Korean conversations are frequently formed while a turn is still in progress (e.g., at a point where a clause or a phrase comes to an end). The phrasal unit boundaries are created in such a way that the speaker of the turn in progress stretches the final sound of a phrasal unit, such as an NP often marked by a post-nominal case or functional marker, with continuing or slightly upward intonation. The speaker's continuing or slightly upward intonation at the boundary is indicated by a comma as seen in line 1 of Excerpt (4), which frequently prompts a brief response from the recipient, usually in the forms of acknowledgment tokens such as *yey*, *ney*, or *ung* as seen in line 2. The recipient's brief acknowledgment displays his/her understanding of the speaker's utterance up to the particular point and signals to the primary speaker that s/he may continue talking and complete the turn in progress. The following excerpt shows an example.

(4) [Modified from Kim, 1999: p. 429, (2)]

1   S: 분당에 막상 진짜 살고 있는 사람들은,

        Pundang-ey maksang cincca sal-ko iss-nun salam-tul-un,

        "Those who are living in Pundang,"

2   Y: 응

        ung.

        'Yes.'

3   S: 속-- 속마음은 안 그렇다네:::

        sok-- sok maym-un an kuleh-tay-ney:::

        "(they) don't actually feel like that, they say."

The phrasal unit boundaries provide opportunities for the interactants to mutually contribute to the ongoing talk. The speaker solicits the recipient's attention and cooperative response to what s/he has said, and the recipient shows his/her understanding and gives the go-ahead to proceed and complete the turn. NPs in these contexts therefore become resources for the joint practice of organizing the structure of ordinary conversation in Korean. Section 3.3 will present further discussions on the structure of discourse in Korean.

3.3 Organizing discourse

This section introduces how writers and speakers organize discourse. It is not enough just to learn how to construct sentences and utterances, but you must learn how to coherently and cohesively combine sentences at a discourse level and interactively co-construct turns and talk. Both written and oral discourse have underlying structural organizations to which learners need to attend. The structure and prominent features of Korean written discourse will be described first, followed by the discussion of Korean spoken discourse.

3.3.1 Structure of written discourse

Like topic management, discourse organization is crucial in establishing discourse coherence, and therefore has been the focus of prior discourse functional linguistics research. There are four basic types of written discourse: narrative (e.g., stories), procedural (e.g., manuals), hortatory (e.g., sermon), and expository (e.g., news articles), and each type of discourse has different aims, components, and linguistics features (Longacre, 1996; Hwang, 2015). Depending on the learners' needs and proficiency levels, each discourse can be incorporated into a class. Narratives can be introduced from the beginning level of learning, while procedural, hortatory, and expository discourses may be more suitable for learners at the advanced level. Narrative is well-known as the meaningful and engaging discourse type for teaching and learning language skills and cultural knowledge (Wajnryb, 2003; Wang, 2008), and therefore the focus of this section is on the discourse structure and features of Korean narratives.

A narrative usually begins with a prologue followed by a series of episodes which comprise a narrative. Each episode may constitute an inciting incident, developing conflict, and climax in the overall discourse structure, as shown below (Hwang, 2015).

(5) [Modified from Hwang, 2015: pp. 289–294]

I. Prologue:

S1 충청남도 동학사 뒤에 오누이 탑이 지금도 우뚝 서 있다.

"Behind the Tonghak Temple in South Chungcheong Province, (there) loftily stands the Brother-and-Sister Pagoda even now."

S2 이 탑에는 낭만과 공포가 서려있는 절이 있다.

"About this pagoda (there) is a legend bearing romance and horror."

II. Stage

S3 어떤 스님이 혼자서 절을 지키며 열심히 불공을 드리고 있었다.

"A monk was keeping the temple alone and earnestly conducting the Buddhist masses."

III. Episode 1 (Inciting incident)

IV. Episode 2 (Climax)

V. Closure

VI. Epilogue

According to Hwang, the analysis of the narrative provides a better understanding of not only the structural features, but also the morpho-syntactic features of the language, because it shows why a certain linguistic form is deployed in the given context of the discourse. For instance, as narrative reports a past story, tense plays an important role in discourse organization. Depending on what role and position the sentence occupies in the narrative structure, different tenses and aspect are deployed. The mainline of the events is usually conveyed in the simple past tense *ess* (었), as in S21 and S23, while supportive information which identifies the setting, characters, and motivation for an action is delivered in the present tense, as in S22 and S24. Sentences which do not report events, but rather ongoing activities or states, may be marked by the progressive, as in S3 or resultative aspect. In particular, when the main characters of the story are first introduced, the progressive form is often used as in S3, while this is not the case in English (Lee, 2006; Hwang, 2015). Teachers can teach these different tense and aspect strategies observed in Korean discourse by utilizing narratives in class.

(6) [Narrative lines from Hwang, 2015: pp. 289–293]

Climax of 미녀와 스님 'The Beauty and the Monk'

S21   스님은 여인에게 곧 상경하도록 **권고했다**.

       "The monk **advised** the woman to go to Seoul immediately."

S22   집에서는 호랑이에게 잡혀가서 죽었으리라고 걱정하고 있었기 **때문이다**.

       "**(It) is** because (people) at home would be worried that (she) must have died, being captured and taken by a tiger."

S23   그러나 이 처녀는 이를 **거절했다.**

       "However, the girl **refused** to do so."

S24   자기의 생명을 구해주신 스님과 평생을 함께 지내야겠다는 **것이다**.

       "**The fact is** that (she) wants to spend (her) life together with the monk who saved her life."

Teachers can further direct learners' attention to many other linguistic features which reflect the boundaries within the discourse structure, such as zero anaphora, discussed in Section 3.2.1. Once the main characters are introduced explicitly in the beginning of the story, they can be omitted (zero anaphora) afterwards in the discourse, as it is given information. However, they are explicitly referred to when a new episode starts, marking a break in discourse structure. Another prominent linguistic feature which separates the peak of the story from the rest of the narrative is that reported speech is often deployed in the peak of the story for dramatic and engaging effect. Single short clause sentences often reflect the tension at the climax of the narrative (Hwang, 2015).

Based on the understanding of the Korean narrative discourse structure and its prominent linguistic features, teachers can develop various activities utilizing narratives. Wajnryb (2003) provides a wide range of detailed and comprehensive narrative activities for the language classroom. Wang's *Frog's Tears and Other Stories* (2008) supplies captivating Korean traditional folktales that can engage beginning- and intermediate-level learners' interests.

3.3.2 Structure of spoken discourse

Now we will focus on unpacking the structure of spoken discourse, in particular conversation. Conversation is constructed and organized by two main practices, turn-taking and sequencing practices. Understanding these practices is important because speakers' utterances are used in and, at the same time, shaped by these systematic operations that underlie talk-in-interaction. This section will also address how the distinct grammatical structure and features of Korean are tied to the interactional practices and resources of Korean speakers (e.g., uniqueness in turn-taking format).

3.3.2.1 Turn-taking practices

Turn-taking is a fundamental practice that learners need to acquire to engage in a conversation. It is not through sentences, but through turns that speakers (co)construct talk and actions in an interaction (Sacks et al., 1974). One of the prominent features of Korean turn-taking is that turns are constructed allusively, because various parts of utterances can be omitted as discussed in Section 3.2.1. These allusively constructed utterances require speakers to fill in the gaps and monitor how the current turn ties back to prior turns. It is essential for learners to have opportunities to learn this feature through awareness-raising activities that utilize authentic or simply modified conversational talk.

Turn-taking practices can be a challenge for learners, because turn-taking cannot be practiced by a single speaker simply constructing the talk, but requires the active participation of recipients who orient to the talk. Recipients display understanding and pass up opportunities to take turns themselves. In English, recipients produce continuers (Schegloff, 1982) or "response tokens," "acknowledgment tokens," "reactive tokens," such as "uh huh" and "yeah," yielding turns or acknowledging that the speaker's turn will continue. Continuers usually occur at or near where the talk is grammatically, intonationally, and pragmatically complete (Ford & Thompson, 1996). However, in Korean, recipients produce such tokens (e.g., *yey, ney, ung,* "yes," "yeah") at turn phrasal boundaries, as discussed in Section 3.2.4. The two excerpts in the following activity show the contrast between English and Korean response tokens in terms of their placement locations and functions. Lee et al. (2017) provide a wide range of procedures and activities for teaching Korean response tokens, which can be easily applied to Korean L2 and KFL classrooms.

Student Activity 2: Identify response tokens in each dialogue and discuss the following questions in small groups.

a. Where is the recipient's response token located in relation to the speaker's turn?
b. Are there any differences in terms of the English and Korean response tokens' locations?
c. What are the functions of response tokens?

[English dialogue, modified from Young & Lee, 2004: p. 383, (1)]

1. AA: Actually I'm I paint (0.3) and I do
2.   some drawing but painting's more my thing.
3. JA: [yeah.]
4. AA: [I have]n't really done much since high school so,
5. JA: yeah.
6. AA: I've really missed it.
7. JA: [mhm,]
8. AA: [and] so it's it's really like fun for me.

[Korean dialogue, modified from Young & Lee, 2004: p. 384, (3)]

1. DK: 저는 (1.0) 엄마[가:,] (0.4) 비비안 리 팬[이라]서, 옛날에
          "Because my mom is a Vivien Leigh fan…"

2. MK: [예]   [예]
                         "yeah"   "yeah"

3. DK: 한국에서 명화 극장인가 [그런]거에서 몇 번을 봤었어요.
          "I must have seen this movie many times on the TV in Korea."

4. MK: [예]
                               "yeah"

3.3.2.2 Sequencing practices

Sequencing refers to how turns-at-talk are ordered (e.g., a sequence-initiating turn and a responding turn) and combined to perform certain actions, such as a summon–answer sequence (엄마 "Mom!" – 응 "Yes."), greeting sequence (안녕 "Hi." – 안녕 "Hi."), "how are you" sequence (어떻게 지냈어요? "How have you been?" – 잘 지냈어요 "I have been well."), request–comply/reject sequence (Excerpt (11)), and offer–acceptance/decline sequence (Excerpt (15)). An understanding of sequencing practice is important, since the absence of a responding turn has consequences in interaction: when someone does not answer a question, the speaker may take it as an addressee's hearing or understanding problem or as a refusal to answer and respond accordingly. Sequencing practice also illuminates the importance of understanding that an action implemented by an utterance is not only affected by the composition of an utterance (i.e., word, word order, some aspect of articulation), but also by its position (i.e., the placement of an utterance in a sequence) (Schegloff, 2007). For example, the word *ney* functions differently depending on the position of the sequence in which it occurs, as shown in Excerpt (7).

(7) [LDC Korean telephone conversation 6783]

1	A:	저기 잘 있어요?	[A sequence-initiating turn]
		ceki cal iss-e-yo?	
		"Have (you) been well?"	
2	B:	네, 그럼요.	[A responding turn]
		ney, kulem-yo.	
		"Yes, of course."	
3	A:	네.	[A sequence-closing turn in third position]
		ney.	
		"Okay."	

As a response to a yes/no interrogative which elicits the speaker's (dis)confirmation, *ney* in line 2 serves as a confirmation response token, "yes." However, where *ney* occurs in the third position in line 3, it serves to close the question-and-answer sequence.

The importance of the sequencing practice will be further discussed in Section 3.4, where we will examine the ways of initiating and responding to talk while carrying out key social actions such as requesting, inviting, and displaying agreement or disagreement.

3.4 Performing social actions

With an understanding of how discourse structures are organized, this section will discuss how we conduct actions using the Korean language in these systems. In daily social interaction, we carry out and come across a wide range of social actions, such as asking for information, expressing opinions, agreeing or disagreeing with someone, making suggestions or requests, providing offers, complaining, apologizing, and more. With research from the perspectives of pragmatics, interactional linguistics, and conversation analysis, this section will provide insights on how participants conduct these various actions in interactional contexts.

3.4.1 Sentence endings for doing actions

We will first discuss how some linguistic forms in Korean, particularly some sentence endings, are employed as devices for performing certain actions. Research on the relationship between form and function in Korean has revealed that many Korean sentence endings are used to do actions in addition to conveying grammatical or semantic meanings. We will select *ci*, *nuntey*, and *kuntey*, and discuss how they become resources for conducting actions in interactional discourse.

3.4.1.1 Ci

Since *ci* (지) is one of the most frequent sentence endings in informal discourse in Korean (Lee, 1999), much research has paid attention to its meanings. By analyzing it from discourse pragmatic perspectives, Lee (1999) provides a comprehensive explanation on the functions of *ci* in actual communication. Building on the findings of previous research, he explicates *ci*'s functions of displaying the speaker's conviction in declarative statements (see Excerpt (8)), asking for confirmation or seeking for agreement in interrogative sentences, and indicating a suggestion in imperative contexts. Then he presents a consistent function underlying all the aforementioned ones; that is, to show that the speaker leans toward committing himself/herself to the conveyed message and to emphasize his/her belief about the message.

> (8) [Modified from Lee, 1999: p. 248, (1), H talking about Dodger Stadium in LA]
>
> 1   H: 여기 딱 들어가면은, 입이 짝 벌어지**지**.
>
>   *yeki ttak tuleka-myen-un, ip-i ccak peleci-**ci**.*
>
>   "If you enter here, your mouth will drop open *ci* [definitely it will]."
>
> 2   S: 그렇게 커요?
>
>   *kulehkey khe-yo?*
>
>   "Is it that big?"

Lee (1999) translates *ci* as "definitely it will" (p. 248) and explains that the use of *ci* expresses the speaker's confidence in what will happen if someone enters Dodger Stadium.

3.4.1.2 Nuntey/kuntey

Nuntey (는데) is a clausal connective with intricate meanings and functions. Park (1999) pays attention to its use in the sentence-final position in conversation because her data reveal that the majority of its occurrences are in this position, rather than in the sentence-medial position. She finds that the use of *nuntey* in the sentence-ending position is closely related to many speech act functions such as requests (Excerpt (9)), disagreements (Excerpt (21)), denials, and rejections, which are interactionally delicate actions. Utterances with *nuntey* in these delicate contexts allow the speaker to avoid explicitly stating his/her intentions and remain indirect. For example, line 1 in Excerpt (9) performs a request by conveying the speaker's intention or wish rather than actually requesting the interlocutor to do the representing prayer (e.g., 대표 기도 좀 해주세요 ["Please do the representing prayer."] or 대표 기도 좀 해주실 수 있어요? ["Can you do the representing prayer?"]). Such an indirect strategy is for "inviting the interlocutor to figure out what the speaker is implying" (Park, 1999: p. 198). The interlocutor responds with a follow-up question regarding the time of the prayer in line 2, implying a reason for not being able to accept the request. This way, both participants show their orientations to the delicate aspect of a request sequence.

(9) [Modified from Park, 1999: p. 194, (6)]

1   L: 제가 대표 기도 부탁드리려구 하**는데**:

*cey-ka tayphyo kito pwuthaktuli-lyekwu ha-**nuntey**:*

"I wanted to ask you to do the representing prayer *nuntey*"

2   T: 그게 일찍 있는 거 아닙니까?

kukey ilccik iss-nun ke ani-pni-kka?

"Isn't that the one in the early part (of the meeting)?"

Another context for the use of *nuntey* is when the "speaker provides what s/he found out, saw or heard from his/her side as circumstantial and evidential ground to be shared and invites the interlocutor to infer the speaker's intention" (Park, 1999: p. 216). She explains such usage as a cultural practice of providing the minimum amount of information, in which case *nuntey* functions as a resource for conveying substantial messages.

Kuntey (근데), another form derived from *nuntey*, becomes a focus of investigation regarding its use in the sentence-final position in disaffiliative actions such as disagreements, refusals, and rejections in Kim and Sohn (2015). They find that *kuntey*, which typically occurs at the beginning of an utterance (see Excerpt (21) in Section 3.4.2.4), is found in the turn-final position as well when the speaker rejects the course of action proposed by the prior speaker and shifts the prior talk's frame to a slightly revised one.

(10) [Modified from Kim and Sohn, 2015: p. 79, (7)]

1   Sylvia: 내 친구가 여기 아파트 summer time에 lease한다는데

nay chinkwu-ka yeki aphathu summer time-ey
lease-ha-n-ta-nuntey

2   그: 생각해봐요. 좀 크고 그런데.

ku: sayngkak-hay-pwa-yo. com khu-ko kule-ntey.

"My friend here is leasing her apartment this summer. Think about it. It's quite big and stuff like that."

3   (0.2)

4   Sally: 방이 너무 작아 **근데**. 그 하나 방이.

*pang-i nemwu cak-a **kuntey**. ku hana pang-i.*

"The room is too small *kuntey*. That one room."

Kim and Sohn argue that the turn-final *kuntey* in interactionally delicate contexts plays a role as a useful resource for the speaker to delay his/her disaffiliative stance and use as a face-saving strategy.

More studies on different sentence endings include *ketun* (거든) for providing background information (Park, 1998; Park & Sohn, 2002), *ney* (네), *kwuna* (구나), and *-ta* (다) for marking newly perceived information (Lee, 1993; Kim, 2004; Kim, 2010), and *telako* (더라고) for marking evidentiality and negotiating epistemic rights (Kim, 2005).

3.4.2 Action formation and responses

While Section 3.4.1 examined how certain linguistic forms are employed as resources for performing particular actions, this section focuses on discussing how different types of actions are constructed and responded to in interaction. We will focus on examining how Korean speakers make requests and offers and display agreements and disagreements. These actions are in particular of importance to learners because they not only frequently occur in daily lives, but they are delicate actions tied to politeness in social interaction.

3.4.2.1 Requests

We seek and receive assistance from others in carrying out daily mundane tasks at home and at work. Requests and offers are recognized as the key action types through which we seek and receive assistance. Requests and offers have a reciprocal relationship to one another. With an offer, the addressee is the benefactor of the service, whereas with a request, the speaker is the benefactor of the act. However, they are not symmetric alternatives (Couper-Kuhlen & Selting, 2017: p. 249). From a politeness perspective, requests can impinge on the other's freedom of action (Pearson, 1989) and thus can be an imposition that threatens the other's face (Brown & Levinson, 1987). From an interactional perspective, offers are preferred over requests. Speakers delay, mitigate, or account for the requests (Schegloff, 2007). Requests are sometimes camouflaged as offers (Leech, 2014).

As requesting bears delicate implications, such as need, obligation, imposition, and constraint, there is a wide range of forms and strategies with which requests are performed in social interaction. It can be directly or indirectly constructed (e.g., 연필 좀 빌려 줘. "Please lend me a pencil." versus 연필 다 썼어? "Are you done using the pencil?"). It can be implemented on-record versus off-record (e.g., 연필 좀 빌려 줄래? "Can you lend me a pencil?" versus 혹시 연필 있어? "Do you have a pencil by any chance?"). Requests can be constructed through imperatives, questions, or statements and with or without mitigators. So, how do speakers choose their forms and strategies?

Studies on Korean request acts show that Korean speakers prefer using indirect strategies, such as interrogatives (Byon, 2006; Koo, 2001; Rue et al., 2007) and that request strategies are also chosen primarily according to social status and social distance between the speakers. Longer sentences with more hedges are considered indirect, and thus polite, while imperative formats are considered impolite compared to other question or statement formats. Although these previous studies are based on written texts or imaginary role plays, these findings are found to be relevant in making high-cost requests in conversation (asking for help from a stranger or imposing a difficult request). As shown in Excerpts (11) and (12), interrogative formats are preferred.

(11) [A person approaches a stranger and asks him/her to take a photo for her]

1   A: 저어, 죄송하지만 사진 좀 찍어 주실 수 있을까요?
         cee coysongha-ciman sacin com ccike cwu-si-l swu iss-ulkka-yo?
         "Excuse me, but could you take a photo for me?"
2   B: 네.
         ney.
         "Yes."

(12) [Modified LDC Korean telephone conversation 6613]

1   A: 내가 부탁이 하나 있는데 들어 줄래?
         nay-ka pwuthak-i hana iss-nuney tule cwu-llay?
         "I have a favor to ask, will you grant the request?"
2   B: 뭔지 말해 봐.
         mwenci malhay pwa.
         "Tell me what it is about."
3   A: 4월 15일에 우리 학교에서 축제가 있거든.
         sa wel sip oil-ey wuli hakkyo-eyse chwukcey-ka iss-ketun.
         "On April 15, our school has a festival."
4   B: 응.
         ung.
         "Yes."
5   A: 근데 파트너하고 같이 가야 돼. 너가 와 줄 수 있나 해서.
         kuntey partner-hako kathi ka-ya tway. ne-ka wa cwu-l swu iss-na hay-se.
         "(You) have to go with a partner. (I) was wondering if you could come."

However, a growing body of empirical research on requests across different languages in social interaction (Sorjonen et al., 2017) shows that the choice of the request format and strategy depends on various pragmatic and interactional factors as well. Some important aspects to consider in constructing a request is the relationship between the directed action and the activity under way (i.e., whether the requested action is "compatible" with the requestee's current situation [Rossi, 2017]), and the cost (low versus high) and the benefit of the requested action to the requester and the requestee (Rossi, 2012, 2017). Let's first look at some cases of here-and-now requests, which require the recipient to immediately comply. The following segment comes from a face-to-face interaction between a newlywed couple (Kim, 2020). After they finished the main course, the wife returns to the kitchen to prepare a noodle dish. As soon as the husband returns to the kitchen, the wife asks for help.

(13) [Modified from Kim, 2020]

1   W: 오빠, 이거 좀 도와 줄 수 [있어?
         oppa, ike com towa cwu-l swu iss-e?
         "Honey, can you help me with this?"

2   H: [응. 너무 맛있겠다.
                               ung. nemwu masiss-keyss-ta.
                               "Yes. It looks so delicious."

3   W: 내가 이렇게 해 주면 고기 좀 저기다 올려 줘.
         nay-ka ilehkey hay cwu-myen koki com ceki-ta ollye cwe.
         "Put some meat on top of (the noodles) for me after I prepare it like this."

4   H: ((The husband assists the wife in preparing the dish.))

As clearly seen in lines 1 and 3, the speaker chooses different forms in making requests to the same recipient: one in an interrogative form (line 1) and the other in an imperative form (line 3). This dialogue demonstrates that the speaker's choice of form is not motivated by the relationship between the speaker and the recipient (e.g., age, social distance, power) here. The speaker chooses different forms according to the relationship between the requested action and the activity or project in which the recipient is engaged. Interrogative forms are usually used when the requester launches a new, self-contained project in which the requestee is not yet involved, as seen in line 1 (Rossi, 2012). Because the requester does not know yet whether the requestee will or can comply, the request is constructed as a question. In contrast, once the requester and the requestee are committed to and engaged in the same project (preparing the noodle dish), the requester formulates the request in an imperative form as seen in line 3. When the request is formulated imperatively, the requester anticipates the requestee will comply with the request. When both interlocutors share the same goal and are engaged in the same activity or project, the use of the imperative is warranted and not considered impolite.

Imperatives are readily used in making requests in Korean even between speakers with social distance. As seen in lines 1 and 5 in Excerpt (14), the optometrist can make requests using imperatives to the customer as both speakers are already mutually engaged in the joint project of checking the eyesight of the customer. Moreover, because the imperatives can be combined with the subject honorific suffix *si* (시) and the polite speech level ending *yo* (요), resulting in *seyyo* (세요)

sentence ender, the use of the imperative is not perceived as impolite (Byon, 2006).

(14) [At an optometrist office, Kim, 2020]
((The optometrist is sitting across from the customer checking her eyesight.))

1   O: 맨 위에 4 자 보**세요**.

       *mayn wi-ey sa ca po-**sey-yo**.*

       "Look at the number 4 on the very top, please."

2   C: ((Looks at the number 4.))

3   O: 눈을 한번 들여다 봐야겠어요.

       nwun-ul hanpen tulye-ta pwa-ya-keyss-e-yo.

       "(I) need to look into your eyes."

4   C: 얼마 전에 병원에 가서 검사 받았는데요.

       elma cen-ey pyengwen-ey ka-se kemsa pat-ass-nuntey-yo.

       "(I) recently got them checked up at the hospital."

5   O: 좀 계**세요**.

       *com kyey-**sey-yo**.*

       "Wait a little, please."

6   ((The optometrist walks to the end of the room to turn off the lights.))

As shown in the data segments, depending on the specific interactional configurations, contexts, and the actions themselves, requesters choose one form or strategy over the alternatives. Request practices may also vary across different registers (e.g., verbal communication versus text messages or emails).

3.4.2.2 *Offers*

As mentioned in Section 3.4.2.1, requesting bears delicate implications, and thus there seems to be a preference for offers over requests (Sacks, 1992). This preference is observed in the following excerpt in which the mother chooses to take the initiative and offer to put her son on the phone even before her daughter requests her to do so.

(15) [Phone call from Daughter to her family]

1   Daughter: 그래 준수는 갔어요?

                 kulay Junsoo-un ka-ss-eyo?

                 "So, is *Junsoo* (Brother) gone?"

2   Mom: 준수 있어.

                 Junsoo iss-e.

                 "*Junsoo* is here."

3   Daughter: 있어? 자?

iss-e? ca?

"Is (he)? Is (he) sleeping?"

4   Mom: 아니 안 자.

ani an ca.

"No, (he) is not."

5   Daughter: 안 자? [그-

an ca? ku-

"(He) is not? Th–"

6   Mom: [바꿔 줄까?

pakkwe cwu-lkka?

"Shall (I) put (him) on the phone?"

7   Daughter: 에: 바꿔 줘요.

ey: pakkwe cw-eyo.

"Yes, put (him) on the phone, please."

The interrogative sentence ending *lkka?* (ㄹ까? "Shall I/we –?") in (15) is frequently employed in offers in Korean. Other forms that are often used in offers are *llay?* (ㄹ래? "Will you –?"), *lkey* (ㄹ게 "I will –"), and imperatives. The following example shows the use of two of these forms.

(16) [Family picnic]

1   Aunt: ((To Nephew 1))   애 이거 갖다 먹**어**.

yay i-ke kacta mek-e.

"Hey, take this and eat."

2   Nephew 2:   *내가 갖다 **줄게**.

nay-ka kacta cwu-lkey.

((standing up and taking food to Nephew 1))

"I will take it to him."

The first one is an offer of food from Aunt to Nephew 1, and the second offer is from Nephew 2 to both Aunt and Nephew 1. Imperatives can be considered impolite, but they are often used with few or no mitigation devices in offers, as illustrated in Excerpt (16) (Yoon, 2019). We could explain it using Clayman's theory on solidary actions (2002). According to Clayman, offers are generally less imposing on the recipient than requests because they involve the transfer of a good or service from speaker to recipient. Therefore, solidary actions such as offers are not mitigated and delivered in ways that maximize the likelihood of their occurrence. The degree of maximization is even higher in offers in Korean which are often constructed in imposing ways (Yoon, 2019). For example, in addition to the use of an imperative in the first offer in line 1 in (16), the offered action in line 2 is conducted immediately, even without being accepted first. Such practices suggest a way in which Korean speakers manage solidary relations in social interactions, which will be beneficial for teaching to KFL learners.

Student Activity 3: Consider the following model conversation on teaching offers and responses. Given what you just read in this section, how does the conversation reflect the ways in which Korean speakers manage solidary relations, or how does it not? How would you modify it if necessary?

[Arirang TV, Let's Speak Korean, Episode 79]

1   A: 우리가 뭘 도와줄까요?

     "How can we help you?"

2   B: 안 도와줘도 괜찮아요. ((thinking face)) 그럼 접시 좀 빌려주세요.

     "It's okay. You don't have to. ((thinking face)) Then please loan me your plates."

3   A: ((head nod)) 내가 접시를 빌려줄게요.

     "((head nod)) I will loan you plates."

4   B: 고마워요.

     "Thank you."

5   C: 그런데 파티가 몇 시에 시작해요?

     "By the way, what time is your party starting?"

6   B: 친구들이 여섯시 쯤 올 거예요.

     "My friends will come at around 6 o'clock."

7   C: 그럼 우리는 다섯 시 쯤 가서 도와줄게요.

     "Then we will come at around 5 o'clock and help you."

8   B: 정말 고마워요.

     "Thank you very much."

3.4.2.3 Alignment and agreement

Alignment in conversation means cooperation for the activity in progress, which the listener provides by "facilitating the proposed activity or sequence, accepting the presuppositions and terms of the proposed action or activity" (Stivers et al., 2011: p. 21). Such cooperation can be applied to a variety of actions in talk, and it can be achieved through small response tokens such as "yes" tokens or head nods. The significance of the usage of such small tokens has been recognized (Gardner, 2001) and examined in the Korean context as well (Kim, 1999; Young & Lee, 2004; Pyun & Yoon, forthcoming). The continuer presented in Section 3.3.2.1 is a type of aligning function performed through "yes" tokens in Korean, and other types include accepting an offer, suggestion, or request as seen in the following examples. These aligning functions are useful to teach because they are preferred actions which progress the course of action and do not threaten sociality (Pomerantz, 1984; Schegloff, 2007) in interactional responses, and the simple formation using "yes" tokens makes it easy to teach.

(17) [Family lunch]

1 Brother: 밥 먹자.

      pap mek-ca.

      "Let's eat."

2 Sister: **음.**

      um.

      "Okay."

(18) [Kay calling Jay, and Jay's husband, Kim answering the call: modified]

1 Kim: 잠깐만 기다리세요.

      camkkan-man kitali-sey-yo.

      "Wait just a minute."

2 Kay: **예 예.**

      yey yey.

      "Ye:s ye:s."

Another aligning function that can be performed through "yes" tokens is agreement, as shown below.

(19) [Office lunch]

1 Jean: 불고기 같은 거는 달아야 맛있잖아

      pwulkoki-kath-un ke-nun tal-aya masiss-canh-a

      "Things like *pwulkoki* are delicious only when they are sweet, right"

2 Sean: **음.** 갈비도 그렇구.

      um. *kalpi-to kuleh-kwu.*

      "Ye:s, so is *kalpi*."

The action of agreement in responses is often extended from a response token to a more substantial clause or sentence, which makes the agreement even stronger, as *kalpi-to kuleh-kwu* ("so is *kalpi*") does in Excerpt (19). Bringing up another beef dish with a desirable flavor displays Sean's opinion about the flavor, and it functions as a strong agreement with Jean's original opinion. Such a strong level of cooperative and supportive response is distinguished from alignment as the concept of affiliation (Stivers et al., 2011), and it is noteworthy because such strong agreement helps the participant accomplish sociability, support, and solidarity (Pomerantz, 1984) at a greater level. Therefore, stronger agreements extended from small response tokens are useful to teach, especially to upper-level learners. The most useful type of agreement for KFL learners may be an assessment, an evaluative reaction to what is being talked about, as illustrated in Excerpt (20).

(20) [KakaoTalk interaction among family members]

1	Mom:	이거 어때 ((posting a picture of a sweater she knit))	
		i-ke ettay	
		"What do you think about this one?"	
2	Daughter:	엄마 솜씨 짱	Assessment 1
		emma somssi ccang	
		"Your skill is the best"	
3	Daughter-in-law:	색깔도 넘 예쁘네요~~	Agreement 1/Assessment 2
		saykkkal-to nem yeyppu-ney-yo	
		"The color is so pretty too~"	
4	Son:	오호~ 멋진데	Agreement 2/Assessment 3
		oho mesci-ntey	
		"Wow~ it's wonderful"	

Assessments occur highly frequently in real interaction, but they do not seem to be well-represented in textbooks. The following activity can serve as a sample exercise for teachers to use.

Student Activity 4: Try to add more lines to the following textbook conversation. How can it be extended as a more friendly and natural conversation?

[Cho et al., 2012: *Integrated Korean, Intermediate 2*, p. 12]

1	All:	생일 축하해, 스티브!
		"Happy birthday, Steve!"
2	Steve:	고마워. 음식 준비하느라고 고생 많이 했겠다.
		"Thank you. You must have had a lot of trouble to make the food."
3	Subin:	아니야, 모두 도와 줘서 금방 끝났어.
		"No, it didn't take long because everyone helped."
4	Steve:	이 국은 무슨 국이야? 처음 보는데.
		"What soup is this? I haven't seen it before."

5 Mark: 미역국이야. 한국 사람들은 생일날 꼭 미역국을 먹거든.

"It is seaweed soup. Korean people have it on their birthdays."

6 Steve: 맛있다. 현우 요리 솜씨가 이렇게 좋은 줄 몰랐네.

"It's delicious. I didn't know *Hyunwoo* cooks this well."

3.4.2.4 Disagreement

It will be beneficial for upper-level learners to learn disaffiliative responses as well as affiliative ones. Numerous studies from different languages and cultures have found that disaffiliative actions such as disagreements, refusals, and rejections frequently occur with mitigating features including pauses, hesitation markers, and/or other types of delaying devices such as *pro forma* agreements (e.g., "yes, but…" Schegloff, 2007). Such mitigating practices are employed to "maximize the likelihood of affiliative, socially solidary actions, and minimize the likelihood of disaffiliative, socially divisive ones" (Heritage, 1984: pp. 265–280). In other words, it is socially important to mitigate the degree, even when speakers misalign with other participants, which pedagogically implies that language learners should learn about it to engage in social interaction appropriately.

Korean speakers are found to frequently utilize a clausal-connective, *nuntey*, and its variation, *kuntey*, to mitigate the degree of disaffiliation as mentioned in Section 3.4.1.2 and as seen in Excerpt (21).

(21) [Park, 1999: p. 202, (9)]
((In previous lines, M explained positive features of a speech-analyzing software.))

1 D: 그렇게 정확하진 않을**텐데** 그거

*kulekhay cenghwakha-ci-n anh-ul-they-**ntey** kuke*

"I don't think that's that accurate *nuntey*."

2 M: (0.5) **근데** 그까 인풋이 좋으면 정확**한데**:

(0.5) ***kuntey** kukka input-i coh-umyen cenghwakha-**ntey**:*

"*Kuntey* I mean if the input is good, it's accurate *nuntey*."

D's remark is a disagreement with a positive description that M presents in the prior lines, and D employs *nuntey* at the turn-final position in carrying out the interactionally delicate action. M subsequently projects a disagreement by issuing *kuntey* at the turn-initial position and completes it with *nuntey* at the final position. Other resources are also utilized for decreasing the degree of disaffiliation. M's disagreement is delayed with a pause at the beginning, and he also produces *kukka* (그까 "I mean") as a device to reformulate his description of the features of the software to effectively handle D's disagreement. The following activity can be used as a sample exercise in class.

Student Activity 5: What disaffiliative actions are conducted in Lines 2, 3, and 4 in the following excerpt? Additionally, what resources are used to mitigate the degree of misalignment in those lines?

1 K: 차를 고쳐야 될래나봐 정말: .h 그래서: (0.2) 음: 너네 차 갖구가두 되겠니?

"It seems like I have to fix my car, really. .h So: (0.2) u:hm can we drive your car?"

2 D: 근데 투도어라서: 괜찮을까 몰라,

"*Kuntey* because it's two-door, I am not sure if it will be okay"

3 K: tch 글쎄 쪼끔 불편은 해두:, .h 불편이 낫지: 아-- 안전보다는 ((chuckle))

4 아니 불안전보단 ((chuckle)) 그렇지 않겠니? ((laugh))

"tch Well even though it's inconvenient a li:ttle bit, .h inconven-ience is better than sa–safety (h), no than unsafety(h) Wouldn't it? ((laugh))"

3.5 Conclusion

Language is always used in context and within a course of action or activity in progress. Language cannot be understood or sustained in isolation from the contextual situation. Accordingly, for communication, it is essential to learn how to use and manage language at the discourse and interactional level. Drawing on findings from functional linguistics, pragmatics, and interactional linguistics studies of the Korean language, this chapter provided an overview of resources for Korean participants displaying and achieving interactional competence, which includes how to produce and understand discourse, reciprocally maintain participation, and accomplish actions and intersubjectivity with other co-participants in everyday social interaction. First, we discussed ways of managing topic and reference to maintain discourse coherence and to communicate ideas. Then we reviewed the fundamental organizations of written and oral discourse. Authentic examples of L1 Korean data showed how the distinct grammatical structure and features of Korean are tied to the interactional practices and strategies of Korean speakers. Concrete activities also suggested some ideas of facilitating or developing awareness of these key structures of L1 Korean for learners of Korean. We also presented ways of performing various social actions in Korean: by employing linguistic devices such as sentence endings and sentence types; and by utilizing different formats and practices to display cooperative or disaffiliative stances in ongoing interaction. Sequences of authentic data showed how speakers design and perform different actions and how recipients recognize and respond to them. We also provided practical strategies and activities using authentic data and textbook materials that can be easily utilized in class. Overall, this chapter provided guidelines on how to increase learners' awareness of how Korean speakers produce and understand language in context.

Discussion questions

1. What is the importance of teaching students how to use and manage language at the discourse and interactional levels? Why?
2. Having read this chapter, can you think of specific activities or tasks you can use for teaching topic and reference management?
3. Have you considered the importance of teaching turn-taking? If you plan to incorporate it in your classroom teaching, how would you teach it and what would be the focus?
4. What are some routine social actions Korean language learners need to perform? How authentic are the textbook materials for teaching these social actions?
5. Having read this chapter, did you learn anything that is different from your expectations or prior knowledge of Korean language? Please explain.
6. When considering your students' proficiency levels, learning goals, ages, etc. how would you design teaching materials to develop their interactional competence? Try to develop a macro-level plan for a whole semester, as well as micro-level ideas for specific activities in class sessions.

References

Arirang, T.V. (2014, January 11). 뭘 도와줄까요? [Video file]. Retrieved from https://www.youtube.com/watch?v=87DazPqfBkQ.

Brown, P., & Levinson, S.C. (1987). *Politeness: Some universals in language usage.* Cambridge: Cambridge University Press.

Byon, A. (2006). The role of linguistic indirectness and honorifics in achieving linguistic politeness in Korean requests. *Journal of Politeness Research, 2*(2), 247–276.

Celce-Murcia, M., Dornyei, Z., & Thurrell, S. (1995). Communicative competence: A pedagogically motivated model with content specification. *Issues in Applied Linguistics, 6,* 5–35.

Chang, S.-J. (1978). Anaphora in Korean. In J. Hinds (Ed.), *Linguistic research* (pp. 223–278). Edmonton, AB: Linguistic Research Inc.

Cho, Y., Lee, H.S., Schulz, C., Sohn, H.-M., & Sohn, S.-O. (2012). *Integrated Korean: Intermediate 2.* Honolulu, HI: University of Hawaii Press.

Clayman, S.E. (2002). Sequence and solidarity. *Group Cohesion, Trust and Solidarity, 19,* 229–253.

Couper-Kuhlen, E., & Selting, M. (2017). *Interactional linguistics: Studying language in social interaction.* Cambridge: Cambridge University Press.

Ford, C.E., & Thompson, S.A. (1996). Interactional units in conversation: Syntactic, intonational, and pragmatic resources for the management of turns. In E. Ochs, E.A. Schegloff, & S.A. Thompson (Eds.), *Interaction and grammar* (pp. 134–184). Cambridge: Cambridge University Press.

Galaczi, E. (2014). Interactional competence across proficiency levels: How do learners manage interaction in paired speaking tests? *Applied Linguistics, 35*(5), 553–574.

Gardner, R. (2001). *When listeners talk: Response tokens and listener stance.* Amsterdam: John Benjamins.

Givón, T. (1979). *On understanding grammar.* New York: Academic Press.

Hall, J.K., & Pekarek Doehler, S. (2011). L2 interactional competence and development. In J.K. Hall, J. Hellermann, & S. Pekarek Doehler (Eds.), *L2 interactional competence and development* (pp. 1–15). Bristol: Multilingual Matters.

Heritage, J. (1984). *Garfinkel and ethnomethodology.* Cambridge: Polity Press.

Hwang, S.J. (2015). Korean discourse structure. In L. Brown & J. Yeon (Eds.), *The handbook of Korean linguistics* (pp. 287–302). Malden, MA: Wiley Blackwell.

Hymes, D. (1972). On communicative competence. In J.B. Pride & J. Holmes (Eds.), *Sociolinguistics: Selected readings* (pp. 269–293). Harmondswarth, Middlesex: Penguin.

Kasper, G. (2006). Beyond repair: Conversation analysis as an approach to SLA. *AILA Review, 19*, 83–99.

Kim, H.-Y. (2012). Development of NP forms and discourse reference in L2 Korean. In H.-M. Sohn (Ed.), *Korean language in America (Special Issue): Innovations in teaching Korean* (pp. 211–235). University Park, PA: Penn State University Press.

Kim, K.-H. (1993). Topicality in Korean conversation: Conversation-analytic perspective. In P.M. Clancy (Ed.), *Japanese/Korean Linguistics 2* (pp. 33–54). Stanford, CA: CSLI, Stanford University.

Kim, K.-H. (1999). Phrasal unit boundaries and organization of turns and sequences in Korean conversation. *Human Studies, 22*(2–4), 425–446.

Kim, K.-H. (2004). A conversation analysis of Korean sentence-ending modal suffixes *-ney, -kwun(a)*, and *-ta*: Noticing as a social action. *The Sociolinguistic Journal of Korea, 12*(1), 1–35.

Kim, M.S. (2005). Evidentiality in achieving entitlement, objectivity, and detachment in Korean conversation. *Discourse Studies, 7*(1), 87–108.

Kim, M.S. (2020). Imperative requests in Korean interaction. In *Japanese/Korean Linguistics 26*. Stanford, CA: CSLI, Stanford University.

Kim, S.H. (2010). A high boundary tone as a resource for a social action: The Korean sentence ender *-ta*. *Journal of Pragmatics, 41*(11), 3055–3077.

Kim, S.H., & Sohn, S.-O. (2015). Grammar as an emergent response to interactional needs: A study of final *kuntey* 'but' in Korean conversation. *Journal of Pragmatics, 83*, 73–90.

Koo, D. (2001). *Realisations of two speech acts of heritage learners of Korean: Requests and apology strategies* [PhD Dissertation]. Ohio State University.

Kramsch, C. (1986). From language proficiency to interactional competence. *Modern Language Journal, 70*(4), 366–372.

Lee, E.-H. (2006). Stative progressive in Korean and English. *Journal of Pragmatics, 38*(5), 695–717.

Lee, H.S. (1986). Topicality and the contrastiveness continuum. In S. DeLancey & R.S. Tomlin (Eds.), *Proceedings of the second annual meeting of the Pacific linguistics Conference* (pp. 271–309). Eugene, OR: University of Oregon.

Lee, H.S. (1987). *Discourse presupposition and the discourse function of the topic marker -nun in Korean.* Bloomington, IN: Indiana University Linguistics Club.

Lee, H.S. (1993). Cognitive constraints on expressing newly perceived information, with reference to epistemic modal suffixes in Korean. *Cognitive Linguistics, 4*(2), 135–167.

Lee, H.S. (1999). A discourse-pragmatic analysis of the committal *-ci* in Korean: A synthetic approach to the form-meaning relation. *Journal of Pragmatics, 31*(2), 243–275.

Lee, H.S., Yoon, K.-E., & Yoon, S.-S. (2017). Teaching listener responses to KFL students. *The Korean Language in America, 21*(2), 250–261.

Leech, G. (2014). *The pragmatics of politeness*. Oxford: Oxford University Press.

Longacre, R.E. (1996). *The grammar of discourse* (2nd ed.). New York: Plenum Press.

Ochs, E., Schegloff, E.A., & Thompson, S.A. (1996). *Interaction and grammar*. Cambridge: Cambridge University Press.

Oh, S.-Y. (2007). Overt reference to speaker and recipient in Korean. *Discourse Studies*, *9*(4), 462–492.

Park, M.-J., & Sohn, S.-O. (2002). Discourse grammaticalization, & intonation: An analysis of -ketun in Korean. In N.M. Akatsuka & S. Strauss (Eds.), *Japanese/Korean Linguistics 10* (pp. 306–319). Stanford, CA: CSLI, Stanford University.

Park, Y.-Y. (1998). A discourse analysis of the Korean connective *ketun* in conversation. *Crossroads of Language, Interaction, and Culture*, *1*, 71–89.

Park, Y.-Y. (1999). The Korean connective *nuntey* in conversational discourse. *Journal of Pragmatics*, *31*(2), 191–218.

Pearson, B. (1989). 'Role-ing out control' at church business meetings: Directing and disagreeing. *Language Sciences*, *11*(3), 289–304.

Pomerantz, A. (1984). Agreeing and disagreeing with assessments: Some features of preferred/dispreferred turn shapes. In J.M. Atkinson & J. Heritage (Eds.), *Structures of social action: Studies in conversation analysis* (pp. 57–101). Cambridge: Cambridge University Press.

Pyun, D., & Yoon, K.-E. (Forthcoming). Discourse functions of Korean 'yes' words. *Korean Linguistics*.

Rossi, G. (2012). Bilateral and unilateral requests: The use of imperatives and mi X? interrogatives in Italian. *Discourse Processes*, 49, 426–458.

Rossi, G. (2017). Secondary and deviant uses of the imperative in Italian. In M.-L. Sorjonen, L. Raevaara, & E. Couper-Kuhlen (Eds.), *Imperative turns at talk: The design of directives in action* (pp. 103–137). Amsterdam/Philadelphia, PA: John Benjamins.

Rue, Y., Zhang, G., & Shin, K. (2007). Request strategies in Korean. *5th Biennial Korean Studies Association of Australasia Conference* (pp. 112–119), Perth, Australia, 12–13 July 2007.

Sacks, H. (1992). *Lectures on conversation*. Oxford: Blackwell Publishing.

Sacks, H., Schegloff, E.A., & Jefferson, G. (1974). A simplest systematics for the organization of turn-taking for conversation. *Language*, *50*(4), 696–735.

Schegloff, E.A. (1982). Discourse as an interactional achievement: Some uses of 'uh huh' and other things that come between sentences. In D. Tannen (Ed.), *Analyzing discourse: Text and talk* (pp. 71–93). Georgetown University round table on languages and linguistics. Washington, DC: Georgetown University Press.

Schegloff, E.A. (2007). *Sequence organization in interaction: A primer in conversation analysis*. Cambridge: Cambridge University Press.

Sorjonen, M.-L., Raevaara, L., & Couper-Kuhlen, E. (2017). *Imperative turns at talk: The design of directives in action*. Amsterdam/Philadelphia, PA: John Benjamins.

Stivers, T., Mondada, L., & Steensig, J. (2011). Knowledge, morality, and affiliation in social interaction. In T. Stivers, L. Mondada & J. Steensig (Eds.), *The morality of knowledge in conversation* (pp. 3–24). Cambridge: Cambridge University Press.

Wajnryb, R. (2003). *Stories: Narrative activities for the language classroom*. Cambridge: Cambridge University Press.

Wang, H.-S. (2008). *Frog's tears and other stories*. Boston, MA: Cheng & Tsui.

Yoon, K.-E. (2019, June). Offer sequences in Korean: Culture and interaction. Paper presented at the conference of the American Association of Teachers of Korean, University of Minnesota, Minneapolis, MN.

Young, R.F. (2008). *Language and interaction: An advanced resource book.* New York/ London: Routledge.

Young, R.F., & Lee, J. (2004). Identifying units in interaction: Reactive tokens in Korean and English conversations. *Journal of Sociolinguistics, 8*(3), 380–407.

4 Culture in language learning and teaching

Lucien Brown and Mi Yung Park

4.1 Introduction

Learning a new language is not just a process of acquiring new linguistic features, such as phonemes, grammatical patterns, and vocabulary. Indeed, a person can know the grammar of a language very well, but still not know how to use that language. When a learner of Korean says to their teacher 늦어서 미안해 "Sorry for being late (plain speech, no honorifics),"[1] there is nothing grammatically "wrong" with this sentence. However, the sentence is still "wrong" in the sense that it is inappropriate, and fails to display sensitivity to cultural values (i.e., respecting status superiors). Effective communication not only requires that the grammar is "right," but also that the speaker is saying the "right" thing at the "right" time in the "right" place and in the "right" way (Gee, 2015: p. 147).

Language is therefore not just a tool for communicating verbal messages, but also a means for speakers to express cultural and social meanings. Whenever anyone talks, their speech simultaneously communicates not just what they want to "say," but also information about who they are as a speaker, what their values are, and what kind of social group or culture they belong to. In Korean, people in positions of respect tend to be addressed with a title, often followed by the honorific suffix –님 (Lee & Ramsey, 2000). The socially normative use of titles such as 선생님, "respected teacher", as a term of address invokes and perpetuates a social system based on hierarchical models of respect. By speaking at all, we inevitably invoke culture and identity.

If we accept that learning a language also involves learning culture, then evidently culture needs to be included within the study of language acquisition and taught in the language classroom. However, to date, SLA and language pedagogy have both been dominated by grammar. In addition, whereas various techniques for teaching grammar have been developed, language teaching still lacks a clear pedagogy for teaching culture, and language teachers often lack training in this area (Crawford-Lange & Lange, 1984). Consequently, culture is often treated in a superficial way (Galloway, 1985) and is rarely included in assessments.

This chapter provides an overview of the learning and teaching of culture in relation to the Korean language. Section 4.2 sets out to define culture, and reviews ways that language is integral to it. Section 4.3 overviews the way that culture (as well as related categories such as "society" and "identity") has been integrated into SLA research. In Section 4.4, we look at the treatment of culture within the language classroom. We conclude with a discussion of future directions for the study of culture in relation to Korean language learning.

4.2 Language and culture

This section offers definitions of culture, and looks at how language and culture are integrally connected. We include an overview of aspects of the Korean language that are closely intertwined with culture.

4.2.1 Notions of culture

Culture is a broad notion that encompasses human behavior, social practices, and rituals, as well as performative and symbolic expressions (e.g., art, music, dance) and the development and consumption of materials goods. The term tends to be reserved for things that are socially structured and transmitted through social learning. Therefore, innate human abilities such as walking, running, or jumping are not culture, but socially structured and transmitted forms of movement (e.g., walking techniques, races, jumping contests, athletics) are culture.

Scholars have attempted to break down the notion of culture into different sub-categories. One distinction is between "big-C culture" and "little-c culture" (e.g., Herron et al., 1999). "Big-C culture" refers to high culture—learning about the great works of art, music, and literature. "Little-c culture," on the other hand, refers to everyday lived culture and the "dos" and "don'ts" of personal behavior (Hadley, 2000).

In North America, the ACTFL standards endorse a tripartite model of culture referred to as the "three Ps": Perspectives (values, beliefs, world views), Practices (patterns of social interaction), and Products (tangible or intangible creations).[2]

One less well-known distinction that we feel is important is Walker's (2000) distinction between "revealed culture," "ignored culture," and "suppressed culture." Walker (2000: p. 232) defines "revealed culture" as "cultural knowledge that a native is generally eager to communicate to a non-native." This corresponds to "normative" aspects of culture about which "natives" have a high conscious awareness and that are reified through power-laden channels. "Ignored culture" is

Table 4.1 "Big-C Culture" and "Little-c culture"

Big-C Culture	Little-c culture
Art	Everyday lived culture
Music	"Dos" and "don'ts"
Literature	(e.g., wait for elders to start eating first)
Great moments in history	

Table 4.2 ACTFL Model: The Three Ps

Perspectives	Practices	Products
Meanings, attitudes, values, and ideas that represent that culture's view of the world	Patterns of social interaction or behaviors accepted in the culture	Books, tools, foods, laws, music, games, etc. that are representative of the culture

to do with knowledge or behavior that "a native is generally unaware of" (i.e., cultural practices that may be specific to a particular community, but whose importance is not recognized. Finally, "suppressed culture" is cultural knowledge or behavior that "natives" are aware of, but "that a native is generally unwilling to communicate to a non-native." These are aspects of culture are considered "nonstandard" or stigmatizing. To give a simple example of Korean food, 김치 "kimchi," 불고기 "bulgogi," and 비빔밥 "bibimpap" are "revealed culture," 보신탕 "dog soup," and 홍어회 "fermented raw skate" are "suppressed culture." Dishes whose status as "Korean food" is questionable may constitute "ignored culture," including 김치버거 "kimchi burger," 토스트 "(Korean style) toast," and certain pizza combinations (e.g., 불갈비 김치 피자 "grilled beef rib and kimchi pizza," 고구마 크러스트 "sweet potato crust").

Walker's (2000) notions of "ignored" and "suppressed" culture remind us of the danger of seeing culture in a deterministic way—as something that is stable, fixed, and which all "natives" have identical and complete knowledge of. Such approaches easily lead to stereotyping. In contrast to this, post-structuralist approaches to culture (e.g., Cameron, 2005; Pennycook, 2006) see culture as something that is dynamic, negotiated, and actively performed during social interaction. From this perspective, the idea of what constitutes "Korean culture" is contested (i.e., different people have different ideas of what it means) and multifarious (i.e., there are many different notions of Korean culture). We can imagine, for instance, that "Korean culture" means something quite different to a young female from Seoul than it would do to an elderly male from South Jeolla Province (let alone a North Korean, or an overseas Korean). People actively "perform" Korean culture through partaking in recognizable and recognized cultural practices such as eating Korean food, drinking soju, performing 제사 "ancestor memorial ceremony," singing karaoke, and using honorific language. Koreans (particularly those overseas) may even appeal to cultural stereotypes in order to emphasize their Korean-ness, such as by saying things along the lines of "like all Koreans, I drink a lot" or "like all Koreans, I like to sing." Other Koreans, however, might purposefully choose to avoid saying such things and even distance themselves from such practices (and/or question if things such as drinking and singing really are "Korean"). As pointed out by Kramsch (2014: p. 44) seeing culture as performative does not mean that everything about culture is relative, subjective, and with no clear boundary. There still *is* something that we can refer to as Korean culture, but seeing Korean culture as a performance underlines the man-made, historically situated, and ideologically invested notion of the concept.

4.2.2 The connection between language and culture

We noted above that the term "culture" is not used to describe innate human abilities, but is instead reserved for things that are socially structured and transmitted through social learning. It may well be that humans are born with at the very least an "innate" disposition to use language, and the extent to which this capacity is "hard-wired" into the brain has been a large debate in linguistics (see Ortega, 2014: p. 111). Putting this debate aside, what is undeniable is that language is also cultural; firstly, in that the structure of a language's lexicon and grammar inherently reflects the social reality in which the language is used, and secondly, in that learning a language involves social learning. In this section, we briefly review some key ways in which this link between language and culture has been conceptualized in linguistic disciplines. The question of language learning as social learning is addressed in Section 4.3.

The idea that culture is encoded in language has traditionally been treated under the concept of linguistic relativity, and more recently in the broader conceptualization of cultural linguistics (or ethnolinguistics). In earlier work on linguistic relativity arose the idea of linguistic determinism (popularly, but inaccurately, known as the "Sapir–Whorf hypothesis"); in other words, that language determines the way people perceive the world (e.g., Whorf, 1956). However, this "strong" version of linguistic relativity has given way to "weaker" versions, where language is seen more as "a guide to social reality" (Sapir, 1949: p. 162), particularly in the moment of speaking (Slobin's 1996 notion of "thinking for speaking"). Different languages require speakers to attend to different grammatical and lexical choices. For instance, in Korean, the existence of an honorifics system "forces" the speaker to attend to the relative social position of the interlocutor (and/or sentence referents) in a way not explicitly needed in English. Through repeatedly forcing its speakers to make these choices, the Korean language, in a sense, "trains" its speakers to attend more carefully to social hierarchy. From this perspective, the existence of honorifics not only reflects Korean culture and the legacy of Neo-Confucian ideology, but also plays a role in perpetuating the importance of age and rank in the way that Korean speakers conceptualize the social world around them (cf. Kramsch, 2014: p. 34).

From the field of linguistic anthropology comes the idea that indexicality is one of the major ways in which linguistic signs communicate cultural meanings (Kramsch, 2014: pp. 34–36). Linguistic choices "index" (i.e., "point to" or "mark") aspects of the context, such as the social identities of the speakers and the activities they are engaged in (e.g., Silverstein, 2003; Ochs, 1990). When a student addresses a teacher as 선생님 "teacher," for instance, the meaning of this word goes beyond a simple job title. It indexes the identity of the speakers (student and teacher), invokes the context of a school, and also marks culture-specific meanings related to status differentiation and respect. These meanings are, however, specific to the context. When two teachers of similar age address each other as 선생님, this may still mark respect, but the meaning of status differentiation is not evoked. When someone addresses a friend, who happens to be a teacher, with 선생님, it may be playful or even sarcastic. Indexical meanings are thus fundamentally different to referential meanings (i.e., literal or "dictionary" meanings) in that they are more dynamic and closely entwined with the context.

This idea that language is made up of different choices that speakers can use to communicate social meanings forms the backbone of the field of systemic functional linguistics, founded by Michael Halliday. Systemic functional linguistics sees language as a semiotic system that orders the world according to meaningful categories (see Eggins, 2004). Take for example the Korean system of lexical items for "sibling" (Table 4.3). Korean speakers organize the conceptual domain of sibship around four factors: (1) gender of sibling; (2) gender of person related to the sibling; (3) relative age; and (4) honorification. There is an interaction between these parameters, generally so that the choices become more complex when talking about older siblings and when the gender of the person related to the sibling is male. The relevance of these parameters and the way that they interact is established by convention rather than nature, which becomes apparent when we compare Korean with a language such as English, which only marks one of these dimensions: gender of sibling. What also becomes apparent through this comparison is that these conventions are culturally established and reflect parameters that are known to be important in Korean social interaction, such as age, gender, and respect. Systemic functional linguistics thus sees language as being "structured for use" (i.e., organized in a way that can make meanings that are relevant to our social experiences as language users).

A paradigm such as that presented for Korean sibship in Table 4.3 may give the impression that language is structured in a way that is tightly rule-based with no freedom for the speaker. This is not necessarily the case, however. There are instances where Korean speakers flaunt these rules. For example, during the 1980s, female university students often addressed older male students as 형

Table 4.3 Commonly Used Korean Kinship Terms for "Sibling"

	Younger		Older	
	Plain	Honorific	Plain	Honorific
Male sibling of a male	[남]동생 (아우)*	–	형	형님
Male sibling of a female	[남]동생 (아우)*	–	오빠	(오라버니/오라버님)*
Female sibling of a male	[여]동생 (누이)*	–	누나	누님
Female sibling of a female	[여]동생 (아우)*	–	언니	–

*These forms are relatively restricted and/or infrequent in contemporary Korean.

"older brother of a man." Kim (1998) argues that this allowed them to create formal institutional identities that were more in line with the atmosphere of college campuses, which were the locus for the pro-democracy movement. Gay men may sometimes address each other as 언니 "older sister of a woman." Speakers can also choose how to say the words, and this can be socially meaningful. 오빠 "older brother of a man," for instance, can become a marker of 애교 "embodied cuteness," but typically only when pronounced with high pitch and elongation on the final vowel (Brown, 2017). Finally, speakers may exercise some degree of choice as to whether to use the kinship term at all, or instead to plump for a title or personal name.

4.2.3 Language and culture in the Korean context

As outlined above, language is a symbolic code that "indexes" social meanings in addition to referential meanings. In every single sentence that we speak, decisions that we make regarding word choices (e.g., 만났어요 versus 뵀어요) mark something about who we are, who we are speaking to, and in which context we are speaking. The same can be said about various pronunciation choices (e.g., pronouncing or not pronouncing the "w" in 뵀어요, with the inclusion of "w" being a marker of more careful and formal speech, and also sounding prestigious (see Silva 1991). Although all language usage is indexical, some areas of language are imbued with particularly rich cultural meanings. In this section, we briefly outline a few such areas for Korean.

Honorifics are known to be closely linked to culture-specific conceptualizations of human relationships (Yoon, 2004). Korean has six speech styles (or hearer honorifics), which are used to mark the relationship between the speaker and the hearer (Table 4.4). In addition, Korean uses the subject honorific marker -시- (as in 하세요, 하시고, 하십시오, etc.) to mark the relationship with the sentence subject, as well as various vocabulary substitutions (분, 잡수시다, 드리다,

Table 4.4 The Six Speech Styles of Korean

English name	Korean name	Declarative	Interrogative	Imperative	Hortative
"Deferential" style	합쇼체	-(스)ㅂ니다	-(스)ㅂ니까?	-(으)ㅂ시오	-(으)십시다
"Polite" style	해요체	-아/어요	-아/어요?	-아/어요	-아/어요
"Semi-formal" style	하오체	-오/소	-오/소?	-오	-(으)ㅂ시다
"Familiar" style	하게체	-네	-나?/-(으)ㄴ가?	-게	-세
"Intimate" style	해체	-아/어	-아/어?	-아/어	-아/어
"Plain" style	해라체	-(ㄴ/는)다	-니?/-(느)냐?	-아/어라	-자

etc.). Readers are referred to Lee and Ramsey (2000: Chapter 7), Brown (2011: Chapter 2), and Brown (2015a).

Contrary to the popular assumption that the system is strictly rule-based, usage of honorifics shows considerable variation. Even when addressing a notable superior, speakers exercise choices over whether to use -요 and -습니다, or whether to use the highest forms of subject honorifics (e.g., 진지 잡수셨어요?) or less formal alternatives (e.g., 식사하셨어요?). Readers are referred to Strauss and Eun (2005), Brown (2015b), and Jo (2018) for discussion of -요 and -습니다 variation, and also to Lukoff (1977), who began work on Korean speech style variation. Brown (2013b) looks at the use of sarcastic honorifics. Through their usage of honorifics, Korean speakers not only mark respect or politeness towards their interlocutors, but also construct their own social roles and personas.

Closely linked to the use of honorifics, Korean address terms are richly imbued with culture-specific meanings. The preference for using titles (e.g., 선생님 "esteemed teacher," 선배님 "esteemed senior," 사장님 "boss") and kinship terms (e.g., 형 "older brother of a male," 이모 "maternal aunt," 아버님 "esteemed father") reflects the group-oriented and relational nature of Korean society. Indeed, the frequent use of kinship terms outside of consanguineal relationships has been claimed to show that many Korean social groups and relationships take the idea of family as their basis (see Harkness, 2015a, 2015b). Korean address terms are also rich in gendered meanings. Brown (2017) discusses the flirtatious usage of 오빠 "older brother of a female" and 누나 "older sister of a male" in Korean popular culture, whereas Kim (2015) discusses the use of teknonymy (e.g., 민준 엄마 "Minjun's mom") versus the pronoun 자기 "you" in interactions between married women negotiating changing gender identities.

The conventional formulation of speech acts (requests, apologies, compliments, etc.) is another area of language that is closely tied to cultural identity. As a prototypical "high context culture," Korean is known to favor indirect forms of communication, where the hearer is required to work out the intended meaning of the utterance in context. This is reflected in the importance placed on 눈치 *nunchi* (Sohn, 1986; Kim, 2003). Korean speakers prefer to make sensitive speech acts such as disagreement and correction in circuitous ways (Yum, 2012). The Korean language is rich in ambiguous expressions such as 글쎄요 (similar to English "well," or "let me see"), which when used in answer to a question can mean either "yes" or "no" and avoids the provision of a direct answer (Kang, 1988).

Korean cultural concepts and values are present in Korean proverbs, maxims, and other conventionalized forms of speech. Lee (2006) notes that Korean proverbs embody a number of properties that reflect Korean culture and consciousness, including vulgarity and commonness, fatalism, realism, and maintaining face:

(1)　a.　Vulgarity and commonness:

똥이 더러워서 피하지 무서워서 피하냐?

"We avoid excrement because it is dirty, not because we are scared of it."

b.   Fatalism:

콩 심은 데 콩 나고 팥 심은 데 팥 난다.

"You plant soybeans, you get soybeans. You plant red beans, you get red beans."

c.   Realism:

사후 술 석 잔 말고 생전에 한 잔 술이 달다.

"One drink in life is sweeter than three drinks after death."

d.   Maintaining face:

양반은 얼어 죽어도 겻불은 안 쬔다.

"Even when a *yangban* is freezing to death, he doesn't make a fire with hulls of rice."

Finally, Korean speakers also make use of non-standard language forms to negotiate their identities. Jeon and Cukor-Avila (2015) found that regional dialects connote specific personal qualities. For instance, Gyeongsang dialect (particularly the version spoken in Daegu) is perceived as the most feminine and *aegyo*-like dialect, at least when spoken by women. Given that many Koreans from the provinces are bidialectal, speakers may choose to use or avoid dialectal forms to shape their personas (see Song, 2005). In the internet age, Korean speakers may also use internet slang and neologisms to mark identity (see Harkness, 2015a).

4.3 SLA research: Language learning as cultural learning

We now look at how SLA has conceptualized language learning as cultural learning.

4.3.1 *Main concepts*

SLA has been dominated by grammatical and cognitive concerns, rather than questions of culture, society, or identity. However, some key questions about the way that language is acquired could not be fully answered without recourse to cultural factors.

One of these questions concerned the presence of variation in L2 learner production. By variation, we refer to speakers producing different versions of referentially identical language. This is a phenomenon that is widespread in native speaker production: 미안해 and 죄송합니다 both mean "sorry," but differ in their social meaning. However, L2 variation differs from L1 variation. First, L2 learners produce forms and combinations that are not found in native speaker grammar. For instance, we have heard learners produce the following for the honorific form of "eat a meal":

(2)   a.   밥을 먹으세요

b.   밥을 드세요

c.   진지 잡수하세요

Here, (a) and (b) may occasionally occur in L1 talk too, but are heavily marked as non-standard ((a) tends to appear in sarcasm). Sentence (c) would probably not occur in native speaker talk.

Also, the L2 variation may occur within a short timespan, even within succeeding utterances (Mitchell et al., 2013: p. 253) and sometimes in a way that is inconsistent and, arguably, "free" or "random" (Ellis, 1999). The same learner may use the correct "진지 잡수세요" correctly in one sentence, then use the incorrect "진지 잡수하세요" in the very next utterance. Some L2 variation is thus no doubt due to issues of linguistic competence, or language development.

However, studies that have applied Labovian sociolinguistic analysis show that at least some L2 variation is patterned according to social factors such as formality, speech style, and the identity of the interlocutor. For instance, Tarone (1998) showed that both Japanese L1 and Arabic L1 learners of English supplied the English third-person singular inflection *-s* more frequently in formal contexts.

These sociolinguistic studies showed that learners who are better integrated with the L2 community display patterns of linguistic variation more similar to the L1 norm. On the other hand, learners whose experience of the language is limited to classroom learning overuse formal variants taught in class (Bayley, 1996; Li, 2010). These findings highlighted that the sociolinguistic repertoires that learners acquire are influenced by the extent to which language socialization takes place. Language socialization refers to the process by which individuals acquire the knowledge and practices that enable them to use language in culturally appropriate ways (Longman, 2008). The concept of language socialization has its origins in the study of how children learn their L1s from birth (e.g., Ochs & Schieffelin, 2001). For instance, in the Korean context, parents socialize children into the culturally appropriate usage of honorifics and associated behaviors through various practices such as modeling honorific language themselves, explicitly correcting children's non-honorific language, and making children bow at appropriate times by lightly pushing their heads downward.

L2 learners are socialized into the culturally appropriate use of language both inside and outside the language classroom. Outside of the language classroom, learners build up increasingly complex repertoires of linguistic variation as they are socialized into the norms of different social groups. In data that we collected from text messages and other online interactions sent by a non-heritage Korean learner (Allison) from the US in a third-year language class who had been extensively socialized into Korean computer-mediated interactions, we found that she had acquired four distinct registers of Korean (shown in Table 4.5). This was despite the fact that her language classes had focused on only one register and had not taught any netspeak.

However, language socialization for L2 learners works somewhat differently to L1 situations. Firstly, L2 learners are cognitively and socially mature and already possess linguistic and cultural knowledge from their L1 (and other previously learned languages). Armed with this knowledge, L2 learners may exert more agency in the extent to which they adopt L2 norms. DuFon (1999) looked at the social acquisition of Indonesian by learners from Western backgrounds. One

Table 4.5 Allison's Use of Four Registers in Online Interactions

Register:	Used to:	Example:
1 Non-honorific with netspeak	Close friends	곧 같이 놀자!!! 보고 싶당!!! ㅋㅋㅋㅋ
2 Semi-honorific with netspeak	Acquaintances of similar age	생일 축하해요! ㅋㅋㅋㅋ 오늘 친구들이랑 즐거운 시간 보내요~!!! :)
3 Semi-honorific no netspeak	More distant acquaintances	한국말로 애기해도 돼요.
4 Full honorific	Her Korean teachers	선생님, 봄 방학 잘 보내셨어요?

learner adopted patterns of egalitarian pronoun usage, since he found it "more comfortable" to "place all on the same footing," despite knowing that this was different to native speaker usage (p. 456).

In addition, whereas L1 children typically become members of the community where the language is spoken simply by being born into it, accessing these communities can be more challenging for L2 learners. The extent to which L2 learners are recognized as legitimate speakers of the language (Norton, 2000) and members of the community of practice (i.e., the social group) in which the language is spoken (Lave & Wenger, 1991) becomes important. In some contexts, the target language community may not expect learners to be socialized into local practices, and learners themselves may not value it either. Iino's (2006) study of American students in Japanese home-stays found that the Japanese hosts had low expectations as to how well the students could speak Japanese, adopt other Japanese practices such as eating Japanese food, and ultimately become members of Japanese society. The host families used simplified honorifics towards the students, avoided local dialect, and were accepting or even welcoming of the students' "cute" mistakes (p. 166). On the other hand, they sometimes negatively evaluated the use of native-like Japanese utterances. For example, when one student used the humble utterance *tsumaranai mono desu kedo douzo* "this is a useless thing but please accept" when giving a gift, the Japanese family perceived the utterance as insincere, since they assumed that there was "no such custom in American's mentality as *tsumaranai mono*" (pp. 166–167).

Attempts to describe the social side of language acquisition increasingly rely on sociocultural theory (Vygotsky, 1978; Lantolf & Thorne, 2006) to model the process of language learning, or an outgrowth of sociocultural theory known as activity theory (Leont'ev, 1978; Engeström, 1987). Sociocultural theory conceptualizes social learning as a process through which novices acquire the use of tools to "mediate" their interactions and relationships with the world around them. The tool *par excellence* through which humans mediate with the social-material world is language. The learning of language and other tools requires scaffolding provided by more competent human interactants, including parents and caregivers, teachers, and more proficient classmates. This learning occurs best when the difficulty level of the task resides in the "Zone of Proximal Development": above what the learner can do unaided, but below what the learner is incapable of doing even with the provision of aid.

Language learning from a sociocultural perspective involves learning a different "tool" which allows for a different mode of mediation with the social-material world. This is the case since, as noted above, languages feature different specific ways of ordering experience which require speaker attention to different culturally embedded parameters. The L2 may not allow the learner to connect with the world in the same way as the L1, but at the same time will allow new ways that are enabled through specific properties of the L2. To give a simple example, a Korean from Busan learning English as an L2 will obviously struggle to find linguistic means to mark their identity as a speaker of Gyeongsang dialect or as a Busanite (since these categories are not normally available in English). However, at least with a certain level of fluency, they can potentially use English to mark other geographically related social meanings. We have met UK-educated Koreans in the US who purposefully keep or even emphasize their British accent in order to mark prestige—an indexical relationship not available in Korea (or even when using British English in Korea, where American English is the prestige variety). Language learning thus "is about developing, or failing to develop, new ways of mediating ourselves and our relationships" (Lantolf & Pavlenko, 2001: p. 145). Naturally, therefore, language learning is constrained by the socio-material conditions of the language-learning environment, including relations of power, although, as noted above, language learners may employ their own agency (Ahearn, 2001) to challenge these conditions.

4.3.2 Application to Korean

Research looking at the social side of Korean language learning has started to take shape in recent years, with a number of studies examining language socialization and identity issues.

Studies have found that Korean language teachers play active roles in socializing learners into the usage of honorifics. Byon's (2003) study of a heritage language classroom in the US found that teachers' use of the polite speech style ending -요 socialized students into two crucial sociocultural norms of Korean: (1) showing respect when addressing someone of higher status, and (2) speaking in a polite manner when addressing the public. In the university KFL classroom, teachers may sometimes shift from the polite style to the intimate style to express solidarity with their students during discussions of intimacy-building topics (Park, 2012, 2016). Park (2014) further demonstrated that teachers shifted to the semi-formal style (the -(으)ㅂ시다 form) to mark transitions between and within activities, with this form reinforcing the teachers' authority and drawing the students' attention. The use of the form effectively socializes students into the student role, that is, following teacher instructions and preparing to be involved in the next activity.

A number of studies have also looked at the social experiences of heritage learners as they navigate their identities and linguistic competency. Heritage learners may be expected to conform to the norms of standard Korean, including erasing non-standard or dialectal forms they may have acquired during family interactions (Jo, 2001) and mastering honorifics (Byon, 2003). Shin (2005: p. 65) noted that Korean-Americans who cannot properly use honorifics may be viewed as "not genuinely Korean." Park's (2011) research on heritage language use and identity among Korean-American university students illustrated the need to consider how learner investment is linked to the (imagined) communities they aspire to join. One participant recounted her desire to speak to, and speak like, a group of native Korean youths she knew, which led her not to speak to older Korean immigrants with whom she did not identify. Another participant distanced herself from what she saw as the overly hierarchical linguistic and cultural practices maintained among first-generation Korean immigrants, such as the use of honorifics, and instead aligned herself with a community of younger, second-generation Koreans who shared her cultural values.

One subset of heritage learners with particularly complex identities is Korean adoptees, especially when they return to South Korea. Higgins and Stoker (2011) showed how "adoptee returnees" in South Korea struggled to integrate and gain acceptance in Korean society. Due to their Korean ethnicity, the local community may expect them to assimilate to Korean linguistic and social norms. Unable to live up to these expectations, the adoptee returnees were frustrated in their search for a sense of belonging in their country of birth. Responding to social exclusion, they sometimes constructed hybrid identities, using labels such as "overseas Korean" or "an adoptee who is a member of the society," indexing both their Korean-ness and their displacement.

Research has explored the language-learning experiences of marriage-migrants in South Korea. Park (2017) showed that Southeast Asian marriage-migrant women faced pressure to adhere to Korean sociolinguistic and cultural norms both within the household and in the workplace. Meanwhile, Park (2020) demonstrated how marriage-migrants' acquisition of a non-standard Korean dialect led to their marginalization, particularly in the workplace. A consequent sense of anxiety and inferiority about their way of speaking created barriers in forming healthy, pluralistic language ideologies. Their experiences motivated them to actively invest in mastering standard Korean and avoid the use of the dialect, at least in formal settings.

Studies have also looked at the language socialization and identity negotiation of non-heritage learners from the US and other Western countries. In contrast to heritage learners and migrants to South Korea, these learners tend to receive less pressure to assimilate to Korean social norms. Brown (2011, 2013a) showed how some learners may take advantage of this to actively flaunt the norms of Korean interaction to pursue their own conversational goals and create identities as status equals, for example, by intentionally choosing to use reciprocal non-honorific language with older interlocutors. However, other learners resisted being positioned as cultural outsiders and therefore made every attempt to adhere to native speaker norms of language use (Brown, 2013a).

Gender identity and sexuality can be complex areas for identity negotiation for learners of Korean. In one application of activity theory to Korean, Brown (2016b) looked at the experiences of a 50-year old lesbian, feminist, and non-traditional student from the US studying in Seoul. Her language learning was constrained by (perceived) hostility towards homosexuality, and also by being consistently paired in the classroom with the one other older male student, with whom she had little in common. Despite this potentially negative environment, she managed to exert her agency to stylize the presentation of "self" and challenge the conditions of her language learning. Meanwhile, Brown (2013c) looked at the contrasting ways in which American learners of Korean perceived and used the kinship term 오빠 "older brother of a woman." Some learners actively used the term to address their Korean boyfriends or to refer to K-pop stars. However, other learners rejected it. One participant saw the 애교 associated with 오빠 as being "in such opposition to how I see myself" (p. 12).

4.4 Teaching and learning culture in the classroom

In recent years, the idea that learning a language involves cultural and social learning has been embraced by the language teaching profession. The propensity for language classes to train learners to operate in a multicultural world is increasingly seen as the *raison d'être* for language programs. Indeed, many language programs now include the word "culture" in their official descriptions or names (e.g., Seoul National University's "Korean Language and Culture Program"). However, as shall be discussed in this section, incorporating culture into language teaching entails diverse challenges.

4.4.1 Intercultural competence

The movement towards incorporating social and cultural elements in language teaching reflected a reconceptualization in the goal of language teaching. Michael Canale and Merrill Swain (Canale & Swain, 1980; Canale, 1983) argued that the profession had to move beyond the paradigm of seeing language pedagogy merely as teaching linguistic competence (i.e., grammar, vocabulary, pronunciation, spelling). They argued that learners needed to acquire "communicative competence" (originally proposed by Hymes 1972), which included not just "grammatical competence," but also "sociolinguistic competence" (the ability to use and understand language appropriately in various contexts), as well as "discourse competence" and "strategic competence."

In addition to "sociolinguistic competence," scholars soon pointed out that learners needed "cultural competence" in order to be effective language users (e.g., Byram, 1997). The idea of "cultural competence" refers to knowledge of the cultural practices, products, and perspectives of the country (or countries) where the language is spoken. The concept focuses on the knowledge of the native speaker, seeing this as the goal that second language learners should aspire to.

In recent years, however, this model of "cultural competence" that targets the culture of the country where the language is spoken and that holds the native speaker as the goal to follow has been questioned. Michael Byram (e.g., Byram et al., 2002; Byram, 2008) has argued that this approach relies on stereotypical representations of national culture, and undervalues the complexity of cross-cultural interactions. It also ignores the fact that in our increasingly globalized world many learners are multilingual individuals. To be sure, learners may require some degree of factual knowledge related to Korean national culture. However, teaching culture in this fact-based way can make some dangerous assumptions, most crucially that all Korean people share exactly the same culture.

Adopting the idea of "intercultural competence," Byram et al. (2002) argue that language classrooms need to prepare learners to accept people from other cultures as individuals with other distinctive perspectives, values, and behaviors. To do this, teachers need to foster in their learners the following attitudes and skills:

1. intercultural attitudes: curiosity and openness, readiness to suspend disbelief about other cultures and belief about one's own
2. knowledge of social groups and their products and practices in one's own and in one's interlocutor's country, and of the general processes of societal and individual interaction
3. skills of interpreting and relating: ability to interpret a document or event from another culture, to explain it and relate it to documents or events from one's own
4. skills of discovery and interaction: ability to acquire new knowledge of a culture and cultural practices, and the ability to operate knowledge, attitudes, and skills under the constraints of real-time communication and interaction
5. critical cultural awareness: an ability to evaluate, critically and on the basis of explicit criteria, perspectives, practices, and products in one's own and other cultures and countries.

These skills place an emphasis on learners interpreting, discovering, and thinking critically about culture for themselves. Going beyond this, Kramsch (2006) argues that learners in the globalized digital era need to be able to interpret and manipulate the increasingly complex symbolic choices of language, which she refers to as *symbolic competence*. Crucially, Kramsch points out the need for the notion of competence in second language learning to encompass written, visual, and electronic modalities of communication, in addition to the spoken modality. Some examples of situations requiring this kind of multimodal symbolic competence in Korean are shown in Figure 4.1.

The advantage of teaching culture as a set of skills is that students can apply these skills to different contexts. A student successfully taught in this way can apply this knowledge not just to interactions with Koreans from Seoul, but also to provincial or overseas populations. Indeed, for some, the focus of language teaching should be on developing skills to survive in a cosmopolitan world (e.g., Canagarajah's 2011 notion of "cosmopolitan practice"). "Not surprisingly," notes Kramsch (2014: p. 42), "speakers of English as a Lingua Franca favor this cosmopolitan view of culture, that befits English as a global language of business and technology." With

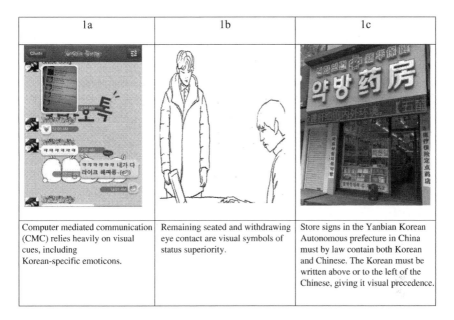

1a	1b	1c
Computer mediated communication (CMC) relies heavily on visual cues, including Korean-specific emoticons.	Remaining seated and withdrawing eye contact are visual symbols of status superiority.	Store signs in the Yanbian Korean Autonomous prefecture in China must by law contain both Korean and Chinese. The Korean must be written above or to the left of the Chinese, giving it visual precedence.

Figure 4.1 Examples of situations requiring multimodal symbolic competence.

Korean language and culture becoming increasingly globalized (e.g., Touhami & Al-Haq, 2017; Luciano & Hernandez, 2018; You et al., 2019), Korean teachers also need to start adopting a more cosmopolitan view of language learning.

4.4.2 Culture in the ACTFL standards

The role of culture has been clearly positioned within the ACTFL standards, which articulate the goals for language teaching in the US. "Cultures" is included as one of the "five Cs" and is defined as being composed of "perspectives," "practices," and "products." The standards include specific progress indicators for assessing the extent to which students understand the relationship between practices and perspectives (Standard 2.1), and between products and perspectives. In addition, culture is explicitly integrated into the "Comparisons" standard, which states that students should "demonstrate understanding of the concept of culture through comparisons of the cultures studied and their own." Table 4.6 shows example objectives for first-year Korean based off the Korean Standards.

4.4.3 Problems in culture teaching

The importance of culture in language learning is supported by modern language pedagogy's focus on "communicative competence" and reified in the ACTFL Standards. Yet many in the field have noted that pedagogy for teaching culture is underdeveloped compared to other areas of language. Hadley (2000: p. 346)

Table 4.6 Example Objectives for Culture (Level 1)

Standard 2.1 Practices and Perspectives	Standard 2.2: Products and Perspectives
• Students use appropriate expressions and gestures for greetings, leave-taking, and common classroom interactions. • Students demonstrate an awareness of the use of speech levels of the Korean language. • Students understand and demonstrate patterns of behavior appropriate to different settings (e.g., using two hands for giving and receiving from elders, Korean table manners). • Students recognize and understand Korean daily practices (e.g., removing shoes before entering homes, sitting and sleeping on the floor, bowing to elders). • Students participate in cultural activities (e.g., holiday celebrations, games) and show an understanding of their significance.	• Students demonstrate an awareness of name of tangible products of Korean culture (e.g., songs, stories, artwork, crafts, food), as well as traditional games and sports. • Students identify both tangible products (e.g., clothing, household items, food) and expressive products (e.g., pop songs, folksongs, modern and traditional dances) of Korean culture. • Students participate in Korean traditional games, sports, and cooking..

Source: Cho et al. (2015), based on the ACTFL Standards for Korean Language Learning.

notes that many teachers struggle to find room to teach culture in their already overcrowded curricula. Teachers may also lack the knowledge and skills needed to teach culture, since it is rarely treated in depth in teacher education. Hence, teachers often fall back on a "facts only" approach, with isolated cultural facts spread across the curriculum in an unstructured way. A classic characterization of this kind of approach (Galloway, 1985) describes four common types of culture teaching:

1. the Frankenstein Approach: a taco from here, a flamenco dancer from there, a gaucho from here, a bullfight from there
2. the 4-F Approach: i.e., folk dances, festivals, fairs, and food
3. the Tour Guide Approach: the identification of monuments, rivers, and cities
4. the "By-the-way" Approach: sporadic lectures or bits of behavior selected indiscriminately to emphasize sharp differences.

Galloway (2015: p. 95) calls these "fast-food approaches" whereby "choice pieces of cultural tissue are plucked and processed." With these underdeveloped techniques, it is easy for the teaching of culture to feature stereotyping, triviality, and political bias (Hadley, 2000: p. 353).

The difficulty of providing cultural training is exacerbated by the sparsity of suitable resources and the limitations of many textbooks. Korean language textbooks tend to oversimplify and misrepresent sociolinguistic aspects of language, particularly honorifics (Brown, 2010; Choo, 1999). Brown (2010) found that textbooks (even at higher levels) tend to over-represent a semi-honorific register of Korean featuring the first name +씨 address pattern, the polite −요 speech style, and the dropping of referent honorifics, as in (3a):

(3) a. 민호 씨, 어디 가요?

"Min-ho, where are you going?" (semi-honorific)

  b. 민호야, 어디 가?

"Min-ho, where are you going?" (non-honorific)

  c. 선생님, 어디 가세요?

"Teacher, where are you going?" (honorific)

This register is non-intimate, but at the same time not fully deferential. It would be appropriate for addressing a non-intimate casual acquaintance of similar age or younger. But it may be too distant for addressing an intimate friend (where 3b would be preferred), and would not be respectful enough for addressing an adult stranger or a person of higher status (where 3c is better). Although sticking to this register may make Korean "easier," it denies language learners the opportunity to develop sensitivity to different registers. Choo (1999: p. 79) is particularly critical of the underrepresentation of intimate speech (반말) in lower-level Korean textbooks. Wang (1999) also points out that textbooks represent speech acts in an impoverished way.

The explicit teaching of culture in many Korean textbooks is often limited to "culture notes" or other culture-related readings. Brown's (2016a) analysis of cultural texts in two Korean textbook series shows that they tend to focus on cultural practices (and to a lesser extent products) without sufficient treatment of underlying perspectives. For instance, a cultural note in one textbook explains the practice of using titles or kinship terms to address elders, but does not mention any reasons for this practice. Brown (2016a) furthermore claims that textbooks present a homogenized, Seoul-centric, and sanitized version of Korean culture. Cultural and linguistic variation is erased, provincial and overseas Korean-speaking communities are overlooked, and critical viewpoints on Korean culture are omitted.

From a slightly different perspective, Ree (2000) points out that Korean language teaching materials also lack sensitivity to the cultural norms of the learners themselves. Textbooks at times contain dialogs and communicative tasks that involve asking and answering personal questions, for example, about dating and marriage preferences (e.g., "When would you like to get married?" "What type of men do you like?"). Such questions can be culturally uncomfortable for some learners (and indeed may not always be appropriate among Koreans). Ree (2000) argues that dialogs embedding distinct Korean cultural values and communication patterns should be accompanied by sufficient explanation to avoid cultural conflict.

In sum, Korean language textbooks are paradigmatically detached from current theory regarding how culture should be taught. They aim for "cultural competence" (i.e., teaching the cultural knowledge of an idealized native speaker of Standard Korean). They fall short of teaching "intercultural competence" or "symbolic competence" because they provide learners with no training in how to interpret culture for themselves or to think critically about it. It would of course be unrealistic to expect language textbooks to fully represent Korean culture in all its complex diversity. However, it is important to understand textbooks' limitations in order for teachers to consider how best to supplement cultural content into their classrooms.

4.4.4 Towards a pedagogy for teaching culture

As noted above, one limitation in culture teaching has been the absence of a clear pedagogy. This situation may now be changing, with recent studies advocating both text-based approaches for teaching culture and experiential project-based learning.

In order to become interculturally competent, learners need to develop the ability to interpret the target culture for themselves. Learners thus require exposure to a wide variety of texts which are rich in symbolic representations of culture. As noted by Kern (2008: p. 367), "texts and the ways that they are interpreted do not merely reflect cultural perspectives; they CONSTITUTE and PROPAGATE much of culture." The texts selected should primarily be authentic texts designed for native speakers, with all textual and visual aspects maintained. Crucially, they should be taught in a critical way in which learners are encouraged to interrogate the viewpoints and symbolic meanings.

Many different kinds of authentic texts can be included at all levels, and there are multiple techniques for encouraging critical reading. Kern (2008) gives the example of including letters from pen-pals in a first-year French class when teaching the topic of "family." Students then compared the descriptions of the pen-pals' families described in the letters (which contained blended families, multicultural families, etc.) with the idealized descriptions of French families in the textbooks. Through this process, they gained critical understanding of the complex realities of the French family and became aware of the ideological restrictions of their textbooks. Further examples of critical cultural reading for Korean can be found in Section 4.4.5 below, whereas the teaching of literacy more broadly is covered in Chapter 6.

If gaining intercultural competence involves learners developing their own experiences of culture and forming new perspectives for themselves, then they need to play an active role in determining the content of their cultural learning. To this end, project work has gained a central role. Project work may involve library or online research and also interacting with the target culture through interviews, field trips, and observations. For project work to foster intercultural competence, it needs to go beyond simply gathering "facts" about the target culture, and must include a critical element. Project work, as well as the analysis of authentic texts, can also be used for teaching sociolinguistic and pragmatic functions of language, as will be fleshed out in Section 4.4.5 below.

As a final observation, language pedagogy practitioners emphasize the importance of integrating culture within the language-related content of the curriculum. Lafayette (1978, 1988; cited in Hadley, 2000: p. 358) makes several suggestions to this end, including that culture is taught in the target language, that cultural knowledge is tested as carefully as linguistic knowledge, and that cultural topics are integrated into language practice activities. Even at lower levels, simple topics can easily be made more culturally connected. Talking about the family can include information about real-world Korean families, talking about daily schedules can feature a comparison of the daily life of a company worker in Seoul with one in New York, and teaching learners how to say months and dates can be centered around the dates of Korean holidays. Also, teachers can ensure that the teaching of "simple" language situations involves Korea-specific cultural routines. For instance, we can find several examples of language routines that occur in Korean restaurant interactions that have no direct correspondences to English:

(4) a. 여기요!

"Over here!" (customer summoning serving staff)

b. 냉면 잘라 드릴까요?

"Shall I cut the noodles?" (serving staff at 냉면 restaurant)

c. 밥 볶아 드릴까요?

"Shall I stir fry the rice?" (serving staff at 닭갈비 restaurant)

d. 간은 빼(고) 주세요.

"Can I have it without liver, please." (customer ordering 순대)

e. 잘 먹었습니다.

"I ate well." (customer expressing thanks to serving staff, or to accompanying diner for paying for the meal)

These culture-specific routines in supposedly "simple" interactions rarely feature in language textbooks.

4.4.5 Teaching culture in the Korean classroom

In contrast to the impoverished representation of culture found in Korean language textbooks, research literature shows that Korean language educators have been experimenting with innovative techniques for teaching culture.

In terms of text-based pedagogies, Korean language educators use films, dramas, and other media materials to cultivate intercultural competence. Cheon and Kim (2010) examined how Korean advertisements can be used to illustrate traditional Korean family structures and values, and changes therein. Although many advertisements are still imbued with traditional family values, certain types of advertisements, such as TV commercials for coffee or cosmetics, display changing gender roles and family values. Brown et al. (2015) used clips from Korean dramas and talk shows to lead discussions of Korean multiculturalism as part of a multiliteracies approach (see Chapter 6). Yoon and Brown (2018) also used multiliteracies to teach the social meanings of nonverbal behaviors associated with politeness in Korean, an important aspect of multimodal symbolic competence. Research also shows that the incorporation of pop culture has added benefits for learner motivation for both non-heritage (Lee, 2018) and heritage learners (Choi & Yi, 2012). For non-heritage learners, pop culture may increase their investment in language learning outside of the classroom and in developing learner autonomy (Lee, 2018), whereas for heritage learners, it may lead them to strengthen their ethnic identities through appreciation of the importance of Korean culture on a global scale (Choi & Yi, 2012).

Korean media materials can also be used for the contextualized teaching of sociolinguistic and pragmatic aspects of language. Byon (2007a) used media materials for teaching the differences between the –습니다 and –요, whereas Brown (2013d) presented a similar study for plain –다 and intimate –어 (see Figure 4.2). Kim and Lee (2010) designed a content-based curriculum featuring media materials for teaching sociolinguistic aspects of Korean (e.g., honorifics and address terms, gender and language, dialects, phatic expressions, loanwords, internet language). Each week, students read academic articles in Korean on one of these topics. They then watched relevant Korean TV shows to facilitate and

---

Brown (2013d) followed Byon (2007a) in using cloze-style activities for teaching speech styles. Students were asked to fill in blanks in the script from the TV drama 파리의 연인 (SBS, 2004) by choosing between intimate and plain styles using their knowledge of pragmatic functions of the styles already learned in class. They then compared their answers to the original materials, which used the forms that are underlined below. For each item, although both answers may be grammatically possible, pragmatic factors influence the choice between intimate and plain styles. For instance, plain style is used in (3) since this is an exclamatory utterance.

1   태영: 아- 떨려요.

2   기주: **(1) 괜찮아 / 괜찮다.**

3   태영: 우와~ [기주의 집을 보며].

4   수혁: **(2) 왔어? / 왔니? 왔냐?** [기주를 보며]

5   왔어요? [태영을 보며]

6   태영: 갑자기 존댓말 하니까 **(3) 이상해 / 이상하다.**

7   수혁: 어른들 안에 계세요.

8   다들 **(4) 기다리셔 / 기다리신다.**

Figure 4.2 Example from Brown (2013d).

expand their understanding of the notions discussed in the readings and during lectures.

Sociolinguistics-related topics have also been featured in project-based assignments. In Jung and Lee's (2018) study, heritage students engaged in a "citizen sociolinguistics" project exploring the use of language in the media and covering topics including "Konglish," neologisms, and gendered language. Byon (2006) taught the speech act of requests through project work involving Discourse Completion Tasks (DCT) that students administered to both English and Korean speakers. The students asked the native speakers to provide forms of requests that they would use in different situations (e.g., asking a professor for a letter of recommendation, asking a roommate to tidy the kitchen). Through analyzing the data they collected, students became aware of how differences in linguistic behavior reflected culture. For instance, Korean respondents frequently prefaced their requests to professors with apologies for causing inconvenience, whereas Americans' request style suggested they saw such requests as their legitimate right.

Korean language practitioners have also developed classroom projects that go beyond sociolinguistic aspects of the language and are designed to lead students to critically engage with Korean society. Byon (2007b) had students in a Korean culture class use project work to explore stereotypes about Korea. Students were first asked to generate their own stereotypes, which they explored through media sources and interviews. They then revised their stated stereotypes in accordance with their findings. Strauss (2015) described project-based work for intermediate and advanced students on the theme of Korean holidays. One strength of this approach was that it involved students thinking critically about how holidays have changed and are viewed in modern society. For 설날 "Lunar New Year," for instance, students were asked to explore whether the maintenance of traditional rituals is "a burden or a blessing." In addition, the materials challenged simplistic comparisons with American holidays by involving students in internet research on holidays across the world. For example, in the unit on 추석 "harvest moon festival," students researched various comparable international holidays such as China's mid-autumn festival, Japan's "Harvest Moon Viewing Festival," Spain's "Grape Harvest Festival" in Andalusia and "Rice Festival" in Valencia, and the Jewish *sukkot* festival.

4.5 Future directions

Research in KFL has started to explore social and cultural aspects of language acquisition and pedagogy. Furthermore, with the implementation of the National Standards for Korean, language programs across the US and beyond are looking at ways to systematically incorporate culture into their curricula.

Nevertheless, the cultural and social side of Korean language learning still lacks status compared to grammar and other organizational and functional aspects of language. Although this situation is common across many languages, it appears to be particularly acute for Korean. One reason for this may be the relatively low status of sociolinguistics and pragmatics in Korean linguistics. On this point, Korean compares rather poorly with languages such as Japanese, where there is a wealth of research on topics such as language variation, gendered language, and politeness. More investment is needed in research on social and cultural aspects of the Korean language and on the influence of these factors in Korean language learning and teaching.

On the practical level of language teaching, this chapter shows that Korean textbook materials appear to lag behind current research and pedagogical practices in how they represent culture, and also do not take the needs and interests of learners into account. Nikitina and Furuoka (2019) suggest exploring language learners' mental images of Korea as one way to assess their learning needs and develop the cultural component of the language curriculum. Going forward, the development of Korean language teaching materials and curricula needs to focus on the best ways to place the critical study of culture and the development of intercultural competence at the heart of the way that language is taught.

4.6 Conclusion

Until recently, cultural and social aspects of language learning and teaching took a backseat to organizational aspects of language, particularly grammar. However, as reviewed in this chapter, culture is now seen as integral to language and the way that it is learned, and language programs increasingly emphasize intercultural competence.

Learning to use language in a culturally appropriate way is difficult for language learners who face daily struggles to navigate across different cultures. This process is complicated by the intense variation that characterizes the symbolic value of language, and the idea of culture itself. Even in a society such as South Korea, which is considered to be relatively homogenous, ideas pertaining to correct language use and the desirable "face" of Korean culture are disputed and unstable. Moreover, expectations as to how learners should assimilate to Korean culture vary according to factors such as the ethno-national identity of the learners. As Galloway (2015: p. 95) remarked, culture learning is "slow food, messy food." It is time to stop treating the learning and teaching of culture in the language classroom as "fast food" or a "side dish" to the main feast.

Discussion questions

1. How important is it to teach culture? Is it as important as the four language skills? How are your views reflected in your teaching practice?
2. Based on the content of this chapter, what aspects of Korean culture do you think should be prioritized in the university-level Korean language classroom? How would your answer change depending on whether your students were heritage learners, non-heritage learners, or a mixture of the two?
3. The authors note that "'Korean culture' means quite different things to a young female from Seoul than it would do to an elderly male from the South Jeolla Province." Do you agree? How might they differ? If the notion of Korean culture is variable, how do we represent it in the language classroom?

4. How do you feel about teaching "suppressed" aspects of Korean culture? Should controversial aspects of culture be taught?

5. How would you teach the use of Korean kinship terms in a first- or second-year Korean class?

6. What kind of cultural project would you do in a third- or fourth-year language class?

7. According to Byram et al. (2002), teachers should foster in their learners "critical cultural awareness" in order to prepare them to communicate with people from diverse cultural backgrounds. What can teachers do to help learners gain "critical cultural awareness?"

8. In some traditional teaching approaches, culture is taught by presenting facts and showing products and artefacts. How might you develop classroom tasks that would present a more elaborate and critical understanding of culture?

9. The authors argue that culture is rarely included in assessment in the language classroom. Please discuss suggestions and techniques for assessing cultural learning.

10. In what ways, if any, was intercultural communication training included in your own teacher education? What characteristics of intercultural communication would you like to see in a teacher training program for future professional development?

Notes

1 Even the direct honorific counterpart of this sentence (i.e., 늦어서 미안합니다) would also not be appropriate for addressing a social superior such as a teacher. 늦어서 죄송합니다 would be preferred.

2 Although the 3 Ps model is widely applied in North America, within South Korea, the most widely used model is the division between achievement culture, informational culture, and behavioral culture advocated by the National Institute for Korean Language.

References

Ahearn, L.M. (2001). Language and agency. *Annual Review of Anthropology, 30*(1), 109–137.

Bayley, R. (1996). Competing constraints on variation in the speech of adult Chinese learners of English. In R. Bayley & D.R. Preston (Eds.), *Second language acquisition and linguistic variation* (pp. 97–120). Amsterdam: John Benjamins.

Brown, L. (2010). Questions of appropriateness and authenticity in the representation of Korean honorifics in textbooks for second language learners. *Language, Culture and Curriculum, 23*(1), 35–50.

Brown, L. (2011). *Korean honorifics and politeness in second language learning.* Amsterdam: John Benjamins.

Brown, L. (2013a). Identity and honorifics use in Korean study abroad. In C. Kinginger (Ed.), *Social and cultural aspects of language learning in study abroad* (pp. 269–298). Amsterdam: John Benjamins.

Brown, L. (2013b). "Mind your own esteemed business": Sarcastic honorifics use and impoliteness in Korean TV dramas. *Journal of Politeness Research, 9*(2), 159–186.

Brown, L. (2013c). "Oppa, hold my purse": A sociocultural study of identity and indexicality in the perception and use of oppa 'Older Brother' by second language learners. *Korean Language in America, 18*, 1–22.

Brown, L. (2013d). Teaching 'casual' and/or 'impolite' language through multimedia: The case of non-honorific panmal speech styles in Korean. *Language, Culture and Curriculum, 26*(1), 1–18.

Brown, L. (2015a). Honorifics and politeness. In L. Brown & J. Yeon (Eds.), *The handbook of Korean linguistics* (pp. 303–319). Malden, MA: Wiley-Blackwell.

Brown, L. (2015b). Revisiting "polite" –yo and "deferential" –supnita speech style shifting in Korean from the viewpoint of indexicality. *Journal of Pragmatics, 79*, 43–59.

Brown, L. (2016a). Ideologies in Korean language teaching. *International Journal of Korean Language Education, 2*, 1–29.

Brown, L. (2016b). An activity-theoretic study of agency and identity in the study abroad experiences of a lesbian nontraditional learner of Korean. *Applied Linguistics, 37*(6), 808–827.

Brown, L. (2017). "Nwuna's body is so sexy": Pop culture and the changing use of kinship terms in Korea. *Discourse, Context and Media, 15*, 1–10.

Brown, L., Iwasaki, N., & Lee, K. (2015). Implementing multiliteracies in the Korean classroom through visual media. In Y. Kumagai, A. Lopez-Sanchez & S. Wu (Eds.), *Multiliteracies in world languages education* (pp. 158–181). London: Routledge.

Byon, A. (2007a). Teaching the polite and the deferential speech levels, using media materials: Advanced KFL classroom settings. In D. Yoshimi & H. Wang (Eds.), *Selected papers from pragmatics in the CJK classroom: The state of the art* (pp. 21–64). Retrieved from http://nflrc.hawaii.edu/CJKProceedings.

Byon, A. (2007b). The use of culture portfolio project in a Korean culture classroom: Evaluating stereotypes and enhancing cross-cultural awareness. *Language, Culture and Curriculum, 20*(1), 1–19.

Byon, A.S. (2003). Language socialisation and Korean as a heritage language: A study of Hawaiian classrooms. *Language, Culture and Curriculum, 16*(3), 269–283.

Byon, A.S. (2006). Developing KFL students' pragmatic awareness of Korean speech acts: The use of discourse completion tasks. *Language Awareness, 15*(4), 244–263.

Byram, M. (1997). *Teaching and assessing intercultural communicative competence.* Clevedon, UK: Multilingual Matters.

Byram, M. (2008). *From foreign language education to education for intercultural citizenship.* Clevedon, UK: Multilingual Matters.

Byram, M., Gribkova, B., & Starkey, H. (2002). *Developing the intercultural dimension in language teaching. A practical introduction for teachers.* Strasbourg: Council of Europe.

Cameron, D. (2005). Language, gender, and sexuality: Current issues and new directions. *Applied Linguistics, 26*(4), 482–502.

Canagarajah, S. (2011). Codemeshing in academic writing: Identifying teachable strategies of translanguaging. *The Modern Language Journal, 95*(3), 401–417.

Canale, M. (1983). From communicative competence to communicative language pedagogy. *Language and Communication, 1*(1), 1–47.

Canale, Michael, & Swain, Merrill. (1980). Theoretical bases of communicative approaches to second language teaching and testing. *Applied Linguistics, 1*(1), 1–47.

Cheon, S.Y., & Kim, K. (2010). Teaching Korean culture with advertisements: Change and persistence in family values and gender roles. *The Korean Language in America, 15*, 1–22.

Cho, Y., Kang, S., Kim, H., Lee, H., & Wang, H. (2015). Overview. *The Korean Language in America, 19*(2), 153–177.

Choi, J., & Yi, Y. (2012). The use and role of pop culture in heritage language learning: A study of advanced learners of Korean. *Foreign Language Annals, 45*(1), 110–129.

Choo, M. (1999). Teaching language styles of Korean. *The Korean Language in America, 3*, 77–95.

Crawford-Lange, L.M., & Lange, D.L. (1984). Doing the unthinkable in the second-language classroom: A process for the integration of language and culture. In T. Higgs (Ed.), *Teaching for proficiency: The organizing principle* (pp. 139–177). Lincolnwood, IL: National Textbook.

DuFon, M. (1999). *The acquisition of linguistic politeness in Indonesian by sojourners in naturalistic interactions* [Unpublished Doctoral Dissertation]. Honolulu, HI: University of Hawai'i at Manoa.

Eggins, S. (2004). *Introduction to systemic functional linguistics*. London: Bloomsbury Publishing.

Ellis, R. (1999). Item versus system learning: Explaining free variation. *Applied Linguistics, 20*(4), 460–480.

Engeström, Y. (1987). *Learning by expanding: An Activity theoretical approach to developmental research*. Helsinki: Orienta-Konsultit.

Galloway, V. (1985). *A design for the improvement of the teaching of culture in foreign language classrooms*. ACTFL Project Proposal.

Galloway, V. (2015). Culture and sustainability: Lessons from the oyster and other metaphors. In P. Swanson (Ed.), *Dimension 2015 anniversary volume* (pp. 94–120). Decatur, GA: Southern Conference on Language Teaching.

Gee, J. (2015). *Social linguistics and literacies: Ideology in discourses*. Abingdon, UK: Routledge.

Hadley, A.O. (2000). *Teaching language in context* (2nd ed.). Boston, MA: Heinle & Heinle.

Harkness, N. (2015a). Basic kinship terms: Christian relations, chronotopic formulations, and a Korean confrontation of language. *Anthropological Quarterly, 88*(2), 305–336.

Harkness, N. (2015b). Linguistic emblems of South Korean society. In L. Brown, & J. Yeon (Eds.), *The handbook of Korean linguistics* (pp. 492–508). Malden, MA: Wiley-Blackwell.

Herron, C., Cole, S., Corrie, C., & Dubreil, S. (1999). The effectiveness of a video-based curriculum in teaching culture. *The Modern Language Journal, 83*(4), 518–533.

Higgins, C., & Stoker, K. (2011). Language learning as a site for belonging: A narrative analysis of Korean adoptee-returnees. *International Journal of Bilingual Education and Bilingualism, 14*(4), 399–412.

Hymes, D. (1972). On communicative competence. In J. Pride & J. Holmes (Eds.), *Sociolinguistics. Selected readings* (pp. 269–293). Harmondsworth, UK: Penguin.

Iino, M. (2006). Norms of interaction in a Japanese homestay setting: Toward a two-way flow of linguistic and cultural resources. *Language learners in study abroad contexts, 15*, 151–176.

Jeon, L., & Cukor-Avila, P. (2015). "One country, one language"?: Mapping perceptions of dialects in South Korea. *Dialectologia: revista electrònica, 14*, 17–46.

Jo, H.Y. (2001). 'Heritage' language learning and ethnic identity: Korean Americans' struggle with language authorities. *Language, Culture and Curriculum, 14*(1), 26–41.

Jo, J. (2018). Korean. 'Formality' endings '-supnita/-supnikka' and '-eyo' in the negotiation of interactional identity in the news interview. *Journal of Pragmatics, 136*, 20–38.

Jung, J.-Y., & Lee, E. (2018). Citizen sociolinguistics: Making connections in the foreign language classroom. *The Korean Language in America, 22*(1), 1–24.

Kang, S. (1988). *Hankwuk munhwa yenkyu [A study of Korean culture]*. Seoul, South Korea: Hyenam.

Kern, R. (2008). Making connections through texts in language teaching. *Language Teaching, 41*(3), 367–387.

Kim, H.-S., & Lee, H.-S. (2010). Enhancing sociolinguistic competency through Korean on-line TV: Advanced level KFL curriculum. *The Korean Language in America, 15*, 23–45.

Kim, M. (1998). Cross-adoption of language between different genders: The case of the Korean kinship terms *hyeng* and *enni*. In S. Wertheim, A. Bailey & M. Corston-Oliver (Eds.), *Engendering communication: Proceedings of the fifth Berkeley women and communication conference* (pp. 271–284). Berkeley, CA: University of California.

Kim, M. (2015). Women's talk, mothers' work: Korean mothers' address terms, solidarity, and power. *Discourse Studies, 17*(5), 551–582.

Kim, S.H. (2003). Korean cultural codes and communication. *International Area Review, 6*(1), 93–114.

Kramsch, C. (2006). *Context and culture in language teaching*. Oxford: Oxford University Press.

Kramsch, C. (2014). Language and culture. *AILA Review, 27*, 30–55.

Lafayette, R.C. (1978). *Teaching culture: Strategies and techniques*. Washington, DC: Center for Applied Linguistics.

Lafayette, R.C. (1988). Integrating the teaching of culture into the foreign language classroom. In A. Singerman (Ed.), *Toward a new integration of language and culture* (pp. 47–62). Middlebury, VT: Northeast Conference.

Lantolf, J., & Pavlenko, A. (2001). (S)econd (L)anguage (A)ctivity theory: Understanding second language learners as people. In M. Breen (Ed.), *Learner contributions to language learning: New directions in research* (pp. 141–158). Abingdon, UK: Routledge.

Lantolf, J., & Thorne, S. (2006). *Sociocultural theory and the genesis of second language development*. Oxford: Oxford University Press.

Lave, J., & Wenger, E. (1991). *Situated learning: Legitimate peripheral participation*. Cambridge: Cambridge university press.

Lee, I. (2018). Effects of contact with Korean popular culture on KFL learners' motivation. *The Korean Language in America, 22*(1), 25–45.

Lee, I., & Ramsey, S.R. (2000). *The Korean language*. Albany, NY: SUNY Press.

Lee, J. (2006). Korean proverbs. In H. Sohn (Ed.), *Korean language in culture and society* (pp. 74–85). Honolulu, HI: University of Hawaii Press.

Leont'ev, A. (1978). *Activity, consciousness and personality*. Upper Saddle River, NJ: Prentice Hall.

Li, X. (2010). Sociolinguistic variation in the speech of learners of Chinese as a second language. *Language Learning, 60*(2), 366–408.

Longman, J. (2008). Language socialization. In J. González (Ed.), *Encyclopedia of bilingual education* (pp. 490–493). Thousand Oaks, CA: Sage.

Luciano, E., & Hernández, T. (2018). Public diplomacy, soft power and language: The case of the Korean language in Mexico City. *Journal of Contemporary Eastern Asia, 17*(1), 27–49.

Lukoff, F. (1977). Ceremonial and expressive uses of the styles of address of Korean. In C. Kim (Ed.), *Papers in Korean linguistic* (pp. 269–296). Columbia, SC: Hornbeam.

Mitchell, R., Myles, F., & Marsden, E. (2013). *Second language learning theories*. Abingdon, UK: Routledge.

Nikitina, L., & Furuoka, F. (2019). Language learners' mental images of Korea: insights for the teaching of culture in the language classroom. *Journal of Multilingual and Multicultural Development*, 40(9), 774–786.

Norton, B. (2000). *Identity and language learning: Gender, ethnicity and educational change*. Harlow: Longman.

Ochs, E. (1990). Indexicality and socialization. In J. Stigler, R. Shweder & G. Herdt (Eds.), *Cultural psychology: Essays on comparative human development* (pp. 287–308). Cambridge: Cambridge University Press.

Ochs, E., & Schieffelin, B. (2001). Language acquisition and socialization: Three developmental stories and their implications. In A. Duranti (Ed.), *Linguistic anthropology: A reader* (pp. 263–301). Hoboken, NJ: Wiley.

Ortega, L. (2014). *Understanding second language acquisition*. Abingdon, UK: Routledge.

Park, M.Y. (2011). Identity and agency among heritage language learners. In K. Davis (Ed.), *Critical qualitative research in second language studies: Agency and advocacy* (pp. 171–207). Charlotte, NC: Information Age Publishing.

Park, M.Y. (2012). Teachers' use of the intimate speech style in the Korean language classroom. *The Korean Language in America*, *17*, 55–83.

Park, M.Y. (2014). A study of the Korean sentence-ender *−(u)psita*: Implementing transitions between activities in the classroom. *Journal of Pragmatics*, *68*, 25–39.

Park, M.Y. (2016). Integrating rapport-building into language instruction: A study of Korean foreign language classes. *Classroom Discourse*, *7*(2), 109–130.

Park, M.Y. (2017). Resisting linguistic and ethnic marginalization: voices of Southeast Asian marriage-migrant women in Korea. *Language and Intercultural Communication*, *17*(2), 118–134.

Park, M.Y. (2020). "I want to learn Seoul speech!": language ideologies and practices among marriage-migrants in South Korea. *International Journal of Bilingual Education and Bilingualism*, *23*(2), 227–240.

Pennycook, A. (2006). *Global Englishes and transcultural flows*. London: Routledge.

Ree, J.J. (2000). Problems of cultural clash in textbooks. *The Korean Language in America*, *4*, 141–159.

Sapir, E. (1949). The status of linguistics as a science. In D.G. Mandelbaum (Ed.), *Selected writings of Edward Sapir in language, culture, and personality* (pp. 160–165). Berkeley, CA: University of California Press.

Silva, D. J. (1991). Phonological variation in Korean: The case of the "disappearing w". Language Variation and Change, 3(2), 153–170.

Shin, S.J. (2005). *Developing in two languages: Korean children in America*. Clevedon, UK: Multilingual Matters.

Silverstein, M. (2003). Indexical order and the dialectics of sociolinguistic life. *Language and Communication*, 23(3–4), 193–229.

Slobin, D.I. (1996). From "thought and language" to "thinking for speaking". In J. Gumperz & S. Levinson (Eds.), *Rethinking linguistic relativity* (pp. 70–96). New York: Cambridge University Press.

Sohn, H. (1986). *Linguistic expeditions*. Seoul: Hanshin.

Song, J.J. (2005). *The Korean language: Structure, use and context*. New York: Routledge.

Strauss, S. (2015). *Korean discourse and genre*. CALPER, The Pennsylvania State University. Retrieved from http://calper.la.psu.edu/content/korean-discourse-and-genre.

Strauss, S., & Eun, J. (2005). Indexicality and honorific speech level choice in Korean. *Linguistics*, *43*(3), 611–651.

Tarone, E. (1998). Research on interlanguage variation: Implications for language testing. In L. Bachman & A. Cohen (Eds.), *Interfaces between second language acquisition and language testing research* (pp. 71–89). Stuttgart, Germany: Ernst Klett Sprachen.

Touhami, B., & Al.-Haq, F.A.A. (2017). The influence of the Korean wave on the language of international fans: Case study of Algerian fans. *Sino-US English Teaching*, *14*(10), 598–626.

Vygotsky, L.S. (1978). *Mind in society: The development of higher psychological processes*. Cambridge, MA: Harvard University Press.

Walker, G. (2000). Performed culture: Learning to participate in another culture. In R. Lambert & E. Shohamy (Eds.), *Language policy and pedagogy: Essays in honor of Richard Lambert* (pp. 221–236). Amsterdam: John Benjamins.

Wang, H.S. (1999). Speech acts in Korean language textbooks: Representations and authenticity. *Journal of Korean Language Education*, *10*(1), 195–220.

Whorf, B.L. (1956). Science and linguistics. In J.B. Carroll (Ed.), *Language, thought, and reality: Selected writings of Benjamin Lee Whorf* (pp. 212–217). Cambridge, MA: MIT Press.

Yoon, K.J. (2004). Not just words: Korean social models and the use of honorifics. *Intercultural Pragmatics*, *1*(2), 189–210.

Yoon, S.Y., & Brown, L. (2018). A multiliteracies approach to teaching Korean multimodal (im) politeness. *The Korean Language in America*, *21*(2), 154–185.

You, Z., Kiaer, J., & Ahn, H. (2019). Growing East Asian words in English: British university students' attitudes to words of East Asian origin in the English language. *English Today*, *36*(2), 17–34.

Yum, J.O. (2012). Communication competence: A Korean perspective. *China Media Research*, *8*(2), 11–17.

5 Korean heritage language teaching and learning

Hi-Sun Kim

5.1 Introduction

In heritage language (HL) acquisition studies, it is well understood that linguistic characteristics differ in HL learners from those of non-HL L2 learners. The recurring attributes of HL learners in the existing definitions of HL learners from HL studies (e.g., Benmamoun et al., 2013; Polinsky, 2015; Polinsky & Kagan, 2007; Rothman & Treffers-Daller, 2014; Valdes, 2001) are as follows: early and significant exposure to heritage language in the home; proficiency in the heritage language; bilingual to some degree; dominant in a language other than the heritage language; and ethnic and cultural connection to the heritage language. These attributes are also evident in Korean HL learners where they have early and significant exposure to Korean language, mostly from home. Upon entering school, they begin to show signs of language attrition and shift as they become dominant in English. In other words, HL learners can be categorized as unbalanced bilinguals, in which they begin as early bilinguals through significant input but are unable to maintain the balance between two languages in their adulthood. As a result, their Korean language proficiency includes high (almost native-like) listening skills, low to moderate accuracy in productive skills, and minimal (or zero) metalinguistic knowledge from the lack of formal instruction. In addition, Korean HL learners, like all HL learners, are linked to a community (often limited to their immediate family), giving them first-hand experience at home that eventually leads them to identify with the Korean culture and community. With such a complex linguistic and cultural profile that Korean HL learners bring into class, different pedagogical approaches that address the linguistic and cultural needs that are unique to Korean HL learners should be implemented in Korean language classes. Hence, this chapter aims to explore the research in the field of HL acquisition studies to examine the linguistic characteristics, language processing issues, and the HL community and identity, in order to provide pedagogical implications for classroom teaching as well as curriculum development for Korean HL learners.

5.2 Linguistic profile of Korean heritage language learners

As a result of language attrition and partial acquisition of their heritage language through their language experience growing up in North America, many second-generation Koreans enroll in Korean language classes in college to (re) learn their heritage language as they begin to notice and explore their Korean identity. In a class with both HL and non-HL L2 learners (L2 learners, hereafter), it becomes apparent that Korean HL learners show differences in their proficiency, processing, and learning from their L2 learner peers due to the language experiences they received from home. While L2 learners generally follow similar and somewhat predictable patterns of L2 acquisition (and despite the same formal L2 instruction that their peer L2 learners receive), Korean HL learners often show different patterns and amount of acquisition, implying that they experience cognitive difficulties in restructuring their interlanguage. To explore such differences, this section will discuss research studies that examine linguistic features and language processing of Korean HL learners to begin constructing a prototype and the linguistic profile of Korean HL learners.

In an empirical study by Kim (2008), the results from a listening comprehension task (with Korean subject-gap versus object-gap relative clause) showed that the sentence processing strategy differed between HL and L2 learners of Korean. In particular, based on the error analysis of the comprehension task, Kim's study revealed that L2 learners (e.g., English speakers) had a tendency to rely on word-order cues (L1 transfer from English), while Korean HL learners had some ability to apply case-marker cues (L1 transfer from Korean) when processing Korean relative clauses. However, for Korean HL learners, the ability to use case-marker cues depended on their HL experience as a child. In this vein, one challenge in HL instruction is accommodating the vast range of levels within Korean HL learners due to their language experience. Hence, Kim (2008) identified three subgroups within Korean HL learners based on their L1, which was defined as the primary language used between the ages 0–5. The three HS subgroups are as follows: HL learners who had Korean as their L1; HL learners with both Korean and English as their L1; and HL learners who had mostly English as their L1. The results further showed that not only were the listening comprehension accuracy scores within the subgroups significantly different, but also the ratio of use of case-marker cues versus word-order cues differed, in that HL learners with more exposure to Korean as their L1 used more case-marker cues, similar to Korean native speakers, while HL learners with English as their L1 used more word-order cues, similar to (English) L2 learners. Therefore, this study showed that HL learners possess language processing aspects that are native-like and L2-like, in which the level of nativeness in their listening comprehension depended on the amount and quality of Korean language exposure that they had received from an early age. However, as English became their dominant language, it was evident that some forms have been stabilized in their HL acquisition and thus may require instruction to destabilize and restructure their interlanguage.

In discussing the process of language development, attrition, and stabilization of Korean in HL learners, Kim (2012) points out the complexities of HL language profiles that include aspects of a native speaker, L2 learner, and bilingual speaker. Hence, in order to investigate the source of stabilization in their Korean of HL learners, Kim (2012) compares and analyzes the errors in the spoken data of Korean HL (college level), L2 learners (college level), and Korean-English bilingual children (4-year-olds). The objective of this study was to identify linguistic errors that are unique to Korean HL learners by comparing them to the errors of Korean-English bilingual children (L1 errors), as well as to those of non-HL L2 learners (L2 errors). The participants included nine Korean HL learners (in 1st, 2nd, and 3rd year levels), five non-HL L2 learners (in 2nd and 4th year level), and two 4-year-old Korean-English bilingual children. The main task for all three groups was to watch a video clip of the "Tortoise and the Hare" and then re-tell the story in Korean with as much detail as possible.

Eighteen error types were identified and analyzed from the spoken data to compare across the three linguistic groups. The results showed that from the 18 error types, five error types were shared in both Korean HL and non-HL L2 learners (lexical choice, particle usage, conjugation of predicates, clausal connectives, and morphemes), which can be interpreted as errors that are L2 learner-like in Korean HL learners. The error types that were found only in non-HL learners (errors related to word order, tense, and inability to omit subject that is recoverable by context) can then be understood as L1 (English) transfer, and the fact that these three error types were not in the spoken data of Korean HL learners can be interpreted as linguistic features that were acquired during their childhood. Looking closer at the errors that were unique just to Korean HL learners, Korean HL learners showed the following error types across the three proficiency levels (e.g., frequent use of English words with the light verb *-hata* "to do" e.g., race-*hata*); conjugation errors that stem from the *-a/e* suffix which is related to the intimate (or polite) speech style ending; and limited usage and over-usage of conjunctive adverbials. While the error types of L2 learners that were not found in Korean HL learners were seen as an indicator of acquired forms from childhood, these error types found in all three levels of Korean HL learners (and not in L2 learners) can then be interpreted as linguistic forms that are stabilized due to the lack of sufficient input and opportunities to develop the forms fully.

When the Korean HL learner error types were compared to those of Korean-English bilingual children, seven out of nine error types made by bilingual children were also found in all levels of Korean HL learners and the other two were found in the lower level of Korean HL learners. Thus, the nature of these error types can be seen as L1 developmental errors that are commonly made by monolingual Korean children. For instance, Kim (2012) discusses the following errors as ones that are related to L1 developmental errors: *-u/e* insertion after consonant ending syllable (e.g., *mek.u.ca** instead of *mek.ca* "let's eat"); exclusive usage of the subject particle *-ka* (e.g., *nun-ka** *apha*, or *nun-i-ka apha** instead of *nun-i apha* "my eyes hurt"), while the errors types shared by Korean HL and English-Korean bilingual children appear to be more representative of the process of bilingual development. That is, while non-HL learners avoided using any English words in their speech, both Korean-English bilinguals and Korean HL learners freely and rather fluently inserted English words, often with the light verb *-hata* ("to do") structure. This is common in bilingual children's lexicon development, in which children mix words from both languages simply based on the accessibility of acquired words of each language.

By comparing and analyzing Korean HL data to that of non-HL L2 learners and Korean-English bilingual children, Kim (2012) revealed that Korean HL learners possess native-like, bilingual-like, and learner-like features in their Korean language. As an outcome of this process of heritage language acquisition and attrition, Korean HL learners are known to have a head-start in their listening comprehension skills, cultural knowledge, and some spoken skills. However, the issue surrounding Korean HL learners' language is that despite formal L2 instruction (in the tertiary level), they continue to exhibit various gaps and weaknesses in their language production and grammar competency. As such, other studies have shown that Korean HL learners are known to have difficulty in aspects of grammar such as case and topic particles (e.g., Kim, 2002, Laleko & Polinsky, 2013; Lee & Zaslansky, 2015), morpho-syntactic cues (e.g., O'Grady et al., 2000), and wh-questions and the pro-drop settings (e.g., Kim, 2001). In addition, studies looking at Korean HL discourse marker use (Kim, 2012) and mental lexicon (Kim, 2013) also indicate challenges in accessing Korean lexicon and structures and thus relying heavily on childhood vocabulary (Shin & Joo, 2015) and stabilized form. Consequently, this brings pedagogical challenges in teaching Korean to HL learners, since Korean language curriculum and teaching approaches are usually implemented to facilitate the learning of L2 learners.

Based on previous discussions on Korean HL learners, it is clear that the difference between Korean HL learners versus non-HL learners stems from the fact that HL learners possess some native-like and bilingual-like quality that reveals attrition and/or partial acquisition in their HL language. Hence, understanding HL learners especially from the perspective of their implicit knowledge and processing, which are features of native language processing, can help identify certain pedagogical methods and approaches that address their different cognitive processing that would be more effective in restructuring the HL interlanguage.

5.3 Theoretical framework for HL learners and issues of attention

In the past few decades, due to an increase of HL learners across foreign languages, the language acquisition of HL learners has been recognized as a unique source of insight into further understanding the theories of language acquisition and theories of second language acquisition, as well as theories of bilingualism (see Montrul, 2016 for detailed discussions). Due to the variation and complexity of the HL language acquisition, as discussed in the previous section, existing theories of L1 and L2 acquisition have been applied from the nativist perspectives (e.g., Bayram, 2013 using Processability Theory), formal linguistics and psycholinguistics perspectives (e.g., Kim et al., 2009), emergentism (e.g., O'Grady et al., 2011), and sociolinguistic perspective (e.g., Silva-Corvalán, 1994). Consequently, HL acquisition, language processing, and proficiency can be examined and explored via the extension and application of the current L1 and L2 acquisition theoretical framework (Montrul, 2016).

In a discussion of constructing an HL prototype learner model, Zyzik (2016) applies the theory of basic-level cognition (BLC) and high-level cognition (HLC) proposed by Jan Hulstijn (2011, 2015) to describe HL learners' cognitive language processing and ability. The BLC-HLC theory describes the language proficiency of native (and non-native) speakers, in which all adult native speakers have BLC, which consists of the following three components of language processing related to the listening and spoken mode (Hulstijn, 2011: 230): (1) the largely implicit, unconscious knowledge in the domains of phonetics, prosody, phonology, morphology, and syntax, (2) the largely explicit, conscious knowledge in the lexical domain (form-meaning mappings), in combination with (3) the automaticity with which these types of knowledge can be processed. In other words, BLC is limited to listening and speaking and includes high frequency lexical and grammatical constructions that are used in routine, everyday conversations. On the other hand, HLC is an extension to BLC, which includes low-frequency vocabulary, uncommon morpho-syntax, and grammatically complex sentences that are associated with written discourse, as well as formal spoken registers. Hulstijn further emphasizes that the BLC-HLC theory should not be understood as a continuum of language acquisition, but rather as a dichotomy. That is, while all adult native speakers have BLC, HLC will vary widely depending on the level of formal education. Thus, language proficiency of all educated and uneducated native speakers can be described under this framework. In this light, Zyzik (2016) points out that research (e.g., Swender et al., 2014) shows that standardized diagnostic tests, such as the ACTFL's Oral Proficiency Interview (OPI) and standards like Common European Framework of Reference for Languages (CEFR), would require HLC in L2 learners' language proficiency, which can only be attained by individuals with higher levels of education. In looking at L2 learners then, Hulstijn suggests that although L2 learners may be capable of acquiring HLC similar to native speakers through formal instruction, whether they can fully acquire BLC (especially post-adolescence) in their L2 is questionable.

As for HL learners, the BLC-HCL theory then provides a framework to examine the nativeness and the non-nativeness of HL learners' language processing and proficiency through its distinction of language modes (e.g., listening, speaking, writing, and reading) as well as their accessibility to their implicit and explicit knowledge. Hence, prior to receiving formal instruction through a Korean language class, Korean HL learners can be described as those who have particular qualities of BLC (but not to the capacity of a native speaker's BLC) and have no, or very limited, HLC. That is, due to the varying degrees of bilingual development and language attrition as a child, some components of BLC exist and thus, show native-likeness in their language processing, but fall short of a complete BLC due to the interruption in their Korean language development as a child. Consequently, Korean HL learners then have BLC components that include: (1) implicit, unconscious knowledge in domains of phonetics, prosody, and phonology, but very limited implicit knowledge in morphology and syntax; (2) explicit, conscious knowledge in the lexical domain that is very limited to knowledge only of high-frequency lexical items used routinely at home; and different from L2 learners, they come to class with (3) the automaticity where the incomplete or limited implicit and explicit knowledge can be processed, especially in the listening mode.

The description of HL learner's BLC in their heritage language proficiency is confirmed by HL studies that examined the implicit versus explicit knowledge in L2 and HL learners. For instance, in Bowles (2011), L2 learners scored higher in the untimed grammatical judgment test (GJT) which tested their metalinguistic knowledge, while HL learners fared better on oral imitation and timed GJT, which both tap into their implicit knowledge. In Potowski et al.'s (2009) classroom research, when it came to the utilization of metalinguistic information in their L2 language output, L2 learners outperformed the HL learners, implying that they benefited in their language output from their access to explicit, metalinguistic knowledge. Similarly, in a study on task-based pedagogy by Torres (2013), L2 learners showed greater improvement in form than HL learners, where HL learners had a tendency to focus more on meaning rather than form. These studies not only provide evidence that HL learners indeed have implicit knowledge (or at least some automaticity in the language processing) similar to native speakers, but also show deficiency in utilizing and accessing explicit knowledge in their language processing. That is, while L2 learners are able to benefit from or access metalinguistic knowledge that they have received from classroom instruction, HL learners appear to mostly rely on their implicit knowledge that is incomplete or incorrect, and are not able to access newly learned explicit, metalinguistic knowledge. If L2 learners are able to attain HLC through explicit knowledge, HL learners are unable to attain it in the same way, because their implicit and automatic meaning processing seem to hinder their access to explicit, metalinguistic knowledge. One way to interpret this is that HL learners have difficulty with noticing and attending to form due to their automatic processing of meaning in the language input.

In second language acquisition theory, as well as in the field of psychology, the notion of attention is necessary, if not essential, for learning or for acquisition to occur (e.g., Baars, 1988; Carlson & Dulany, 1985; Gass, 1988; VanPatten, 1994; Schmidt, 1995, 2001). That is, studies have found that attention plays a key role in guiding perception of language input toward being selected and encoded to become part of the long-term memory, which then becomes final intake or acquisition (Chaudron, 1985). Thus, the noticing hypothesis (Schmidt, 1990) states that for language input to turn into intake, the learner must notice the gap or discrepancy between the current linguistic system and the target language system available as input. In this vein, as L2 acquisition requires attention to form and access to metalinguistic knowledge for monitoring, HL learners are often unable to notice discrepancies between their stabilized forms and the correct forms in the input. That is, even though HL learners' acquisition may be incomplete, they have sufficient semantic knowledge and sociolinguistic competency that allows them to comprehend most input and at times even the complex structures. Consequently, the effects of instruction and outcome of language acquisition between L2 and HL learners differ, especially in grammar competency, due to the fast processing of meaning by HL learners which hinders their access to their explicit knowledge. From this, it is apparent that HL learners lack the ability to access metalinguistic, explicit knowledge in order to accommodate a more efficient method to restructure HL learners' interlanguage. The pedagogical implication for HL learners then would be two-fold: (1) to develop metalinguistic (and lexicon) knowledge for them to have access to for restructuring; (2) to implement cognitive intervention to perhaps slow down meaning processing in order for them to bring their attention to form and to have them notice any discrepancy between the input and their interlanguage. In other words, the HL pedagogical approach can be summed up as explicit grammar/lexical instruction with the goal of altering and restructuring the existing implicit knowledge of HL learners.

5.4 Korean HL pedagogical approaches

Based on the description of Korean HL learner's proficiency and linguistic profile, this section will discuss key pedagogical approaches and goals that will address the cognitive processes and language background of Korean HL learners by focusing on methods that can maximize attention to form. For non-HL L2 learners, attentional resources for L2 learners are directed first at those elements in the input that carry message meaning, primarily lexicon and only later, when the cost comes down, towards communicatively redundant formal features of language (e.g., VanPatten, 1990, 1994, 1996). In this view, for HL learners, research has shown that the attentional resources are significantly different from those of non-HL L2 learner where due to automaticity and meaning processing, formal features cannot be attended to. For both L2 and HL learners, a classroom activity should always be meaning-based and designed in such a way that a meaningful interaction is the main goal for the student, rather than simply practicing the target form. Assuming that attention is still necessary for HL acquisition, language instruction must still prioritize the idea that a linguistic form is best acquired also by HL learners when it is experienced in a way that is meaningful to them. Hence, the discussion in the following sections will explore the meaningful and meaning-based contents, topics, and types of interaction and activities in the classroom that are more relevant to HL learners and would draw such attention to linguistic forms.

5.4.1 Apperception and attention for HL acquisition

For something to be "meaningful" to a person means something that is of high relevance, value, or significance. For one to place meaning onto something requires an experience that involves emotion. Hence, by tapping into one's past or prior experience that has been attached to meaningfulness, it can draw the level of attention that would benefit learning. The notion of *apperception* is related to attention and noticing. As discussed in Kim (2016), apperception refers to the mental process in which new information is brought into connection with an existing system of information and thus results in giving a new understanding and meaning. The notion of apperception had been first discussed in philosophy and psychology in the 17th century, which was later applied to education theory in the 19th century by the German philosopher Johann Herbart, one of the founders of the scientific study of modern pedagogy. According to Herbart, the mental interaction of the old and the new in the learner's pedagogical experience is the crucial process that results in new associations or new conclusions through modification or development of knowledge (McMurry, 1903). Similar to the notion of noticing in SLA, what gets apperceived is highly dependent on the interest or the past experience of a student, and therefore identifying the interest of a group of students would be key in achieving apperception. When we experience something new that sparks our interest, the source of our interest in a new idea can be explained by our conscious and/or unconscious connection to our past experience. Hence, in Herbart's education theory, understanding and focusing on the mental development in relation to prior knowledge of the learners can be vital to teachers in order to implement the materials in the way that would direct the learner's attention to target information. As such, the idea of apperception is also relevant in SLA research which is discussed as "the process of understanding by which newly observed qualities of an object are related to past experiences ... the selection of what we might call noticed (apperceived) material" (Gass, 1988: p. 201). Thus, apperception is one of the first stages of language processing, and while perception is often implicit, peripheral, and unnoticed, apperception involves a process that triggers noticing of the input as it is connected to one's prior knowledge or experience.

In this vein, prior knowledge becomes one of the key factors that determine whether the apperceived force will select input for further processing. From this viewpoint, understanding and identifying the student's prior experience, intellectual interest, and mental development becomes pivotal in being able to draw interest and the level of attention necessary for learning to occur for L2 learners. Considering that prior knowledge and experience for HL learners includes significant exposure to the heritage language and culture, the application of apperception in the pedagogical approach for HL and L2 learners should be different. For instance, while prior knowledge and experience for L2 learners can be topics related to their major, hobby, or popular culture, for HL learners, their prior HL knowledge received from home, as well as their cultural experience as a Korean-American can be also incorporated into HL language instruction. Hence, teachers of HL classes should become fully acquainted with HL learners' prior knowledge of the heritage language that they bring to class, and incorporate it into the curriculum.

In operationalizing the apperception framework into the HL curriculum, it is vital to first identify and understand the linguistic and cultural context and experiences that a Korean-American student might bring into class. In other words, considering that the primary language exposure for Korean HL learners is from home (and from their parents), it would be most sensible to examine the language spoken at home growing up, and in particular, to identify linguistic forms, phrases, and content that would have been used at home with high frequency. For instance, as KFL textbooks are designed for non-HL L2 learners' curriculum, it often begins with introduction to the polite or deferential speech ending in which the rules of conjugation are first taught. However, for HL learners (and L1 children), they have been exposed mostly to the intimate speech style (i.e., *panmal*), which is the speech style frequently used between parents and their children. Therefore, with understanding that their prior experience of Korean is frequently in the intimate speech style, it may be beneficial to factor this into the Korean HL instruction. This can also explain the common errors made by Korean HL learners where they conjugate from the intimate form rather than the stem of a predicate for different speech levels (e.g., deferential speech ending), (e.g., **poapnita* instead of *popnita* "to watch [TV]") rather than from the stem. Thus, from such knowledge, instructors may implement a different pedagogical sequence for Korean HL learners, where they begin from the conjugated form of the intimate speech style (i.e., what they already know/apperception) and go backwards to explain the rules of conjugation and the infinitive form of predicates, rather than the other way around. Similarly, when teaching the grammar pattern *-ci malta* (prohibition), rather than first providing rules of conjugation of a grammatical structure, starting with a high-frequency familiar phrase that Korean HL learners would have heard from home growing up, such as "*haci ma!*" ("stop doing that!"), would provide an opportunity that triggers apperception, in which then the phrase that they are familiar with can be deconstructed to discuss the grammar aspect of the phrase (e.g., *hata + -ci malta*). That is, by first triggering the prior familiar language memory of HL learners, it will bring them to an optimal processing moment to attend to form. Such HL pedagogical instruction will bring new structural understanding to the communicative phrase, which will then allow them not only to build their metalinguistic knowledge, but also allow a form-meaning mapping process to efficiently access their metalinguistic knowledge through instruction. It is also worth noting here that instructors should understand that in a way, the process of HL acquisition may be cognitively more challenging compared to those of L2 non-HL learners.

In the discussion of attention and noticing in SLA, what is important in language pedagogy is not only selecting instructional materials and topics that are meaningful, but also sequencing them appropriately to maximize noticing opportunities. In this vein, a deductive and deconstructive pedagogical sequence and approach starting with what HL learners are most familiar with may trigger apperception in Korean HL learners, which in turn may maximize their attention to form to develop their metalinguistic knowledge. In other words, understanding and identifying the Korean L2 target forms from the context of Korean HL learners' language experience from home may bring different cognitive processing for HL learners. While methods such as processing instruction (e.g., VanPatten, 1996) are designed to bring attention to form through meaning-based activities for L2 learners, apperception can add another layer to the cognitive process in HL learning by bringing attention to form through their existing system (i.e., BLC).

5.4.2 Fine-tuning HL proficiency: bringing attention to accuracy

According to the *World-Readiness Standards for Learning Languages* (2015), there are five goal areas for language learning: Communication, Cultures, Connections, Comparisons, and Communities. These five goal areas provide a roadmap for language learners to develop communicative and cultural competence to effectively participate in multilingual communities at home and around the world. Considering the different language backgrounds and experiences of HL learners, it is apparent that the roadmap to building language proficiency for non-HL L2 learners should be different for HL learners. For instance, in applying the three modes (interpersonal, interpretive, presentational) of Communication to the development of HL curriculum, rather than focusing on the interpersonal skills, it is important to identify aspects of the Communication modes that HL learners lack and need, such as reading (interpretive) and writing/formal speaking (presentational) skills. In developing the HL curriculum based on the 5 Cs, it is equally crucial to determine how the HL linguistic goals are operationalized in the classroom activities that optimizes their language acquisition.

The noticing hypothesis proposed by Schmidt emphasizes the subjective experience of noticing as a necessary and sufficient condition for converting input to intake. The second condition for acquisition to occur is that learners must notice the gap between the current state of their developing linguistic system, as realized in their output, and the target language system available as input. As HL learners have a tendency to process meaning more like native speakers, they are unable to utilize processing mechanisms and fail to notice the gap. Hence, in a HL curriculum, adjusting of the modes may influence the processing issue of HL learners. While L2 classes tend to focus on the interpersonal mode of the communication with the goal of building automaticity in their processing, HL learner instruction should focus on slowing down their automaticity and their native-like meaning processing by enforcing writing as a medium. In other words, assuming that HL learners have difficulty noticing the input-output discrepancy, writing tasks that include corrective feedback followed by self-revision may be helpful to begin slowing their processing to notice the gap. In other words, as HL learners build their metalinguistic knowledge through classroom (grammar) instruction, a self-revision component for all written assignments would push them to explicitly access their metalinguistic knowledge to monitor their input–output discrepancy. Through such exercise, this will strengthen and fine-tune the form-meaning mapping in their processing, which will lead to attaining higher accuracy in their language.

One interesting finding reported in a study by Park et al. (2016) that looked at corrective feedback, was that out of the four error types (tense and conjugation; orthographic; particle; lexical), HL learners produced significantly more orthographic errors in relation to other errors, implying their reliance on spelling by sound. Hence, another important application of writing in Korean HL learner instruction is providing the explicit metalinguistic explanation of the phonetic-orthographic mapping to connect their existing spoken Korean to the written form. Consequently, writing tasks can be an extremely important medium for HL processing which would not only fine-tune their existing pronunciation, but also more importantly reinforce and fill the metalinguistic and orthographic gap in their implicit knowledge. In this vein, when delivering a presentation from written (script or composition) to spoken form, while the goal for L2 learners is the ability to summarize what they have written to the audience for a more natural and efficient interaction, the goal for HL learners is to deliver the written form as close to the script as possible in order to force them to use more complex forms outside their usual HL everyday (home) language.

As discussed above, a processing issue for HL learners may be the lack of ability to access their explicit knowledge due to their native-like BLC proficiency. Despite their native-like processing of the input, the difference between HL learners and native speakers is that due to their incomplete acquisition, they need to develop their explicit knowledge through instruction (similar to L2 learners) in order to build a system that monitors their input to notice the input-output discrepancy. In this vein, one pedagogical approach for HL learners may be to provide an explicit metalinguistic (i.e., grammar) instruction that optimizes their noticing of the gap. As stated in the *World-Readiness Standards for Learning Languages* (2015), one of the standards for the Comparisons goal area is for the learners to "use the language to investigate, explain, and reflect on the nature of language through comparisons of the language studied and their own." While the language of comparison for L2 learners of Korean would be between Korean and their own language (e.g., English, Chinese, etc.), for Korean HL learners, it would have to be between Korean, English, *and* their incomplete Korean. Since Korean-Americans have been exposed to various forms of grammar growing up, rather than introducing each structure separately, introducing clusters of similar linguistic structures (e.g., multiple speech levels: intimate, deferential, polite, plain speech levels) for comparing and contrasting its usage grammatically and sociolinguistically may be a useful pedagogical tool in HL instruction. Moreover, a comparison of similar grammatical structures that already implicitly exist in HL learners may be another effective way to bring attention to forms, as well as a deeper understanding of each structure. Thus, a comparative, explicit, and grammar-based instruction could make a significant contribution toward directing them to metalinguistic awareness and noticing of their stabilized features (i.e., input-output discrepancy) which would begin the process of restructuring of the HL interlanguage. In this vein, altering the sequence of grammatical structures for comparison and implementing self-correction of their errors, especially in their written output, may increase the noticing of input-output discrepancy.

5.4.3 Empowering Korean HL learners: Bringing critical consciousness

Although more explicit grammar instruction would be beneficial for HL learners, solely grammar-based instruction is not adequate in and of itself for optimal acquisition, due to the lack of meaningful interaction. Therefore, as discussed through the literature in SLA instruction, it is imperative to provide grammar instruction through meaning-based activities that are also meaningful to maximize opportunities for noticing to occur. Just as the pedagogical approach for teaching linguistic forms should be different for HL, the choice of topics or contents for class activities or assignments must also differ from those for HL learners. For example, rather than having students compare and re-learn the target culture, discussions should also incorporate topics that compare and examine the notion of Korean-ness versus American-ness to further explore what it means to them to be a Korean-American between the two cultures. In fact, giving HL learners an opportunity to discuss and analyze their Korean-American identity through the use of HL language instruction is crucial in bringing critical consciousness of what it means to be a heritage speaker in the larger social context of the US.

One important difference between HL and L2 learners that instructors should understand is that while L2 learners go through an individual transformation within themselves as they acquire a new language and culture, for HL learners, their relationship and connection to their HL community changes simultaneously as they experience a transformation within themselves through HL language learning experience. For instance, with the immediate family often being their closest in their HL community circle, as Korean HL learners begin to (re-)learn their heritage language, it begins to positively affect the quality of their relationship with their Korean-speaking family members, enabling their discussion to go beyond the daily home conversation. The idea that all HL learners are connected to the HL community, and that any changes brought to their interlanguage and proficiency through instruction could also affect their interaction and relationship with their connected community, brings insight into the importance of developing a community-based HL curriculum.

One crucial goal for Korean HL instruction and curriculum then should be the inclusion of content that addresses issues of HL identity within the sociopolitical context to foster understanding that their HL language is not limited to developing deeper family relationships, but rather is an asset that can bring impact to the Korean-American community. That is, as discussed in Parra (2016) through a theoretical framework of critical pedagogy (Freire, 1970), HL curriculum must be a venue for exploring the intricacies of HL learners' identities, which has a sociocultural and political dimension growing up as the children of immigrants. By bringing such topics into HL instruction, it will raise the awareness of Korean HL learners of how their language and lived experience as a Korean-American relates to the mainstream culture of the US and Korea. As stated in Parra (2016: p. 170), "the ultimate goal is for students to embrace their own language and use it to develop their social consciousness and voice to become agents of constructive action toward positive change in their communities and beyond." With such awareness, HL instruction can empower them by providing an understanding of how advancement in their heritage language can open up opportunities to change and impact society.

Consequently, rooted in theories by Freire (1970), Dewey (1942), and Vygotsky (1986), service-learning courses which incorporate meaningful and authentic social experiences into the curriculum have been on the rise in language education, which has been found to foster language learning as well as community understanding due to its hands-on interactive nature. Moreover, service-learning has been known to be especially effective for HL learners because it enhances their critical thinking skills in analyzing their own communities in relation to the power structures that shape them (Parra, 2016). This was apparent for Korean HL learners in the study by Kim and Sohn (2016), which documented the implementation of a Korean service-learning class at UCLA, in which 50 Korean HL students enrolled in a course titled, "Advanced Korean with Service-Learning." The instructors established community service work for the students at four community partners located in Koreatown in Los Angeles: Korean Cultural Center (for assisting language instructors); a cardiology hospital (for assisting English to Korean translation); Korean-English dual-language elementary schools (for assisting teachers); and Koreatown Youth and Community Center (for assisting low-income Korean-American families). In addition to a minimum of 20 hours of work at the community site of their choice, the HL learners met twice a week on campus for in-class discussions to reflect on their hands-on experience at each community sites. Based on a survey from both students and the community partners, as well as students' reflective writings and final research papers addressing linguistic and sociocultural issues based on their experience, the authors came to the conclusion that service-learning is an essential component of heritage language education.

First of all, the results of the data show that it has significantly fostered student awareness of heritage and sociocultural identity through their experience of applying their heritage language at an authentic professional work context. That is, by giving them the opportunity to use their heritage language outside of home and family, it pushed them to examine and notice the gap in their own language and thus provided insight as to how the language register differs at home and at a work. Thus, in their self-assessment of their language, not only have they indicated general improvement in their communication skills, they also provided details about their awareness of specific linguistic aspects that they improved in (e.g., honorifics, complex sentence constructions for translation, etc.). In essence, this study demonstrates that incorporating the HL community into the curriculum brings meaningfulness to HL learners, which optimizes their attention and noticing in their language use, allowing them to ultimately build an explicit tool to begin fine-tuning their existing language. Thus, for teachers of HL learners, it is crucial to understand a HL learner not as an individual language learner, but as an individual with various levels of HL community connected to them.

5.5 Conclusion and future directions

In this chapter, the key theoretical and pedagogical underpinning for HL language teaching and learning is discussed through the notion of attention and awareness. Due to the native-like, bilingual-like, and L2 learner-like processing nature of HL learners, different pedagogical approaches and sequencing should be implemented with the goal of optimizing HL learners noticing the input-output discrepancy.

Although the notion of attention is critical and applicable to both HL learner and non-HL L2 learners, it is important to recognize that due to their dissimilarity in their language processing of the input, the instructional approach to facilitate each type of processing should also be different. That is, while the pedagogical goal for L2 learners is to build automaticity in their explicit knowledge, the goal for HL learners is to first slow down their automaticity to begin building their metalinguistic knowledge in order to help them access it as a self-monitoring tool for the restructuring of their HL interlanguage. Moreover, as the notion of apperception is especially relevant to HL learners and may be useful to bringing attention to form, it is essential to teachers to understand and incorporate the HL language experience from home into classroom activities, tasks, and the curriculum as a whole. In other words, utilizing what they already know and what they have heard growing up in terms of their HL may be a useful tool in maximizing attention in HL instruction.

As this chapter emphasized the importance of HL linguistic processing and attention in their language acquisition, HL learners' awareness and understanding of their own HL identity and community is as crucial to their heritage language development. This brings me to the issue of motivation of Korean HL learners. In a survey study by Carreira and Kagan (2011), which examines the HL learners across different heritage languages (22 languages) and geographic regions in the United States, it reveals particular aspects of Korean HL learners that differed from HL learners of other languages. Despite the access to community resources (e.g., weekend Korean language schools) and significant language input and exposure from home, Korean HL learners rated their HL skills considerably lower than Spanish HL learners (who had similar profiles). Moreover, when asked about top four priorities for the HL maintenance, according to the authors, the Korean HL learners showed to have the least ambitious of the goals commonly cited when compared by other survey respondents. Specifically, the results revealed that Korean HL learners reported their highest priority for learning their Korean is for fulfilling a language requirement or for communicating with family and friends in the United States, while HL respondents of other languages indicated their priority to be for future careers or to connect with cultural and linguistic roots. This brings insight to how much social and global value Korean HL learners see in their heritage language, which can be changed through HL instruction. As discussed in Parra (2016) and Kim and Sohn (2016), HL curriculum must strive to go beyond communication and address the social, cultural, and political context surrounding the HL learner and their community to foster critical thinking and analysis through materials, classroom discussion, projects, or community service learning.

One issue that is noteworthy for HL instructors of Korean is how the Korean HL learner demographic is changing, in that the range of Korean HL learners' language is becoming wider and more diverse with the third generation of Korean-Americans beginning to enroll to Korean language classes. In other words, before applying HL instruction, it is crucial to first identify which profile type of HL learners would benefit most from HL pedagogical approaches. Hence, along with more classroom research and empirical data examining their language processing, research on issues of HL placement and assessment is also needed. Furthermore, another area for further research is the exploration of mixed HL and non-HL group interaction in classrooms and its pedagogical implication for Korean language classes. Overall, more research for an effective Korean HL instruction and curriculum can fast-track their language acquisition to higher levels and raise their social awareness of their HL community, which will empower them to use their language in a more meaningful way at home and beyond.

Discussion questions

1. How do we define Korean HL learners? How are Korean HL learners different from other HL learners? What linguistic aspects do you find native-like and what linguistic aspects do you find L2-like in Korean HL learners? What are the sources of their nativeness and L2-ness?
2. Based on the linguistic profile of Korean HL learners, what should be the goals for HL language teaching that might differ from those for L2 learners? For instance, how can the National Standards' 5 Cs be applied to Korean HL learners?
3. How are the Korean HL learners' errors similar or different from L2 learners? What are the possible sources of HL learners' errors that differ from L2 learners? For instance, what type of language input have they been exposed to from home that can be linked to the error types? Are HL learner errors comparable to those in L1 acquisition (i.e., errors made by Korean children)?
4. How is it that HL learners are able to process and comprehend input despite their low accuracy and lack of metalinguistic knowledge? What effective pedagogical approaches can be used to address issues of attention (or lack of attention to form) for HL learners? For example, how do we address errors of HL learners that keep recurring despite having provided repeated corrective feedback and/or grammar explanation? Are there methods or classroom tasks that can slow down implicit processing of HL learners in order for them to attend to form or errors?
5. How should Korean culture be (re)introduced to Korean HL learners? How can culture be implemented into the HL classroom that will aid the (re)formation of a Korean HL identity?
6. In what ways will HL instruction bring changes to the immediate community around Korean HL learners? What role can HL instruction have in expanding HL learners' interaction with the Korean community beyond their family?
7. What are the challenges and benefits of having a mixed class of HL and non-HL learners? What pedagogical methods can be used that apply and balance the strengths and weaknesses to benefit both HL and non-HL learner's acquisition?
8. With globalization and access to (and popularity of) Korean popular culture, what changes are occurring in terms of language maintenance, acquisition, and attrition to the next generation of Korean HL learners? Are there sub-prototypes of Korean HL learners that require a different pedagogical approach?

Reference

Baars, B.J. (1988). *A cognitive theory of consciousness*. Cambridge: Cambridge University Press.

Bayram, F. (2013). *Acquisition of Turkish by heritage speakers: A processability approach* [Unpublished Doctoral Dissertation], University of Newcastle, UK. Retrieved from http://hdl.handle.net/10443/1905.

Benmamoun, E., Monstrul, S., & Polinsky, M. (2013). Heritage languages and their speakers: Opportunities and challenges for linguistics. *Theoretical Linguistics, 39*(3–4), 129–181.

Bowles, M. (2011). Measuring implicit and explicit linguistic knowledge: What can heritage language learners contribute? *Studies in Second Language Acquisition, 33*(2), 247–271.

Carlson, R., & Dulany, D. (1985). Conscious attention and abstraction in concept learning. *Journal of Experimental Psychology: Learning, Memory, and Cognition, 11*(1), 45–58.

Carreira, M., & Kagan, O. (2011). The results of the national heritage language survey: Implications for teaching, curriculum design, and professional development. *Foreign Language Annals, 44*(1), 40–64.

Chaudron, C. (1985). Intake: On models and methods for discovering learners processing of input. *Studies in Second Language Acquisition, 7*(1), 1–14.

Dewey, J. (1942). *Democracy and education*. New York: Macmillan.

Freire, P. (1970). *Pedagogy of the oppressed*. Trans. Myra Bergman Ramos. New York: Herder.

Gass, S. (1988). Integrating research areas: A framework for second language studies. *Applied Linguistics, 9*(2), 198–217.

Hulstijn, J. (2011). Language proficiency in native and nonnative speakers: An agenda for research and suggestions for second language assessment. *Language Assessment Quarterly, 8*(3), 229–249.

Hulstijn, J. (2015). *Language proficiency in native and non-native speakers: Theory and research*. Philadelphia, PA: John Benjamins.

Kim, E. (2002). Investigating the acquisition of Korean particles by beginning and intermediate learners. In J. Ree (Ed.), *The Korean Language in America, 7,* 165–176. Tallahassee, FL: The American Association of Teachers of Korean.

Kim, H. (2008). Heritage and non-heritage language learners of Korean: Sentence processing differences and its pedagogical implications. In K. Kondo-Brown & J.D. Brown (Eds.), *Teaching heritage students in Chinese, Japanese, and Korean: Curriculum, needs, materials, and assessment* (pp. 99–134). (ESL & Applied Linguistics Professional series.) New York: Lawrence Erlbaum Associates/Taylor & Francis.

Kim, H. (2012). Identifying the source of stabilization in Korean heritage learners: A comparative data analysis of HL learners and bilingual children in. In A. Byon & D. Pyun (Eds.), *Teaching and learning Korean as a foreign language: A collection of empirical studies* (pp. 209–227). Columbus, OH: The Ohio State University Foreign Language Publications.

Kim, H. (2016). Attention, apperception, and illusion in Korean language pedagogy. *International Journal of Korean Language Education, 1,* 1–22.

Kim, I. (2012). Phenomena of discourse marker use of bilingual children and implications for heritage language education. *The Korean Language in America, 17*(1), 24–54.

Kim, J. (2001). The degree of L1 interference among heritage and non-heritage learners of Korean: Do heritage students have advantages over non-heritage students? In J. Ree

(Ed.), *The Korean Language in America, 6*, 285–296. Honolulu, HI: The American Association of Teachers of Korean.

Kim, J., Monstrul, S., & Yoon, J. (2009). Binding interpretation of anaphors in Korean heritage speakers. *Language Acquisition, 16*(1), 3–35.

Kim, M. (2013). The mental lexicon of low-proficiency Korean heritage learners. *Heritage Language Journal, 10*(1), 17–35.

Kim, S., & Sohn, S. (2016). Service learning, an integral part of heritage language education: A case study of an advanced-level Korean language class. *Heritage Language Journal, 13*(3), 354–381.

Laleko, O., & Polinsky, M. (2013). Marking topic or marking case: A comparative investigation of heritage Japanese and heritage Korean. *Heritage Language Journal, 10*(2), 40–64.

Lee, E., & Zaslansky, M. (2015). Nominal reference in Korean heritage language discourse. *Heritage Language Journal, 12*(2), 132–158.

McMurry, C. (1903). *The elements of general method based on the principles of Herbart.* New York: MacMillan.

Montrul, S. (2016). *The acquisition of heritage languages.* Cambridge, UK: Cambridge University Press.

O'Grady, W., Lee, M., & Choo, M. (2000). The acquisition of relative clauses by heritage and non-heritage learners of Korean as a second language. In S. Sohn (Ed.), *Korean Language in America 5*, 245–256. Los Angeles, CA: American Association of Teachers of Korean.

O'Grady, W., Lee, O., & Lee, J. (2011). Practical and theoretical issues in the study of heritage language acquisition. *The Heritage Language Journal, 8*, 23–40.

Park, E., Song, S., & Shin, Y. (2016). To what extent do learners benefit from indirect written corrective feedback? A study targeting learners of different proficiency and heritage language status. *Language Teaching Research, 20*(6), 678–699. doi: 10.1177/1362168815609617.

Parra, M. (2016). Critical approaches to heritage language instruction: How to foster students' critical consciousness. In M. Fairclough & S. Beaudrie (Eds.), *Innovative Strategies for Heritage Language Teaching: A practical guide for the classroom* (pp. 166–190). Washington, DC: Georgetown University Press.

Polinsky, M., & Kagan, O. (2007). Heritage languages: In the "wild" and in the classroom. *Language and Linguistics Compass, 1*(5), 368–395.

Polinsky, M. (2015). When L1 becomes an L3: Do heritage speakers make better L3 learners? *Bilingualism: Language and Cognition, 18*(2), 1–16.

Potowski, K., Jill, J., & Morgan-Short, K. (2009). The effects of instruction on linguistic development in Spanish heritage language speakers. *Language Learning, 59*(3), 537–579.

Rothman, J., & Treffers-Daller, J. (2014). A prolegomenon to the construct of the native speaker: Heritage speaker bilinguals are natives too! *Applied Linguistics, 35*(1), 93–98.

Schmidt, R. (1990). The role of consciousness in second language learning. *Applied Linguistics, 11*(2), 129–158.

Schmidt, R. (1995). Consciousness and foreign language learning: A tutorial on the role of attention and awareness in learning. In R. Schmidt (Ed.), *Attention and awareness in foreign language learning* (Technical Report #9) (pp. 1–64). Honolulu, HI: University of Hawaii, Second Language Teaching and Curriculum Center.

Schmidt, R. (2001). Attention. In P. Robinson (Ed.), *Cognition and second language instruction* (pp. 1–32). Cambridge: Cambridge University Press.

Shin, S., & Joo, A. (2015). Lexical errors in Korean-Australian heritage learners' compositions. *Journal of Korean Language Education, 26*, 129–162. doi: 10.18209/iakle.2015.26.129.

Silva-Corvalán, C. (1994). *Language contact and change: Spanish in Los Angeles.* Oxford: Clarendon.

Swender, E., Martin, C., Rivera-Martinez, M., & Kagan, O. (2014). Exploring oral proficiency profiles of heritage speakers of Russian and Spanish. *Foreign Language Annals, 47*(3), 423–446.

The National Standards Collaborative Board. (2015). *World-readiness standards for learning languages,* 4th ed. Alexandria, VA: Author.

Torres, J. (2013). *Heritage and second language learners of Spanish: The roles of task complexity and inhibitory control* [PhD Diss.]. Georgetown University.

Valdes, G. (2001). Heritage language students: Profiles and possibilities. In J.K. Peyton, D. Ranard & S. McGinnis (Eds.), *Heritage languages in America: Preserving a national resource* (pp. 37–80). Washington, DC: Center for Applied Linguistics.

VanPatten, B. (1990). Attending to form and content in the input. *Studies in Second Language Acquisition, 12*(3), 287–301.

VanPatten, B. (1994). Evaluating the role of consciousness in second language acquisition: Terms, linguistic features & research methodology. *AILA Review, 11*, 27–36.

VanPatten, B. (1996). *Input processing and grammar instruction.* New York: Ablex.

Vygotsky, L. (1986). *Thought and language.* Cambridge, MA: MIT Press.

Zyzik, E. (2016). Toward a prototype model of the heritage language learner: Understanding strengths and needs. In M. Fairclough & S. Beaudrie (Eds.), *Innovative strategies for heritage language teaching: A practical guide for the classroom* (pp. 19–38). Washington, DC: Georgetown University Press.

6 Literacy and multiliteracies in Korean language learning and teaching

Joowon Suh and Ji-Young Jung

6.1 Introduction

When one first attempts to learn a foreign language, the typical first step would be learning its writing system, including orthography. When one tries to acquire knowledge through any language, it mostly involves learning to read and eventually learning to write. In higher education, literacy has occupied a central place in foreign language (FL) pedagogy in that it makes a connection between FL courses with different foci, such as literature and history, which in turn characterizes the overall FL program. It is often assumed that being literate in a language includes being familiar with and knowledgeable about literature (Kern, 2000). In this sense, reading and writing have become two of the most fundamental skills and functions when learning and teaching languages, and thus literacy has long been a core interest in language education.

In the field of teaching Korean as a foreign language (KFL), literacy has become all the more pressing an issue in connection with heritage language learners (HLLs), who make up a significant part of the KFL learner population. It has been well documented in heritage language (HL) acquisition studies that HLLs' literacy skills often lag behind their oral proficiency. For an extensive period of time in KFL education, particularly in the North American setting, both researchers and practitioners have sought to understand HLLs' literacy needs and develop an effective pedagogy to promote their literacy competence. In this context, literacy development deserves a separate and careful consideration in discussing KFL teaching and learning.

With ever-increasing globalization through various modes of communication and the advancement of technology, the notion of literacy has evolved significantly. Specifically, multimodality and multiculturality have become crucial components of literacy. According to the report by the MLA Foreign Languages Ad Hoc Committee (2007), the notion of multiliteracies, an expanded view of literacy with strong critical lenses into language learning, has attracted growing attention in the field of FL education. Especially in teaching a less commonly taught language, cultivating culturally literate speakers is vital to prepare students to function competently in various personal, academic, and professional contexts in today's multicultural and multimodal society.

This chapter focuses on theoretical and pedagogical issues of literacy and multiliteracies in FL education in general, and KFL education in particular. We first review literacy research in language education, from a traditional understanding to a more sociocultural perspective. We then extend our discussion to the notion of multiliteracies that includes multimodality and critical literacies. Finally, we examine in detail how such analytical notions and instructional practices on literacy and multiliteracies are implemented in KFL classrooms.

6.2 Literacy in language education

Undoubtedly, literacy has long been one of the most important goals in general education. In earlier years, literacy was considered to be what makes some people—*literate* people—more intelligent than *illiterate* people (Gee, 2015). Gee (2015) further argues that "literacy is what freed some of humanity from a primitive state … what makes some of us 'civilized'" (p. 28). Bull and Anstey (2019) share a similar concept of literacy to Gee that literacy is "a collection of knowledge and skills that enabled individuals to participate effectively in the society of the time" (p. 2). This very notion of literacy is often associated with school literacy and academic literacy in first language (L1) education in institutional settings and with functional literacy and workplace literacy in the everyday real-life environment. Literacy was considered to be conventions and a set of skills that students needed to acquire to enter into a socially sanctioned workforce. Furthermore, "being literate" itself was considered a pre-requisite for financial success, social promotion, civic responsibility, and cultural integration (Baker et al., 2010; Lankshear & Knobel, 2011).

In the context of language learning, literacy is traditionally defined as, simply, the ability to read and write in a language. Being literate in a language implies that one can read a written text and write a text that is readable. August and Shanahan (2006) define literacy acts as three types of activity. *Pre-reading* skills denote knowledge of the printed alphabet, whereas *word-level* skills include reading and understanding words and spelling words, and *text-level* skills refer to overall fluency in comprehending and composing a text. As shown thus far, literacy has been treated as an isolated and compartmentalized goal, skill, function, and practical tool, rather than an integrative ability or communication. This conventional view of literacy tends to dismiss its interactional and social aspects by focusing only on the mental, cognitive, and individual processes of literacy acts.

Shifting away from a purely mental and cognitive view of literacy, Gee (1989a, 1989b, 2015) suggests the concept of *Discourse*, as opposed to *discourse* with a little "d." Discourse with a capital "D" is "a socially accepted association among ways of using language, of thinking, and of acting that can be used to identify oneself as a member of a socially meaningful group or social network" (Gee, 1989b: p. 18). To Gee, acquiring literacy is conceptualized as a way of claiming membership in the society. He (1989b) also argues that literacy generates pedagogical issues on which both psycholinguistics and sociolinguistics have equal bearing, and that the discussion on ideology, identity, and socialization becomes indispensable.

The field of language education has accepted that literacy should be understood not only as the act of reading, writing, and thinking, but also as meaning construction from text within a sociocultural context (Pérez & McCarthy, 2004). Many have agreed that literacy development should be viewed as social and cultural activities involving interactional and interpersonal phenomena. That is, the acquisition of literacy requires the acquisition of the social and cultural norms and practices surrounding literacy. As Kern (2000) argues, acquiring literacy involves far more than just learning grammar and vocabulary to put together words to produce texts. He emphasizes that, in addition to linguistic and structural knowledge, the literacy act involves identifying and understanding cultural beliefs and values underlying the given discourse, focusing on what the writer "meant" by his/her words, not what is written.

Kalantzis and Cope (2012) have effectively summarized the purposes of this changing notion of literacy as *communications* and *representations*. The communication purposes of literacy include literacies for the new workplace, public participation, and personal and community life, while the representation purposes of literacy involve literacies to make sense of the world, for thinking and learning, and for identity. In literacy education, all linguistic, cognitive, and sociocultural dimensions of written language need to be considered, in that the primary goal of literacy is to interpret and create cultural, social, and historical meanings through texts (Kern, 2000).

6.3 From literacy to multiliteracies

6.3.1 Conceptualizing multiliteracies

With the increase of different modes of communication and multicultural and multilingual interactions via rapid technological advances, the traditional sense of literacy was seriously challenged. In their seminal paper, the New London Group (1996) first introduced the notion of multiliteracies, a modified, adjusted, and expanded concept of literacy. Multiliteracies recognize the multiplicity of contexts and communication modes, and emphasize both "local diversity" and "global connectedness" (p. 64). It is believed that meanings do not reside in texts; rather, learners draw meanings from the texts by engaging in dynamic and collaborative activities to achieve their own goals. Therefore, language learners are "decoders of language" and become "users as designers of meaning" (p. 74).

The notion of multiliteracies is particularly valuable in FL learning and teaching, since it includes strong pedagogical applications based on the notions of multiplicity, diversity, interculturality, and multimodality. It recognizes the multiplicity of literacy in language skills, modalities, genres, contents, meanings, contexts, and actions. Literacy in this framework is redefined as "being able to communicate or make meaning—as a producer or receiver—using signs, signals, codes, graphic images" (Lankshear & Knobel, 2011: p. 21). The essence of multiliteracies is effectively presented in Table 6.1.

Table 6.1 The Two "Multis" of Multiliteracies

| Multi- | |
contextual	modal
community setting	written
social role	visual
interpersonal relations	spatial
identity	tactile
subject matter	gestural
	audio
	oral

Modified from Kalantzis & Cope, 2012: p. 2.

Kress (2009) also points out that the "multi" of multiliteracies refers to the multiplicity of modes and the multiplicities of socially distinct uses and forms of language. Within the framework of multiliteracies, there are no absolute, standard conventions of meaning-making or communication, but diverse ways of speaking (e.g., dialects and minority varieties of the given language), behaving, thinking, and acting are given equal consideration and treatment in the FL classroom. The two "multis," in terms of *multimodality* and *critical literacies*, are discussed in more depth in the following two sections.

6.3.2 Multimodality

With rapid technological development in the 21st-century interconnected world, the most relevant and urgent interest that the multiliteracies theory has focused on is multimodal aspects of language learning and teaching. Based on the belief that the text in literacy education goes beyond mere traditional printed materials, Kalantzis and Cope (2012) define multimodality as "the use of different and combined modes of meaning" (p. 39) through a meaning-making process. According to them, multimodality further deals with how these various modes of meaning are combined, integrated, and interconnected in literacy practices of communication and representation. In this sense, literacy education needs to recognize and utilize a wide range of communication modes that exist with the advancement of technologies, including digital and media resources.

In language education, therefore, developing learners' multimodal competence has become an essential task. Multimodal competence, first proposed by Kress (2003), is broadly adopted as "the ability to understand and use the power of images and sounds, to manipulate and transform digital media, to distribute them pervasively, and to easily adapt them to new forms" (cited in Guichon & Cohen, 2016: p. 515). Watching a Korean entertainment show on TV, for instance, requires multimodal competence in order to fully appreciate it: listening competence in Korean (i.e., what is being said by the entertainers) and the competence to comprehend the subtitles for the native audience provided on the screen to enhance, usually, entertaining effects (i.e., the purposes and visual placements of subtitles). A simple act of watching TV now involves a completely different multimodal experience than decades ago. Royce (2007) applies the notion of multimodality to FL contexts and proposes the term *multimodal communicative competence*. Digital story-telling projects, in which various modes of meaning-making (i.e., written, oral, and visual for certain, and possibly gestural, tactile, and spatial), can be an exemplary activity to promote learners' multimodal communicative competence.

In relation to multiliteracies perspectives of multimodality, Lankshear and Knobel (2011) point out that the term *literacy* has become "a metaphor for competence, proficiency, or being functional" (p. 22), as in digital literacy and media literacy. Digital literacies refer to the "practices of communicating, relating, thinking and 'being' associated with digital media" (Jones & Hafner, 2012: p. 13). The currently available technological tools and digital modes include, but are not limited to, internet searches, social networking sites (SNSs), sites for sharing audiovisual materials, individual blogs, and even online games.

Overlapped with digital literacies, media literacy can be defined "as a set of capabilities applied to media messages and experiences" (Scheibe & Rogow, 2012: p. 19). They further provide the components of social actions and practices comprising media literacy: access, comprehension, awareness, analysis, evaluation, reflection, production, and collaboration. The modes targeted in media literacy generally include traditional mass media forms such as radio, television, newspapers, magazines, and movies. Media literacy expands to include music, cell phones, games, advertising, and visual media such as signs, posters, and flyers.

Digital and media literacy, often requiring strong critical thinking, have deepened and widened the scope of literacy education "to critically analyze relationships between media and audiences, information and power" (Keller & Share, 2007: p. 4). According to Jones and Hafner (2012), understanding digital and media literacies further implies understanding how these media may interact with our literacy practices. After all, one of the goals of multiliteracy education is to foster multiliterate learners capable of consuming and creating a wide range of semiotic systems available to them in a critical way. They then warn us about technological determinism, the fallacy that "new practices of reading and writing are determined solely by the affordance and constraints of the new digital tools available" (p. 13).

6.3.3 Critical literacies

The second "multi" in the multiliteracies theory represents critical thinking through literacy practices to acknowledge and understand linguistic, social, and cultural diversity and plurality (Cope & Kalantzis, 2000, 2009; Gee, 2009; Kress, 2009; NLG, 1996). According to Kalantzis and Cope (2012), critical literacies refer to "approaches to literacy which focus on texts that communicate student interests and experiences and address challenging social issues such as discrimination and disadvantage" (p. 167). Within this framework, learners are encouraged to recognize many differing voices that may exist in the meaning-making processes of texts. For example, we expect our learners to not only comprehend the contents presented in different types of media, but also to differentiate and appreciate the voices and stances represented in a wide range of media, and to incorporate them into their own views of the world.

Learners also should learn how to apply their own critical thinking to texts by bringing their own experiences and expectations to their language learning processes by understanding texts or "any other kind of representation of meaning, as a site of struggle, negotiation, and change" (McKinney & Norton, 2008: pp. 195–196). In this sense, identity formation and negotiation has become one of the most crucial research interests. Identity, encompassing "a person's ways of thinking, communicating and being, based on their life experiences and aspirations" (Kalantzis & Cope, 2012: p. 167), can become extremely tricky in second or foreign language classrooms when having to deal with target language and culture (Block, 2007; Kramsch, 2009).

In fact, the critical literacies theory attempts to answer the very question, *why should we care about multiliteracies in the 21st-century language classroom?* There are three aspects in our "knowledge society" and "new economy" (Cope & Kalantzis, 2009: p. 168) that literacy education aims to impact: workers in their working lives, citizens in their public lives, and identities of people in their private lives (NLG, 1996). In critical literacies education, the equality and equity of the diverse and multiple voices heard in these three aspects of our changing times need to be looked at critically via the analysis of multimodal texts.

Kalantzis and Cope (2012) have proposed the goals in critical literacies as follows: (1) addressing discrimination and disadvantage; (2) focusing on voice and agency; (3) engaging with real-world issues and active citizenship; (4) investigating social issues and moral dilemmas; and (5) exploring human differences and social justice. Thus, social justice and peace have become new focal points of literacy education, and the primary purpose of literacy education has shifted to develop and foster learners as *languagers*, agents, and language activists. Hull and Hernandez (2008) argue that literacy competence includes the ability to grasp multiple and fluid meanings and the purposes of multimodal texts beyond the simple ability to read and write in a language, implying "its emancipatory potential, linking it to heightened political awareness and collective movements" (p. 328).

6.3.4 *Pedagogy of multiliteracies*

Thus far, we have reviewed what multiliteracies means in literacy education and why it is important in the changing times of present-day language learning and teaching. One of the reasons why the notion of multiliteracies has become more and more important in FL language education is that it has presented rather concrete and useful guidelines for practitioners to apply the notion to the language classroom, what to teach, and how to teach.

As for the "what" of a pedagogy of multiliteracies (i.e., what it is that students need to learn), the NLG (1996) has introduced the notion of *design*, simply defined as what one is expected to do in the process of making and creating meanings. For this active and dynamic *design* process, in which participants "are seen as designers of learning processes and environments" (NLG, 1996: p. 73), three aspects are proposed: Available Designs, Designing, and The Redesigned. *Available Designs* refer to a series of activities in which learners analyze linguistic forms, styles, and culture presented in the given texts. *Designing* includes meaning-making activities through various modes, and *The Redesigned* involves learners reproducing and transforming meanings.

For example, in Lee-Smith's (2016) study on Korean TV public service announcements (PSAs), the semiotic system of PSAs itself functions as Available Designs, meaning-making acts performed by learners using PSAs as Designing, and finally the meanings produced by learners based on their experiences and purposes as The Redesigned. To summarize, in the process of designing or meaning-making, learners and teachers utilize resources available to them, and the outcomes produced via the process can be used for a new designing process as resources or transformed meanings, and a new cycle starts all over again.

When it comes down to the "how" of literacy pedagogy, the NLG (1996) has identified four pedagogical components within the range of appropriate learning relationships: Situated Practice, Overt Instruction, Critical Framing, and Transformed Practice. *Situated Practice* implies learners **experiencing** the utilization of available discourses. *Overt Instruction* refers to the **conceptualizing** process of requiring explicit metalanguages to interpret different modes of meaning. *Critical Framing* involves interpreting and **analyzing** the social and cultural context of particular meanings. Lastly, *Transformative Practice* implies **applying** and transferring the transformed and created meanings to other contexts. Cope and Kalantzis (2009) argue that, in the FL classroom, learners' needs, current knowledge and affective state, different skill sets, and backgrounds should be considered, and that the teacher should accordingly guide them to modify and reassess the text presented.

The feasibility and effectiveness of multiliteracies pedagogies in FL curricula has been steadily tested and re-examined at various levels (Allen & Paesani, 2010; Bull & Anstey, 2019; Cope & Kalantzis, 2015; Warner & Dupuy, 2018). The romance novel as a textual genre was adopted in an elementary German course (Maxim, 2006), paintings were used in elementary Spanish classes (Meyer, 2009), and a semester-long travel guide project was conducted in a French class (Mills, 2009). The whole curriculum has successfully adopted the multiliteracies framework in French (Allen & Paesani, 2010) and German (Byrnes et al., 2010). Warner and Dupuy (2018) call attention to two challenges of implementing multiliteracies pedagogy in FL programs: the professional development of FL instructors, and instructional materials that have adopted a multiliteracies approach. Allen and Paesani (2010) have discussed three issues when implementing a multiliteracies pedagogy specifically within communicative language teaching (CLT) by pointing out the differences between the two approaches: collaboration, language use, and conventions.

Despite these challenges remaining, the potentials of multiliteracies pedagogy for college-level FL programs are simply too commanding to discount. A pedagogy of multiliteracies enables learners: (1) to develop substantive abilities across a range of personal and public contexts of language use; (2) to develop intellectually substantive target cultural knowledge and critically engage with their own cultures; and (3) to develop their positions in relation to the target language culture and fine-tune their identities. In this sense, the new goal of FL teachers should be to lead learners to be problem-solvers, meaning-makers, and code-breakers, and active and informed citizens (Anstey & Bull, 2006).

6.4   Practices in KFL language classrooms

This section discusses empirical studies on KFL literacy. The studies reviewed are categorized into four groups based on their dealings with literacy: (1) literacy as a semiotic means (*learning to read and write*); (2) literacy as a learning tool (*reading and writing to learn*); (3) literacy as a social action (*reading and writing to "do"*); and (4) literacy as a translingual and transformational activity (*reading and writing to "be"*). As extensively discussed in the previous sections, the conceptualization and the implementation of literacy have evolved significantly. We begin our discussion with the most traditional treatment of literacy practice as a series of cognitive activities designed to teach learners how to read and write in the target language. Later on, KFL teachers began to realize that reading and writing themselves serve as powerful learning tools, which enable learners to obtain and convey knowledge about the target language and culture. In recent years, literacy has received renewed attention and been discussed in a handful of studies as a social act through which learners interact with each other not only to make and convey meanings, but to negotiate and reconstruct meanings. More recently, many studies set out to explore literacy development by HLLs of Korean through multimodal means of communication. These studies discuss identity construction as a crucial aspect of heritage literacy development.

6.4.1   Learning to read and write

More than a decade ago, Street (2004) pointed out that writing prevailed in academia as a privileged semiotic mode. In KFL teaching today, literacy is still considered a higher-order learning objective. This is particularly so for writing, which many teachers adopt as an ultimate assessment tool to determine learning in advanced-level language-and-content courses. In lower-level language courses, literacy is often conceptualized in its narrowest sense, and adopting this notion of literacy naturally entails orthographic accuracy being the focal point for many teachers.

Shin's (2007) study, for example, examined spelling errors made by 167 English-speaking KFL students in their writing examinations. Shin found that the most frequent errors were the substitution of *ch* (ㅊ) by *c* (ㅈ), *ay* (ㅐ) by *ey* (ㅔ), and *e*

(ㅓ) by *o* (ㅗ), and attributed phonetic proximity as the source of confusion. To the researcher, it is important to identify orthographic errors and their sources, because misspellings are not merely typographical errors but oftentimes reveal and reinforce learners' incorrect mapping between sound, meaning, and symbol.

In contrast to Shin's study that investigated traditional KFL learners, Pyun and Lee-Smith (2011) attempted to identify the types of orthographic errors commonly made by HLLs of Korean. The researchers examined writing assignments submitted by 76 HLLs who were enrolled in intermediate-level Korean classes. Drawing upon data collected over 5 years, the researchers classified spelling errors into 12 categories. Among these, errors involving resyllabification (e.g., *iss-e-yo* 있어요 written as *i-sseo-yo* 이써요) and consonant assimilation (e.g., *ip-ni-ta* 입니다 written as *im-ni-ta* 임니다) were found to be the most commonly occurring. The researchers attributed the cause of these errors to HLLs' heavy reliance on aural cues. The two instructors in the study focused improving orthographic accuracy by providing phonological and morphological explanations and having students work on online dictation exercises. Results of pre- and post-test analysis indicated a statistically significant increase in spelling accuracy. Although HLLs' weakness in sound–symbol mapping is argued by many researchers, Pyun and Lee-Smith's study is the first KFL study that offers strong empirical evidence and a practical pedagogical intervention for improvement.

In a more recent study, Joo and Shin (2016) report similar findings on spelling errors committed by 321 HLLs of Korean. Their findings are consistent with most existing studies: (1) a lack of knowledge of inflectional and derivational morphology was the primary cause of spelling errors; and (2) a head-start in oral and aural skills, which are regarded as "advantages" that heritage learners have over non-heritage learners, actually have disadvantageous effects on their acquisition of literacy skills. In line with Pyun and Lee-Smith's claim, the researchers underscore the importance of explicit grammar instruction to prevent HLLs from committing spelling errors.

As shown thus far, orthographic accuracy is often considered a fundamental component of literacy, because literacy inexorably involves the use of written language and, thus, is naturally assumed to be a foundation for mastery of the writing system. Kim (2013), however, points to the caveat of emphasizing "rules" in teaching HLLs. She emphatically states that "the obsession with orthography has cost teachers and learners of KHL [Korean as a heritage language] dearly" (p. 84). In her view, teachers' stressing their students' orthographic "correctness," approximating "educated" native speakers' proficiency, has contributed to higher attrition rates in enrollment in college Korean courses. The complexity of, and oftentimes illogical, rules of spelling and spacing discourages HLLs in taking an upper-level course. It is true that, in Kim's own words, "simply learning the alphabet (or how to spell words better) does not improve one's functional literacy" (p. 85).

Vocabulary is a fundamental process of meaning-making, and thus is often considered to be a key component of literacy. To our knowledge, there is only one empirical study that explores vocabulary in literacy development. Shin and Joo (2015) conducted an error analysis of lexical usages by 69 KHL learners enrolled in community schools in Australia. The researchers identified a total of 217 lexical errors and categorized them into 6 types of errors. The most frequent errors were simplification and redundancy (omission of the necessary word, and addition of an unnecessary word), followed by code-switching (replacement of the target word by an English word). Errors resulting from semantic similarity and nonconventional register were the third most frequent type of errors. The researchers argue that HLLs' lexical repertoire tends to be limited to home or childhood vocabulary, and that "remedial teaching" (p. 156) involving explicit instruction is required (e.g., explanations and pattern drills).

It is generally accepted that approximately 60–70% of Korean vocabulary consists of Sino-Korean words (*hanjaeo*). Since the *hangul*-only language policy for public publication was enforced in 1971, there have been heated debates among policy-makers and scholars on whether Chinese characters (*hanja*) should be included in the curriculum as early as elementary education. In KFL education, Jung and Cho (2006) argue for the integration of *hanja* in the curriculum because, in their view, knowledge of *hanja* enhances "textual comprehension" (p. 64) and helps learners advance beyond an intermediate level of proficiency by expanding their Sino-Korean vocabulary. According to the researchers, teaching *hanja* is not only beneficial in literacy development, but also in developing higher-level thinking skills and making language learning a meaningful life experience.

Bang (2007) also advocates including *hanja* in KFL pedagogy. She conducted a survey study with English-speaking learners who were enrolled in advanced-level Korean courses over two semesters. The results show that learners recognized the need to learn *hanja* in order to obtain an advanced-level proficiency in Korean, although they found learning *hanja* highly challenging. The results also show that most learners were using the strategy of photographic memory using flash cards, and repetitive writing of individual *hanja* on paper. The researcher calls for more effective and systematic methodologies, including assignments and tasks appropriate to the learner's learning style and proficiency level, and providing the teacher's prompt feedback.

Lastly, based on the premise that literacy is a set of skills to read and write, some researchers put forward strategy as a literacy component. For example, Lee and Cho (2010) implemented "concept mapping pre-writing strategies" and "collaborative planning" with 123 KFL students in beginning, intermediate and advanced Korean classes. Results show that students who used collaborative concept mapping outperformed those who did not on composition scores in content, structure, vocabulary, and language use. The collaborative planning strategy was shown to be particularly beneficial for beginning-level students in a mixed class of heritage and non-heritage classes.

6.4.2 *Reading and writing to learn*

As we discussed earlier, the concept of literacy is much more dynamic and complex than the way most KFL teachers have typically dealt with teaching literacy in their classroom. However, probably due to the paucity of theoretical frameworks and empirical evidence specific to KFL, there is still a lack of plausible models for teaching literacy in KFL. Yet, a handful of KFL researchers advocate multiliteracies approaches and offer convincing evidence for their benefits.

Yoon and Brown (2017) demonstrate that literacy practice utilizing multimodal texts, such as TV dramas and shows, helped learners learn pragmatic components—i.e., how to express rudeness—through both verbal and non-verbal means. A multiliteracies approach was found to be useful for facilitating multimodal (im)politeness due to its critical analysis of various means of communication shown in the materials. Learners were critically engaged with the target texts and evaluated the observed meanings in question. Therefore, a multiliteracies approach was particularly useful to promote learners' identity negotiation, because learners were encouraged to discuss their own perspectives on the behavior in question. In addition, according to the researchers, adopting a multiliteracies approach addresses "the need for literacy pedagogy in the digital age" (p. 157).

Indeed, being "literate" is not limited to the ability to decode and encode semiotic modes. Cultural literacy is an emerging research topic in recent years, which refers to the ability to understand, analyze, and critically engage with diverse cultural practices in today's globalized world. Also adopting a multiliteracies approach and utilizing TV drama clips, Lee-Smith and Roh (2016) show that using clips from a TV drama *Misaeng* improved the sociocultural competence of advanced KFL learners through in-depth discussions and critical analysis of the prevalent cultural practices in Korean workplaces. The learners in the study also positively evaluated the activity on the end-of-semester survey: they not only learned about the distinct workplace culture in Korea and linguistic features associated with it, but had a meaningful opportunity to discuss the gap between Korean and American culture and relate it to their own lives as Korean-Americans.

6.4.3 Reading and writing to "do"

Over the past decade, there has been a major shift in perspective on literacy practice. In the 1990s, reading and writing activities focused on products, emphasizing structural and lexical accuracy (e.g., spelling and vocabulary), well-formedness of sentences and paragraphs (e.g., sentence structures, coherence, rhetoric), and whether the communicative purpose is achieved (e.g., genre). Accordingly, reading and writing were considered as primarily mental and cognitive activities. In the broader field of FL education, "attention began to shift away from texts to writers" as early as the 1960s (Kern, 2000, p. 181). However, this shift in perspective occurred much later in KFL education. A process-oriented view of literacy avoids a teacher-centered approach, modeling "good" writing, and teaching prescribed rules. Rather, in a process-oriented, student-centered approach to literacy, learners are allowed to explore new ideas and thoughts, and come to "redesign" meanings through the process of drafting, editing, and revising (Kern, 2000).

This new approach to literacy has motivated a number of researchers to explore feedback on writing. For example, Byon (2005) investigates the efficacy of peer feedback on composition assignments. Over four weeks, Byon had 11 advanced learners of KFL decide on the genre in which they wanted to write, brainstorm to decide the topic, and conduct two peer-editing activities. In the fourth week, the learners submitted peer comments, brainstorming sheets, and checklists for editing activities, with their final draft. During the peer-editing activities, learners were specifically instructed to examine their peers' writing, with foci placed on the organization, clarity, logicality, grammaticality, and content. At the end of semester, the researcher distributed a feedback form, asking the students to express freely how they felt about the peer-editing activities. Overall, the learners showed positive responses, by answering that comments on the content was most helpful, followed by topic development. They also enjoyed the fact that their "authority" as a writer was acknowledged. Byon's study is a meaningful contribution to the existing body of literature because he was able to demonstrate that the role of readers is crucial in literacy practice.

Kim's study (2016) is another valuable addition in that it addresses the recently emerging view of literacy as a social action, through which learners develop not only grammar and vocabulary but also critical-thinking skills and meaningful self-presentation, and, more importantly, a sense of community. She examines third-year KFL students' development of writing skills over two semesters within the person/context approach to writing. The overall objective of the study was to explore if content-based writing tasks are indeed beneficial for developing literacy. The participants were asked to write five to six commentaries in each semester after viewing movies on Korean culture, such as the cultural history of Korean food and South Korea's educational system. The students also posted their comments on their classmates' commentaries on the course website. The results show growth in the development of writing skills in fluency, grammatical complexity, and lexical diversity.

Globalization and digitalization highlight the contemporary communication landscape in the 21st century. The affordances of new media and communication devices such as laptops and smartphones have led FL teachers to inevitably add a new dimension to the traditional way of teaching literacy. In recent years, more and more studies on FL literacy underscore increased interactivity and the reconceptualization of literacy as a socially constructed practice, aided by digital technologies. As we have seen in the previous section, multimodality utilizing digital technologies has widened the scope and speed of communication, and opened up very new possibilities for engaging language learners in literacy practice. These venues include social media, Wikipedia, fanfiction, online role-playing games, online interest communities, reaction videos on YouTube, captioning, and so on.

Incorporating a digital medium in literacy education presents several difficulties. Most of all, incorporating digital literacy in pedagogy assumes users' proficiency in the required technology to some degree. Many older and experienced teachers struggle to understand a new technology or to learn how to make use of the newly learned technology in their pedagogy. As "digital immigrants," teachers are now facing a great challenge in teaching "digital natives." Yet, implementing digital literacy also brings about many benefits. Most importantly, digital literacy readily enables both consumption and production of literacy work. For example, in Kim and Jung's study (2018), learners enjoyed their own webzine articles on Korean culture, created using the free digital publishing platform *Issuu*, and actively participated as both writers and readers. The researchers found that the online magazine facilitated learners' creative-thinking and problem-solving skills, and induced learners' playful engagement with texts.

Earlier studies on developing digital literacy utilize digital story-telling. Angay-Crowder et al. (2013) had 12 middle school students of ESL conduct a digital story-telling project during a four-week summer program, using the computer software *Photostory 3* to incorporate text, images, and sounds. The researchers designed the project following the four steps of multiliteracies pedagogy. Through the project, learners were able to create a collaborative environment—not only among themselves, but between the teacher and students—and experience interdisciplinary learning. For KFL literacy, Yi (2008) explores electronic literacy practices by Korean-American adolescents, involving their voluntary writings, instant messaging, postings on an online community, online diary, scheduling, and shared notes. Yi observes that those digital resources offered authentic and meaningful opportunities for the adolescents to use their heritage language in daily lives—e.g., socializing, pursuing personal interests, and identity maintenance as Koreans. Kim and Omerbašić (2016) examine and compare adolescents' literacy practices in two online forums for Korean dramas, *DramaCrazy* and *Tete Pasta*; participation in these forums enabled the adolescents not only to informally and accidentally learn Korean language and culture, but also to construct imagined identities and practice transnational literacies.

In this section, we have shown several empirical studies on literacy that conceptualize literacy practice as a purposeful social act with the presence of the audience. Teaching literacy within this approach presumes that any literacy practice is an interpersonal and discursive practice occurring for a social purpose (Gee's big "D" Discourse), which integrates language, actions, interactions, technologies, and values. Gee (2015) argues that "learning within a Discourse leads to the mastery of a literacy tool-kit" (p. 127). He gives videogames as a good example of Discourse, in which actors (learners) utilize the learning system in hand—in his own term, "affinity space"—through "guidance, mentoring, smart tools, well-designed and well-organized problems, feedback, and language just-in-time and on demand" (p. 129). In fact, we frequently witness non-Korean gamers, who never formally learned Korean, speaking Korean, acting like a Korean (e.g., using expletives), and interacting with Koreans, in multi-player online games (and Korean gamers acting so in English). In a Discourse episode, learners come to establish a new identity which is socially significant to them at the moment. In the next section, we examine how "designing a new meaning" is intrinsically correlated with identity negotiation.

6.4.4 *Reading and writing to "be"*

When we utilize a social-oriented approach to literacy, there are two things that should be ensured in designing a literacy activity: learner agency and transformation. In critical literacy, readers analyze the text in hand through a critical lens, constantly asking a "why" question and looking for the underlying social and historical contexts. Writers write to expose reality, to exercise power, to influence the social reality or social injustice that they see. In doing so, the writer's personal views and points of opinion are embedded in the newly created discourse, which in turn (re)shapes his/her sense of identity. In critical literacy, the learners' agency is enhanced because they take a social action by reading and writing and "choose" to learn how to communicate their views and beliefs through wordings.

Choi's study (2015) is one of the first KFL studies that looked at how learners construct their L2 identity through literacy practice. She designed literacy activities by incorporating the four steps of implementing multiliteracies—situated practice, overt instruction, critical framing, and transformed practice. As the instructor, Choi had her ten third-year HLLs of Korean write autobiographic essays, movie reviews, poems, and a research paper on the topic of their own choice. In each activity, learners used both print-based and multimodal materials, and recorded their responses on their language logs. In analyzing results, Choi focused on one learner, Jenny, who was born in the US, barely spoke Korean, and had not had any prior experience with reading and writing in Korean before coming to college. Despite her lower proficiency in Korean, Jenny took an "agentive take" on learning by actively engaging in identifying her problematic areas and searching for ways to improve her writing (p. 121). Furthermore, the researcher observed that Jenny gained nuanced understanding and confidence in Korean, and transformed her identity as "an English reader, writer, and storyteller to an emerging Korean literate individual" (p. 124).

In a similar vein, Brown et al. (2015) utilized a multiliteracies approach and illustrate how third-year learners of Korean positioned themselves in the context of the fast-globalizing Korean society. The researchers selected clips from a TV drama *My Lovely Sam Soon* as the multimedia texts because the drama portrays characters of diverse cultural and ethnic backgrounds, including a 혼혈인 "mixed-race person." Like Choi, the instructor, one of researchers followed the four steps of multiliteracies, and encouraged learners to critically engage in discourse surrounding the increasing multi-ethnicity and multiculturalism, and the semiotic systems used to represent the social reality. The retrospective interviews with the learners show that they came to "create their own meanings" and "redefine their own identities" as 교포 "overseas Korean" or 외국인 "foreigner" by relating the sociocultural and linguistic features shown in the drama with themselves (p. 167).

Jung and Lee's study (2018) provides learner-produced texts in which transformed identities are manifested, also following the four steps of multiliteracies in which learners: (1) immersed themselves in the sociolinguistic practice of their choice using open-source, participatory resources on the internet (e.g., YouTube videos and comments, blogs, vlogs, and memes); (2) identified the linguistic features associated with particular social groups; (3) critically analyzed and evaluated the practices; and (4) presented their own opinions and beliefs in relation to the target practices in both writing (final essay with multiple drafts) and speaking (final in-class presentation). Results showed that the learners, who were all heritage speakers of Korean, formulated a hybrid identity that practiced beliefs and values held by both cultures, and strengthened their transnational and translingual identity as 교포 "overseas Koreans."

So far, we have discussed different perspectives on what literacy practice is and how it has been implemented in KFL education. In earlier years, KFL teachers were primarily concerned with teaching how to read and write, and increasing accuracy and lexical repertoire of linguistic conventions. Later, there were shifts in perspective in the conceptualization of literacy, from a cognitive activity to a social one, and from a product-oriented activity to a process-oriented one. Teachers began to assign students multiple roles as writer, reader, and editor, and facilitate reading and writing as purposeful social acts and thus making them more engaging for students. More recently, multiliteracies have gained increasing attention. In the contemporary globalized and digitalized world, multimodality and multiculturalism have emerged as important components of literacy, which teachers should inevitably incorporate in their pedagogy to prepare students to become competent global citizens. Today, KFL teachers actively utilize a variety of multimodal materials, genres, and new technologies to help learners develop critical awareness and establish a sense of identity as Korean speakers and writers. The latest movement is much welcomed by KFL researchers and practitioners alike, since it is indeed our ultimate goal of teaching Korean to guide our students to be Korean speakers/writers beyond the classroom.

6.5 Conclusion

This chapter has reviewed the concepts and roles of literacy in language education, the development of multiliteracies, and the pedagogical practices of literacy and multiliteracies in KFL classrooms. In the context of a digitalized global community, the primary communication tools have shifted from oral to written (and typed) modes. In the 1980s and 1990s, when CLT was the prevailing approach to teaching foreign languages, orality triumphed over literacy. FL teachers primarily focused on developing learners' communicative competence by having students practice spoken conversations—i.e., talking about and with, and doing things by talking. As most communication modes have rapidly been digitalized, however, there has been renewed and increasing interest in literacy-based pedagogy. This major shift in perspectives and approaches to communication, from textual to sociocultural thinking, also entails changes in the ways of teaching literacy. As discussed thus far, recent studies on multiliteracies suggest that FL teachers incorporate additional dimensions into their teaching. Teaching reading and writing is not limited to decoding and encoding semiotic means, but has expanded to include a wide range of meaning-making activities realized through multiple modes and multiple parties. This calls for serious reconsideration of the notion of text in language teaching and reconceptualization of literacy as multifaceted, sociocultural practice rather than a transferrable skill (Paesani, 2018).

Building upon the findings of these studies, we suggest that teachers transcend the normative view of literacy—i.e., teach the standard language and enforce conforming views of the mainstream culture. As mentioned earlier in the chapter, critical thinking holds the central place in the multiliteracies pedagogy. In our view, learner-centered, top-down approaches, applying learners' own cultural and real-world knowledge to reading the given text, can effectively motivate our students to read and write, and help them gain a sense of transformed identity through literacy practice. Avoiding bottom-up approaches (e.g., correcting spelling, writing drills, reading comprehension practice) may enable us to motivate them to use literacy outside and beyond the classroom.

Yet, challenges remain as we move away from the traditional view of literacy and recognize literacy as a social act rather than a cognitive one. Adopting this view of literacy requires thoughtfully designed learning activities which involve sufficient and authentic context, elements of human interaction, collaboration, existing knowledge—cultural and linguistic—as well as language skills. Approaching literacy practice as a social act is not new. However, incorporating multimodality into the curriculum today unescapably entails utilizing digital literacy, an emerging notion of literacy pedagogy. FL teachers are just beginning to realize that their digital-native students communicate in quite different ways from most KFL instructors. Although keeping up with new digital tools of communication and proliferation of social media may be immensely challenging, it may be an important component in implementing multimodality into the curriculum.

Lastly, we suggest that teachers keep in mind that the ultimate goal of a literacy-oriented curriculum is not teaching new linguistic codes, but cultivating intercultural readers and writers, by providing them with access to new TL communities outside the classroom (Kern, 2000). To this end, teachers should play the role of a mediator who allows different interpretations and perspectives, and facilitates discussion across multiple cultures and languages.

Discussion questions

1. What does "being literate" mean in a language? Is being literate in L1 different than L2? If so, how? What does "being literate" mean in Korean as a foreign language?
2. How important do you think grammatical accuracy (including spelling and punctuation) is in literacy instruction?
3. What types of assignments would you give to your students to have them read and write in Korean in their everyday lives outside the classroom?
4. What are some examples of person-oriented literacy practice as opposed to text-oriented literacy practice?
5. If you were to give your students a peer-editing task, what would you include in the guidelines for peer editors? What types of peer feedback would be more beneficial for student authors?

6. How do you think incorporating authentic media texts may impact the development of literacy? What types of texts would you use to prepare your students for today's technologically mediated, global community?
7. How important do you think technology is in literacy development? Do you think KFL teachers should also be familiar with the technology prevalently used by their students? Why? Why not?
8. What are the roles of social media in your students' daily literacy practices? Do you think we should incorporate social media in teaching KFL literacy? Why? Why not?
9. Research findings report that young students tend to use non-standard varieties of language in a digital format of communication (e.g., newly coined and shortened words). Do you think you need to teach those varieties in class? Why? Why not?
10. What are the essential elements in designing a lesson using a multiliteracies framework for a lower-level KFL class? Are these elements different from the ones for an advanced-level KFL class? If so, how are they different, and why?
11. Are literacy and multiliteracies pedagogies different for HLLs and non-HLLs? If so, how?

References

Allen, H.W., & Paesani, K. (2010). Exploring the feasibility of a pedagogy of multiliteracies in introductory foreign language courses. *L2 Journal, 2*, 119–142.

Angay-Crowder, T., Choi, J., & Yi, Y. (2013). Putting multiliteracies into practice: Digital storytelling for multilingual adolescents in a summer program. *TESL Canada Journal/ Revue TESL du Canada, 30*(2), 35–45.

Anstey, M., & Bull, G. (2006). *Teaching and learning multiliteracies: Changing times, changing literacies*. Newark, DE: International Reading Association.

August, D., & Shanahan, T. (2006). *Developing literacy in second-language learners: Report of the National Literacy Panel on Language Minority Children and Youth*. Mahwah, NJ: Erlbaum.

Baker, E.A., Pearson, P.D., & Rozendal, M.S. (2010). Theoretical perspectives and literacy studies: An exploration of roles and insights. In E.A. Baker (Ed.), *The new literacies: Multiple perspectives on research and practice* (pp. 1–22). New York, NY: The Guilford Press.

Bang, Y.H.S. (2007). An analysis of English native speakers' needs and strategies in leaning Chinese characters. *Bilingual Research, 34*, 185–220.

Block, D. (2007). *Second language identities*. London: Continuum.

Brown, L., Iwasaki, N., & Lee, K. (2015). Implementing multiliteracies in the Korean classroom through visual media. In Y. Kumagai, A. López-Sánchez, & S. Wu (Eds.), *Multiliteracies in world language education* (pp. 158–181). New York: Routledge.

Bull, G., & Anstey, M. (2019). *Elaborating multiliteracies through multimodal texts: Changing classroom practices and developing teacher pedagogies*. New York: Routledge.

Byon, A.S. (2005). Teaching composition in the advanced KFL class. *Journal of Korean Language Education, 16*(1), 299–325.

Byrnes, H., Maxim, H.H., & Norris, J.M. (2010). Realizing advanced foreign language writing development in collegiate education: Curricular design, pedagogy, assessment. *Modern Language Journal [Suppl.]*, *94*, 1–235.

Choi, J. (2015). A heritage language learner's literacy practices in a Korean language course in a U.S. university: From a multiliteracies perspective. *Journal of Language and Literacy Education*, *11*, 116–133.

Cope, B., & Kalantzis, M. (2000). Introduction: Multiliteracies: The beginning of an idea. In B. Cope & M. Kalantzis (Eds.), *Multiliteracies: Literacy learning and the design of social futures* (pp. 3–8). London: Routledge.

Cope, B., & Kalantzis, M. (2009). "Multiliteracies": New literacies, new learning. *Pedagogies: An International Journal*, *4*(3), 164–195.

Cope, B., & Kalantzis, M. (2015). The things you do to know: An introduction to the pedagogy of multiliteracies. In B. Cope & M. Kalantzis (Eds.), *A pedagogy of multiliteracies: Learning by design* (pp. 1–36). New York: Palgrave Macmillan.

Gee, J.P. (1989a). Literacy, discourse, and linguistics: Introduction. *Journal of Education*, *171*(1), 5–17.

Gee, J.P. (1989b). What is literacy? *Journal of Education*, *171*(1), 18–25.

Gee, J.P. (2009). Reflections on reading Cope and Kalantzis' "'Multiliteracies': New literacies, new learning.". *Pedagogies: An International Journal*, *4*(3), 196–204.

Gee, J.P. (2015). *Literacy and education*. New York: Routledge.

Guichon, N., & Cohen, C. (2016). Multimodality and CALL. In F. Farr & L. Murray (Eds.), *The Routledge handbook of language learning and technology* (pp. 509–521). New York: Routledge.

Hull, G.A., & Hernandez, G. (2008). Literacy. In B. Spolsky & F.M. Hult (Eds.), *The handbook of educational linguistics* (pp. 328–340). Malden, MA: Blackwell Publishing.

Jones, R.H., & Hafner, C.A. (2012). *Understanding digital literacies: A practical introduction*. New York: Routledge.

Joo, A., & Shin, S.-C. (2016). Characteristic features of English-L1 KHL learner orthographic errors. *Journal of Korean Language Education*, *27*, 1–36.

Jung, J.-Y., & Lee, E. (2018). Citizen sociolinguistics: Making connections in the foreign language classroom. *The Korean Language in America*, *22*(1), 1–24.

Jung, M., & Cho, Y.Y. (2006). Chinese character education in teaching Korean as a foreign language: A new paradigm of cognitive expansion. *The Korean Language in America*, *11*, 64–83.

Kalantzis, M., & Cope, B. (2012). *Literacies*. Cambridge, UK: Cambridge University Press.

Keller, D., & Share, J. (2007). Critical media literacy, democracy, and the reconstruction of education. In D. Macedo & S.R. Steinberg (Eds.), *Media literacy: A reader* (pp. 3–23). New York: Peter Lang.

Kern, R. (2000). *Literacy and language teaching*. Oxford, UK: Oxford University Press.

Kim, E., & Jung, J.-Y. (2018, June). The development and assessment of literacy through digital media. Paper presented at the 23rd Annual Conference of AATK (American Association of Teachers of Korean), University of Toronto, Canada.

Kim, G.M., & Omerbašić, D. (2016). Multimodal literacies: Imagining lives through Korean dramas. *Journal of Adolescent and Adult Literacy*, *60*(5), 557–566.

Kim, H.-Y. (2016). Socially engaged writing in the KFL class: A post-product, post-process approach. *Language Facts and Perspectives*, *37*, 119–148.

Kim, S. (2013). When keeping up means falling behind: The dear price of stressing "correct" orthography in teaching Korean as a heritage language. *The Korean Language in America, 18*, 71–91.

Kramsch, C. (2009). *The multilingual subject*. Oxford: Oxford University Press.

Kress, G. (2003). *Literacy in the new media age*. London, UK: Routledge.

Kress, G. (2009). Comments on cope and Kalantzis. *Pedagogies: An International Journal, 4*(3), 205–212.

Lankshear, C., & Knobel, M. (2011). *New literacies*. New York, NY: McGraw Hill Open University Press.

Lee, Y., & Cho, S. (2010). Using concept map prewriting strategies in Korean writing classes. *Korean Language in America, 15*, 46–61.

Lee-Smith, A. (2016). Pedagogy of multiliteracies for Korean language learners: Developing Standards-based (the 5Cs) teaching-learning materials using TV public service announcements. *Journal of Korean Language Education, 27*(2), 143–192.

Lee-Smith, A., & Roh, J. (2016). Promoting socio-languacultural competence in advanced Korean curriculum: Using drama [Misaeng]. *The Language and Culture, 12*(2), 113–142.

Maxim, H.H. (2006). Integrating textual thinking into the introductory college-level foreign language classroom. *Modern Language Journal, 90*(1), 19–32.

McKinney, C., & Norton, B. (2008). Identity in language and literacy education. In B. Spolsky & F.M. Hult (Eds.), *The handbook of educational linguistics* (pp. 367–382). Malden, MA: Blackwell.

Meyer, C. (2009). The role of thinking on the college language classroom. *ADFL Bulletin, 41*(1), 86–93.

Mills, N. (2009). A guide du Routard simulation: Increasing self-efficacy in the standards through project-based learning. *Foreign Language Annals, 42*(4), 607–639.

Modern Language Association Ad Hoc Committee on Foreign Languages. (2007). Foreign languages and higher education: New structures for a changed world. *Profession, 2007*, 234–245.

New London Group. (1996). A pedagogy of multiliteracies: Designing social futures. *Harvard Educational Review, 66*(1), 60–92.

Paesani, K. (2018). Researching literacies and textual thinking in collegiate foreign language programs: Reflections and recommendations. *Foreign Language Annals, 51*(1), 129–139.

Pérez, B., & McCarthy, T.L. (2004). *Sociocultural contexts of language and literacy*. Mahwah, NJ: Lawrence Erlbaum Associates.

Pyon, D.O., & Lee-Smith, A. (2011). Reducing Korean heritage language learners' orthographic errors: The contribution of online and in-class dictation and form-focused instruction. *Language, Culture and Curriculum, 24*(2), 141–158.

Royce, T. (2007). Multimodal communicative competence in second language contexts. In T. Royce & W. Boweher (Eds.), *New directions in the analysis of multimodal discourse* (pp. 361–390). Mahwah, NJ: Lawrence Erlbaum Associates.

Scheibe, C., & Rogow, F. (2012). *The teacher's guide to media literacy: Critical thinking in a multimedia world*. Thousand Oaks, CA: Sage.

Shin, S.-C. (2007). Types and patterns of English L1 students' misspellings in Korean. *Journal of Korean Language Education, 18*(3), 99.

Shin, S.-C., & Joo, A. (2015). Lexical errors in Korean-Australian heritage learners' compositions. *Journal of Korean Language Education, 26*, 129–162.

Street, B.V. (2004). Futures of the ethnography of literacy? *Language and Education, 18*(4), 326–330.

Warner, C., & Dupuy, B. (2018). Moving toward multiliteracies in foreign language teaching: Past and present perspectives... and beyond. *Foreign Language Annals, 51*(1), 116–128.

Yi, Y. (2008). Relay writing in an adolescent online community. *Journal of Adolescent and Adult Literacy, 51*(8), 870–880.

Yoon, S.Y., & Brown, L. (2017). A multiliteracies approach to teaching Korean multimodal (Im)politeness. *The Korean Language in America, 21*(2), 154–185.

7 Korean language assessment

Sun-Young Shin and Hyo Sang Lee

7.1 Introduction

Language assessments are used for making informed decisions about students, which are intended to bring about beneficial consequences for the students, programs, and institutions. In a Korean language program context, language assessments are usually used for assisting placement of students into an appropriate level of classes and for checking on students' progress or achievement towards the course objectives. In addition to such curriculum-related decisions, language assessments are also often used to measure students' overall language proficiency levels to see if they meet some predetermined language proficiency standards. The growing interest in and need for assessing language ability and related skills have generated much attention to how we can ensure that a language assessment fulfills its intended purposes and functions. Likewise, language teachers should be able to know how to evaluate whether the instruments we use are of high quality, test scores are reliable, and the inferences and uses made on the basis of test scores are appropriate. It is also important to note that language assessment can, and should, be integrated with language teaching to promote student learning by providing teachers with information about student progress in relation to learning objectives. Foreign language instructors should thus be equipped with sufficient background and knowledge to develop, select, and use language tests and interpret test results. To that end, this chapter on Korean language assessment addresses an array of fundamental issues to consider in developing and using language assessments properly for diverse purposes carried out in the Korean language teaching context.

7.2 Standardized Korean language proficiency assessment

The Test of Proficiency in Korean (TOPIK), the Korean Scholastic Aptitude Test (SAT) Subject Test, and the Oral Proficiency Interview (OPI) are the most well-known large-scale standardized Korean language proficiency tests. TOPIK is developed and administered for learners of Korean either as a second or foreign language, whereas the Korean SAT Subject Test is used to assess the Korean language proficiency of US high school students who need to demonstrate their overall level of foreign language proficiency to the US universities they apply to.

This section provides an overview of each of these standardized Korean proficiency tests.

7.2.1 Test of Proficiency in Korean (TOPIK)

The Test of Proficiency in Korean (TOPIK) is most widely used as a measure of general proficiency in Korean as a foreign language for both academic and employment purposes in Korea. TOPIK was first launched in 1997 and is administered by the Ministry of Education under the supervision of the National Institute for International Education (Kim & Lee, 2014). Originally, TOPIK consisted of six separate levels from Level 1 to 6. Since the 35th test administration in 2014, TOPIK is available in two modules: TOPIK I for Level 1 and Level 2; and TOPIK II for Levels 3, 4, 5, and 6. TOPIK I includes only listening (30 multiple-choice items for 40 minutes) and reading (40 multiple-choice items for 60 minutes) sections, whereas TOPIK II contains a writing section (50 minutes) involving sentence completion questions and descriptive essays for intermediate levels (Levels 3 and 4) and argumentative essays for advanced levels (Levels 5 and 6), in addition to more lengthy listening (50 multiple-choice items for 60 minutes) and reading (50 multiple-choice items for 70 minutes) sections (National Institute for International Education, 2019). TOPIK is administered to examinees who learn Korean as a foreign language, six times annually to examinees in Korea, and twice outside of Korea.

TOPIK items have been developed and revised based on multiple pilot testing results, and an item bank system was implemented to safeguard the convenience and fairness of the test (Kim & Lee, 2014). Despite the use of the TOPIK test scores for high-stakes purposes such as admission into academic programs and employment for companies, very little research has thus far been conducted and published for validating newly developed TOPIK. In particular, more research should be conducted to ensure the appropriateness of item difficulty and cutoffs in determining the general Korean proficiency levels of examinees. Unlike other more established standardized English proficiency tests, to date, TOPIK does not measure examinees' speaking abilities, underrepresenting the intended construct. However, it plans to include a speaking section starting in 2023, delivered in an internet-based format (The Korea Herald, 2019).[1]

7.2.2 The Korean Scholastic Aptitude Test (SAT) Subject Test

The Korean Scholastic Aptitude Test (SAT) Subject Test is administered by College Board. It started in 1997, and a few thousand college-bound high school students take it annually, even though the number of test-takers has been decreasing in recent years; after having reached the peak in 2009 at 4,625, it was down to 1,712 in 2017, a decrease of 9% from 1,891 in 2016 (Korea Daily, 2017).[2] The test consists of three parts: listening, usage, and reading. The listening and reading test items are not much different from other SAT foreign language subject tests. A prompt of a conversational sequence or narration is given and two or more questions are asked for students to respond in a multiple-choice format. As in most of the paper-based language tests, the listening and reading test items in the Korean SAT Subject Test are able to measure only receptive comprehension skills, while the test items in the structure section assess only students' knowledge of grammar and vocabulary without measuring production skills.

7.2.3 The Oral Proficiency Interview (OPI)

The Oral Proficiency Interview (OPI) is a standardized, face-to-face or telephone interview between a trained interviewer and the interviewee, whose overall speaking proficiency is being assessed (Proficiency Standards Division, 1999). The OPI has long been used as a measure of foreign language oral proficiency, including Korean, in the US. It originated from the Interagency Language Roundtable (ILR) proficiency scales formed by the Foreign Service Institute (FSI) and other US government agencies (Thompson et al., 2016). The American Council on the Teaching of Foreign Languages (ACTFL) adapted the ILR scale and created its proficiency guidelines for use in educational contexts, and developed an OPI protocol accordingly (Liskin-Gasparro, 2003). It tests the interviewee's oral language proficiency, ranging from Novice to Superior levels, based on the elicited speech samples. It also has three sublevels (low, mid, and high) for each Novice, Intermediate, and Advanced levels. The OPI ratings awarded by certified interviewers are based on four main criteria: the functions performed, the social contexts and content areas, the accuracy, and the oral text types (Proficiency Standards Division, 1999). Speech samples are rated by a second OPI rater, and any discrepancy between the assigned scores from the two raters is resolved by a third OPI rater. Since the OPI features adaptive, interactive, and learner-centered assessment, the interviewer tries to elicit different hierarchical functions such as description, narration, comparison, explanation, and justification during the interview, based on their judgment of the interviewee's oral proficiency. Thus, the questions that are being asked are not fixed for all interviewees, although OPI interviewers follow the standardized sequence of the OPI protocol. The OPI also has a role-play section in which the interviewer selects the role-play card based on the interviewee's performance during the interview and plays the role of questioner. Of particular note about the OPI is that a level is determined by the test-taker's sustained performance of target functions or tasks. In other words, a lower rating will be given if an interviewee fails to function consistently both in linguistic fluency and accuracy at the target level. The OPI is found to be a reliable measure of oral language proficiency (Surface & Dierdorff, 2003) despite its criticism of being a one-way conversation, resulting in failing to assess learners' interactional oral language skills involving turn-taking and initiations of conversations (Kramsch, 1986; Galaczi & Taylor, 2018).

7.3 Issues in classroom-based Korean language assessment

Classroom-based language assessments are broadly categorized into two different types: formative and summative assessments (Bachman & Damböck, 2018). Formative assessments are usually given before the language program starts to place students into the most appropriate levels to maximize efficiency in their language learning, but they can be provided in the midst of teaching as well to identify students' strengths and weaknesses, to direct their learning, and to monitor their progress towards the predefined goals and objectives of the program. The results of formative assessments can also be used to inform changes in teaching materials and tasks presented to students to ensure their effectiveness. In contrast, summative assessments are often understood as achievement tests that are used to assess how well students have mastered course content and objectives at the end of the course. They can be used to ensure that students are ready to move to the next level or to confirm whether students can be certified to meet a certain designated level by satisfying a minimum requirement (Bachman & Damböck, 2018).

In a Korean as a Foreign Language (KFL) context, language assessment has usually been used as a tool for making placement and achievement decisions of students. Developing proper placement tests is particularly challenging for many KFL programs because heritage and non-heritage learners of Korean are often mixed together from the beginning, despite the fact that heritage learners and non-heritage learners have different language profiles, including cultural backgrounds, motivation for learning the target language, and oral proficiency, and thus different instructional needs (Brinton et al., 2008; Kondo-Brown, 2005). Such differences between the two groups pose pedagogical challenges for many KFL teachers when they have both heritage language and non-heritage Korean learners in the same classroom because they tend to have different linguistic profiles and instructional needs (Kondo-Brown, 2010; Lee & Kim, 2008). In particular, many heritage Korean learners have better listening skills than non-heritage Korean learners, in spite of their relatively weak literacy and productive skills in Korean (Kim, 2002). These notable differences in spoken language abilities between the two distinctive groups of learners are challenges confronting KFL teachers and testers, especially when they attempt to design and implement placement tests (손성옥, 2005; Sohn & Shin, 2007; Cho & Chun, 2015). This is of particular concern to many Korean language programs in North American universities, where student populations are often polarized between high (heritage Korean learners) and low oral proficiency levels (non-heritage Korean learners). 손성옥 (2005), Sohn and Shin (2007), and Cho and Chun (2015) thus recommend that a Korean composition test should be given to heritage Korean learners to increase discrimination power among them. In addition, many existing placement tests utilizing a standardized proficiency language exam rarely reflect classroom materials and tasks, and thus fail to inform instructional decisions (Green, 2012). Such a gap between test items on placement tests and curricular objectives would seriously limit the meaningfulness of the information we can gather from the results of placement tests (Long et al., 2018; Shin & Lidster, 2017). In that sense, computer adaptive tests (CATs) are recommended as a placement testing tool, which can make each item tailored to the ability of the student. However, CATs cannot be easily implemented into local, small-scale testing contexts due to its technical and practical problems, and instead, a "semi-adaptive" web-based test has been suggested as an alternative testing tool (Ockey, 2009). For example, the Korean language program at Indiana University has developed a semi-adaptive Korean placement test in which there are sections of four different course levels consisting of multiple sets of items, and students can advance to the next level of the test only when they get enough correct responses in each section (Shin & Lee, 2014).

Another common use of language assessments in a KFL context is grading student performance in the form of an achievement test. Multiple assessment tasks for the language use activities of reading, listening, speaking, and writing are developed and used to measure the level of students' mastery of course objectives. Steps for developing classroom-based tests for achievement purposes will be discussed in detail in the next section, but it is important to point out that grades are composite measures which include many factors beyond the mastery of stated course learning outcomes and which are subject to variation in the means of assessment and rating severity across instructors. Teachers also should keep in mind that general language proficiency is not equivalent to achievement as a result of instruction (Norris, 2006). It is thus crucial to create classroom-based assessment tasks and rubrics to truthfully reflect curriculum content and goals so that achievement-based assessment can be useful for evaluating program effectiveness and demonstrating to stakeholders what students in the program actually become able to do through instruction.

7.4 Steps for developing classroom-based language assessment

Davidson and Lynch (2002) provide step-by-step guidelines to develop a criterion-referenced language test whose focus is on determining the absolute level of language ability or knowledge as specified in a course syllabus, not on identifying the relative standing of each student, as in a norm-referenced language test. According to Davidson and Lynch (2002), teachers or test developers should first decide on the constructs to be measured, usually informed by certain internal (i.e., curricula goals or objectives) or external (i.e., American Council on the Teaching of Foreign Languages (ACTFL)/the Common European Framework of Reference for Languages (CEFR) scales) mandates. In the context of Korean language programs, such external mandates can be found in the set of learning objectives for the Standards-Based College Curriculum for Korean Language Education published in the journal *The Korean Language in America* (Cho et al., 2015). It includes six consecutive levels and two heritage levels for the 5 Cs: Communication (C1), Cultures (C2), Connections (C3), Comparisons (C4), and Communities (C5). (See Cho et al., 2015, for the full description of learning objectives in the 5 Cs in all levels.)

Test item specification should then be generated to guide test construction. It is made up of four main required components: 1) the general description; 2) the prompt; 3) the response; and 4) the sample item (Davidson & Lynch, 2002). The general description refers to the specific language knowledge or skills to be measured, which is often rephrased as "student learning outcomes (SLOs)" in a class syllabus. It is important to note that when language teachers define SLOs, they should ensure that SLOs are observable and measurable. For that purpose, the

SLOs should be specific and concrete. Consider the following example of general description that was adapted from Korean Level 1 curricular specifications for interpretive communication (Park et al., 2015: 179–182).

The general description for Korean Level 1 for interpretive communication:
It is important for KFL learners to understand simple kinship terms and questions about their immediate family. Students will be able to identify basic information from simple conversation and texts on family members.

The second component of test specification is the prompt attribute, which indicates both the instructions and the input students receive in the test. The prompt attribute provides a detailed description of what students will be presented with in terms of the genre, length, and topic of test input. The following is the example of a prompt description for assessing KFL learners' ability to understand simple conversations.

The prompt attribute for Korean Level 1 for interpretive communication:
The aural text consists of a short monologic passage (40–50 words) about one's family members. Students will also be given the family tree picture matching with the aural description of family members. The aural text is then followed by four to five multiple-choice questions with four options written in Korean. Each question is not shown but audio-recorded at regular speed and played only once to students.

The third component, the response attribute, describes the type of response task format that will be delivered to students (Carr, 2011). For example, response formats can be selected from various task formats including true/false, matching, or multiple-choice questions in which students do not need to provide any language in their responses to the given test input. These task formats are commonly used for discrete-point tests where one specific feature of a construct is measured at a time (Cheng & Fox, 2017). In contrast, limited production tasks normally require students to provide responses to the input in a word, phrase, or short-sentence level. Fill-in-the-blank, short-answer questions, or cloze tests exemplify this type of response task format. Lastly, extended production tasks are used to elicit responses that are beyond a single sentence. Interviews and compositions are good examples of extended production tasks.

An example of the response attributes for selected response task format in assessing students' ability to understand the simple, aural text in Korean is given below:

The response attribute for Korean Level 1 for interpretive communication:
Students will click on the correct option of the four alternatives on the online listening multiple-choice test format.

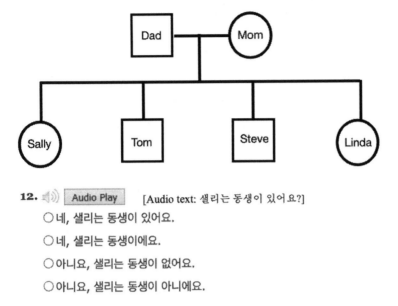

12. 🔊 [Audio Play]   [Audio text: 샐리는 동생이 있어요?]

○ 네, 샐리는 동생이 있어요.

○ 네, 샐리는 동생이에요.

○ 아니요, 샐리는 동생이 없어요.

○ 아니요, 샐리는 동생이 아니에요.

Figure 7.1 An example of selected response task format.

The final component of test specifications is the sample item, which will give a solid example for test developers to follow when they should replicate multiple items based on the same characteristics of prompt and response formats. Consider the following sample item, adapted from Indiana University's Korean placement test.

The sample item for Korean Level 1 for interpretive communication:
Read to the questions in Figure 7.1 and choose the most appropriate answer based on the picture of the family tree. (Note: the sibling on the right is older than the one on the left.)

7.5 Practical tips for constructing Korean language achievement tests

Given the goal of foreign language teaching and learning to enhance language proficiency and communicative competence of the target language, the most ideal test format should be open-ended, discourse-based, and naturalistic. Nevertheless, classroom-based language tests should also measure whether students have mastered the specific learning materials of the course, that is, specific level-appropriate grammar points, vocabulary, or set expressions such as passive and causative constructions, indirect discourse, noun-modifying forms, honorific expressions, or expressions specific to a given situation (e.g., taxi ride, restaurant scenes, shoe stores, telephone conversations, etc.). Such discrete-point language items can be better assessed in a convergent item format, although it should still be contextualized, reflecting real-life situations as closely as possible, while avoiding some mechanical grammatical conversion questions. In the following section we review some of the test items commonly used in the KFL contexts and provide alternative test item formats.

Quoting someone's speech is a common communicative transaction, although mastering its use is quite challenging to many KFL learners. Thus, many test items on indirect or direct quoting in Korean often utilize convergent item formats, as shown in Example 1. In this example, while a mini-dialogue is given in the test input, the dialogue cannot be said to be natural, and the tasks asked in these test items are not contextualized, but simply force students to mechanically change the predicate endings to the plain style and to attach it to the indirect discourse pattern ~고 해요.

Example 1. Sample test items modified from the final exam obtained from University A[3]

VI. Change the following conversation into indirect quotations. [3 points each]

소피아: 오늘이 내 생일이야.
마이클: 오늘 같이 저녁 먹자.

1. 소피아가 마이클한테 오늘이 _____.
2. 마이클이 소피아한테 오늘 같이 _____.

In order to measure the students' mastery of executing indirect discourse in a more communicative manner, test items should reflect real-life communication situations, as given in Example 2 below.

Example 2. A sample item modified from the midterm exam obtained from University B

[김탄 left a phone message to 은상, who had told him that she is going back to Korea. Listen to his message and complete the conversation between 은상 and 지원.][4]

[AUDIO: "어디야? 누구랑 있어? 언제 가? 안 가면 안 돼? 가지마. 나랑 더 있어. 보고 싶어. 전화 해 줘."]

은상: 김탄이 내 핸드폰에 메시지를 남겨 놨더라구요.

지원: 뭐라고(그러던가)요?

은상: _____고요.

When a student's learning of specific grammar points learned during a semester is assessed, a cloze test format is commonly used, as can be seen in Example 3 below.

Example 3. Sample items modified from the final exam obtained from University A

IV. Complete the dialogue or sentence by filling in the blank with the given word, choosing one of the grammar structures in <보기>. Each grammar structure can be used ONLY ONCE. Change the form when necessary to make the sentence grammatical. [3 points each]

[보기: -기로 하다, –아/어 보이다, –아/어 있다, -는 데에, 아무리 -아도/어도]

1. 스티브: 유진 씨는 지금 어디에 있어요?
   마크: 유진 씨는 지금 한국에 (가다)_____.
2. 우진: 스티브, 마크랑 같이 오기로 하지 않았어?
   스티브: 응, 그런데 마크한테 (전화하다)_____ 안 받아서 그냥 혼자 왔어.

In this test format, while students need to understand what is conveyed in order to select a correct target pattern in each test item, only minimum contextual information is provided in a made-up mini-dialogue format. A better item type for assessing the same construct would be to have students answer questions that are related to their real-life situations, as shown in Example 4.

Example 4. Sample items modified from the final exam obtained from University C

III. Give responses to the following questions in Korean by using any of the grammar patterns below. If necessary, you can make complex sentences.

[Grammar patters: ~어야/아야 돼요, ~기로 하다, ~(으)면 돼요, ~거든요, ~게 되다, ~(으)려면, ~려고 하다, ~(으)ㄴ 지 . . . 되다, ~(으)면 좋겠다, ~어야/아야지요, ~(으)ㄴ 적이 있다]

1) 가: 이번 학기가 시작한지 얼마나 되었어요?
   나: _____.

2) 가: 한국 하숙집에서 살아본 적이 있어요?
   나: _____.

3) 가: 우체국에서 소포를 보낼 때 뭐가 제일 중요해요?
   나: _____.

4) 가: 서울에서 지하철을 타려면 승차권을 어디서 구해요?
   나: _____.

The questions asked in this format can be given either in writing or orally. When questions are given in writing, some questions may already reveal in them the target patterns which the students are tested on, as found in Example 4. To avoid revealing the target patterns, questions can alternatively be given in English, with an option for students to translate them, as shown in Example 5.

Example 5. Sample test items modified from a final exam of University B

(Translate and) answer the given questions in Korean.

Q: How long has it been since you moved to the current place from the previous place?

_____

A: [Make a reference to the type of your residence (apartment, dorm, house) and the length of the residence in your previous place.]

_____

Q: How many years of Korean do you have to take if you would like to major in Korean?

_____

A: _____

Q: Have you ever made your parents angry?

_____

A: _____

Q: Have you had an occasion when you almost got into an accident because the car in front of you suddenly stopped?

_____

A: _____

Questions can be formulated so as to elicit the grammar patterns covered in a given term. In these test items, the target grammar points that are expected to be executed are: ~(으)ㄴ지 … 되다, ~다가, ~(으)려면, ~(으)면 되다, ~(으)ㄴ 적이 있다/없다, ~게 하다, ~는 바람에, ~(으)ㄹ 뻔하다, etc. The question and answer format used in Examples 4 and 5 are more likely to lead to communicatively meaningful, authentic language production with focused grammar points covered in the course than the one in Example 3, as the test items simulate more real-life interactions.

One of the challenges in a paper-and-pencil test is to assess learners' conversational or interactional abilities. The most common test format to measure such conversational skills has been a discourse completion task in the fill-in-the-blank question format, requiring an examinee to complete a conversational sequence. Sample test items from a final exam in an intermediate level class are shown in Example 6 below.

Example 6. Sample test items modified from the final exam obtained from University D

Complete the conversation with the given information. (2점)

마크: 택시!
(택시 안에서)
기사: 1._____ (Where are you going)?
마크: 2._____ (Go to the airport, please).
기사: 네.

(15 분 후에)

마크: 길이 많이 막히네요.

기사: 3. _____ (There's a lot of traffic because it
        is the weekend).

마크: 공항까지 얼마나 걸릴까요?

기사: 글쎄요, 적어도 두 시간은 걸리겠는데요.

마크: 알겠습니다.

(1시간 30분 후에)

기사: 손님, 공항 4. _____ (We almost arrived at
        the airport). 79,000원입니다.

마크: 여기 있어요. 5: _____ (Thank you for your
        effort [Literally: Keep working on!]).

기사: 감사합니다.

In these test items, the parts that need to be filled in are given in translation, and
so it is not so much to complete the conversation as to translate the given English,
except that the translation task is to be carried in a conversational context. A better
test version with the same material is shown in Example 7.

**Example 7. An alternative version for the same
test material as shown in Example 6**

Complete the conversation between 마크 and a taxi driver.

[마크는 공항에 가려고 택시를 탔습니다.]

마크: 택시!

(택시 안에서)

기사: 1. _____ [asking for destination]

마크: 2. _____ [giving a destination]

기사: 네.

(15 분 후에)

마크: 길이 많이 막히네요.

기사: 3. _____ [giving an explanation for a
        traffic situation due to its being a weekend]

마크: 공항까지 얼마나 걸릴까요?

기사: 글쎄요, 적어도 두 시간은 걸리겠는데요.

마크: 알겠습니다.

(1시간 30분 후에)

기사: 손님, 공항 4. _____ [informing of being
near the destination] 79,000 원입니다.

마크: 여기 있어요. 5. _____ [expressing gratitude
for the driver's efforts or trouble).

기사: 감사합니다.

In this revised version, simple instructions or descriptions of the situation are provided to help students to complete the conversation, referring to communicative
acts in question, rather than giving direct translations of what needs to be filled in.

In a paper-and-pencil test, the only practical production test that can be open-
ended, discourse-based, and naturalistic is a free composition or essay test. An
essay test is usually conducted by giving a single topic or having a topic selected
from a number of given options, which limits the range of vocabulary and expressions to be utilized. In order to solicit more specific ranges of vocabulary and
expressions, one can give a set of small and more specific topics that have been
covered in the class for shorter paragraph writing, as in the following example.

**Example 8. Sample short essay questions in an
advanced level final exam from University B**

가. 문화 차이에 대하여 다음 의제 중 하나를 골라 이야기해 보십시오.

1. 한국에서는 가끔 식당에서 여러 사람이 식사를 하고 한 사람이
계산을 하는 경우가 있습니다. 이와 관련된 에피소드나 여러분의
느낌을 이야기해 보십시오.

2. 미국에서 A.S를 받거나 어떤 일을 처리할 때, 시간이 너무 걸려
답답하거나 불편할 때가 많습니다. 이에 반해 한국에서는 뭐든지
"빨리빨리" 해야 하는 문화가 있습니다. 한국의 "빨리빨리" 문화에
대한 에피소드나 여러분의 생각을 이야기해 보십시오.

3. 문화 차이로 인해 당황했던 경험에 대해 이야기해 보십시오.

나. 날씨와 계절과 관련해서 의제(discussion topic)들에 대해
답하십시오.

4. 여러분은 날씨를 타는 편입니까? 날씨와 관련하여 자신의 호불호
(좋아하고 싫어하는 것)를 이야기하고 날씨 때문에 고생한
에피소드를 이야기해 보십시오.

5. 폭우나 태풍 등 험한 날씨(severe weather)로 생기는 일들을 실제
사건이나 에피소드를 들어서 이야기해 보십시오.

다. 물건을 구입하고 나서 마음에 들지 않아 반품하거나 불만을 소비자
게시판이나 상담원에게 이야기한 적이 있습니까? 구입, 반품, 교환,
환불 과정에서 기분이 나빴던 경험, 기분이 좋았던 경험 등에 대해서
이야기해 보십시오.

The topics given in this test have all been covered in class, and so the students can utilize vocabulary and expressions that are familiar from the coursework.

The most effective testing tool for measuring the students' achievement in enhancing communicative competence should be an oral exam. The most commonly utilized oral exam format is an oral interview by an instructor. In fact, many programs use an Oral Proficiency Interview (OPI) (Swender, 1999) as a final exam to certify whether or not students have achieved a target proficiency level set for a given course. The problem with the OPI is two-fold: practicality and the issues inherent in the format itself. Firstly, it is time-consuming if there are a large number of students to test. It is simply not feasible to give substantial interviews to a large number of students. Secondly, as pointed out by Kramsch (1986) with regard to the OPI, the interview format is not quite suitable in nature for drawing spontaneous and natural interaction from the interviewee; it often winds up with the instructor alone asking questions and the interviewees responding to them, being heavily skewed toward assessing the testee's production skills. The interview format scarcely provides mechanisms and contexts through which students utilize and execute interactional features such as reactive tokens, meaning negotiation tactics such as repair-initiating, aligning or non-aligning with the interlocuters' utterances, and requesting and providing clarification, etc. (Luoma, 2004; 이효상, 2016). To facilitate more natural and spontaneous interaction, a format of having conversations among students themselves might be a better option. It could be a one-on-one conversation between two students or a multi-party conversation with three or more people, depending on time constraints. One issue that could be critical is how the pair or group is formed. Students prefer pairing or grouping in advance so that they can practice among themselves. A danger with pre-arranged pairing or grouping, however, is that students would write a script and participate in a conversational session using the pre-written script, which would lessen the spontaneity and naturalness of the conversation. Another potential drawback of this format is that students may not explore all the material whose mastery the instructor would like to assess. A panel-like conversation format with an instructor being a moderator can resolve these issues, akin to a famous TV program "비정상 회담," in which foreigners living in Korea are engaged in a fairly free spontaneous conversation on a given topic with a couple of native Korean moderators.[5] Each panel could consist of four to five students with an instructor-moderator, and the instructor-moderator can set the agenda to control the topics, pace, and content of conversation based on the course material. Students can freely interact with each other and among themselves as well as responding to the moderator's questions and/or cues. Since the moderator controls the content and the material, instructors can explore the targeted material, and students cannot prepare a script in advance and cannot help but produce spontaneous and naturalistic language, although the students may be able to prepare themselves with the familiar materials from the coursework. Example 9 below exhibits possible agendas for the prompts given by the instructor-moderator for an intermediate level oral exam.

**Example 9. An example of oral final exam questions in an
intermediate level class obtained from University B**

--날씨가 추워졌죠? 벌써 겨울이 온 것 같아요.... 씨는 어느 계절을
좋아하세요?

--왜요?

--요즘은 아침에는 춥고 낮에는 따뜻해서 옷 입기가 어려운데,
...씨는 어떤 옷을 잘 입으세요? ... 씨, ... 씨한테 ... 스타일 옷이 잘
어울리는 같아요? ... 씨한테는 어떤 옷이 잘 어울릴까요?

--여행 하는 거 좋아하는 사람 있어요? 제일 가 보고 싶은 데가
어디예요? 어디 가 봤어요? ... 갔을 때 제일 인상적인 게 뭐였어요?

--... 씨는 지금 어디 사세요? ...-에 이사 오기 전에는 어디 살았어요?
전에 살던 데서 지금 사는 ... -로 이사 온지 는 얼마나 됐어요?

This format is useful not only to solicit students' production of learned material,
but also to control the pace and balance of the interactions among participants,
as the instructor-moderator directs the discussion and exercises the authority to
select speakers at any given time.

7.6 Alternative Korean language assessment

Authenticity is an important aspect of test quality, and it is usually achieved in
open-ended, discourse- or interaction-based, and natural formats. Such assessment tasks can be implemented in some alternative assessment formats such as
E-portfolios and role-plays. Compared to structure-oriented and discrete-point
test items, alternative assessments could include naturally contextualized tasks
and better simulate real-life activities while eliciting more meaningful and natural
conversational exchanges. It is important to note that many alternative methods of
assessment have been introduced and increasingly adopted in a foreign language
classroom context in response to multiple criticisms of standardized language
assessment (Brown & Hudson, 1998; Coombe et al., 2012). On the other hand,
alternative assessment tools do not seem to be widely used in a KFL context. This
section discusses several options and issues in using alternative language assessment in a KFL teaching context with a focus on self-assessment, E-portfolio, and
role-plays.

7.6.1 Self-assessment

Among many possible assessment forms for evaluating student learning outcomes,
a self-assessment has been widely used as a cost-effective and time-efficient measurement tool (Ross, 1998; Ross, 2006). It has also gained substantial attention as

a potential means of facilitating learning by helping students to self-monitor their own language learning processes and progress against the standards or the course objectives, thereby enhancing learner autonomy (Butler & Lee, 2010). However, previous literature on self-assessment has shown that a commonly used off-task self-assessment, which is constructed by abstract and decontextualized can-do statements, often fails to reliably capture students' learning progress (Brown et al., 2014) and tends to be affected by student attitude and personality factors (Butler & Lee, 2006). On the contrary, an on-task self-assessment tool, which provides sample tasks along with statements to assist students to better evaluate their language performance, has been suggested as an alternative (Butler & Lee, 2006). It is thus recommended that self-assessment should be equipped with specific exemplifying tasks so as to be implemented as a beneficial tool for involving students in assessment of themselves and for enhancing interaction between teachers and students during instruction.

The National Standards for Korean (2012) and the Standards-Based College Curriculum for Korean Language Education in six levels developed by AATK (Cho et al., 2015) could be used as excellent resources for developing Korean self-assessments. However, level descriptors alone would make it difficult for either teachers or students to situate an individual performance in relation to the specific levels. For example, under Communication Standard 1.2 (Students understand and interpret written and spoken Korean on a variety of topics), one of the sample progress indicators (Grade 12) states,

> students summarize orally or in writing the content of articles or documentary films intended for native speakers of Korean, to discuss historical or contemporary issues (e.g., Korea's rapid economic growth, separation of family members in North and South Korea, etc.).

Typically, off-task self-assessment contains this level descriptor only, leaving students to decide whether or not they are able to perform this successfully, although they are not often assured of their judgments of self-evaluation. In contrast, students would feel better able to determine their level of success with an on-task self-assessment tool, allowing students to evaluate their performance after their completion of representative level-specific tasks. This will make students more aware of their goals and expectations, and better able to monitor and evaluate their learning progress. In this example, students could be asked to write a summary of a documentary about Korea's economic success and then receive feedback on their accuracy and coverage of the main points of content covered in the documentary by teachers. This will help them better judge their progress on this specific standard and understand the types and amount of assistance and effort needed to accomplish a given goal and standard. However, it will still be difficult for students and teachers to determine the level of students' progress towards the target goal based on a single task, and thus monitoring students' performance through multiple tasks in a longitudinal manner is still necessary to more reliably evaluate students' achievements on these standards. This will necessitate using the online portfolio system which is discussed in the following section.

7.6.2 E-portfolios

Recently, various online classroom management systems such as "Canvas" or "OnCourse" have been extensively used in secondary and tertiary education contexts. Such technological changes may lead to more active use of an E-portfolio as an alternative assessment tool in a KFL assessment situation. An E-portfolio refers to a purposeful online collection of students' works and allows language teachers to evaluate students' language samples based on specific criteria and students to reflect on those works, follow up on teachers' comments, and reload their updated samples. E-portfolios can also be constructed to represent multiple linguistic and situational contexts while making multimedia input and response formats possible (Shin, 2013). Teachers are thus able to create different folders to construct various tasks and to store students' performance along with teachers' feedback and scorings. Different tasks can be ordered and structured to reflect various levels across three communication modes: interpretive, presentational, and interpersonal in the E-portfolio system. For more detailed information and examples of E-portfolios, refer to Shin (2013).

Other than communicational language abilities, cultures and comparisons among the 5 Cs of language learning can also be integrated into and assessed in the portfolio system (Byon, 2007; Zapata, 2019). Byon (2007) demonstrated that students could gain insights into a particular aspect of Korean culture, minimizing their own stereotypes of Korean culture while enhancing their cross-cultural awareness as a result of completing their semester-long culture portfolio projects. Likewise, E-portfolios could make possible more project-based language learning (PBLL), in which students are engaged in authentic problem-solving tasks (Beckett & Miller, 2006), by allowing them to collect, select, and reflect their linguistic productions when they participate in various types of real-world tasks (Green, 2014). For example, Ko et al. (2015) designed and developed a "Digital Story-telling" project as a part of a PBLL-based curriculum for KFL classroom settings. This project has four steps: students are first introduced to previous samples and brainstorm their ideas with other students. Secondly, they write scripts in class while receiving feedback on them from their peers and a teacher. Thirdly, students construct their digital stories and practice their speech with other classmates with feedback from a teacher. Lastly, they show their digital presentation to the rest of class. Likewise, E-portfolios can be a useful platform to realize PBLL because students can receive both formative and summative feedback on their task performance throughout all stages of collaborative in-class and out-of-class activities.

7.6.3 Interactive role-plays

Currently, interactional competence (Kramsch, 1986), that is, the ability to participate in interaction, has been increasingly considered as important as the ability to produce and comprehend language accurately in the field of language assessment (Roever & Kasper, 2018). Nevertheless, many foreign language teachers, including KFL instructors, have difficulty in choosing or constructing appropriate assessment instruments to elicit interactional competence and rating rubrics to score students' performance on such tasks. Although the OPI implements the role-play tasks during the OPI interview, it is quite limited in that the interviewer always plays the role of questioner and the interviewee plays only the role of reporter or respondent. Such fixed role-plays might not be appropriate to assess interaction-involved pragmatic performances, including interactive listening and turn-management, which are essential to interactional competence in various speech act contexts (Galaczi & Taylor, 2018). Different role-play cards can be used to represent multiple situations in which students are asked to interact with each other or a teacher. Using role-play cards can help establish standardization of assessment practices while eliciting spoken interaction imitating naturally occurring talk. However, it is important to design rating criteria for assessing students' role-play performance and to let them be familiar with each aspect of the rubric before they are engaged in role-plays. Youn (2015) created the five rating domains (Content Delivery, Language Use, Sensitivity to Situation, Engaging with Interaction, and Turn Organization) on a scale of 1 to 3 points based on the Conversation Analysis (CA) findings to evaluate students' performance in role-play with a professor and a classmate in different situations. Although these rating categories were constructed for English role-plays, they can be easily adapted into Korean role-play situations. This rating rubric will help teachers to decide how well KFL students can choose linguistic expressions and take turns appropriately in conversations, depending on various speech acts and interlocutors. Meanwhile, teachers should be trained and calibrated on the rating rubrics to safeguard the reliability of their role-play scorings, which involves creating anchor samples and comparisons and discussions of scoring results with other teachers.

7.7 Conclusion

This chapter has addressed various issues in developing and using language assessment in a KFL context. The current large-scale standardized Korean language proficiency tests—TOPIK, the Korean SAT Subject Test, and the OPI—are introduced. Specific cautions were discussed for the development and use of Korean placement and achievement tests, particularly when students from different language backgrounds (heritage versus non-heritage Korean language learners) are mixed in the same classroom. The guidelines for developing classroom-based language assessment with specific Korean language samples were also provided to assist KFL teachers when they develop and use their own assessment tasks in a more reliable and valid manner. Finally, some alternative language assessment tools were suggested, including self-assessment, E-portfolios, and interactive role-plays, which could make classroom language learning more useful and meaningful to students.

Discussion questions

1. Compare your experience in taking or administering Korean language tests versus other foreign language tests. What are the similarities and differences you could identify?

2. What different test qualities should be examined for classroom-based and large-scale language tests?
3. What challenges do you expect to encounter, or have you encountered, while assessing both heritage and non-heritage Korean language learners in your classroom?
4. How would you respond to the needs of students who need to prepare for TOPIK or the Korean SAT Subject Test in your regular KFL classroom contexts?
5. If you have taught a Korean language course, take one sample item from your midterm or final exam, evaluate it based on the step-by-step guidelines in Section 7.4 and the practical tips in Section 7.5, and present a modified/improved version.

Acknowledgments

We would like to thank Dr Young-mee Yu Cho, Dr Mi Yung Park, Dr Seongyeon Ko, Dr Beomyong Choi, and other teachers from the KFL Pedagogy Textbook Manuscript Workshop at Harvard University for their valuable insights that helped us improve earlier versions of this manuscript. Any mistakes, however, are our own.

Notes

1 http://www.koreaherald.com/view.php?ud=20190120000128.
2 http://www.koreadailyus.com/students-no-longer-take-sat-korean-subject-test/.
3 We would like to thank the following universities for providing exam samples and granting permission to cite them: (in alphabetical order) Arizona State University, Indiana University, Northwestern University, University of Illinois at Urbana-Champaign, and University of Iowa.
4 The content of the phone message is reconstructed from a scene in the SBS TV drama "상속자들" ("The Heirs").
5 https://youtu.be/3ODmLmuIzTA.

References

Bachman, L.F., & Damböck, B. (2018). *Language assessment for classroom teachers.* Oxford: Oxford University Press.

Beckett, G.H., & Miller, P.C. (2006). *Project-based second and foreign language education: Past, present, and future.* Charlotte, NC: Information Age.

Brinton, D., Kagan, O., & Bauckus, S. (Eds.). (2008). *Heritage language education: A new field emerging.* Mahwah, NJ: Lawrence Erlbaum.

Brown, J.D., & Hudson, T. (1998). The alternatives in language assessment. *TESOL Quarterly, 32*(4), 653–675.

Brown, N.A., Dewey, D.P., & Cox, T.L. (2014). Assessing the validity of can-do statements in retrospective (Then-Now) self-assessment. *Foreign Language Annals, 47*(2), 261–285.

Butler, Y.G., & Lee, J. (2006). On-task versus off-task self-assessments among Korean elementary school students studying English. *The Modern Language Journal, 90*(4), 506–518.

Butler, Y.G., & Lee, J. (2010). The effects of self-assessment among young learners of English. *Language Testing, 27*(1), 5–31.

Byon, A.S. (2007). The use of culture portfolio project in a Korean culture classroom: Evaluating stereotypes and enhancing cross-cultural awareness. *Language, Culture and Curriculum, 20*(1), 1–19.

Carr, N.T. (2011). *Designing and analyzing language tests.* Oxford: Oxford University Press.

Cheng, L., & Fox, J. (2017). *Assessment in the language classroom.* London, UK: Palgrave.

Cho, Y., & Chun, H.C. (2015). Integrated assessment in a college level heritage curriculum in the United States. *Bilingual Research, 61,* 163–189.

Cho, Y., Kang, S., Kim, H., Lee, H., Wang, H., Kim, H.-Y., ... Suh, J. (2015). Overview. *The Korean Language in America, 19,* 153–177.

Coombe, C., Purmensky, K., & Davidson, P. (2012). Alternative assessment in language education. In C. Coombe, B. O'Sullivan, P. Davidson & S. Stoynoff (Eds.), *The Cambridge guide to language assessment* (pp. 147–163). Cambridge: Cambridge University Press.

Davidson, F., & Lynch, B.K. (2002). *Testcraft: A teacher's guide to writing and using language test specifications.* New Haven, CT: Yale University Press.

Galaczi, E., & Taylor, L. (2018). Interactional competence: Conceptualizations, operationalizations, and outstanding questions. *Language Assessment Quarterly, 15*(3), 219–236.

Green, A. (2012). Placement testing. In C. Coombe, B. O'Sullivan, P. Davidson, & S. Stoynoff (Eds.), *Cambridge guide to language assessment* (pp. 164–170). Cambridge, UK: Cambridge University Press.

Green, A. (2014). *Exploring language assessment and testing.* New York, NY: Routledge.

Kim, C., & Lee, J. (2014). Assessing Korean. In A. Kunnan (Ed.), *The companion to language assessment* (pp. 1–10). Hoboken, NJ: Wiley-Blackwell.

Kim, H.-S.H. (2002). Heritage and nonheritage learners of Korean: Sentence processing differences and their pedagogical implications. In K. Kondo-Brown & J.D. Brown (Eds.), *Teaching Chinese, Japanese and Korean heritage language students: Curriculum needs, materials, and assessment* (pp. 99–134). New York: Erlbaum.

Ko, K., Lee, S., Lee, M., Park, J., Chang, S.-E., Kim, M., & Kim, J. (2015, June). Incorporating project-based language learning (PBLL) to college-level KFL curriculum. *Workshop presented at the 20th annual meeting of American Association of Teachers of Korean.* Monterey, CA.

Kondo-Brown, K. (2005). Differences in language skills: Heritage language learner subgroups and foreign language learners. *The Modern Language Journal, 89*(4), 563–581.

Kondo-Brown, K. (2010). Curriculum development for advancing heritage language competence: Recent research, current practices, and a future agenda. *Annual Review of Applied Linguistics, 30,* 24–41.

Korean National Standards Task Force. (2012). *Standards for Korean language learning.* ACTFL.

Kramsch, C. (1986). From language proficiency to interactional competence. *Modern Language Journal, 70*(4), 366–372.

Lee, J.S., & Kim, H.Y. (2008). Heritage language learners' attitudes, motivations and instructional needs: The case of postsecondary Korean language learners. In K. Kondo-Brown & J.D. Brown (Eds.), *Teaching Chinese, Japanese and Korean heritage language students: Curriculum needs, materials, and assessment* (pp. 159–186). New York: Erlbaum.

Liskin-Gasparro, J.E. (2003). The ACTFL proficiency guidelines and oral proficiency interview: A brief history and analysis of their survival. *Foreign Language Annals, 36,* 484–490.

Long, A., Shin, S.-Y., Geeslin, K., & Willis, E. (2018). Does the test work? Evaluating a web-based language placement test. *Language Learning and Technology, 22,* 137–156.

Luoma, S. (2004). *Assessing speaking.* Cambridge: Cambridge University Press.

National Institute for International Education. (2019). Test details of the test of proficiency in Korean (TOPIK). Retrieved February 13, 2020 from http://www.topik.go.kr/usr/cmm/subLocation.do?menuSeq=2210101

Norris, J.M. (2006). The why (and how) of assessing student learning outcomes in college foreign language programs. *The Modern Language Journal, 90*(4), 576–583.

Ockey, G. (2009). Developments and challenges in the use of computer-based testing (CBT) for assessing second language ability. *The Modern Language Journal, 93,* 836–847.

Park, M., Choi, B., Kim, H., Yu, Y., & Pyun, D. (2015). Level 1 curriculum. *Korean Language in America, 19*(2), 179–182.

Proficiency Standards Division. (1999). *OPI 2000 Tester Certification Workshop.* Monterey: Defense Language Institute Foreign Language Center.

Roever, C., & Kasper, G. (2018). Speaking in turns and sequences: Interactional competence as a target construct in testing speaking. *Language Testing, 35*(3), 331–355.

Ross, J.A. (2006). The reliability, validity, and utility of self-assessment. *Practical Assessment, Research, and Evaluation, 11,* 1–13.

Ross, S. (1998). Self-assessment in second language testing: A meta-analysis and analysis of experiential factors. *Language Testing, 15,* 1–20.

Shin, S.-Y. (2013). Developing a framework for using E-portfolios as a research and assessment tool. *ReCALL, 25*(3), 359–372.

Shin, S.-Y., & Lee, H. (2014, June). Validating a semiadaptive web-based Korean placement test. *Paper presented at the 19th annual meeting of the American Association of Teachers of Korean (AATK),* Boston, MA.

Shin, S.-Y., & Lidster, R. (2017). Evaluating standard setting methods in an ESL placement testing context. *Language Testing, 34*(3), 357–381.

Sohn, S., & Shin, S.-K. (2007). True beginners, false beginners, and fake beginners: Placement strategies for Korean heritage speakers. *Foreign Language Annals, 40*(3), 407–418.

Surface, E., & Dierdorff, E. (2003). Reliability and the ACTFL oral proficiency Interview: Reporting indices of interrater consistency and agreement for 19 languages. *Foreign Language Annals, 36*(4), 507–519.

Swender, E. (Ed.). (1999). *ACTFL oral proficiency interview tester training material.* Yonkers, NY: ACTFL.

Thompson, G.L., Cox, T.L., & Knapp, N. (2016). Comparing the OPI and the OPIc: The effect of test method on oral proficiency scores and student preference. *Foreign Language Annals, 49,* 75–92.

Youn, S.J. (2015). Validity argument for assessing L2 pragmatics in interaction using mixed methods. *Language Testing, 32*(2), 199–225.

Zapata, G.C. (2019). L2 Spanish university students' perceptions of the pedagogical benefits of culture portfolios. *Language, Culture and Curriculum, 32*(1), 94–110.

손성옥. (2005). 영어권 학습자를 대상으로 한 한국어 능력 평가의 실제와 과제. 제*15*회 국제한국어교육학회 국제학술대회 발표집, 139–155. [Korean language assessment for English speakers: principles and practices. *Proceedings for the 15th International Conference on Korean Language Education*, 139–155.]

이효상. (2016). 대화분석과 한국어 교육의 융합: 학습자들의 대응표지 구사를 통해 보는 상호대응 능력 측정. 제*18*회 서울대 국어교육연구소 국제학술회의 발표집 335–345. [Convergence of conversation analysis and Korean language education: Measuring interactional competence through learners' usage of reactive tokens. *Proceedings for the 18th International Conference on Korean Language Education*, 335–345. Korean Language Education Research Institute, Seoul National University.]

8 KFL program building and professional development

Young-mee Yu Cho, Ahrong Lee, and Hye-Sook Wang

8.1 The development of KFL programs in North America

8.1.1 A brief history of Korean language programs

Historically, all foreign language programs have emerged from a particular socio-political milieu of the time, therefore, given 20th-century history, it is no surprise that Korean language education in the US was initiated in the 1940s by a handful of military contractors in the Cold War environment. Private NGOs and military contractors were only interested in language instruction with the narrow goal of US security in mind. For example, the University of Washington Korean program started as part of the Army Specialized Training Program in 1944. Before the 1960s, a handful of universities (e.g., Harvard in 1952, the University of Hawaii in 1946, the University of California at Berkeley in 1943) followed suit by offering courses on Korean language, history, literature, and culture. However, these early programs were by no means fully developed; some offered KFL courses, while others mostly concentrated on training a small number of Korea experts.

After a period of relative inactivity in the 1960s and 1970s,[1] the turning-point arrived in the mid-1980s through the early 1990s which saw the largest expansion. A number of factors played a key role during this phase of "first renaissance." Firstly, the remarkable economic development of South Korea raised the status and the visibility of the country, along with international events such as the 1986 Asian Games and the 1988 Seoul Summer Olympics. Secondly, some universities responded positively to the demographic changes on campus. A massive influx of Korean immigration to the US was recorded during the 1970s, initiated by the Immigration Act of 1965 and fueled by an unstable political atmosphere in Korea (e.g., the 18-year dictatorship of the Park regime). The children of these immigrants reached college age during the 1980s and the vast majority of students enrolled in language classes were heritage students from the Korean-American immigrant population. This trend continued until the beginning of the 21st century when *Hallyu*, "the Korean Wave," reached North America. Thirdly, academic interests in multilingualism and multiculturalism, as well as emerging foreign language policies of the US government, bolstered foreign language education, and the Korean language was certainly one of the beneficiaries. In addition to continuing immigration, globalization has resulted in a growing number

of Korean international students and transnationals. The political environment of
the hostility between the US and North Korea, coupled with America's alliance
with South Korea, is one of the compelling reasons for expanding Korean language programs. North Korean nuclear issues have been, and still are, an important motivator for learning Korean for national security at the Defense Language
Institute and other government agencies.

Most notably, one of the key contributing factors in the expansion of the
Korean language program is the systematic funding support from the Korea
Foundation (KF) since its establishment in 1991, especially for the creation of
faculty positions. KF has supported the creation of 123 faculty positions world-
wide from 1992 to 2016, of which 86 positions were created in North American
institutions.[2] It is not an overstatement to say that nearly all the major institutions that have a Korean program benefited from KF in one way or another at
some point in the development of their Korean programs.[3] The Academy of
Korean Studies also provides major funds for activities related to Korea, including sending lecturers to schools overseas. This program can best be used for
newly developing programs that desperately need an additional faculty member. While it is a temporary measure rather than a permanent solution, strategic use of this program might eventually lead to a regular faculty hiring, or at
least pave the way to such hiring by increasing student enrollment. Schools that
already have a strong infrastructure in Korean studies can benefit from applying for the Core University Program for Korean Studies by the Academy of
Korean Studies. In addition, US federal funding agencies (e.g., the Fulbright
Program, Title VI programs, the Language Flagship program) have proved to
be beneficial for Korean programs. The Fulbright Foreign Language Teaching
Assistant Program grant enables the awardees to receive a short-term teaching staff. A Title VI grant is typically awarded to an Asian/East Asian Studies
Center at which Korean faculty can be hired. Flagship programs funded by a
US Department of Defense are specifically designed to provide students with
opportunities to reach a professional level of Korean proficiency; for the past
16 years the University of Hawaii has been running a Korean MA Flagship program, while the University of Wisconsin-Madison started a new undergraduate
Korean Flagship program in 2018.

Against this historical backdrop, this chapter provides an overview of the current state and future prospects of KFL programs, curricular concerns, and professional development within the context of general foreign language education
in North America, as, for instance, exemplified in the four categories of K–12,
University, Government, and International Learning in Berbeco (2016).

8.1.2 The current status of KFL programs in higher education

Korean language education in 2018 has a very different look to that of 1988 or
even 1998. According to the MLA 2016 Report on foreign language enrollments
in higher education, Korean enrollments show the highest increase of 95% from
2006 to 2016, while Chinese and Japanese show a 2–5% increase and all the other

languages experienced decreases.[4] The Korean language is ranked as the 11th most popularly taught foreign language in the US, and the quantitative growth of KFL learners over the past three decades has caused a keen interest in KFL education as an academic discipline.

Not only has the number of US colleges and universities offering Korean courses dramatically increased, but many of them have also grown into full-fledged programs (Kim, 2017). According to the American Association of Teachers of Korean's (AATK henceforth) homepage, over 80 institutions in North America out of the 109[5] listed currently offer more than three years of Korean language courses, while 29 schools offer only two years of Korean language courses. Furthermore, approximately half of the schools listed also offer Korean content course(s) in addition to language courses.

Korean language programs in American institutions can be divided into three main groups based on their status with respect to the program history and the number of faculty and course offerings: 1) newly established programs; 2) developing programs; and 3) developed programs. Newly established programs usually have one full-time faculty member who runs the program single-handedly as program director or is assisted by one or more part-time faculty members. They typically first offer two or three years of Korean language instruction on a regular basis. Some of these programs barely sustain the status quo even after many years due to a lack of support from their own institutions, as well as the inability to bring in external grants. Developing programs are those that are seeking expansion to full Korean studies programs beyond language courses. Programs in this group typically offer a three-year sequence in the Korean language on a regular basis, taught by at least two language specialists. Many of these programs also offer a course on Korean culture or literature. Developed programs are those that already have a fully established curriculum with a major or minor degree in Korean language and/or Korean studies in place, have two or more language faculty members, and offer several non-language courses (e.g., history, literature, culture) taught by a Korean studies faculty. These programs either already have a graduate program (e.g., University of Hawaii, University of California at Los Angeles) or seek an opportunity to expand the program to include a graduate program.

Alternatively, these programs can be categorized into three models, simply based on whether they confer major or minor degrees in Korean, and from a perspective of program goals. In Section 8.3, we will give concrete examples based in the categorization given here.[6]

Model 1: train prospective students to achieve an advanced level of proficiency in the Korean language with a special focus on practical language training.
Model 2: allow prospective students obtain an academic degree (i.e., major or minor) in Korean language or Korean studies.
Model 3: in addition to a robust undergraduate program, also offer a graduate program in Korean studies with the goal of producing the next generation of Korean studies scholars.

8.1.3 The current status of KFL programs in K–12 education

While we have detailed information on college-level KFL programs, it is beyond the scope of this chapter to delve into K–12 KFL programs throughout North America for several reasons. Firstly, K–12 programs are not widely available enough to derive generalizations regarding their structure, content, teacher profiles, and other aspects. Secondly, K–12 programs are much more restricted by the parameters of each state and local school district. Therefore, it is not possible to chronicle a pattern of program development and suggest overall program evaluation measures, as we do for college-level courses.

As formal instruction, KFL at the high school level has been steadily increasing, from 60 schools in 2007 to over 100 schools in 2016 across the US, while it is still quite limited at elementary- and lower secondary-levels. According to the homepage of the Foundation for Korean Language and Culture in USA (한국어진흥재단), a total of 114 K–12 schools are reported to offer Korean language classes as of August 2018.[7] Among these, 55 schools (almost 50%) are located in the state of California, 22 schools in New York, and 8 schools in New Jersey, totaling 85 schools (75%) concentrated in three states. This, of course, is not surprising given a strong presence of the Korean communities in these locations.[8] Besides California and New York/New Jersey, Texas and Washington rank next, each with six K–12 schools offering Korean language.

Other notable facts can be summarized as follows. Firstly, half of these schools are high schools (56 out of 114: 49%), followed by elementary schools (27 out of 114: 24%), and middle schools (18 out of 114: 16%).[9] Secondly, at least one school in 16 states (i.e., AZ, CA, CO, GA, HI, IL, KY, MD, MI, MN, NY, NJ, OH, TX, VA, WA) is currently providing Korean language instruction at the K–12 level. Eight states have only one school, five of which are high schools.

The focus of Korean language and culture education in America has been on higher education, and consequently less attention has been paid to K–12 schools. However, it has become more important than ever to connect primary and secondary education to university programs for better articulation between the two. An advanced or superior level of Korean language proficiency beyond exploring heritage and personal interests is expected for students who wish to use Korean for academic purposes (e.g., advance to graduate schools) and/or business purposes (e.g., find a job in Korea or in multinational corporations). Often, four years of Korean language training in college is not sufficient to accomplish academic and career goals. Exposure to the Korean language, either as a heritage language or a legitimate foreign language, from early in the education system is not only meaningful to heritage students for their personal pursuits but also beneficial to non-heritage students in the 21st-century globalized world.

Even though the current state of affairs regarding K–12 Korean language education is not as robust as that of the tertiary level, it is encouraging to note a modest but steady increase in schools offering Korean language, and serious suggestions have been made to improve the picture. For instance, Cheon (2017) addresses the lack of coordination between a small number of public K–12 Korean programs and over 1,400 Korean community schools and suggests enhanced teacher training workshops as a way to pool the available resources together. Chun and Cho (2018) identify the paucity of qualified K–12 Korean teachers and propose a locally relevant KFL education curriculum for teacher certification that ultimately builds communication between university faculty and K–12 teachers.

8.2 National standards and local concerns

8.2.1 National standards for Korean language education

Since the mid-1990s in the US, there has been a call for action towards designing national standards in the field of foreign language education. Initially funded by the US Department of Education and the National Endowment for the Humanities, "The National Standards in Foreign Language Education Project" was a collaborative effort between the American Council on the Teaching of Foreign Language (ACTFL) and many associations of foreign language teachers. The first set of languages are French, German, Italian, Spanish, Portuguese, classical languages (Latin and Greek), Russian, Chinese, and Japanese, while the second set includes Arabic, Korean, and Scandinavian languages. In 2015, American Sign Language and Hindi were added.

Standards for Korean Language Learning (2012), a collaborative effort between the AATK and a group of K–12 teachers, was built on the framework of *Standards for Foreign Language Learning in the 21st Century* (2006).[10] It is based on three core assumptions: (1) competence in more than one language is an educational goal; (2) all students can be successful language learners; and (3) language and culture education is part of the core curriculum. On the foundation is laid out a set of clearly articulated content and performance standards for an idealized K–16 Korean language program. On the content side, the five main goals of Communication, Cultures, Connections, Comparisons, and Communities are comprised of specific sub-goals.

It is not an overstatement to say that *Standards for Korean Language Learning* marks a milestone in KFL education by placing KFL in the proper context of foreign language education in North America. It has served as a blueprint for the implementation of the extended sequence of study for the full K–16 range. Although we have yet to see the full sequencing from kindergarten to college in the real education landscape, these standards are designed to ensure the effective transition from primary to secondary, and secondary to post-secondary levels. For the past several years the document has facilitated new curriculum development and the improvement of existing programs. As the first KFL learning standards that provide a common framework for all KFL shareholders, it has begun to play an important role in areas such as teacher education, professional development, curricula design, and KFL pedagogical research. While it establishes the common goals for KFL learners of all backgrounds, it specifically acknowledges the educational challenges of the mixed group of heritage and non-heritage learners. Therefore, it has a good potential for the large Korean heritage language community in North America; as a guide for reflecting on language maintenance, it could provide a missing link in connecting Korean as a Heritage Language (KHL) curricula with formal K–16 programs. There are more than 1,400 Korean community weekend schools through the US (Overseas Koreans Foundation, 2007) with over 10,000 students. Unfortunately, however, there is little coordination between Korean community schools and the formal educational sector of K–16 programs, and we have yet to see concerted efforts to enhance KFL/KHL instruction (Sohn et al., 2007).

Korean instruction at the university level is geographically widespread, and most major universities in North America offer KFL from elementary to advanced levels. Since the K–12 level is a feeder system to the university programs, there should be meaningful interactions between the two components in the education system. Both learners and teachers are mutually connected through teacher certification, teacher training, testing (such as the SAT II in Korean), and shared teaching materials. For instance, K–12 public schools often hire Korean teachers who have been certified by either obtaining university degrees or individually obtaining credits in the required fields from local universities (e.g., Stonybrook University, Rutgers University).

Another remarkable change to note is a demographic shift in the learner profile. Unlike at the beginning stage of KFL instruction in North America, for the past decade non-heritage learners and international students from diverse cultures and language backgrounds have been rapidly increasing across the continent. In many cases non-heritage learners are no longer the majority of the class, particularly at the elementary level. Given the current concentration of KFL instruction in universities, it made most sense to address the highest need and to focus on the area of the broadest impact—that is, producing a coherent and comprehensive curriculum based on National Standards. The special issue of *Korean Language in America* (vol. 19, no. 2, 2015), entitled *College Korean Curriculum Inspired by National Standards for Korean*, is a result of the coordinated efforts by 25 KFL faculty members from 20 universities. The document begins with the curricula overview and framework. It spans seven levels, from Novice to Advanced High (Levels 1–6 and Heritage Level). The overview is a progress map of learning objectives defined by the 5 Cs on the one hand, and layered by ACTFL proficiency guidelines on the other, that roughly correspond to years of college-level instruction. Heritage Level straddles the first and the second levels, reflecting a common practice of covering two years of non-heritage curriculum in a year in most collegiate heritage curricula.

Just as *Standards for Korean Language Learning* functions as a blueprint for the college curriculum, this explicitly spelled-out curriculum is a detailed blueprint for developing Korean textbooks and teaching materials. It is a useful template for revising, expanding, and evaluating an existing curriculum as well as for creating new courses and textbooks.[11] There are a few follow-up projects in progress (e.g., designing level-specific textbooks, developing assessment tools). Recently, researchers have started to explore the influences of standards for language programs, in particular for assessment and language learning (Cox et al., 2018).

8.2.2 *Locally relevant curriculum design*

The majority of college-level programs consist of a multi-level language curriculum that is designed to satisfy the learning goals of foreign language proficiency and general humanities requirements, namely, "Korean for a general academic purpose." In contrast, "Korean for Specific Purposes" (KSP) by definition is created by local needs with specific results in mind, as illustrated by such examples as university-level business Korean, Korean for diplomacy, and Korean for students of hospitality (Trace et al., 2015). There is some interest in developing Korean Translation and Business and Professional Korean curricula at the tertiary level, but such courses are closely connected to specific fields of interest (e.g., Entertainment, Finance, Teaching English, Healthcare, and Government) and are hard to generalize within the framework of KFL education.

Another area of critical needs in KFL pedagogy concerns both K–12 and college KFL. Any pedagogy program needs a coherent curriculum dealing with Korean language, applied linguistics, KFL education, Korean culture, and teaching practicum. Moreover, an ideal curriculum contextualizes KFL pedagogy within the proper disciplinary areas (foreign language teaching, Korean studies, humanities, etc.) on the one hand, and creates "content connections" on the other, with an ultimate goal of enabling students to explore personal interests in the culture on their path from "communicative competence" to "symbolic competence" (Kramsch, 2011).

Even across different localities and diverse educational levels, a set of common learning goals of KFL education emerges: (1) understand the theoretical and practical application of KFL instruction within SLA; (2) use identifiable principles in order to design lesson plans and activities; (3) understand the practicalities of being a classroom teacher; (4) understand the history and current issues in language teaching; and (5) acquire teaching techniques for developing overall language and cultural proficiency and in specific skill areas (Chun & Cho, 2018). These goals, when properly implemented, will successfully address KFL-specific issues of heritage/non-heritage learners, grammar instruction, proper incorporation of sociolinguistic and cultural aspects as well as properly aligning KFL instruction in the professional context of general foreign language education. In addition, K–12 teachers benefit from hands-on guidelines, such as "Program standards for the preparation of foreign language teachers" (ACTFL, 2013) and "Teacher Effectiveness for Language Learning (TELL) Project," adopted by each school district or state, according to local concerns. Korean teachers learn to align themselves with other foreign language teachers, in particular with those in less commonly taught languages in the local school system.

8.3 Next stage of program building

8.3.1 *Degree programs*

A quick study of the development history of Korean programs tells us that there were times when growth took place at a fast pace and there were times when growth was slower, influenced by various internal and external factors at the time. As we have seen, over the course of eight decades since the first Korean language instruction began in the US, the number of schools that have Korean programs has steadily increased. However, the recognition of KFL as an academic discipline, distinct from traditional Korean language education, conceived as "Korean for Korean Native Speakers," has taken more than four decades to be established. Fortunately, a strong institutional presence of KFL programs in Korea,[12] North America, and elsewhere in the world, gives us an opportunity to reassess program articulation beyond immediate classroom needs such as securing teaching staff and teaching materials. While no-one questions the quantitative growth, it is time to focus on qualitative development of curricular content and program cohesion of KFL as a Less Commonly Taught Language (Gor & Vatz, 2009).

Now we will analyze college-level Korean programs in North America along the three models we suggested in Section 8.1.2. We determine that half of the institutions listed in the AATK website are still at the initial stage of offering lower level KFL courses (precursor to Model 1), while the other half aims to train students to achieve an advanced level of proficiency. Our data on 60 major universities that offer a 3–5-year sequence of language instruction[13] show that 50 universities belonging to Model 2 offer an academic degree. Nine institutions offer a minor in Korean only (sometimes as part of Asian Studies), while 24 universities offer an Asian Studies major with a concentration in Korean. Only seven universities specifically provide a Korean Major and Minor. The remaining ten universities offer multi-level Korean language courses without degree or certificate programs (Model 1), where KFL courses are often conceptualized either as one of the Less Commonly Taught Languages or as add-on service courses for related disciplines. The most common model is the one embedded in (East) Asian Studies, and a few programs belong to a larger unit of Modern Languages. Only a handful of universities have active doctoral programs that produce Korean Studies specialists (Model 3).[14]

Undoubtedly, the current status reflects big progress when compared to the situation in the 1990s. What is notable is the three stages of program development: 1) offering multi-level language courses without a degree program; 2) offering a Korean minor; and 3) offering a Korean major. Even with limited resources, about two-thirds of the 60 universities have established major or minor programs beyond an unstructured array of language and content courses over the past two decades. While a Korean minor essentially contributes to stabilizing language course offerings, a Korean major could not be conceptualized without a clear articulation of program goals, articulated in parallel to the other East Asian majors. It is instructive to note that all institutions with only a minor in Korean offer Chinese and Japanese majors where the language program is well-developed and integrated into culture courses. Obviously, a Korean major is the next logical step in program development in these institutions.

Now we will illustrate how it is possible to establish a Korean major in relatively newer KFL programs, even without abundant faculty positions, once a well-articulated curricular map is followed. Through the map one can gauge the degree of language–content connection and determine whether or not the language program is well-developed and integrated into culture and the rest of the Korean Studies program.

Firstly, the Korean Major within Asian & Middle Eastern Studies at Duke University exemplifies how a relatively small program can offer a coherent yet flexible degree program that requires ten courses (3–6 language courses and 3–7 culture courses). By stipulating levels of language courses (all in Intermediate and beyond, and two at the 300 level or above), it ensures the desired level of minimum language proficiency. In addition, the course offerings in culture comprise not only Korean literature, sociolinguistics, religion, and cinema but also Inter-Asian or Asian-American fields, thus making organic connections with other components in the department.

A slightly different example, the Korean Major at Rutgers, the State University of New Jersey, newly established in September 2018, sets the following program goals of acquisition of in-depth knowledge of the Korean language and culture within the larger context of East Asia. The broad goals focus on what students will be prepared to do with the credential: 1) acquisition of linguistic/cultural competency needed for post-graduate study or employment; 2) ability to demonstrate oral, reading, and written proficiency in Korean; and 3) development of critical skills in analyzing and interpreting literary and cultural texts. The program goals are closely connected with an evaluative matrix in such a way as to measure the students' linguistic and content competency directly, and to indirectly assess program robustness through such means as enrollment/completion rates, admission to graduate programs, teaching evaluations, peer reviews, student surveys, focus groups, and job placement data (Ross, 2009).

The development paths taken by a number of universities are easy to follow: from an introductory language program to a multi-level KFL sequence (Model 1) and then towards Model 2 (a Korean minor often requiring six language courses and a Korean major requiring 12 courses of language and content courses). Whereas Model 3 is not a realistic goal for many universities, Model 2 is a reachable and worthwhile step many institutions could strive to achieve once a multi-level language program is established.

8.3.2 *Program evaluation and curricular articulation*

Once the program goals are articulated, it is imperative to implement a set of evaluative tools to measure how much the needs of a program are met. There are a range of methodologies available, from simply generating tangible outcomes (e.g., test scores, course completion rates) to more comprehensive, qualitative methods of interpretation. Depending on the circumstances of a particular evaluation process, the scope and the goal of evaluation will differ. Sometimes top-down measures are needed to evaluate the program against the goals of general foreign language education, liberal arts education, National Standards, and others, while bottom-up measures are called for in order to fine-tune the language program and address locally relevant and region-specific needs of diverse stakeholders (students, teachers, curriculum developers, administrators, the department, the institution, policy-makers, parents, and community, etc.).

Improving the coherence of a KFL curriculum is important within a language program, but we should consider the contemporary issue of the so-called "High School Challenge" in foreign language education. According to Egnatz (2016, p. 67), there is a big gap between K–12 language programs and college programs. Only 15% of public elementary schools in the US offer FL programs, compared to 90% of elementary schools that offer foreign language instruction in Europe. Therefore, for the majority of US students, second-language learning begins in high school. Although 91% of high schools offer world language courses, only 41% of high school students enroll. Moreover, less than 1% of high school students study Arabic, Chinese, Farsi, Japanese, Korean, Russian, or Urdu (US Dept. of Education).

It is well-known that several years of foreign language education in K–12 and community schools are not properly acknowledged at the college level, and many university students are placed in elementary courses despite their prior FL education. In order to achieve better articulation (transition between levels of study) between secondary and post-secondary FL education, student assessment in high school should be aligned to that of the university student learning outcomes— namely, reaching the goal of culturally appropriate, meaningful communication with target language speakers. Students should be given comprehensive input to achieve communicative goals (articulated in the *World Readiness Standards*) and the assessment should focus on what they *can do* in the language (following Integrative Performance Assessment), rather than on traditional multiple-choice exams. Some innovative ways are proposed by a number of scholars working on the articulation issue (Latoja, 2001; Lally, 2001; Barrette & Paesani, 2004): 1) aligning the FL curricula between high schools and universities through local collaborative projects; 2) instituting mandatory entrance and exit requirements; and 3) using the National Standards as a guide. In addition, college-level placement has been adopting a more personalized approach that consists of interviews, essay writing, and communicative tasks.

For KFL programs in higher education, program evaluation is one of the most important tools to ensure curricular articulation. Before conducting an evaluation, decisions have to be made in three areas. Firstly, determine the audiences for the evaluation (e.g., the board of directors of the university, the dean of the college, the department chair, the department faculty). Secondly, identify specific areas for the evaluation (e.g., teacher effectiveness, teacher satisfaction, placement and achievement tests, adequacy of KFL curriculum, teaching methods and materials, course development and delivery, faculty structure). Finally, decide on the kind of evaluation data (whether qualitative or quantitative) (e.g., interviews with faculty and students, student evaluations, class observation, test results, teacher self-report, focus group meetings). For instance, the KFL program at Rutgers University is required to satisfy the following three assessment criteria: 1) is there a clearly articulated plan for program assessment?; 2) is it clear how the program learning goals are achieved?; and 3) is it clear how the program learning goals are sustainably assessed? On the practical level, an assessment plan has been developed on the basis of outcome (Brindley, 1998, 2001), and assessment data have been collected and analyzed in order to develop plans for addressing areas of concern. Then, clear and appropriate benchmarks (e.g., the 6th semester of KFL learning) were designed to gauge student achievement. Finally, assessment tools are reviewed periodically to ensure consistency and improvement over time.

Based on recommendations by Kiely (2006), Watanabe et al. (2009) and Norris (2016), we suggest six useful ways an evaluation could be employed to address local concerns: 1) evaluate how the program works and what the learning goals of the program are; 2) evaluate the program against other language programs in the same unit; 3) understand the value of the program in the institution; 4) enhance the program accountability through explicit assessment tools; 5) contextualize KFL education within larger educational goals; and 6) get the program accredited or create a minor/major.

8.4 KFL faculty

8.4.1 KFL faculty profile

Growth of a Korean language program necessitates hiring of teaching staff. Naturally, the sheer number of Korean language instructors has increased over the past few decades. A glimpse into job opening data in KFL helps us get a sense of how demanding the field has been. During the academic year of 2017–2018, 32 job opening announcements were made through the AATK listserv and website. Similar openings of 30 positions were made during the previous academic year. The vast majority of these openings look for language teachers at the lecturer/instructor level.

Despite such quantitative growth, however, the status of the faculty does not paint a rosy picture. According to Wang (2014, 2018), the majority of Korean language teachers are woman lecturers in their 40s and 50s from South Korea,[15] with over 10 years of teaching experience, holding a doctoral degree in either Applied Linguistics/Second Language Acquisition (61%) or Theoretical Linguistics (24%), whose degrees were earned from an American higher institution. Fewer than 20 universities[16] have professorial positions in the Korean language, while the majority (i.e., nearly 70%) rely on contractual faculty running the programs (i.e., senior lecturer, lecturers/instructors), reflecting a prevalent view that foreign language education is hardly considered an academic discipline worthy of tenure-track positions. One encouraging aspect is that while a good number of these faculty members are not tenure-track or tenured professors, many of them, unlike in other foreign language programs, hold PhDs in linguistics, language education, or related fields. The data also capture a notable change in the specialty of the KFL faculty over time. While those with theoretical linguistic backgrounds (e.g., syntax, morphology, phonology, semantics) have decreased, those with Applied Linguistics, Second Language Acquisition, and Foreign Language Education backgrounds have been increasing. The field has also started to produce East

Asian Studies or Korean Studies specialists in more recent years. In particular, the University of Hawaii, the largest Korean program in the nation, has been producing KFL specialists, and their active presence in the field is strongly visible. However, as teacher education at the graduate level in general for Korean teachers is not widely available, the AATK has assumed the role of KFL faculty training at its annual conferences and professional development workshops as well as through a number of collaborative projects.

8.4.2 Faculty training venues

Korean language teachers, especially those teaching in colleges and universities, receive their training internally at their own institutions and externally through professional organizations. Wang (2018) reports that 75% of the respondents in her survey answered that they participate in language pedagogy workshop in their institutions. Of these, 42% do so once per semester/quarter and 26% more than twice per semester/quarter. Also, 80% of the respondents answered that they attend workshops outside of their institutions; of these, 60% do so once a year and 34% once per semester/quarter—an encouraging sign for the KFL field.

While teachers get their training readily at their institutions, AATK, as the sole organization for Korean language teachers of K–16 in North America, has also been a venue for teacher training since its inception in 1994. One of its main missions and activities specified on its homepage is to "host annual workshops for professional development" and "encourage the development and demonstration of instructional materials, teaching methods, and curricula".[17] Its annual meetings devote the first half of the three-day conference to pedagogical hands-on workshops centering around the conference theme of each year (e.g., Korean Language Assessment, Integrating Technology, Global Competence for Diverse Learners, Diverging Korean Language Across Boundaries).

Given AATK's role in faculty training that exclusively focuses on KFL matters, a new direction could be considered for more effective workshops. For instance, novice and experienced teachers could be placed into different components of a workshop. It has been shown that pre-service and novice teachers are amenable to change as a result of instruction and professional development, whereas experienced teachers are already well-grounded and more resistant to change (Macdonald et al., 2001). Also, thematic workshops run by specialists could be systematically implemented to enhance expertise. Organization-wide needs analysis will provide insightful guidelines for further discussion.

8.5 Professional development

8.5.1 Definition and forms

It is commonly recognized that teachers are among the most essential and fundamental elements in foreign language education, and professional development should be designed to understand the complex process of learning to teach

(Freeman, 1989, 2002). For instance, successful implementation of *National Standards for Learning Korean* into the KFL curriculum and the further development of KFL programs in North America would not have been possible without the teachers' ability to understand the framework and willingness to implement it. In order for teachers to be equipped with the competence and expertise that can lead to building and maintaining a successful language program, continuing self-development or (re)education is indispensable. Indeed, many researchers in the field of language education underscore the importance of teacher training and development for the long-term progress not only of teachers, but also for the success of the language programs themselves.

The terms *teacher training* and *teacher development* are sometimes used interchangeably in education literature, but they can be differentiated; while teacher training refers to activities that provide "trainable" skills or knowledge to a specific group of teachers within a specific period of time, teacher development involves career-long processes in both pre- and in-service programs designed to enable teachers to enhance their expertise and commitment to high-quality education (see Freeman, 1989 for detailed distinctions). Professional development, then, is a superordinate concept that encompasses both training and development. Thus, professional development includes participation in workshops at conferences for Korean teachers on specific themes that may interest them (e.g., how to build an online course, how to incorporate Korean popular culture products into the classroom), as well as the lifelong discipline to increase self-awareness of their performance as language educators (e.g., how to improve understanding of individual learners, of teaching, of themselves as teachers).

Various forms of language teacher professional development have been proposed since the early 1990s to enhance teacher competence and to address their diverse needs. For instance, Diaz-Maggioli (2003) offered six strategies: peer coaching, study groups, dialog journals, professional development portfolios, mentoring, and participatory practitioner research. Similarly, Richards and Farrell (2005) proposed eleven ways to educate teachers, including workshops, self-monitoring, teacher support groups, keeping a teaching journal, peer observation, teaching portfolios, analyzing critical incidents, case analysis, peer coaching, team teaching, and action research. In the field of KFL education, past proposals include workshops, lectures, peer supervision, mentor supervision, open-classes, peer discussions, and self-reflection and research (Baek, 1991; Choi, 2013).[18]

8.5.2 Pre-service teacher training

Previous studies on professional development in the field of language teacher education revolve primarily around training in-service teachers on the premise that they have completed the mandatory subject-matter curriculum in a formal setting. Due to a rather short immigration history and the subsequent scarcity of qualified teachers, however, most K–12 Korean schools in North America in the past have employed teachers who, as a minimum qualification, hold a bachelor's degree (in any field) and have native proficiency in Korean. Fortunately, with the recent growth in KFL, the importance of KFL teacher expertise and professional development has begun to be noticed. While the emphasis has been primarily for novice teacher trainees, the curricula established in the past decade also play a crucial role in professional development for both pre- and in-service teachers in North America.

The passage of the Korean Education Act in 2005 in Korea has ensured the production and promotion of qualified teachers via the Korean Language Certificate issued by the Ministry of Culture, Sports and Tourism. Teachers can either earn a degree in Korean education as a foreign language or complete mandatory coursework followed by the examination administered by the National Institute of the Korean Language. Although there is regional variation (see Section 8.2.3), more or less equivalent training seems to be needed for KFL teacher certification in North America. Currently, certification programs are limited to California, New York, and New Jersey, regions of dense Korean population. Unless the infrastructure for developing a curriculum for KFL teacher education can readily be set up using local resources, KFL teachers often lack opportunities for formal training, with the result of Korean courses available only in non-public sectors (i.e., community schools, weekend schools, religious facilities, etc.). Promoting Korean courses in public schools, with the requisite professional preparation, should be a long-term goal for KFL in North America. But, in practice, schools often implement teacher training programs under a cooperative format using materials already available in Korea. In fact, a number of universities and government organizations in Korea offer lectures on mandatory subject matter that are available online for pre-service teachers. In this way, core disciplines can be taught remotely, while special training programs centered on the educational practices of their country of assignment help resolve issues that may arise from discrepancies in linguistic and cultural backgrounds among teachers and learners.

An example of this kind of design for teacher training is found in Toronto, Canada, introduced in fall 2017 at the University of Toronto–Ontario Institute for Studies in Education (OISE), as a joint effort from the Korean Education Centre in Toronto at the Consulate General of Korea and the Language Education Institute (LEI) at Seoul National University. Trainees in this non-degree certificate program hosted at the School of Continuing Education at OISE are required to complete 40 hours of online lectures provided by LEI on the theoretical fundamentals of teaching and learning KFL, attend 38 hours of lectures focused on the practical components and the application of academic knowledge in the classroom, and observe 12 hours of KFL classroom instruction from K–12 through university-level in the area. Five KFL faculty members from local universities apply their respective expertise in the 14-week-long curriculum, concentrating on varied teaching methodologies with hands-on teaching materials and real-life experience with local students. Upon completion of the program, one-year teaching opportunities at community classrooms are given to those who earned the highest scores, which are intended to serve as a stepping-stone to more concrete teaching positions.

The combination of online materials from language source country and local resources can be tailored according to varied circumstances and needs in each of the states and provinces, as long as both academic knowledge and experiential training components are included in the program. The US National Association for Korean Schools (NAKS) started a program with a similar design in 2011 in coordination with the Digital Seoul Culture Arts University in Korea, aimed at enhancing teacher expertise and competence in KFL education in America. A common challenge is to establish a system in which teacher trainees who are equipped with requisite knowledge and skills can be led onto a solid career path. In order to build a thriving and long-lasting program, public teacher certification should be developed with the local authority and appropriately integrated into the curriculum.

8.5.3 In-service teacher training

Recent studies have reported on the perceptions of KFL teachers as to the utility of re-education, irrespective of their educational background and formal training. And the institutional perspective concurs with teachers' demand for continuous training. In view of constant changes in pedagogical paradigms, KFL instructors in most schools at the K–12 and collegiate levels today are expected, if not required, to keep up-to-date on current trends in delivery methods (online, blended, flipped-classroom), language for specific purposes (business Korean, academic Korean), lesson plans, and so on. A number of academic institutions and government organizations in KFL education now offer programs for training Korean language educators, under various formats, via regular courses, short-term workshops, and a range of specialized academic activities (e.g., 2018 Boston University's STARTALK Online Korean Teacher Training).[19]

The most commonly offered and widely preferred form of professional development activity is in the form of a workshop that responds to immediate needs within a short period of time. And, as expected, the results of several needs analyses and surveys conducted among KFL teachers indicate that teachers find workshops to be the most effective and useful. Depending on the focus of individual instructors and the context of their teaching environment, the priorities for workshop themes vary slightly, and can be quite comprehensive. Im et al. (2013) show that teachers registered with the Washington Association for Korean Schools expressed a need for further training that concentrates on developing class activities, understanding students, planning lessons, reconstruction of teaching materials, techniques to make students concentrate on class, knowledge of Korean, technical support, and English proficiency. Approximately 80% of the respondents are under the age of 50, who, per the authors' remarks, experienced student-centered learning, task-based learning, and/or activity-based learning during their own K–12 education in the 1980s and 1990s in Korea. Moreover, many of the teachers did not major in a relevant field in language education nor do they hold a teaching certificate. Thus, these teachers are highly motivated to make use of opportunities to improve their knowledge and skills. Similarly, other needs analyses revealed that KFL teachers requested training opportunities that focus on developing class activities, establishment of professional groups, delivery of cultural components, and reconstruction of teaching materials with multimedia materials and innovative applications of technology (Bang, 2016; Cheon, 2017; Sohn et al., 2007). Overall, in-service teachers recognize the necessity of, and articulate a desire for, continuing self-development so that they can perform better with updated pedagogical methods and effective teaching materials.

It should also be noted that there is a gap between pre-service teacher education and in-service teacher professional development. In closing this gap while updating their professional knowledge and skills, teachers can take part in various activities such as workshops, team teaching, and action research. The teacher training program for novice teachers mentioned above is in use at annual workshops at the NAKS. The aim of teacher education is to encourage experience, and teacher education will need to support new relationships between new and experienced teachers.

Whether for pre-service or in-service teachers, the impact of education programs and professional development on beliefs and instructional practices is known to be enormous. Research on the impact of teacher professional development holds several pedagogical implications for Korean language educators: 1) a pressing need for the acquisition of innovative instructional strategies and techniques; 2) in-depth understanding of the student learning process; and 3) growing awareness of collegial communication and collaboration (teacher learning communities) for best practice standards. In addition to the impact on individual teachers, professional development will benefit the institutions, as the students can also be supported by the new teaching methods adopted by the instructor. It cannot be emphasized enough that social and institutional context plays a significant role in teacher education. Because individual teachers, due to time constraint and workload, may not be able to engage in teacher-initiated, self-directed professional development, institutional support for professional development is all the more essential in keeping KFL teachers pedagogically up-to-date and culturally competent.

8.6 Conclusion

This chapter has provided an overview of the current state and future prospects of KFL programs, curricular concerns, program evaluation, and professional development within the context of FL education in North America. The past two decades or so have witnessed remarkable growth in KFL programs, particularly at the university level. Such rapid growth has been accompanied by collaborative efforts by KFL educators through AATK projects. Such an approach is useful as a conceptual tool for organizing KFL curricula, and helpful as an objective evaluative measure. The next stage of KFL program development concerns program cohesion and setting program goals. In order to be taken seriously as an independent discipline beyond its role as a service program, it is imperative to promote the Korean major and minor within the department and to align rigorous program evaluation with curricular articulation.

Having identified KFL instructors as the key component in the success of a language program, we argue for the need for structured and sustainable systems for professional development that help teachers to effectively respond to changes in the educational environment by acquiring knowledge and strategies in curriculum design, student needs, technology, cultural competency, and other emerging issues.

Discussion questions[20]

1. Imagine you have been asked to design a new course or a curriculum in the area where a special need has been identified (e.g., KSP courses, multiliteracies curricula). Discuss the content and the structure of your contribution in a program that you are familiar with.
2. Design one learning scenario based on *Standards for Korean Language Learning* (2012) for one specific level you are familiar with.
3. What are the best ways to measure the effectiveness of a language program? Make suggestions based on a program you are familiar with.
4. According to the program evaluation rubric of Weir and Roberts (1994: 134), classroom observations should be constructed along the following categories: Teacher Belief, Teacher Abilities, Teacher Practices, Student Behaviors, and Student Learnings. Name a list of concrete procedures (e.g., interviews, questionnaires, unit tests) that you recommend for each category.
5. What do you believe to be the characteristics of "an ideal KFL teacher" in the level you are most familiar with?
6. What conditions are needed to support teachers to become engaged in professional development?
7. To what extent are there opportunities for teachers in your context to engage in teacher education, and what are the potential challenges in pursuing teacher-directed initiatives in professional development?
8. What are the theme(s) and the structure of a workshop that you want to organize and/or participate in?

Appendix A

Korean Programs in Universities in Canada (N = 12)

	School	Degree	Number of instructors	Number of courses offered	Province
(1) Programs with KFL courses only	Carleton University	N/A	2 (part-time)	Korean languages—3 levels	Ontario
	George Brown College	N/A	1 (part-time)	Korean languages—2 levels	Ontario
	Seneca College	N/A	5 (all part-time)	Korean languages—4 levels	Ontario
	University of Manitoba	N/A	1 (part-time)	Korean Language—1 level	Manitoba
	University of Winnipeg	N/A	1 (part-time)	Korean languages—2 levels	Manitoba
	University of Prince Edward Islands	N/A	1 (part-time)	Korean language—1 level	PEI
(2) Developing program	University of Waterloo	Certificate/diploma in Korean OR Minor in East Asian Studies	4 (1 full-time, 3 part-time)	Korean languages—3 levels Content course (culture, literature, etc.)	Ontario
	York University	Certificate in Korean	5 (1 tenured, 1 tenure-track, 3 part-time)	Korean languages—4 levels Content courses (culture, film, food, and linguistics)	Ontario
(3) Developed program	McGill University	Major in East Asian Studies	2 (1 tenure-track, 1 part-time)	Korean language—4 levels Content courses (culture, film, translation, etc.)	Quebec
	University of Alberta	Major in East Asian Studies	7 (1 tenured, 1 full-time, 5 part-time)	Korean languages—4 levels Content courses (culture, linguistics, literature)	Alberta
	University of British Columbia	Major in Asian Studies—Area of focus: Korea	6 (3 tenured, 3 part-time)	Korean languages—4 levels Content courses (literature, culture, etc.)	British Columbia
	University of Toronto	Major in East Asian Studies	4 (1 tenured, 2 full-time, 1 part-time)	Korean languages—4 levels Content courses (culture, history, political science, etc.)	Ontario

[Compiled by Ahrong Lee]

Korean Programs in Universities in United Kingdom (N = 16)

School	Degree	Number of instructors	Number of courses offered	Region
(1) Programs with KFL courses only				
Durham University	N/A	1 (part-time)	Korean language—1 level	Durham, England
Imperial College of Science, Technology & Medicine	N/A	1 (part-time)	Korean language—2 levels	London, England
King's College of London	N/A	1 (part-time)	Korean language—1 level	London, England
Queen's University of Belfast	N/A	1 (part-time)	Korean language—2 levels	Northern Ireland
University of Bradford	N/A	1 (part-time)	Korean language—1 level / Content course (language and culture)	Bradford, England
University of Exeter	N/A	1 (part-time)	Korean Language—2 levels	Exeter, England
University of Manchester	N/A	1 (part-time)	Korean language—1 level	Manchester, England
London School of Economics and Political Science	N/A	1 (part-time)	Korean language—1 level / Content courses (history, etc.)	London, England
(2) Programs with separated KFL-Korean studies				
University of Edinburgh	Major	1 (1 tenured)	Korean language—1 level / Content course (politics, etc.)	Edinburgh, Scotland
University of York	MSc/PhD in Korean Studies / N/A	1 (1 full-time)	Korean language—1 level / Content course (linguistics)	York, England
University of Oxford	Minor (B.A.) with Chinese/Japanese Studies / MSt in Korean Studies	3 (2 tenured, 1 part-time)	Korean Language—1 level / Content courses (culture, history, etc.)	Oxford, England
University of Leeds	Major in East Asian Studies (Chinese/Japanese only)	2 (1 tenured, 1 part-time)	Korean language—1 level / Content course (politics, etc.)	Leeds, England

(Continued)

(Continued)

	School	Degree	Number of instructors	Number of courses offered	Region
(3) Developed program	Cambridge University	Major in East Asian Studies	2 (1 tenured, 1 part-time)	Korean language—1 level (Part of Japanese) Content courses (politics, history, cinema, etc.)	Cambridge, England
	SOAS	Major in Korean	6 (2 tenured, 2 full-time, 2 part-time)	Korean language—4 levels Content courses (literature, history, culture, etc.)	London, England
	University of Central Lancashire	Major in Modern Languages, TESOL, or Asia Pacific Studies	8 (2 tenured, 3 full-time, 3 part-time)	Korean language—5 levels Content courses (culture, politics, linguistics, etc.)	Lancashire, England
	University of Sheffield	Major in East Asian Studies	6 (1 tenured, 2 full-time, 3 part-time)	Korean language—4 levels Content courses (culture, cinema, politics, etc.)	Sheffield, England

[Compiled on the basis of data provided by Jae Hoon Yeon (London, SOAS)]

Korean Programs in Universities in Oceania (N = 8)

	School	Degree	Number of instructors	Number of courses offered	Province, Country
(1) Newly established program	University of Melbourne	Major/Minor in Asian Studies	7 (1 full-time, 6 part-time)	Korean language—1 level (6 to be offered by 2022) Content courses (politics)	Victoria, Australia
(3) Developed program	Australian National University	Major/Minor in Korean language	7 (2 tenured, 5 part-time)	Korean language—4 levels Content courses (culture, literature, history, politics)	Australian Capital Territory, Australia
	Monash University	Major/Minor in Korean MA, PhD with specialization in Korean	9 (3 tenured, 6 part-time)	Korean language—3 levels Content courses (literature, linguistics, and culture)	Victoria, Australia
	University of Auckland	Major/Minor in Korean MA in Asian Studies PhD in Korean	7 (2 tenured, 5 part-time)	Korean language—3 levels Content courses (culture, film, history)	Auckland, New Zealand
	University of New South Wales	Major/Minor in Korean MA in Applied Linguistics PhD in Korean Studies	8 (3 tenured, 5 part-time)	Korean language—3 levels Content courses (culture, translation)	New South Wales, Australia
	University of Queensland	Major/Minor in Korean MPh, PhD	11 (2 tenured, 1 tenure-track, 8 part-time)	Korean language—3 levels Content courses (culture, film, translation)	Queensland, Australia
	University of Sydney	Major/Minor in Korean Studies	3 (3 tenured)	Korean language—3 levels Content courses (culture, linguistics, literature, media, history, translation and interpretation)	New South Wales, Australia
	University of Western Australia	Major in Korean Studies MA, PhD in Asian Studies	4 (3 tenured, 1 part-time)	Korean language—3 levels Content courses (history, society)	Western Australia, Australia

[Compiled on the basis of the data provided by Mi Yung Park (U. of Auckland)]

Appendix B

Number of Korean Language Users in the US[21]

State	Number of users	%	State	Number of users	%
California	370,062	33.5	Florida	20,936	1.9
New York	103,229	9.3	Hawaii	18,116	1.6
New Jersey	78,100	7.1	Massachusetts	16,298	1.5
Texas	56,688	5.1	Michigan	15,605	1.4
Virginia	54,623	4.9	Colorado	15,095	1.4
Washington	47,892	4.3	North Carolina	14,761	1.3
Georgia	45,221	4.1	Ohio	11,394	1.0
Illinois	44,848	4.1	Nevada	10,969	1.0
Maryland	37,819	3.4	Oregon	10,115	0.9
Pennsylvania	29,158	2.6	Arizona	9,942	0.9

Notes

1 Indiana University started its Korean program in 1962, and a handful of institutions such as Brigham Young University, University of Illinois Urbana-Champaign, University of Kansas, and University of Pittsburgh started their programs in the 1970s.

2 https://www.data.go.kr/dataset/3064822/fileData.do, retrieved on July 26, 2018.

3 Wang (2015) chronicles the history of 17 universities and illustrates how each program, whether private or public, has managed to grow into a major Korean language program with solid enrollment and diverse course offerings during this period.

4 https://www.mla.org/content/download/83540/2197676/2016-Enrollments-Short-R eport.pdf and https://www.insidehighered.com/news/2018/03/19/mla-data-enrollments -show-foreign-language-study-decline, retrieved on July 18, 2018.

5 Retrieved from www.aatk.org on July 18, 2018. It may not reflect the most recent data despite the AATK's constant efforts to update changes. The actual number could go up to 130 or 140 with an exhaustive list of schools. Appendix A provides up-to-date information on Canada, England, and Oceania.

6 Our focus is mainly on college-level KFL programs and presents some issues in secondary schools, excluding elementary schools, community colleges, summer intensive programs, foreign service institutions, Defense Language Institute, and other private-sector programs.

7 www.klacUSA.org, retrieved on August 14, 2018. KlacUSA is the main source for information on Korean language education for K–12 schools, as its mission statement states: "The Foundation for Korean Language and Culture in USA (formerly known as the Foundation for SAT II Korean) is a private, non-profit organization whose primary mission is to promote Korean language and cultural education in American elementary, middle and high schools throughout the United States."

8 According to the 2012–2016 American Community Survey Five-Year PUMS (Public Use Microdata Sample) provided by the US Census Bureau, California has the highest number of Korean language users with 33.5% of about one million users, followed by New York with 9.3% and New Jersey with 7.1%. See Appendix B for detailed information.

9 Among 114 schools, 13 are listed as either Elementary–Middle School, or Middle–High School, or Elementary to High School.

10 For detailed information, the reader is referred to the revised version in *World-Readiness Standards for Learning Languages* (2015). https://www.actfl.org/publicat ions/all/world-readiness-standards-learning-languages.

11 *Integrated Korean: Accelerated* will be the first textbook specifically designed with the World-Readiness Standards in mind for heritage learners (Cho et al., 2020).

12 KFL education in South Korea began at Yonsei Korean Language Institute in 1959. The establishment of KFL as a related yet distinct discipline from *kukekyoyuk* (Korean language education for Koreans) only started in the late 1990s, but after two decades, there are more than 90 programs that correspond to our Model 3.

13 The data collected here are from the AATK homepage accessed in October 2018, as well as from the online Korean program websites of 60 universities selected for their multi-level KFL and "culture" courses. Here we use the term "culture" as a cover term for all non-language courses in literature, history, civilization, anthropology, religion, etc.

14 These include University of Hawaii, UCLA, Harvard University, Columbia University, University of Michigan, University of Chicago, University of Washington, University of British Columbia, Indiana University, Ohio State University, and University of Toronto.

15 One notes the apparent lack of 1.5 generation- or second-generation teachers as well as non-heritage teachers.

16 Those schools are Arizona State University, Brown University, Brigham Young University, Claremont McKenna College, Georgia Institute of Technology, Indiana University, Michigan State University, Middlebury College, Ohio State University, Queens College-CUNY, Rutgers University, SUNY-Albany, SUNY-Buffalo, SUNY-Binghamton, UCLA, Hawaii (multiple positions), UNC at Chapel Hill, University of N. Georgia, University of Wisconsin. Eleven other schools have teaching-focused professorial positions using various titles such as assistant/associate/professor of practice or instruction, teaching assistant/associate/professor, professorial lecturer, or sessional professor.

17 See www.aatk.org.

18 These procedures, recommended in the context of EFL (English as a Foreign Language) and KSL (Korean as a Second Language) could be applied to KFL education with modifications tailored to the North American context.

19 STARTALK started as part of the National Security Language Initiative in 2006 to expand the learning of strategically important foreign languages not commonly taught in the US. It has two components: student programs and teacher programs.

20 The following discussion questions are inspired by Richards (2001).

21 Retrieved from 2012–16 ACS (American Community Survey) five-year PUMS (Public Use Microdata Sample) data, US Census Bureau (https://factfinder.census.gov/faces /tableservices/jsf/pages/productview.xhtml?pid=ACS_16_5YR_B16001&prodType =table).

References

ACTFL. (2013). Program standards for the preparation of foreign language teachers. Retrieved from https://www.actfl.org/sites/default/files/CAEP/ACTFLCAEPStandards2013_v2015.pdf, retrieved on July 20, 2018.

ACTFL. (2015). World-readiness standards for learning languages. ACTFL. Retrieved from https://www.actfl.org/publications/all/world-readiness-standards-learning-languages, retrieved on July 20, 2018.

Baek, B.-J. (1991). Teacher training in Korean as a second language and its method. *Bilingual Research*, 8, 507–525.

Bang, S.-W. (2016). A study on the issues and tasks of Korean teachers' re-education. *Journal of Korean Language Education*, 27(2), 79–103.

Barrette, C.M., & Paesani, K. (Eds.). (2004). *Language program articulation: Developing a theoretical foundation*. Boston, MA: Thomson Heinle.

Berbeco, S. (Ed.). (2016). *Foreign language education in America: Perspectives from K-12, university, government, and international learning.* New York: Palgrave Macmillan.

Brindley, G. (1998). Outcomes-based assessment and reporting in language programs: A review of the issues. *Language Testing, 15,* 45–85.

Brindley, G. (2001). Outcomes-based assessment in practice: Some examples and emerging insights. *Language Testing, 18,* 393–407.

Cheon, S.-Y. (2017). The design, implementation and evaluation of Korean K-12 teacher training workshops. *Journal of Less Commonly Taught Languages, 21,* 145–165.

Cho, Y., Jung, J., & Ha, J. (2020). *Integrated Korean: Accelerated 1 & 2.* University of Hawaii Press.

Choi, E.-G. (2013). Current situation and future for teacher reeducation at the Korean language education institute. *The Society for Korean Language and Literary Research, 41*(1), 443–475.

Chun, H., & Cho, Y. (2018). Building a locally relevant curriculum for Korean language teachers. *Korean Language in America, 22*(1), 46–70.

College Korean Curriculum Inspired by National Standards for Korean. (2015). *The Korean Language in America, 19*(2), 149–460.

Cox, T., Malone, M., & Winke, P. (2018). Future directions in assessment: Influences of standards and implications for language learning. *Foreign Language Annals, 51*(1), 104–115.

Diaz-Maggioli, G. (2003). Professional development for language teachers. *Eric Digest* EDO-FL-03-03. Retrieved from https://www.unitus.org/FULL/0303diaz.pdf on July 20, 2018.

Egnatz, L. (2016). The high school challenge. In S. Berbeco (Ed.), *Foreign language education in America: Perspectives from K-12, university, government, and international learning* (pp. 66–84). New York: Palgrave Macmillan.

Freeman, D. (1989). Teacher training, development, and decision making: A model of teaching and related strategies for language teacher education. *TESOL Quarterly, 23*(1), 27–45.

Freeman, D. (2002). The hidden side of the work: Teacher knowledge and learning to teach: A perspective from North American educational research on teacher education in English language teaching. *Language Teaching, 35*(1), 1–13.

Gor, K., & Vatz, K. (2009). Less commonly taught languages: Issues in learning and teaching. In M.H. Long & C.J. Doughty (Eds.), *The handbook of language teaching* (pp. 234–249). Malden, MA: Wiley-Blackwell.

Im, C.-S., Suh, H., Jung, Y., Shin, H.-Y., & Choi, J. (2013). A study on the state of Korean school instructors and measures to develop their professionalism in the U.S., specifically in WAKS' case. *Journal of the International Network for Korean Language and Culture, 10*(2), 247–274.

Kiely, R. (2006). Evaluation, innovation, and ownership in language programs. *The Modern Language Journal, 90*(4), 597–601.

Kim, S. (2017). A survey on postsecondary Korean language programs in the United States. *Journal of Less Commonly Taught Languages, 21,* 99–126.

Kramsch, C. (2011). The symbolic dimensions of the intercultural. *Language Teaching, 44*(3), 354–367.

Lally, C.G. (Ed.). (2001). *Foreign language program articulation: Current practice and future prospects.* London: Bergin and Garvey.

Latoja, L. (2001). Foreign language placement examinations: A brief history of the standardized test. In C.G. Lally (Ed.), *Foreign language program articulation: Current practice and future prospects.* London: Bergin and Garvey.

Macdonald, M., Badger, R., & White, G. (2001). Changing values: What use are theories of language learning and teaching? *Teaching and Teacher Education, 17*(8), 947–963.

Norris, J. (2016). Language program evaluation. *The Modern Language Journal,* 100(Supplement 2016), 169–189.

Richards, J.C. (2001). *Curriculum development in language teaching.* Cambridge, UK: Cambridge University Press.

Richards, J.C., & Farrell, T. (2005). *Professional development for language teachers: Strategies for teacher learning.* New York: Cambridge University Press.

Ross, S.J. (2009). Program evaluation. In M.H. Long & C.J. Doughty (Eds.), *The handbook of language teaching* (pp.756–778). Malden, MA: Wiley-Blackwell.

Sohn, H., Huh, S., & Choi, Y. (2007). Needs analysis of Korean community schools in Hawai'i. *Proceedings of the 17th international conference on Korean Language Education* (pp. 587–603). Seoul: The International Association for Korean Language Education. Retrieved from http://www.iakle.com/contents/bbs/bbs_content.html?bbs_cls_cd=002002002&cid=07111211113700&bbs_type=B

Trace, J., Hudson, T., & Brown, J.D. (2015). *Developing courses in languages for specific purposes.* Honolulu, HI: University of Hawai'i. doi: http://hdl.handle.net/10125/14573. Retrieved from https://scholarspace.manoa.hawaii.edu/bitstream/10125/14573/5/NW69.pdf.

Wang, H.-S. (2014). Korean language teachers in higher education: Profile, status and more. *Journal of the National Council of Less Commonly Taught Languages, 16,* 147–187.

Wang, H.-S. (2015). *Rise of Korean language programs in U.S. institute of higher education: A narrative history.* Seoul: Korea University Press.

Wang, H.-S. (2018, June). *The state of current affairs: Korean language teachers in U.S. higher education.* Paper presented at the 23rd Annual Meeting of the American Association of Teachers of Korean. Toronto, ON: University of Toronto.

Watanabe, Y., Norris, J.M., & Gonzalez-Lloret, M. (2009). Identifying and responding to evaluation needs in college foreign language programs. In J.M. Norris, J.M. Davis, C. Sinicrope, & Y. Watanabe (Eds.), *Toward useful program evaluation in college foreign language education* (pp. 5–56). Honolulu, HI: National Foreign Language Resource Center, University of Hawaii.

Weir, C.J., & Roberts, J.R. (1994). *Evaluation in ELT.* Oxford: Basil Blackwell.

Part II
Annotated bibliography on KFL pedagogy

Annotated bibliography on KFL pedagogy

Ho Jung Choi, Ji-Young Jung, and Hee Chung Chun

Introduction

Korean language education in the United States has a long history, dating back to 1930s and 1940s, when the first Korean language courses were offered at Columbia University and University of California, Berkeley. It is, however, no exaggeration to state that the first six decades of Korean language education were devoted to day-to-day language instruction in the classroom, and there were few conscious efforts for Korean as a Foreign Language (KFL) research of any significance. When the American Association of Teachers of Korean (AATK), the first professional organization in North America, was founded in 1994, its mission statement clearly indicated promoting "research in second language acquisition, applied linguistics, and language pedagogy," as well as providing "a forum for presenting research findings" and publishing a journal (www.aatk.org). As a result, *Korean Language in America* (KLA), the first journal exclusively dedicated to Korean language education, has served as the most popular venue for KFL research. Decades-long growth in enrollments in Korean courses in secondary and post-secondary institutions helped place KFL research in the proper context so that interesting articles now appear in major scholarly journals such as *Foreign Language Annals, The Modern Language Journal, Heritage Language Journal*, and others.

In the past, there have been a couple of attempts to understand the overall trend of the field by compiling a more or less comprehensive list of KFL studies (Wang, 2003, 2013; and Lee, 2014), but they narrowly focus on the articles published in KLA and deal only with topics explicitly discussed in the articles, not paying enough attention to the current state of KFL research in the context of foreign language education. Therefore, it is high time to provide a comprehensive profile of KFL research, to examine recent inquiries and to identify notable trends by expanding the scope beyond KLA to scholarly journals on language acquisition and education, including those published in Korea, the UK, Australia, and Canada. The overarching goal of this section of Annotated Bibliography (AB) is, therefore, to offer a bird's eye view of KFL research of the past two decades or so. In particular, we attempt to provide an overview of salient research inquiries of KFL studies within appropriate theoretical frameworks, identify notable trends in the field, and finally, suggest directions for future research. In addition, we offer an annotated bibliography of important studies that we believe to have made significant contributions to the development of KFL pedagogy.

Methods

We constructed a database of over one thousand entries based on the survey of articles in peer-reviewed journals and doctoral dissertations published in the US and South Korea between 1995 and 2019 (see Appendix 1 for the list of 74 journals initially examined for this project and the list of 35 journals used for our database). We decided to exclude KFL studies in the format of book chapters, due to their limited accessibility, not being easily downloadable from online databases, and the difficulty in determining the relevance and applicability of their research findings. The final database included 21 major journals published in North America and the UK, as well as 14 journals published in South Korea.

All 35 journals specialize in foreign language teaching and learning as one of their primary research topics and include at least one article on KFL pedagogy written in English. The final database comprises 524 studies (including 29 doctoral dissertations), all of which focus exclusively on teaching and learning of KFL (as opposed to Korean as a Native or First Language), and deal with English-speaking learners of Korean. As expected, articles in KLA comprise about half of the data (46.9%), while articles in journals published in Korea comprise about one-third of the data (31.5%). Only about 22% of the data comes from journals other than KLA, arguably because research on KFL pedagogy in the broader field of foreign language education only began in the late 2000s. Both our quantitative and qualitative analyses were conducted based on this final database.

Based on the results of data analysis we were able to select a handful of noteworthy studies for annotation consisting of brief evaluative summaries for each of the eight areas of KFL research which were identified in the first part of this monograph. The numbers of annotated references in each field vary widely, ranging from 4 to 13 due to factors in KFL history such as initial emphasis on immediate pedagogical concerns and recently emerging fields of inquiry. As the goal of AB is to inform the readers of the relevance and usefulness of the selected studies, we relied on the following criteria for selecting an article: (1) the significance of findings in terms of its relevance and connection to the broader field; (2) its pedagogical influences; (3) the applicability in practice; and (4) the validity of findings in terms of research methods, theoretical framework, and data. After examining research topics, we were able to construct a manageable body of important KFL research: 69 out of 495 journal articles that promise significant implications for teaching practice and offer new insights for future research. We believe this version of AB is by no means exhaustive, but it is sufficiently comprehensive. As such, it is useful and meaningful for KFL practitioners for its pedagogical values.

Analysis

Quantitative analyses

Bibliometric information

Once the database was completed with 524 entries, the data analysis was conducted, using both quantitative and qualitative methods. Studies were grouped into the eight research areas identified in Part I of this book: (1) learner language and language processing; (2) pedagogical approaches and practices, (3) language in use; (4) culture; (5) Korean as a heritage language (KHL); (6) literacies; (7) assessment; and (8) program building and professional development. Within each of these areas, the entries were tagged with more specific keywords (or sub-topics) for a large-scale bibliometric analysis and the selective annotations. Subsequently, information visualizations were carried out. Information visualization has long been utilized in a variety of research fields and addresses various information service issues such as the diffusion of ideas, knowledge flow, and research evaluation (Chen, 2003; Zhao & Strotmann, 2015). Informative visualizations of bibliometric data in this study were created by a visualization tool, Visualization of Similarities (VOS) viewer (Chen, 2003). VOS viewer was utilized to produce informative visual maps, which provide a quick overview of the major topics and relevance of the topics in the bibliometric data (Van Eck & Waltman, 2009).

Our quantitative analyses reveal a number of notable trends over the past 24 years. As Figure A.1 shows, the three research topics most actively discussed in the field since 1995 are: (1) pedagogical approaches and practices; (2) Korean as a heritage language; and (3) learner language and language processing.

Using information visualization, frequent research topics and trends were identified for each of five periods: 1995–2000, 2001–2005, 2006–2010, 2011–2015, and 2016–2019. Interestingly, the results show a couple of noticeable changes over two decades. As Figure A.2 indicates, although pedagogical approaches and practices is the most frequently explored topic, its frequency dramatically

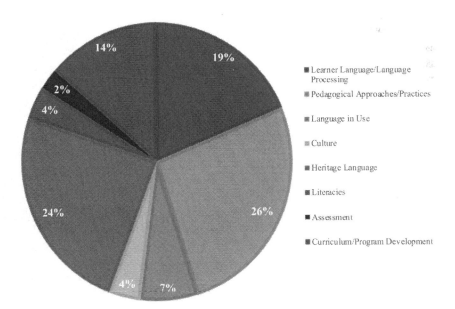

Figure A.1 Research topics in Korean language pedagogy.

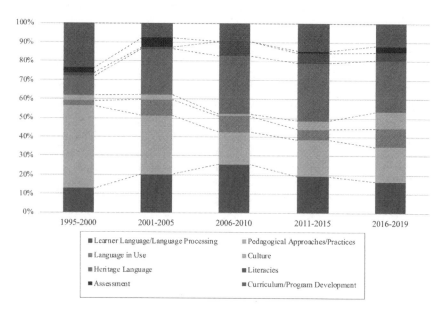

Figure A.2 Trends in Korean language pedagogy research.

decreases over time. For example, it takes up only slightly over 18% during the last period. In contrast, it can be seen that the topic of culture and curriculum and program development received increasing attention in recent years.

In addition, a chronological analysis of the data clearly indicates that culture, literacies, and assessment are consistently underexplored. These understudied research areas could be attributed to an unprecedented pace of KFL development during the past two decades. While early research on KFL research focused on understanding various pedagogical approaches, pinpointing pedagogical issues, and developing teaching materials for such issues (Lee, 2014), only recently have a wider array of topics in literacies, culture, and assessment started to be explored. Because these studies are mostly interdisciplinary in nature, researchers were able to frame their studies specifically on the latter topics only in the mid-2000s. The small number of studies in culture, literacies, and assessment may be due to our categorization method that assigned only one primary topic to each study. For example, a study on heritage learners' literacy development or the use of pop culture in heritage language learning was classified under heritage language, although it was tagged with other keywords such as literacies and culture. For instance, Choi and Yi's "A Pop Culture in Heritage Language Learning" (2012) is categorized under one primary topic, "Heritage Language," but is tagged with such searchable keywords as #literacy, #culture, #identity, #intertextuality, #multimedia, and #proficiency level advanced. In an effort to minimize this limitation, we employ keyword search to increase search results in culture, literacies, and assessment categories, and include them in AB.

In the next phase of quantitative analyses, bibliometric maps were created by using VOS viewer. Figure 9.3 shows the relations and dynamic associations between the key concepts found in studies published from 1995 to 2019. Bibliometric maps provide a low-dimensional visualization in which the distance between any two items reflects the similarity or relatedness of the items. For example, "syntax" in Figure A.3 is far from "culture," implying less frequent co-occurrence, whereas "pedagogical grammar" and "corpus" are located close to each other, indicating similarity or frequent cooccurrences.

Bibliometric maps present both the current landscape and the development of the field (i.e., chronological changes) over the last two decades. For example, "pedagogical approaches" and "learner language" colored in dark gray were investigated mostly in the early 2000s, while "heritage language" colored in light gray was most actively discussed in the mid-2000s and the early 2010s. "Pedagogical approaches" and "learner language" are densely intertwined with several tags, such as "beginning proficiency level," "pedagogical grammar," "syntax," and "textbook analysis," all of which were popular research topics prior to the mid-2000s. Emerging topics in recent years are colored in light gray, including "identity," "teacher background," "K–16 education," and "community school."

The bibliometric networks of literacy and assessment are presented separately in Figures A.4 and A.5, respectively. Despite the small number of entries

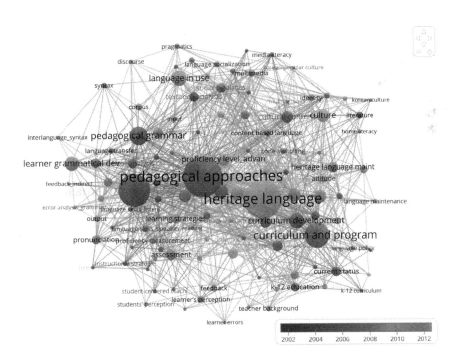

Figure A.3 Network visualization map in the database.

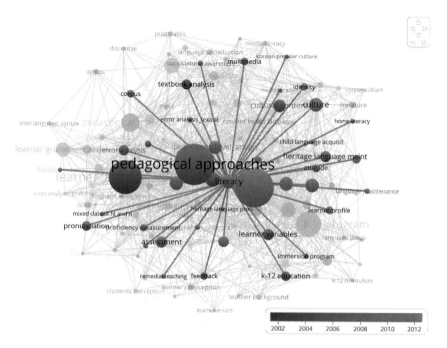

Figure A.4 Visualization map of literacy.

in the database, these research topics reveal dynamic relations and chronological changes.

Figure A.4 illustrates that literacy is associated with such topics as pedagogical approaches, culture, heritage language, feedback, and learner profile.

Figure A.5 demonstrates that assessment was connected with pedagogical approaches, heritage language, curriculum development, interlanguage, and proficiency. As the bibliometric networks provide both co-occurrences and the timeline-based information at the same time, they can offer useful information for KFL researchers in identifying dynamic relationships between important concepts in the field and gaining a comprehensive understanding of the latest developments in KFL research.

In addition, it is noteworthy that research articles with the exclusive focus on KFL pedagogy began to appear between 2006 and 2010 in major journals on foreign language education, such as *Foreign Language Annals, Modern Language Journal, Heritage Language Journal,* and *Language, Culture and Curriculum.* Interestingly, these studies mostly deal with KHL. For example, in *Foreign Language Annals,* Sohn and Shin (2007) focus on placement strategies for heritage students, and Choi and Yi (2012) examine the use and role of pop culture in heritage language learning. In *Modern Language Journal,* Kang (2010) examines the effectiveness of negative evidence in KHL learning.

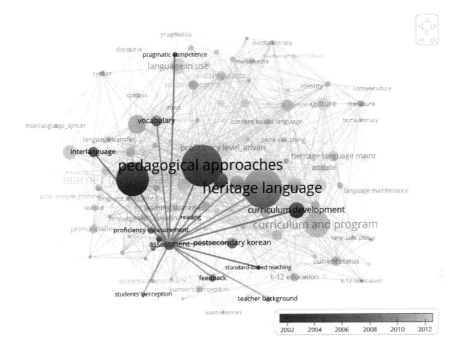

Figure A.5 Visualization map of assessment.

Qualitative analyses

Research trends

SHIFT OF RESEARCH FOCUS

The most common topics in the earlier periods of KFL research were the application of teaching strategies and methods, and their pedagogical efficacy and implications from the teacher's perspective. Accordingly, during those time periods, a wide range of topics in pedagogical approaches and practices, and curriculum and program development were investigated. For example, Sohn (1995) proposes performance-based principles and proficiency criteria for KFL textbook development, while Kim (2005) explores the acquisition of language and culture in a content-based class. Although assessment seems to be underrepresented in our database, Korean language researchers and educators often deal with the issue of assessment as a major component of their curriculum. For example, between 1995 and 2005, frequently discussed topics included standardized testing such as Oral Proficiency Interviews (OPIs) and the development of online placement tests to accurately measure students' proficiency levels and place them appropriately (Kim, 2004; Lee, 2000). In short, in earlier years KFL research focused on the teachers' strategies for curriculum development and placement of students.

Recently, however, there has been a shift of focus from a top-down, teacher-oriented view to a learner-oriented view in research on pedagogical approaches and practices. An increasing number of studies investigate learner language, language processing, and individual factors such as motivation, anxiety, and learner strategy. For example, Kong (2012, 2017) explores the learners' input processing, "focus on form," and reading comprehension in task-based classes, and Pyun (2013) explores the learners' attitudes and motivational states in a task-based class. Kim et al. (2017) examine the learners' cognitive processing in a content-based, flipped classroom. This shift of research focus is partly due to the recent attempts by KFL researchers to adopt theoretical frameworks and take advantage of advances made in Second Language Acquisition (SLA), applied linguistics, and educational linguistics.

Evolution of scholarship in KHL

Research on KHL learning has steadily increased because heritage learners still take up a larger portion in KFL learner demographics. Earlier studies on KHL focused on curricular design (e.g., differentiated instruction, a two-track system, placement issues) on the one hand, and particular needs and motivations of heritage learners such as affective factors, anxiety levels, integrative motivations, on the other hand (Jee, 2016; Kim, 2004; Shin & Kim, 2000; Sohn & Shin, 2007). For example, there exist a handful of studies on program development and placement strategies (Cho & Chun, 2015; Sohn & Merrill, 2008; Sohn & Shin, 2007). Earlier KHL research also centered on unique psycholinguistic processes of heritage learners, distinct from foreign language acquisition by non-heritage learners (Kim, 2004). A closer look at the data reveals interesting patterns. Earlier studies viewed heritage learners as unbalanced bilinguals whose literacy skills lag behind their aural/oral skills, and made efforts in identifying heritage learners' weaknesses and suggesting effective pedagogical interventions for such "problems."

In contrast, recent studies tend to view heritage learners as potentially advanced-level (and above) users of Korean with a higher level of language exposure and cultural literacy. These studies focus on instructional approaches and practices that aim to help learners become competent in using Korean in various personal, academic, and professional settings (Kim & Sohn, 2016), rather than viewing them as deficient in reading and writing, and thus employing skill-oriented instruction. Naturally, an increasing number of studies in later periods tend to integrate KHL learners as part of the FL/SL teaching community (Huh & Choi, 2015; Kim & Sohn, 2016; Park et al., 2016). In accordance with the most recent trends in FL/SL research, KHL research has turned away from deficiency-oriented views of learners and has begun to explore how heritage learners develop intercultural competence to become a member of the global community, enhance critical thinking skills, and experience transformation and renew their sense of identity through language learning (Choi & Yi, 2012; Jee, 2016; Kim & Pyun, 2014).

Emergence of standards-based and proficiency-based assessment and teaching

In the earlier periods, it was common for KFL assessment researchers to collect data from small-scale pilots, often resulting in limited validity and reliability of their findings. It is also observed that qualitative and longitudinal studies in the earlier periods were rare. With the development of ACTFL proficiency guidelines and Standards for Learning Korean (2012), however, standards-based teaching and proficiency-based assessment/teaching have received increasing attention. Recently, many Korean language educators set out to develop and apply formative and constructive assessment tools based on ACTFL's World-Readiness Standards for Language Learning, Integrated Performance Assessment (IPA), proficiency guidelines for speaking and writing, and Interagency Language Roundtable (ILR) (Kang & Lim, 2011; Kim, 2016; Shin, 2016).

Attention to digital tools of communication

In recent years, KFL educators have actively explored and showcased digital tools of communication to address the communicative needs of the students known as digital natives. From the very first period of scholarly works on Korean language education, studies demonstrated the usefulness and validity of technology in their pedagogy, such as computer-assisted language learning (CALL). In the 21st-century multimodal society, it is only natural that diverse technology-based resources, including web-based resources and digital media, are conceived as more than mere teaching tools and are ultimately incorporated into foreign language curricula in order to help learners become competent members of their own community of practice. In this context, the development of literacy skills through multimodal venues has emerged as an important research topic. More and more KFL studies are based on the premise that the ultimate goal of language teaching is to prepare students to participate fully and effectively in intercultural interactions in their digitally connected, globalized world. In addition, flipped learning, mobile-assisted language learning (MALL), and hybrid courses have been adopted in KFL pedagogy (Fouser, 2010; Kim et al., 2017; Yong & Ko, 2018). Also noticeable is a trend towards multiliteracies; a number of articles discuss the use of digital media such as video clips, internet TV shows, webtoons, and advertisements to enhance learners' sociolinguistic competence (Brown, 2013b; Kim & Lee, 2010) and cultural literacy (Cheon & Kim, 2010; Roh, 2011; Strauss, 1999).

Emergence of intercultural competence

Although the total number of research studies on culture is relatively small compared with other areas of research in KFL, the existing studies show an important shift in dealing with the complex nature of culture in language teaching. In the earlier periods in our database, most culture studies regarded culture as tangible products and observable norms that need to be explicitly taught to students as objective knowledge or a skill set that completes successful language learning. Studies during the late 1990s and the early 2000s focused on proposing a list of cultural materials to be included in the curriculum (Hong, 2004; Jung, 1995; Kim, 1995; King, 2004; Koo, 1999; Lee, 2002; You, 2002). Such studies tended to limit the content of learning to Korean literature, etiquette, and traditional customs, and exposing students to idioms and proverbs. From the late 2000s on, however, more studies began to consider culture an essential component of global competence that needs to be discussed and negotiated, rather than explicitly taught and learned. Recently, there have been studies dealing with cultural awareness (Byon, 2005, 2007), and individual differences of learners (e.g., identity, motivation, autonomy, L2 self). Furthermore, we observe novel topics emerging in the field, such as translingual and intercultural competence (Lee, 2017), and learner identity as a member of the global community (Brown, 2016; Jung & Lee, 2018; Shin, 2013).

Limitations

The authors recognize that our review has limitations due to several factors. Firstly, it is possible that some research articles and dissertations in KFL pedagogy could have been omitted despite our utmost efforts to carry out as thorough a search as possible. Secondly, we compiled research papers meeting the following criteria: (1) published in English in peer-reviewed journals; (2) studying English-speaking learners of Korean as a foreign language; and (3) carrying pedagogical suggestions and implications of value. As mentioned earlier, research papers published in the Korean language or dealing with KFL learners in non-English-speaking environments, however valuable the findings might be, were not included in the database. We also excluded book chapters for reasons of accessibility. Lastly, the analyses and annotations are based on our own interpretations of the database, although we communicated with the authors of each chapter of this monograph. Keenly aware of possible biases embedded in the review process, we have made every effort to reduce the risk of potential biases and to mitigate errors by cross-checking categorizations by topic, and keyword tags in each research topic.

Concluding remarks

The objective of this broad overview and the following annotated bibliography is to provide KFL educators with a useful and ready-to-use resource. We have identified a list of prominent research topics and trends in KFL pedagogy to date, by highlighting topological characteristics of KFL research. Interestingly, new trends are observed in relatively understudied areas such as culture, literacy, and teacher education, which will lead future researchers to meaningful and fruitful areas of exploration. Topics such as multimodality, technology, multiculturalism, and identity seem to be particularly important and interesting in the fast-changing era of globalization.

In addition, we observe that findings in the data analyses point to a major shift in research focus, from a top-down, teacher-oriented pedagogy to a more learner-centered pedagogy. In other words, while a huge number of studies were conducted in pedagogical practices in earlier years, many of those studies were action research carried out from the teacher's point of view and motivated by immediate teaching environment issues. As Wang (2003) points out, in the early 2000s, then-current KFL studies began shifting towards data-based research or applying general teaching theories to KFL, both being part of a natural growth pattern in KFL scholarship. Our findings call attention to the demand for empirical research based on robust data and sound research methodology, beyond collecting anecdotal evidence and casual pedagogical practices.

The results also point to an ever-growing number of KHL studies. Based on the assumption that heritage learners typically lag behind in literacy skills, earlier KHL studies tend to focus on finding effective pedagogical interventions to improve orthographic and structural accuracy. More recent KHL studies in bilingualism have begun to look at language loss and maintenance, relating them to identity issues. Also, recent studies increasingly adopt a sociocultural orientation and explore the use of multimedia and digital tools in connection with cultivating intercultural competence, motivated by a higher level of cultural proficiency of heritage learners.

However, the analysis of the bibliometric data reveals certain limitations of KHL studies. First of all, most studies, especially earlier studies, rarely utilize longitudinal data, a severe limitation to understanding learners' acquisition and language processing over time. Many of the earlier studies rely on the researcher's intuitions, speculations, and personal experiences in putting forward pedagogical recommendations. In fact, a large number of these studies are action studies setting out to deal with immediate pedagogical issues or difficulties (e.g., fixing persistent spelling errors and fossilized grammatical forms). We note that future KHL research should be carried out in the theoretical context of other heritage language studies.

Also, the bibliometric maps reveal a number of strong connections, hitherto unrecognized, among keywords across different disciplines such as linguistics, cultural studies, psychology, social sciences, and anthropology. Publications in peer-reviewed journals is a way of expanding the scope of KFL research and reaching out to related interdisciplinary fields of foreign language education, which, in turn, will make an invaluable contribution to KFL pedagogy.

Appendix 1. A complete list of journal titles reviewed[1]

1. Annual Review of Applied Linguistics*
2. Applied Linguistics*

---

1 The 35 journals in our database are marked with an *.

3. Applied Psycholinguistics
4. Bilingual Research (이중언어학)*
5. Bilingual Research Journal*
6. Bilingualism
7. Brain and Language
8. Bulletin of Science, Technology and Society
9. CALICO Journal
10. Classroom Discourse*
11. Communication Education
12. Communication Quarterly
13. Communication Reports
14. Communication Research Reports
15. Communication Teacher
16. Computer Assisted Language Learning
17. Dyslexia
18. Educational Research
19. Educational Technology and Society
20. Foreign Language Annals*
21. Foreign Languages Education*
22. Harvard Educational Review
23. Heritage Language Journal*
24. Innovation in Language Learning and Teaching
25. International Journal of Bilingual Education and Bilingualism*
26. International Journal of Bilingualism
27. International Journal of Multilingualism
28. International Review of Applied Linguistics in Language Teaching
29. Issues in Applied Linguistics
30. Journal of Applied Communication Research
31. Journal of Asian Pacific Communication*
32. Journal of Child Language Education*
33. Journal of Curriculum Studies
34. Journal of Interactive Learning Research*
35. Journal of Research in Childhood Education*
36. Journal of the International Network for Korean Language and Culture* (한국언어문화학)
37. Journal of Korean Language Education* (한국어교육)
38. Journal of Language & Literacy Education
39. Journal of Language Sciences* (언어과학)
40. Journal of Less Commonly Taught Languages*
41. Journal of Multilingual and Multicultural Development*
42. Journal of Pragmatics*
43. Korean Journal of Applied Linguistics* (응용언어학)
44. Korean Language Education Research* (국어교육학연구)
45. Language and Education*

46. Language Assessment Quarterly
47. Language Awareness*
48. Language Facts and Perspectives* (언어사실과 관점)
49. Language Learning
50. Language Learning and Technology
51. Language Learning Journal
52. Language Research (어학연구)
53. Language Teaching Research*
54. Language, Culture and Curriculum*
55. Linguistics and Education *
56. Qualitative Inquiry*
57. Research on Language & Social Interaction
58. Review of Research in Education
59. Studies in Foreign Language Education (외국어교육연구)
60. Studies in Second Language Acquisition*
61. System
62. Teaching and Learning Inquiry
63. Teaching Korean as a Foreign Language* (외국어로서의 한국어교육)
64. Teaching Sociology
65. The Canadian Modern Language Review*
66. The International Review of Research in Open and Distributed Learning
67. The Journal of Educational Research
68. The Journal of Korean Language Education (국어교육)
69. The Journal of Korean Language and Literature Education* (국어교육연구)
70. The Korean Language and Literature (국어국문학)
71. The Korean Language in America*
72. The Language and Culture* (언어와 문화)
73. The Modern Language Journal*
74. Theory into Practice

Annotated bibliography for Chapter 1 Second Language Acquisition and its implications for teaching Korean

Kim, E. (2002). Development of writing accuracy through error feedback. *Journal of Korean Language Education, 13*(1), 279–306.

This research investigates the effects of error correction on the development of Korean as a Second Language (KSL) writing accuracy. A total of 135 writings were collected from five intermediate-level Korean heritage learners, on which the instructor corrections and feedback on the errors in spelling, grammar, vocabulary, and discourse/pragmatic consistency were given. This study indicates that there was a long-term effect of corrective feedback on the development of writing accuracy in Korean, but error feedback was effective only for some types of errors. Kim finds that Korean learners did not benefit from comprehensive error feedback on their writing. It was suggested that selective error correction may be more useful than comprehensive feedback since the learners do not pay equal attention to all types of errors.

Kim, H.-Y. (2012). Development of NP forms and discourse reference in L2 Korean. *KLA, 17*, 211–235.

By examining data collected from a film re-telling task performed by intermediate/advanced level heritage and non-heritage learners, this study demonstrates development of discourse reference forms. This study presents pedagogical implications of how language instructors help KFL learners in acquiring the discourse reference system for text cohesion and effective referential communication as their oral fluency is developed. Kim argues for the need to provide more opportunities to process natural uses of reference forms in longer stretches of speech in the development of discourse reference forms.

Kim, M. (2000). Mnemonic vocabulary learning strategies of non-heritage Korean language students. *The Korean Language in America, 5*, 303–316.

This study focuses on how non-heritage students retain and recall Korean vocabulary. Learners' mnemonic approaches and successful vocabulary retention are examined by analyzing data from 25 KFL learners. Results show that non-heritage Korean learners in the study adopted four mnemonic approaches: sound associations, morphological associations, word groupings, and keyword techniques. It was found that the high-scoring group used a wider variety of vocabulary learning strategies than the low-scoring group did. Diverse mnemonic approaches for teaching and learning Korean vocabulary (e.g., a vocabulary network) are suggested for diverse groups of Korean learners.

Kim, M. (2010). Korean language learners' collocational word association and its implication for classroom teaching. *Teaching Korean as a Foreign Language, 35*, 1–21.

Kim compares how KFL learners and native speakers store their words in their mental lexicon and produce them as chunks. The study deploys the word association method and examines the word association tests of 40 native Korean speakers and 40 non-heritage learners. Results show that beginning-level KFL learners organized and associated words in a limited environment and found collocations to be difficult to acquire. A variety of activities and strategies (e.g., guessing a common collocate or a missing headword) were suggested to help integrate collocations in all levels of Korean classes and enhance the learners' fluency and accuracy.

Kim, Y. (2008). The contribution of collaborative and individual tasks to the acquisition of L2 vocabulary. *The Modern Language Journal, 92*(1), 114–130.

This study focuses on learner collaboration to facilitate the acquisition of L2 vocabulary. Data collected from 32 KSL learners compared the effectiveness of collaborative tasks (e.g., dictogloss in pairs) and individual tasks (e.g., think-aloud) on the acquisition of Korean vocabulary. Results indicate that the learners who participated in the collaborative task performed significantly better on the vocabulary tests. Kim presents the pedagogical implication for the effective use of pair or group activities for Korean vocabulary learning in the classroom.

Lee, E., & Kim, H.-Y. (2007). Reference to past and past perfect in L2 Korean. *KLA, 12,* 67–84.

Eighty-one journal entries written by nine college students in an intermediate-level Korean language class were collected and analyzed to examine tense marking in the learner corpus. Lee and Kim show that intermediate-level Korean language learners have very little understanding of the past perfect in the double past form, on the basis of the learners' understanding of the past and double past markers, *-ess* and *-essess*. Noting the scarcity of instructional materials explaining the function of the past perfect, this study suggests explicit instructional treatment designed for more appropriate uses of the past tense markers.

Lee, E., & Zaslansky, M. (2015). Nominal reference in Korean heritage language discourse. *Heritage Language Journal, 12*(2), 132–158.

Employing the Interface Hypothesis, this study compares Korean narrative discourse from ten Korean heritage speakers with those of five native Korean speakers and five L2 speakers. Data reveal that the form-meaning mapping patterns among the three groups were quite different from one another. Results from a film re-telling task show that heritage speakers used nominal reference of zero anaphora as frequently as Korean native speakers, in contrast to the findings in previous studies. Different from native speakers, however, Lee and Zaslansky find that heritage speakers employed topic/subject shifts across sentences more frequently.

O'Grady, W., Lee, M., & Choo, M. (2003). A subject-object asymmetry in the acquisition of relative clauses in Korean as a second language. *Studies in Second Language Acquisition, 25,* 433–448.

Formulating the linear and structural distance hypothesis, O'Grady et al. investigate the acquisition of relative clauses in Korean as a second language. The interpretation of subject and direct object relative clauses by 53 beginning and intermediate learners of Korean as a Second Language (L2) was investigated and compared with data from nine native speakers. Results show that English-speaking learners of Korean prefer subject relative clauses to direct object relatives. This paper provides useful information regarding English-speaking learners' comprehension and acquisition of relative clauses in Korean.

Shin, S.-C. (2009). Language instructors' use of learners' L1 and L2 in classroom: Perceptions by students and teachers of Korean. *Journal of Korean Language Education, 24,* 165–195.

Shin investigates perceptions by both Korean instructors and learners about the roles of teachers and the teacher's use of learners' L1 and L2 in classroom settings. Adopting a survey method, data were collected from 27 language instructors working in two institutions and 38 students studying Korean in college. The evidence of this study reveals that the teachers had a conservative or negative opinion overall on the use of the language learner's L1 in class, while the students were more positive or had a more flexible attitude towards the use of the L1. The results provide useful information in choosing an instructional language in a Korean language classroom.

Strauss, S., Lee, J., & Ahn, K. (2006). Applying conceptual grammar to advanced-level language teaching: The case of two completive constructions in Korean. *The Modern Language Journal, 90*(2), 185–209.

Focusing on constructions expressing the completive aspect in Korean (e.g., V-*a/e pelita* and V-*ko malta*), this study introduces Conceptual Grammar combining corpus, discourse analysis, and cognitive linguistics, an alternative approach to more traditional pedagogical analyses in teaching Korean grammar. Samples of pedagogical materials developed using this model were presented for advanced-level Korean learning environments. The combined qualitative and quantitative results demonstrate a positive reaction to both the teaching and learning of the target grammar patterns. The pedagogical implication of conceptual grammar is that this approach enables teachers and students of advanced Korean to formulate new rules derived from the relationship between the target form and its meaning in discourse.

Türker, E. (2017). The acquisition and development of the Korean adverbial particle -*ey* by L1 English learners of Korean. *Journal of Korean Language Education, 28*(4), 337–366.

Acknowledging the fact that particles are one of the most challenging grammatical features for Korean L2 learners to acquire, Türker investigates the acquisition order of the multiple meanings of the Korean adverbial particle, -*ey*. Data were collected from 45 students in beginning, intermediate, and advanced proficiency levels. Results indicate that the advanced learners acquired four meanings out of five: the time, goal, stative location, and contact meanings, but not the unit meaning; whereas the beginner- and intermediate-level learners had acquired the time, goal, and stative location meanings, but not the contact and unit meanings. The study suggests more factors, including L2 frequency and the availability of explicit grammar instruction, should be the focus for better understanding of the acquisition of the particle -*ey* in the future.

Ahn, H. (2015). *Second language acquisition of Korean case by learners with different first languages* [Doctoral Dissertation]. University of Washington, Seattle, Washington.

Ahn, M. (2017). *Student perception of language achievement and learner autonomy in a blended Korean language course: The case study of defense language institute foreign language center* [Doctoral Dissertation]. Northcentral University, Prescott Valley, Arizona.

Byon, A. (2003). Analysis of a KFL learner's spoken performance variation. *Journal of Korean Language Education, 14*(1), 343–366.

Byon, A. (2012). Vocabulary learning strategies of advanced KFL learners: Using vocabulary journal assignment. *KLA, 17*, 236–254.

Cheon, S., & Lee, T. (2013). The perception of Korean stops by heritage and non-heritage learners: Pedagogical implications for beginning learners. *KLA, 18*, 23–39.

Cho, I. (2001). Recognition of English loanwords by learners of Korean. *KLA, 6*, 69–74.

Choi, B. (2016). Collostructional analysis of Korean auxiliary verbs *-e twu-* and *-e noh. KLA, 20*(1), 29–208.

Choi, G. (2016). A study on using the learning strategies of (in)effective Korean language learners. *Journal of International Network for Korean Language and Culture, 13*(3), 231–259.

Choi, J., Choi, J., & Koheng, B. (2015). A research on the effects of English learning experience as l2 on Korean audio-morphological awareness as l3. *Journal of Korean Language Education, 26*(2), 239–258.

Damron, J. (2009). A study on the students' error feedback preferences according to proficiency level. *International Journal for Korean Language Education, 20*(3), 337–358.

Forsyth, J., & Damron, J. (2012). Korean language studies: Motivation and attrition. *Journal of Less Commonly Taught Languages, 12*, 161–188.

Fouser, R. (2000). Too close for comfort sociolinguistic transfer from Japanese into Korean as an L3. *Journal of Korean Language Education, 11*(2), 211–237.

Ha, J. (2001). English speaking students' written language development in Korean in a Korean/English two-way immersion program. *KLA, 6*, 297–307.

Ha, K., & Choi, S. (2012). Adult second language learners' acquisition of word order and case markers in Korean. *KLA, 17*, 1–23.

Han, S. (2006). Does L2 proficiency make a difference in choosing between WDCT and ODCT? *KLA, 11*, 17–42.

Jee, M. (2012). Effects of language anxiety on three levels of classes of Korean as a foreign language. *Journal of Korean Language Education, 23*(2), 467–487.

Jee, M. (2014). Affective factors in Korean as a foreign language: Anxiety and beliefs. *Language, Culture and Curriculum, 27*(2), 182–195.

Jee, M. (2017). Heritage language proficiency in relation to attitudes, motivation, and age at immigration: A case of Korean-Australians. *Language, Culture and Curriculum, 31*(1), 70–93.

Jeon, K., & Kim, H.-Y. (2007). Development of relativization in Korean as a foreign language: The noun phrase accessibility hierarchy in head-internal and head-external relative clauses. *Studies in Second Language Acquisition, 29*(2), 253–276.

Jeon, M. (2018). Attitudes toward accents in less commonly taught language education: A Korean case in Canada. *Journal of Less Commonly Taught Languages, 23*, 132–152.

Jeon, M., & Kang, I. (2005). Investigating student preferences in error correction in Korean-language teaching. *KLA, 10*, 19–49.

Jeong, W.-D. (2004). Suprasegmental sounds in Korean teaching. *KLA, 9*, 302–307.

Kang, S. (1995). Anaphora in the acquisition of Korean as a second language: An attempt to bridge the gap between linguistic studies and language teaching. *KLA*, *1*, 125–136.

Kim, C.-W., & Park, S.-G. (1995). Variation in onset timing of *Hangul* and its impact on the formation of il phonology "A case study involving Korean liquid." *Bilingual Research*, *12*(1), 141–162.

Kim, D. (2015). *Temporal phenomena in the Korean conjunctive constructions* [Doctoral Dissertation]. University of Hawai'i at Manoa, Honolulu, Hawai'i.

Kim, E.-J. (2000). Phonological, syntactic, and semantic linking in Korean vocabulary learning. *KLA*, *5*, 291–301.

Kim, E.-J. (2002). Investigating the acquisition of Korean particles by beginning and intermediate learners. *KLA*, *7*, 165–176.

Kim, E.-J. (2003). Effects of word clustering on L2 Korean vocabulary learning. *Journal of Korean Language Education*, *14*(1), 367–388.

Kim, H.-S. (2006). Learning and teaching Korean intonation: A case study of English-speaking learners. *Journal of Korean Language Education*, *17*(2), 69–94.

Kim, H.-Y. (2000). Strategies for improving accuracy in KSL writing: Developmental errors and an error-correction code. *KLA*, *5*, 231–248.

Kim, J. (2003). Accounting for back-vowel under-differentiation: An acoustically-based study of English-speaking learners of Korean. *KLA*, *8*, 51–64.

Kim, K.-R. (2008). A study on main factors influencing proficiency of Korean language learners. *Bilingual Research*, 25–42.

Kim, M.J. (2000). Treatment of loan words in Korean proficiency tests. *KLA*, *5*, 249–255.

Kim, M.-R., & Lotto, A. (2002). An investigation of acoustic characteristics of Korean stops produced by non-heritage learners. *KLA*, *7*, 177–187.

Kim, M.-R., Lotto, A., & Kim, J.-K. (2006). Influence of prosody on Korean word production by non-heritage learners. *KLA*, *11*, 102–111.

Kim, M.-S. (2005). Perception and production of Korean /L/ by L2 learners and implications for teaching refined pronunciation. *KLA*, *10*, 71–88.

Kim, O., & Park, E. (2017). The utility of indirect written corrective feedback for learners with different proficiency levels. *Bilingual Research*, *68*, 1–26.

Kim, Y., & Damron, J. (2015). Foreign language reading anxiety: Korean as a foreign language in the United States. *Journal of Less Commonly Taught Languages*, *17*, 23–55.

Kim, Y., & McDonough, K. (2008). The effect of interlocutor proficiency on the collaborative dialogue between Korean as a second language learners. *Language Teaching Research*, *12*(2), 211–234.

Kim, Y., Nam, J., & Lee, S.-Y. (2016). Correlation of proficiency with complexity, accuracy, and fluency in spoken and written production: Evidence from L2 Korean. *Journal of Less Commonly Taught Languages*, *19*, 147–181.

Kim, Y., Tracy-Ventura, N., & Jung, Y. (2016). A measure of proficiency or short-term memory? Validation of an elicited imitation test for SLA research. *The Modern Language Journal*, *100*(3), 655–673.

Lee, D. (2006). Markedness and L2 acquisition of numeral classifiers. *Bilingual Research*, *31*, 153–169.

Lee, D. (2006a). L2 retention and attrition of Korean numeral classifiers. *Korean Journal of Applied Linguistics*, *22*(2), 49–64.

Lee, E., & Zaslansky, M. (2015). Nominal reference in Korean heritage language discourse. *Heritage Language Journal*, *12*(2), 132–158.

Lee, H. (2017). Effects of fine-tuning instruction on second language pronunciation. *KLA*, *21*(1), 89–119.

Lee, H., & Lee, M. (2008). Genre-based study of oral presentation and its pedagogical implications. *KLA, 13,* 21–42.

Lee, H., & Pyun, D. (2015). Vocabulary learning strategies of learners of Korean as a foreign language: A case study. *Journal of Korean Language Education, 26,* 29–53.

Lee, I. (2015). US-based KFL college students' Korean language learning strategies. *Bilingual Research, 60*(60), 201–227.

Lee, J. (2011). The study on reading-to-write task for KAP learners. *Journal of Korean Language Education, 22*(4), 83–108.

Lee, J.-H. (2003). The effectiveness of web-based listening comprehension assignments for non-heritage students. *KLA, 8,* 233–244.

Lee, K. (1995). Age differences in second language acquisition: An educational perspective. *KLA, 1,* 281–291.

Lee, K. (1997). Motivational type and second language achievement in schools. *KLA, 2,* 87–98.

Lee, M. (1997). Acquisition of Korean referent honorifics by adult learners of Korean as a second language. *KLA, 2,* 99–110.

Lee, M. (2003). Subject case drop vs. object case drop in L2 Korean. *KLA, 8,* 65–73.

Lee, M., Song, M., O'Grady, W., & Park, J. (1999). Word order preferences for direct and indirect objects in children learning Korean. *KLA, 3,* 69–76.

Lee, S. (2003). Age differences in auditory discrimination and pronunciation of Korean phonemes. *KLA, 8,* 85–94.

Lee, S.-I. (2000). An analysis of a speaking practice in Korean. *KLA, 5,* 257–271.

Lee, S.-I. (2001). An analysis of errors in speaking practice. *KLA, 6,* 225–248.

Mueller, J., & Jiang, N. (2013). The acquisition of the Korean honorific affix (*u*)*si* by advanced L2 learners. *The Modern Language Journal, 97*(2), 318–339.

Murray, B. (2010). Students' language learning strategy use and achievement in the Korean as a foreign language classroom. *Foreign Language Annals, 43*(4), 624–634.

Murray, B. (2007). Metacognitive strategies and the achievement of listening proficiency in the language classroom. *Korean Journal of Applied Linguistics, 23*(1), 1–15.

O'Grady, W., Lee, M., & Choo, M. (2000). The acquisition of relative clauses in Korean as a second language. *KLA, 5,* 345–356.

O'Grady, W., Lee, M., & Choo, M. (2001). The acquisition of relative clauses by heritage and non-heritage learners of Korean as a second language. *Journal of Korean Language Education, 12*(1), 283–294.

Oh, K., & Cheon, S. (2016). Motivational orientations and variables of Korean learners. *KLA, 20*(2), 131–151.

Oh, M., & Kim, Y. (2011). The production of Korean stops and intonation by English speakers. *Teaching Korean as a Foreign Language, 36,* 139–158.

Oh, S. (2000). Korean verbs of location, possession, and identity and some pedagogical issues in their acquisition by American students. *KLA, 5,* 357–372.

Park, B. (2001). An error analysis in relation to typological differences. *KLA, 6,* 249–254.

Park, B. (2004). Relationship between motivation and language learning. *KLA, 9,* 308–313.

Park, E. (2009). Learners' perception of indirect written feedback and its impact on their classroom performance. *Bilingual Research, 41,* 179–207.

Park, E. (2013). Learner-generated noticing behavior by novice learners: Tracing the effects of learners' l1 on their emerging L2. *Applied Linguistics, 34*(1), 74–98.

Park, J., & Hong, G. (2003). A remedy for grammatical errors related to two Korean sequential Conjunctives −*ko* and −(*e*)*se* by means of "consciousness raising tasks." *KLA, 8,* 113–129.

Park, J., & Jo, J. (2009). A comparative analysis of summary of Korean text by Korean and foreign students. *Korean Journal of Applied Linguistics*, *25*(2), 227–250.

Park, M.-J. (2000). Incorporating intonation in Korean language instruction. *KLA*, *5*, 373–384.

Park, M.-J. (2009). Perception and production of Korean obstruents through prosody. *Journal of Korean Language Education*, *24*, 143–163.

Park, S. (2013). A study of the case marking of English speaking learners of Korean in complements and adjuncts. *KLA*, *18*, 92–114.

Pyun, O. (2001). Crosscultural variations in personal essays: Second language writing by American learners of Korean as compared to native Koreans' writing. *KLA*, *6*, 309–324.

Shim, W. (2002). A contrastive study of the words '중에 (서)' and "among" in Korean and English, *KLA*, *7* (pp. 239–246).

Shin, E. (2005). The perception of foreign accents in spoken Korean by prosody: Comparison of heritage and non-heritage speakers. *KLA*, *10*, 103–118.

Shin, E. (2007a). How do non-heritage students learn to make the three-way contrast of Korean stops? *KLA*, *12*, 85–105.

Shin, S.-C. (2007b). Lexical errors caused by semantic similarity in Korean. *Teaching Korean as a Foreign Language*, *32*, 141–170.

Shin, S.-C. (2002). Students' lexical errors in Korean. *Journal of Korean Language Education*, *13*, 307–338.

Shin, S.-C. (2006). Acceptability of some Korean lexical items judged by Korean L1 and L2 speakers. *Teaching Korean as a Foreign Language*, *31*, 153–171.

Shin, S.-C. (2008). Locative substitution errors by English L1-KFL learners. *The Language and Culture*, *4*(1), 23–43.

Shin, S.-C. (2009). Language instructors' use of learners' L1 and L2 in classroom: Perceptions by students and teachers of Korean. *Journal of Korean Language Education*, *24*, 165–195.

Shin, S.-C. (2012). Learners' perceptions on text types: Understanding, preferences and necessity. *Journal of Korean Language Education*, *23*(4), 471–493.

Shin, S.-C. (2016). *English* L1-Korean L2 learners' cognitive knowledge and difficulty of grammatical error items. *Language Facts and Perspectives*, *37*, 173–201.

Shin, S.-C., & Kang, S. (2015). L1-Korean L2 learners' grammatical knowledge on high frequency grammatical error items. *Journal of Korean Language Education*, *26*, 59–99.

Song, H., & Schwartz, B. (2009). Testing the fundamental difference hypothesis. *Studies in Second Language Acquisition*, *31*(2), 323–361.

Song, Y., Kim, S., & Rhee, S.-C. (2018). The role of VOT and F0 in production of Korean word-initial stops by non-native learners of the Korean language. *Teaching Korean as a Foreign Language*, *50*, 95–113.

Tark, E. (2016). *Acquisition of Korean obstruents by English-speaking second language learners of Korean and the role of pronunciation instruction* [Doctoral Dissertation]. California State University, Los Angeles, California.

Türker, E. (2017b). The interaction of affective factors in L2 acquisition of Korean formulaic language: A critical overview. *KLA*, *21*(1), 120–145.

Wang, H.-S. (1997). The effects of topic on lexical errors in writings by intermediate learners of Korean. *KLA*, *2*, 39–56.

Wang, H.-S. (2003). A review of research as Korean as a foreign language. *KLA*, *8*, 7–35.

Yang, J. (2003). Motivational orientations and selected learner variables of East Asian language learners in the United States. *Foreign Language Annals*, *36*(1), 44–56.

Annotated bibliography for Chapter 2 Pedagogical approaches and practices in teaching Korean

Brown, L. (2010). Questions of appropriateness and authenticity in the representation of Korean honorifics in textbooks for second language learners. *Language, Culture and Curriculum, 23*(1), 35–50.

Brown investigates how Korean honorifics are represented in dialogs of three Korean language textbooks in terms of frequency, appropriateness, and authenticity, and finds that the use of honorifics is under- or mis-represented with oversimplification. This paper specifically argues that overly simplistic explanations often lead to misunderstandings and inauthentic presentations of honorifics. It suggests that language educators need to understand ideologies and preconceptions affecting their decisions in choosing textbook language.

Byon, A. (2005a). Teaching pragmatic competence through speech acts: American KFL instructional settings. *Teaching Korean as a Foreign Language, 30,* 77–112.

This paper emphasizes the importance of teaching Korean pragmatic ability through speech acts and raises KFL educators' pragmatic and pedagogical awareness. The Korean speech act of refusal in a KFL classroom setting is analyzed. This study emphasizes teaching speech acts through authentic texts and in an interactional framework. It argues for expanding the use of pragmatic learning activities and linking classroom learning to learners' needs and their real-world experiences beyond the school setting. This paper asserts that teaching socio-pragmatic elements is crucial in order to incorporate cultural knowledge in action into an existing syllabus. Byon suggests practical pedagogical applications to stimulate KFL learners' motivation and expedite the process of learning in a broader cultural context.

Chang, M., Cho, Y., Jeon, S., & Jeon, S. (2003). A new strategy to teach Korean grammar: Implementation of output activities in KFL classrooms. *The Korean Language in America, 8,* 181–198.

Chang et al. analyze grammar items from three Korean language textbooks to develop a new grammar activity to be used as classroom instruction. Two units were developed and implemented for consciousness-raising tasks and for output activities to improve performance. Results from student feedback suggest that grammar instruction for output activities should be effective in maintaining the grammar knowledge and interesting to motivate their participation. Overall findings provide insightful suggestions to encourage students to understand and produce the target grammar in a meaningful context.

Cheon, S. (2007). Content-based language instruction through Korean film. *KLA, 12,* 15–30.

Advanced Korean language learners should acquire not only the second language, but also learn about social issues, history, and the culture of the target language. Cheon introduces a content-based language course, which integrates films into language curricula in a college setting. The course *Korean Proficiency Through Film* adopted Content-Based Language Instruction (CBLI) to enhance advanced learners' language skills as well as to broaden their knowledge of Korean studies. Taking KFL learners' language backgrounds, learning experiences, and interests into account, this paper provides practical guidelines to develop a Korean language course utilizing film and assess learners' performance.

Cheon, S., & Kim, K. (2010). Teaching Korean culture with advertisements: Change and persistence in family values and gender roles. *KLA*, *15*, 1–22.

Changes in Korean family life, family values, and gender roles reflected in advertisements were taught and discussed in a Korean language course at the University of Hawaii called *Language and Culture of Korea*. Utilizing advertisements in classroom instruction, Cheon and Kim explored contemporary cultural values and stereotypical social and gender roles based on a hierarchical structure in family and society to facilitate advanced language learners' understanding of Korean culture. Upon the close examination of Korean advertisements, interesting phenomena were found, including the disjuncture between traditional values and new relationships. A theme-based instruction course, one of three content-based instruction models, was introduced and dealt with such topics as a low birth rate, an aging population, and an increased divorce rate in South Korea.

Kang, S. (2002). The effect of the use of Korean and English in KFL classrooms of non-heritage learners. *KLA*, *7*, 28–37.

Starting with a wide range of opinions on the degree of L1 (English) use, Kang points out that there is still very little research that provides quantitative data on how much the primary language of instruction should be the language learners' L1. Data consist of class observations, survey questions, proficiency scores, and students' evaluations. Results reveal that the instructors' use of Korean varies a great deal from 16% to 91% based on 12 hours of sample utterances. Direct correlations between the proficiency scores and the use of Korean and English in the classrooms were not identified. This article calls for detailed and long-term research to find more "effects" on the use L1 and L2 in Korean learning.

Kim, H.-Y. (2005). Construction of language and culture in a content-based language class. *KLA*, *10*, 50–70.

Kim focuses on heritage learners in upper-level Korean courses and presents a content-based curriculum for advanced students. Since content-based instruction (CBI) has been tested as one of the most promising ways to teach foreign languages, CBI is proposed to accommodate a broad range of Korean heritage learners and address their unique needs. Adopting the methodology of ethnography of communication, data were collected from seven learners in a college-level Korean class. The classroom discourse data reveal that the content of CBI such as literature and social issues motivated learners for engaged discussion and students' interview data confirm the effectiveness of the curriculum. Kim provides helpful guidelines to design CBI classes and proposes CBI as a more effective method to yield enriched curricula for both heritage learners and other advanced students.

Kim, J.-E., Park, H., Jang, M., & Nam, H. (2017). Exploring flipped classroom effects on second language learners' cognitive processing. *Foreign Language Annals*, *50*(2), 260–284.

A flipped instructional model has been adopted more into second language (L2) curricula and is expected to differentially affect the L2 learners' cognitive processes. Kim et al. investigate the pedagogical effectiveness of flipped classrooms for KFL learners. The effects of the flipped classroom approach in a content-based instructional context were compared with the traditional classroom approach. Research data were collected from a flipped classroom with 26 students and a traditional classroom with 25 students. Kim et al. found evidence of the positive effects of a flipped classroom format on higher-order thinking processes and cohesive discussion in the content-based language classroom. The students in the flipped classroom demonstrated significantly more use of reasoning skills and produced significantly more cognitive comments than did the traditional classroom students.

Kim, N. (2002). The importance of grammar in Korean language teaching. *Teaching Korean as a Foreign Language*, *27*(1), 119–139.

This research argues that grammar should still be considered one of the major components for acquisition of communicative competence in language teaching and material development. Starting with the historical overview of major language teaching approaches or methods, this study focuses on communicative language teaching (CLT) where grammatical competence is a component of language competence under communicative competence. Kim also mentions that language-teaching practitioners advocate for balanced teaching of grammar through the use of appropriate techniques in recent communicative language teaching. Three factors of grammar instruction in Korean language teaching were suggested: teaching grammar as meaning, teaching grammar as discourse, and teaching grammar as a social function.

Kong, D.-K. (2012). Task-based language teaching in an advanced Korean language learning program. *KLA*, *17*, 32–48.

Kong provides practical information on the implementation of a task-based approach and demonstrates real task-based language teaching (TBLT) classes in the Korean Language Flagship Center (KLFC) at the University of Hawaii. Defining TBLT as a meaning-focused approach, this paper introduces seven stages of TBLT. Some key principles of learning such as rich input, focus on form, and individualized instruction are discussed, and sample target tasks (e.g., debates) are presented to show the interconnectivity of the tasks. Actual implementation of TBLT in an advanced Korean language program are described, along with challenges to this innovative approach such as material development and teacher training.

Kong, D.-K. (2017). Effects of text elaboration on Korean reading comprehension. *The Korean Language in America, 21*(1), 53–88.

Text modification is not actively addressed in KSL/KFL situations. This study aims to verify the effects of text modification with multiple elaboration types and multiple levels of learner proficiency in Korean. A total of 160 intermediate- and advanced-level participants were randomly assigned to one of five elaborated versions of texts. Assessing comprehension and perceived comprehension, Kong finds that text modification (especially elaboration) is an effective tool to promote KSL reading comprehension, and based on their scores on reading comprehension tests, concludes that the KSL learners benefited from the modification task. The results of this study can affect the current practice of materials development and provide a useful framework for future study of the effects of text modification on reading comprehension in KSL/KFL.

Lee, Y.-G. (2001). Effects of task complexity on L2 production. *The Korean Language in America, 6*, 53–67.

Lee investigates the effects of differing degrees of task complexity on learner production and shows that differing degrees of task complexity affects the accuracy and complexity of learners' oral production. Data were collected from three advanced KFL learners and analyzed in terms of complexity and accuracy. It was found that more complex language was produced on a more complex task and more accurate language on a simpler task.

Oh, S.-S. (2012). A project-based curriculum for an advanced Korean class: Teaching Korean in the post-modern era. *KLA, 17*, 128–148.

This study presents actual cases of project-based curricula in upper-level college KFL classes and discusses the course design and learners' self-evaluation. Project-based instruction (PBI), a teaching method leading to active learning through the production of an end-product, was adopted to encourage learners to produce comprehensible output through meaningful interaction in FL/SL education. Presenting case studies of PBI with the course syllabus and content of fourteen actual individual projects, Oh identifies specific benefits and challenges of the project-based curriculum. KFL learners' feedback data were collected and analyzed, and the students' overall assessment of a PBI class was very positive. KFL learners identified positive elements of the PBI classes as the ability to help KFL learners to improve their language skills, and to deepen their knowledge of content.

Park, H. (2002). Grammar instruction in task-based classrooms. *KLA*, *7*, 7–24.

Park argues that the attitudes of FL/SL teachers and researchers toward grammar instruction have been either negative or indifferent due to the communicative language teaching (CLT) approach's emphasis on meaning and authentic language learning rather than on language form. One of the weaknesses of CLT is its exclusive focus on fluency at the cost of accuracy, so task-based language teaching (TBLT) was proposed as a way to overcome this weakness. Following TBLT, Park explores ways to incorporate grammar instruction into task-based Korean language classes. Some examples of possible grammar activities in Korean language instruction were developed to encourage learners to engage in language analysis.

Pyun, D. (2013). Attitudes toward task-based language learning: A study of college Korean language learners. *Foreign Language Annals*, *46*(1), 108–121.

Focusing on FL/SL learners' attitudes toward task-based language teaching (TBLT), Pyun examines the relationship between these attitudes and learner variables (e.g., anxiety and integrated motivation). Questionnaire data were collected from 91 KFL learners who received task-based language instruction and analyzed to identify any correlations. Findings demonstrate that FL/SL learners' perception of TBLT varies depending on their affective or motivational state. Results suggest that FL/SL educators should be more sensitive to learners' motivational levels for effective language learning.

Sohn, H.-M. (1995). Performance-based principles and proficiency criteria for KFL textbook development. *Journal of Korean Language Education*, *6*, 67–98.

Foreign language educators in the United States reorganized and redirected foreign language curricula, textbooks and other teaching materials, and classroom instruction toward a performance-based approach, based on ACTFL (American Council on the Teaching of Foreign Languages) Proficiency Guidelines. Definitions of performance-based language education and performance-based principles were reviewed and presented. Sohn argues for applying the performance-based principles and proficiency criteria to KFL textbook development and KFL instruction in general. It is also recommended for KFL textbook developers to follow a set of performance-based principles such as contextualization, personalization, student-centeredness, and the use of authentic language.

Sohn, H.-M. (2001). Teaching politeness routines in Korean. *KLA*, *6*, 25–35.

This study focuses on politeness, which is crucial in successful intercultural communication and interpersonal communication. Research questions regarding politeness such as the concept of linguistic politeness and linguistic devices for politeness were examined and shared with preservice and in-service teachers of Korean. Sohn argues that explicit teaching of politeness routines to adult learners of Korean is more desirable because it takes time to learn politeness routines through awareness-raising only, and the acquisition could be only fragmentary. Techniques for teaching speech acts are proposed for the effective teaching of Korean politeness routines.

Strauss, S. (1999). Using television commercials as aids for teaching language, grammar, and culture. *KLA*, *3*, 235–252.

This research is one of the early attempts to utilize Korean TV commercials as part of authentic discourse and a rich source of linguistic input, such as vocabulary and grammar in the FL/SL classroom. Forty commercials were recorded and used as sources of linguistic and cultural input in class. Strauss suggests that FL educators use a variety of authentic multimedia materials in the classroom and show that television commercials are effective resources for both building and recycling vocabulary items and grammar.

You, S.-H. (1999). Incorporating the internet resources into various levels of KFL classes. *The Korean Language in America*, *3*, 267–280.

This study points out the great potential of integrating the internet into KFL curricula. Internet-incorporated classes were designed and proposed to make the learning of Korean language more interesting than learning in conventional classes. This study is one of the earliest attempts to adopt what was then the latest technology into KFL teaching in the late 1990s, where the pros and cons of various tools and resources on the internet are discussed for KFL learners. Interactive and dynamic internet activities are suggested for KFL classes.

Bong, M.-K. (2017). The development of a new Korean synonyms dictionary for learners. *Language Facts and Perspectives*, *40*, 31–47.

Brown, L. (2013). Teaching 'casual' and/or 'impolite' language through multimedia: The case of non-honorific *panmal* speech styles in Korean. *Language, Culture and Curriculum*, *26*(1), 1–18.

Byon, A. (2000). Teaching Korean honorifics. *KLA*, *5*, 275–289.

Byon, A. (2005). Composition in the advanced KFL class. *Journal of Korean Language Education*, *16*(1), 299–325.

Chang, M., Cho, Y., & Jeon, S. (2003). A new strategy to teach Korean grammar: Implementation of output activities in KFL classrooms. *KLA*, *8*, 181–198.

Chang, S. (2012). Approaching L2 listening comprehension for advanced learners: Using reading as a pre-listening task. *KLA*, *17*, 166–186.

Cheon, S. (2012). Culture learning curriculum for advanced learners of Korean. *KLA*, *17*, 18–31.

Cho, I. (2000a). Constructivist approaches to development of web courses. *KLA*, *5*, 43–56.

Cho, I. (2000b). Integrating Technology into Korean language education: Teaching today's students for tomorrow's society. *KLA*, *5*, 57–69.

Cho, S. (1999). Review of KFL textbooks: Grammar, culture and task/function. *KLA*, *3*, 297–307.

Cho, S., & Carey, S. (2001). Increasing Korean oral fluency using an electronic bulletin board and wimba-based voiced chat. *KLA*, *6*, 115–128.

Cho, Y.-M., Chun, H., & Jung, J.-Y. (2014). Using film in the college-level KFL classroom: Applying theories and developing activities. *Journal of Korean Language Education*, *25*(4), 249–275.

Choi, H.-W., Choi, H.-W., & Koh, S. (2001). Interactive online exercises: Retention of non-heritage learners in a mixed class. *KLA*, *6*, 129–140.

Choi, S. (2000). Integrating the World Wide Web into Korean language instruction. *KLA*, *5*, 81–90.

Choo, M. (1999). Teaching language styles of Korean. *KLA*, *3*, 77–95.

Chung, H. (2001). Reflective journal writing in the Korean II class. *KLA*, *6*, 325–333.

Chung, Y.-G., Graves, B., Wesche, M., & Barfurth, M. (2005). Computer-mediated communication in Korean-English chat rooms: Tandem learning in an international languages program. *The Canadian Modern Language Review/La revue canadienne des langues vivantes*, *62*(1), 49–86.

Daniel, J., & Chang, S.-J. (2004). Spelling variations of English loan words in KFL textbooks and their pedagogical problems. *KLA*, *9*, 273–281.

Foard, M. (1999). What teachers of Korean and teachers of Japanese can learn from each other: The student centered classroom. *KLA*, *3*, 15–22.

Fouser, R. (2010). Developing web-based multimedia tools to evaluate sociolinguistic proficiency in learners of Korean as a second language. *Journal of Korean Language Education*, *25*, 3–29.

Ganter, S. (1996). Teaching Hanja in Korean language courses. *Bilingual Research*, *7*, 275–280.

Hardy, A., & Kim, M. (2000). Developing content materials for computer-assisted study for enhancing listening comprehension skills in Korean. *KLA*, *4*, 51–62.

Jeon, J. (2004). On-site study of online Korean courses: Current analysis of online Korean courses. *KLA*, *9*, 210–224.

Jeon, S. (2006). Vocabulary teaching and learning in the Korean language: Strategies and activities. *KLA*, *11*, 43–63.

Ju, Y., & Lee, C. (2018). Music as an important Korean learning tool. *Journal of Korean Language Education*, *29*, 1–19.

Jung, J.-H. (1997). Distance language education using multimedia. *Journal of Korean Language Education*, *8*, 235.

Jung, J.-Y. (2010). Classroom study on the efficacy of interactional feedback for Korean particles. *Journal of Korean Language Education*, *21*(4), 255–282.

Jung, J.-Y., & Cho, Y.-M. (2011). An integrated approach to the teaching of business Korean. *KLA*, *16*, 1–40.

Kang, I. (1999). The clause conjunction marker *ko* in Korean. *KLA*, *3*, 97–123.

Kang, I. (2006). Active learning: A new approach to improving students' proficiency in a foreign language. *KLA*, *11*, 84–101.

Kang, S. (1995). Chapter 1.[2]

Kang, S. (1997). Teaching for proficiency: Designing four-skill integration for interactive grammar activities. *KLA*, *2*, 15–25.

Kang, S. (1999). Higher order thinking skills in language education. *KLA*, *3*, 35–40.

Kang, S. (2001). Teaching Korean grammar in context: Teaching of -*myen* and -*ttay*. *KLA*, *6*, 13–23.

Kang, S., & Lim, B.-J. (2011). Implications of ILR/ACTFL proficiency guidelines and text typology in teaching and testing college level Korean. *KLA*, *9*(1), 126–143.

Karlsson, A. (1997). Teaching Korean society and culture through language. *Journal of Korean Language Education*, *8*, 251–259.

Kim, C.-W., & Park, S.-G. (1995). Chapter 1.

Kim, D., & Koh, T. (2017). Tandem translation classroom: A case study. *Journal of Multilingual and Multicultural Development*, *39*(2), 97–110.

Kim, E.-J. (2003). Chapter 1.

Kim, G.-S. (1999). Understanding communication pitfalls. *KLA*, *3*, 161–168.

Kim, K.-O. (2003). Teaching the verb tense in conjunctive clauses in Korean. *KLA*, *8*, 131–140.

Kim, O., & Park, E. (2017). Chapter 1.

Kim, S. (2006). Hangul and teaching pronunciation to beginners. *Journal of Korean Language Education*, *18*, 217–244.

Kim, S., & Elder, C. (2005). Language choices and pedagogic functions in the foreign language classroom: Across-Linguistic functional analysis of teacher talk. *Language Teaching Research*, *9*(4), 355–380.

Kim, S.-C. (1995). Teaching for cultural proficiency in Korean language courses. *KLA*, *1*, 59–64.

Kim, Y. (2006). Culture in the advanced KFL reading class: Using an information-processing approach. *Journal of Korean Language Education*, *17*(3), 27–54.

Kim, Y. (2007). Discourse-based grammar instruction in the advanced KFL writing class. *Bilingual Research*, *33*, 1–34.

Kim, Y., & Kim, Y. (2000). Intermediate Korean web-based instruction. *KLA*, *5*, 91–98.

Kim, Y., Kong, D.-K., Lee, J.-H., & Lee, Y.-G. (2001). Implementation and evaluation of an approach to task-based Korean language teaching. *KLA*, *6*, 45–51.

Kim, Y., & McDonough, K. (2008). Chapter 1.

Kim, Y.-H. (1995). Teaching Asian women's literature in translation. *KLA*, *1*, 43–50.

King, R. (2004). Teaching Korean language through literature. *Journal of Korean Language and Literature Education*, *14*, 295–335.

Ko, K. (2003). Typing in language classes? A study on the effect of learning how to type Korean. *KLA*, *8*, 245–254.

Koo, E.-H. (2001). Using hyper studio for teaching Korean. *KLA*, *6*, 141–149.

Koo, H. (1999). Teaching classical Korean literature: *Hyang'ga*. *KLA*, *3*, 193–208.

Kwon, Y., & Choi, J. (2017). Proposing a Korean teaching method and evaluation tool using paraphrasing in learning. *Journal of Korean Language Education*, *28*(2), 265–289.

Leaver, B., Ehrman, M., & Lekic, M. (2004). Distinguished-level learning online: Support materials from LangNet and RussNet. *Foreign Language Annals*, *37*(4), 556–566.

---

2 In the interest of space, only the author(s) and year are listed here. See the relevant chapter for the full reference.

Lee, D. (2015). Relation between recast and uptake: A longitudinal study in KSL context. *Bilingual Research, 61*, 191–214.

Lee, D.-J. (1995a). A top-down approach to pronunciation teaching and teaching of Korean intonation. *KLA, 1*, 111–124.

Lee, D.-J. (1995b). The state of the art in and desiderata for Korean language textbook compilation. *Journal of Korean Language Education, 6*, 121–158.

Lee, D.-J. (1999). Teaching pronunciation and 한글: Strategies in Korean for English speakers I (preliminary version (5/15/97) by KLEAR). *KLA, 3*, 55–67.

Lee, E.-J. (1997). Effects of task familiarity on second language oral production. *KLA, 2*, 73–85.

Lee, H.-J., & Lim, B.-J. (2018). Interdisciplinary learning and linguistic development in an ICT-based collaborative videoconferencing. *Korean Journal of Applied Linguistics, 34*(1), 169–198.

Lee, J. (2011). Chapter 1.

Lee, J.-E. (1997). A model of video activities in Korean language teaching for elementary to intermediate level learners. *Journal of Korean Language Education, 8*, 279–294.

Lee, J.-H. (2004). "Can you play tennis today?": The distinction between *-(u), l swu issta* and *-(u)l cwul alta. KLA, 9*, 99–112.

Lee, J.-H. (2005). Korean particles: *-to* and *-(i)lato. KLA, 10*, 89–102.

Lee, M. (1997). Chapter 1.

Lee, M. (2002). The role of corrective recasts in L2 Korean: Object relatives and the honorific morpheme *-si. KLA, 7*, 291–306.

Lee, M., & Bonk, C. (2013). Through the words of experts: Cases of expanded classrooms using conferencing technology. *Language Facts and Perspectives, 31*, 107–138.

Lee, S. (2002). Using TV commercials to teach culture. *KLA, 7*, 121–127.

Lee, S. (2017). Qualitative study on genre recognition of native Korean speakers - Based on the comparison between authentic texts and textbook reading materials. *Journal of Korean Language Education, 28*, 81–105.

Lee, S., & Mcvannel, M. (1999). Internet activities for Korean language classes. *KLA, 3*, 253–266.

Lee, S.-I. (2000). Review of introductory unit by DLI. *KLA, 4*, 95–107.

Lee, S.-I. (2004). Role of loan words in teaching Korean. *KLA, 9*, 282–301.

Lee, Y. (2000). Environments for student initiative in intermediate Korean language classroom. *KLA, 5*, 331–344.

Lee, Y., & Cho, S. (2010). Using concept map prewriting strategies in Korean writing classes. *KLA, 15*, 46–61.

Lee, Y.-G. (2000). Task-based approach to syllabus design for Korean as a foreign language. *Journal of Korean Language Education, 11*(1), 111–130.

Lee, Y.-G. (2001). Effects of task complexity on L2 production. *KLA, 6*, 53–67.

Lim, B.-J. (2003). How to teach Korean collocation. *KLA, 8*, 157–163.

Lim, B.-J., & Lee, H.-J. (2015). Videoconferencing for Korean language education: Synchronous online interactions between learners of Korean and English beyond the classroom. *Journal of Korean Language Education, 26*, 1–8.

Nguyen, H., & Yi, H. (2008). The representation of culture in selected Korean textbooks. *KLA, 5*(4), 209–222.

Oh, S.-S. (2004). A corpus-based analysis and teaching of Korean causal connectives: *-nula(ko)* and *-nun palamey. KLA, 9*, 78–98.

Oh, S.-S., & Jeong, H.-J. (2014). Who is talking? From teacher-led to student-led discussion in advanced Korean classes. *Journal of Korean Language Education, 25*(2), 79–112.

Park, B. (2002). Teaching Korean in an integrated four-skills way with pictures and maps. *KLA, 7*, 157–164.

Park, C.-H. (2015). A new approach to selection of academic and technical vocabularies for second language learners of Korean. *Journal of Korean Language Education, 26*, 93–127.

Park, H.-Y. (2008). On Korean subject case-marking rules: Implication for Korean as a foreign language learners. *Journal of Korean Language Education, 19*(1), 113–140.

Park, M.-J. (2000). Chapter 1.

Park, M.Y. (2014). *Teachers' use of speech styles in the Korean language classroom* [Doctoral Dissertation]. University of Hawai'i at Manoa, Honolulu, Hawai'i.

Park, Y.-Y. (1997). Teaching authentic conversation: How to incorporate discourse into teaching. *KLA, 2*, 27–37.

Park, Y.-Y. (1999). Incorporating discourse into classroom activities and teaching grammar in pragmatics: Teaching the connectives *kulentey* and *kulehciman*. *KLA, 3*, 145–160.

Pyun, D. (2004). The role of group work in the second language classroom. *KLA, 9*, 169–191.

Ree, J. (2000). National standards and reinforcement of task-based teaching. *KLA, 5*, 149–166.

Richards, K. (1995). Interactive teaching methods for Korean language instruction. *KLA, 1*, 67–78.

Roh, J. (2011). The development of the cultural video project and its impact on Korean learning. *KLA, 16*, 73–100.

Roh, J. (2016). Teaching poetry in Korean language classes. *KLA, 20*(1), 4–28.

Roh, J., & Kim, T. (2019). Fostering learner autonomy through CALL and MALL in a Korean class: A case study. *Journal of Interactive Learning Research, 30*(2), 215–254.

Shim, Y.-S. (2003). The use of asynchronous CMC in a beginning Korean class. *KLA, 8*, 199–220.

Shin, S.-C. (2009). Chapter 1.

Shin, S.-C. (2014). Focused instructional strategies in remedial teaching on L2 Korean errors: A methodological proposition. *Language Facts and Perspectives, 33*, 219–245.

Sim, S. (2007). A comparison of quantitative and qualitative research method in KSL reading. *Korean Language Education, 124*, 127–149.

Son, J.-B. (1997). An experimental computer-assisted reading practicum in a foreign language classroom. *Korean Journal of Applied Linguistics, 13*(1), 35–61.

Sung, J.B. (2013). Effects of multimodal input on Korean L2 learners' vocabulary acquisition. *Teaching Korean as a Foreign Language, 38*, 133–162.

Sung, K.-Y., & Wu, H.-P. (2011). Factors influencing the learning of Chinese characters. *International Journal of Bilingual Education and Bilingualism, 14*(6), 683–700.

Wang, H.-S. (1999). Speech acts in Korean language textbooks. *Journal of Korean Language Education, 10*(1), 195–220.

Wang, H.-S. (2000). Culture, commercials and teaching Korean. *Journal of Korean Language Education, 11*(1), 85–109.

Wang, H.-S., & Kwa, J. (2019). Investigating gender bias in KFL textbooks. *Teaching Korean as a Foreign Language, 52*, 159–190.

Won, H.-Y. (2018). A study on class activities for Korean sentence pattern applying task-essential language. *Language Facts and Perspectives, 43*, 203–225.

Yang, J. (2004). A writing project integrating cultural aspects, computer technology, and writing skills. *KLA, 9*, 152–168.

Yeon, J. (1996). Some problems in teaching Korean speech levels. *Bilingual Research, 7*, 281–295.

Yi, H. (1999). Culture content analysis of Korean textbooks: A reconsideration of the current theoretical models. *KLA*, *3*, 309–318.

Yoon, S.-S., & Lee, D.-E. (2012). Contexts of the deferential style of Korean. *Journal of Korean Language Education*, *23*(4), 495–516.

You, C. (2000). Oral presentation enhancement. *KLA*, *5*, 181–187.

You, S.-H. (1995). Teaching benefactive construction to KFL learners: A contrastive perspective. *KLA*, *1*, 137–152.

You, S.-H. (2000). K-Buddy: A near-spontaneous and an interactive Korean conversation program. *KLA*, *5*, 105–114.

You, S.-H. (2002). Teaching Korean kinship terms to foreign learners of Korean language: Addressing and referencing. *KLA*, *7*, 307–329.

Yuen, S.-A.K. (2003). Strategies to develop cultural understanding in lower-level Korean classes. *KLA*, *8*, 393–406.

Annotated bibliography for Chapter 3 Language in use

Byon, A. (2003). KFL students' abilities to assess an appropriate speech act. *KLA*, *8*, 95–112.

This study explores how 30 KFL learners enrolled in a second-year Korean class assessed the appropriateness of different scenarios involving performing the speech act of request. Both HLLs and non-HLLs recognized indirectness as a politeness device. However, more HLLs misjudged the appropriate speech level to be used, whereas more non-HLLs failed to recognize euphemistic verbs (e.g., humble expressions such as *yeccwupta* "to ask" and *tulita* "to give"). Byon concludes that teachers should include socio-pragmatic aspects of language use in their pedagogical goals, for both HLLs and non-HLLs.

Byon, A. (2005c). Teaching refusals in Korean. *KLA*, *10*, 1–18.

This study reiterates the importance of teaching pragmatic competence. The researcher suggests effective approaches to teaching the face-threatening speech act of refusal, which is more likely to result in pragmatic failure than other speech acts: (1) help learners identify the target speech act; (2) present explicit strategies to perform the target act (e.g., suggesting an alternative, expressing regret, explaining the reason, etc.); (3) raise learners' awareness of the important socio-pragmatic features of the given situation (e.g., power and social distance); and (4) guide learners to actually perform the given act (e.g., role-play). Byon argues that pragmatic competence is a "vital" component in teaching KFL.

Chung, H. (2017). Pragmatic functions of *ettehkey* as a discourse marker in Korean spoken data. *KLA*, *21*(1), 25–52.

This study makes an important pedagogical suggestion that teaching discourse markers will help KFL learners know how to conduct spoken interactions more appropriately and effectively. Chung examines pragmatic functions of the discourse marker *ettehkey* used in 50 naturally occurring phone conversations between native speakers of Korean. Through a Conversation Analytic method, the researcher was able to identify two primary functions of the marker: (1) a hedging device which allows the listener to mitigate the imposition of the question; and (2) a marker indicating the speaker's affective stance toward what has just been said, typically expressing surprise or perplexity. This study offers empirical evidence that discourse markers play a crucial role in engaging the interlocutors in the conversation.

Kim, J., & Sohn, S.-O. (2012). Repair initiation by advanced non-heritage Korean learners. *KLA*, *17*, 151–165.

This study provides naturally occurring learner data that is rare in Conversation Analysis studies. The researchers investigate how native speakers' and non-native speakers' "other-initiated repair" practices (i.e., treating a problem detected by the interlocutor) are different. When the interlocutor indicated a problem, non-native speakers tended to repeat what their interlocutor has just said, treating the problem source as a simple hearing problem. In contrast, native speakers tended to treat the other-initiated, hearing repair as indicating an understanding problem and thus responded to help their interlocutor's understanding over multiple turns. Moreover, advanced speakers tended to produce understanding repair initiations, whereas lower-proficiency speakers produced more hearing repair initiations. The researchers suggest that teaching repair techniques may help learners effectively communicate with native speakers by utilizing repair initiation to hold a turn at talk (i.e., buying time to produce a response).

Kim, M. (2012). Advanced Korean language learners' use of formulaic language. *KLA*, *17*, 255–268.

This study demonstrates the importance of formulaic language in developing writing proficiency beyond the intermediate level. The researcher examines collocations, lexical bundles, and idiomatic expressions used by advanced KFL learners in their essays. The most frequent errors were found with collocations, mostly produced from word-for-word translations of English expressions. Kim suggests that learners be exposed to more native uses of formulaic language, especially low-frequency expressions, and be explicitly taught to avoid literal translation of English into Korean.

Pyon, D. (2009). A Corpus-based analysis of Korean 'yes' words *yey*, *ney*, and *ung*: A pedagogical perspective. *KLA*, *14*, 25–46.

As a corpus-based study, this study underscores the importance of exposing learners to real-life language use by analyzing the functions of *yey*, *ney*, and *ung*. Pyon points out that traditional textbooks only present the dictionary meaning of those expressions ("yes"), and that teachers should help learners become aware of their functional meanings as important conversational features (e.g., hesitation filler, self-affirmation, repair initiator, etc.).

Song, J. (2016). Language socialization and code-switching: A case study of a Korean–English bilingual child in a Korean transnational family. *International Journal of Bilingual Education and Bilingualism, 19*, 1–16.

This ethnographic study illustrates how a five-year-old Korean–English bilingual child was socialized into the acceptable social types of person (i.e., personae) through code-switching. For example, when he was objecting to or disagreeing with his mom, he switched to English, distancing himself away from Korean and associating aggressiveness and assertiveness with English. In contrast, when he was seeking permission from his mom, he switched to Korean, using a softer tone.

Walker, C. (2016). Identifying pragmatic uses of evidentials in Korean discourse: Observations from native and non-native speaker data. *Language Facts and Perspectives, 37*, 91–116.

This study shows that discourse competence is difficult to acquire, even for advanced-level learners who live in Korea and use Korean as an L2. The researcher compares evidentiality markers (e.g., *-tamye, -telako, -tae,* and *-tako*) used by native speakers of Korean and Japanese learners of Korean in naturally occurring conversations. Results show that native speakers used a much wider range of such markers, while the learners' use of evidentiality markers was limited to certain reportative and quotative markers such as *-tako* and *-tako hata,* possibly due to L1 transfer. These results imply that some clausal connectives and sentence endings should be treated as having discursive and social functions, whereas traditional textbooks treat them as mere grammar items.

Brown, L. (2013). Chapter 2.

Byon, A. (2000a). The analysis of *yo* "the politeness marker in Korean": From language socialization point of view. *KLA, 4*, 115–140.

Byon, A. (2000b). Chapter 2.

Byon, A. (2006). Language socialization in Korean-as-a-foreign-language classrooms. *Bilingual Research Journal, 30*(2), 265–291.

Choi, H.-K. (2002). A study of politeness in Korean requests. *Teaching Korean as a Foreign Language, 27*(1), 271–299.

Choi, J. (2003). The functions of *mwusun* in discourse: Its question/non-question usage and highly discourse dependent nature. *KLA, 8*, 143–155.

Hong, J. (2008). Students' trouble source and signal types in the negotiation of meaning process. *Journal of Korean Language Education, 19*(2), 353.

Jee, H.-S., & Jee, H.-S. (2017). Error analysis of Korean learners' speaking comparing between storytelling and opinion task. *Language Facts and Perspectives, 40*, 147–166.

Jeon, M. (2003). Linking words to the world: The Korean language learners in the United States. *KLA, 8*, 327–336.

Jeong, K.-O. (2005). Use of the first person plural possessive pronoun *woorie* in Korean language. *Journal of Korean Language Education, 16*(3), 405–422.

Kang, H.-S. (2004). Compliment responses by Korean speakers. *KLA, 9*, 113–125.

Kang, I. (2005). Foreign students' views of academic listening and speaking skills in Korean universities. *Bilingual Research, 27*, 21–40.

Kim, H.-G., Kang, B.-M., & Hong, J. (2007). 21st century Sejong corpora (to be) completed. *KLA, 12,* 31–42.

Kim, K.-T. (2007). The relative tense-aspect in emergent discourse: Theoretical and pedagogical implications. *KLA, 12,* 43–66.

Kim, S.-J., & Nam, J.-M. (2009). A discourse analysis of a KFL classroom using English in America. *The Language and Culture, 5*(3), 161–191.

Lee, H. (2013). Perception and production of Korean discourse marker *com* (좀) by KFL and KHL students. *Teaching Korean as a Foreign Language, 38,* 197–226.

Lee, J.-H. (2008). A corpus-based study of short-form and long-form negations in Korean. *KLA, 13,* 43–57.

Lee, S.-H., Dickinson, M., & Israel, R. (2016). Challenges of learner corpus annotation: Focusing on Korean learner language analysis (KoLLA) system. *Language Facts and Perspectives, 38,* 221–251.

Park, H. (2012). Discourse marker *kunyang* in Korean as a second language. *Bilingual Research, 49,* 137–162.

Park, M. Y. (2012). Teachers' use of the intimate speech style in the Korean language classroom. *KLA, 17*(1), 55–83.

Pyun, D. (2009). Pedagogical application of corpora: A speech act analysis of responses to thanks in Korean. *Journal of Korean Language Education, 18*(2), 135–154.

Walker, C. (2018). Sentence Final Particles (SFPs) and audience sensitivity in Korean discourse: A multimodal discourse approach. *Language Facts and Perspectives, 43,* 179–201.

Walker, C. (2019). L1 and L2 Korean evidential use: Using the discourse completion task (DCT). *Language Facts and Perspectives, 46,* 31–55.

Wang, H.-S. (1999). Pragmatic errors and teaching for pragmatic competence. *KLA, 3,* 127–143.

Yoon, K.-E. (2007). Application of conversation analysis to teaching Korean language and culture, *KLA, 12,* 126–144.

Yuen, S.-A. (2001). Socio-pragmatic functions of the interactive sentence ender *-ney* from the politeness perspective. *KLA, 6,* 337–356.

Annotated bibliography for Chapter 4 Culture in language learning and teaching

Brown, L. (2013a). "Oppa, hold my purse:" A sociocultural study of identity and indexicality in the perception and use of *oppa* "older brother" by second language learners. *KLA, 18,* 1–22.

This study examines the perception of the address term *oppa* by female learners of KFL in college. While most HLLs used the term to conform to the Korean norm of their diasporic community, some non-heritage KFL learners viewed it as childish, manipulative, and implicative of gender inequality. The researcher points to the need to include the social meaning and indexicality of the kinship term *oppa* in teaching address terms, in addition to its referential meaning.

Brown, L. (2013b). Teaching 'casual' and/or 'impolite' language through multimedia: The case of non-honorific *panmal* speech styles in Korean. *Language, Culture and Curriculum, 26*(1), 1–18.

This study explores the teaching of impolite speech styles, less commonly taught pragmatics in KFL teaching, and suggests multimedia as a useful instructional resource for intermediate-level learners. Brown provides a personal anecdote in which, as an advanced learner of KFL himself, he felt frustrated to realize that he had never learned how to express anger in Korean. He observed that using drama clips effectively engaged learners in learning and raised their awareness of contextual features and linguistic features associated with them. The instructor designed an activity in which learners identified social relationships and hierarchies among the characters, and when and how they selectively use *contaymal* and *panmal*. Despite the prevalent assumption that teaching *panmal* may lead to learners' overuse and simplification of it, Brown argues that non-polite language should be taught from an earlier stage of learning to help learners learn to function in the "real world" when speaking the target language.

Brown, L. (2016). An activity-theoretic study of agency and identity in the study abroad experiences of a lesbian nontraditional learner of Korean. *Applied Linguistics, 37*(6), 808–827.

In this research, several claims are made by analyzing one lesbian non-traditional KFL learner's journal entries. Brown suggests that a contradiction and the agentive resolution of it is important for defining language-learning trajectories, and that more attention be paid to agency in language learning. He also confirms activity-theoretic perspectives' demonstration of defining self and its emphasis on the historicity of a learner. Finally, his conclusions contradict findings from previous research on L2 English and homosexuality: homosexuality may not necessarily empower Western homosexual learners when studying abroad at non-Western countries.

Byon, A. (2007). The use of culture portfolio project in a Korean culture classroom: Evaluating stereotypes and enhancing cross-cultural awareness. *Language, Culture and Curriculum, 20*, 1–19.

After qualitatively analyzing students' written and spoken reports, Byon reports that a semester-long culture portfolio project helped students gain insights into a particular aspect of Korean culture by minimizing their own stereotypes of the culture. Students' cross-cultural awareness was also enhanced, and this positive learning experience of the target culture had positive impacts on students' language learning.

Lee, I. (2017). Cultural contacts and intercultural sensitivity of KFL college students in the US. *Journal of Korean Language Education, 28*, 19–43.

This research explores the relationships between cultural contact, intercultural sensitivity, and KFL proficiency of college-level KFL students in the US. The research findings suggest that learners' experience with native speakers and contacts through social networking services (SNS) had an impact on their intercultural sensitivity. Lee claims that multimedia is one of the most familiar cultural contacts for learners and is significantly correlated to their intercultural sensitivity and KFL proficiency. A statistically significant correlation is also found between the learners' perception of Korean class and their proficiency levels.

Semaan, G., & Yamazaki, K. (2015). The relationship between global competence and language learning motivation: An empirical study in critical language. *Foreign Language Annals, 48*(3), 511–520.

The researchers explore the relationship between global competence and second language learning motivation in critical language classrooms. Among 137 learners of other critical languages, 11 students of Korean answered a 30-item Likert scale survey. A significant positive relationship between global competence and language learning motivation was found. In addition, global competence was also found to be interconnected with three of the four subcategories of motivation: integrativeness, instrumental orientation, and attitudes and beliefs.

Brown, L. (2010). Questions of appropriateness and authenticity in the representation of Korean honorifics in textbooks for second language learners. *Language, Culture and Curriculum, 23*(1), 35–50.

Byon, A. (2003). Language socialisation and Korean as a heritage language: A study of Hawaiian classrooms. *Language, Culture and Curriculum, 16*(3), 269–283.

Byon, A. (2004). Teaching culture skills to elementary KFL students. *KLA, 9,* 15–30.

Byon, A. (2006). Developing KFL students' pragmatic awareness of Korean speech acts: The use of discourse completion tasks. *Language Awareness, 15*(4), 244–263.

Chan, W., & Chi, S. (2016). Language and culture learning through project work: Perceptions of university students of Korean as a foreign language. *Journal of Korean Language Education, 27,* 133–173.

Cheon, S., & Kim, K. (2010). Teaching Korean culture with advertisements: Change and persistence in family values and gender roles. *KLA, 15,* 1–22.

Choi, A. (2001). The film, the poem, and the story: Integrating literature into the language curriculum. *KLA, 6,* 91–98.

Choi, J., & Yi, Y. (2012). The use and role of pop culture in heritage language learning: A study of advanced learners of Korean. *Foreign Language Annals, 45*(1), 110–129.

Choo, M. (1999). Chapter 2.

Fouser, R. (2009). "Multiculturalization" of Korean language education. *Journal of Korean Language Education, 24,* 119–141.

Gearing, N., & Roger, P. (2017). I'm never going to be part of it: Identity, investment and learning Korean. *Journal of Multilingual and Multicultural Development, 39*(2), 155–168.

Higgins, C., & Stoker, K. (2011). Language learning as a site for belonging: A narrative analysis of Korean adoptee-returnees. *International Journal of Bilingual Education and Bilingualism, 14*(4), 399–412.

Hong, Y. (2004). Cultural integration in Korean language instruction. *KLA, 9,* 1–14.

Hong, Y. (2005). *The role of culture as a social construct in learning Korean as heritage language* [Doctoral Dissertation]. University of Southern California, Los Angeles, California.

Huh, S. (2015). Same music, same genre. Same stance and same purpose? *KLA*, *19*(1), 58–83.

Jee, M. (2019). Foreign language anxiety and self-efficacy: Intermediate Korean as a foreign language learners. *Language Research*, *55*(2), 431–456.

Jeon, M. (2008). Korean language and ethnicity in the United States: Views from within and across. *Qualitative Inquiry*, *14*(1), 28–45.

Jo, H. (2001). 'Heritage' language learning and ethnic identity: Korean Americans' struggle with language authorities. *Language, Culture and Curriculum*, *14*(1), 26–41.

Jung, J.-Y., & Lee, E. (2018). Citizen sociolinguistics: Making connections in the foreign language classroom. *KLA*, *22*(1), 1–24.

Jung, S. (1995). Teaching of Korean literature in Korean language courses. *KLA*, *1*, 51–57.

Karlsson, A. (1997). Chapter 2.

Kim, G. (2018). Applying positioning analysis to interview narratives: A Korean-language learner's experience studying abroad. *Journal of Korean Language Education*, *29*, 21–48.

Kim, H. (1999). The spirit of liberation in modern Korean poetry: Poems by Soe Jungjoo and Kim Sooyoung. *KLA*, *3*, 171–181.

Kim, H.-S., & Lee, H.-S. (2010). Enhancing sociolinguistic competency through Korean on-line TV: Advanced level KFL curriculum. *KLA*, *15*, 23–45.

Kim, K. (2000). Dimensions of Korean culture. *KLA*, *5*, 199–208.

Kim, Y. (2006). Chapter 2.

Kim, Y.-H. (1995). Chapter 2.

Kim, Y.-H. (1997). Teaching Korean culture: Its challenges and significance. *KLA*, *2*, 185–192.

Lee, D. (2014). Motivations of learning Korean and their influence on cultural content. *Korean Language Education Research*, *49*(4), 191–218.

Lee, I. (2018). Effects of contact with Korean popular culture on KFL learners' motivation. *KLA*, *22*(1), 25–45.

Lee, J. (2002). The Korean language in America: The role of cultural identity in heritage language learning. *Language, Culture and Curriculum*, *15*(2), 117–133.

Lee, S. (2002). Chapter 2.

Lee, S., & Cho, H. (2017). Understanding the language learner from the imagined communities perspective: The case of Korean language learners. *Journal of Korean Language Education*, *28*(4), 367–402.

Nguyen, H.T., & Yi, H. (2008). Chapter 2.

Park, E. (2008). Intergenerational transmission of cultural values in Korean American families: An analysis of the verb suffix -ta. *Heritage Language Journal*, *6*(2), 173–205.

Park, H.-Y. (2009). Raising 'ambi-cultural' children: Korean immigrant parents' ambitious project for bilingual education. *Bilingual Research*, *39*, 113–145.

Park, M. (2012). Chapter 3.

Park, M. Y. (2014). A study of the Korean sentence-ender −(u)psita: Implementing transitions between activities in the classroom. *Journal of Pragmatics*, *68*, 25–39.

Park, M. Y. (2016). Integrating rapport-building into language instruction: A study of Korean foreign language classes. *Classroom Discourse*, *7*(2), 109–130.

Ra, C. (2017). A pedagogical study on understanding of "Shinmyoung"(神明) in modern Korean novels for foreign learners. *Journal of the International Network for Korean Language and Culture, 14*(3), 147–172.

Ree, J. (2000). Problems of cultural clash in textbooks. *KLA, 4,* 141–159.

Roh, J. (2016). Chapter 2.

Shin, S.J. (2013). Transforming culture and identity: Transnational adoptive families and heritage language learning. *Language, Culture and Curriculum, 26*(2), 161–178.

Spagnoli, C. (1999). Storytelling: A bridge to Korea. *KLA, 3,* 183–192.

Wang, H.-S. (1999). Chapter 2.

Wang, H.-S. (2000). Chapter 2.

Yi, H. (1999). Chapter 2.

Yoon, S., & Brown, L. (2017). A multiliteracies approach to teaching Korean multimodal (im)politeness. *KLA, 21*(2), 154–133.

You, S.-H. (2002). Chapter 2.

Yuen, S.-A. (2003). Chapter 2.

Annotated bibliography for Chapter 5 Korean heritage language teaching and learning

Carreira, M., & Kagan, O. (2011). The results of the national heritage language survey: Implications for teaching, curriculum design, and professional development. *Foreign Language Annals, 44*(1), 40–64.

The researchers point to Community-Based Instruction (CBI) as a way of promoting HL learning at the college level. Their nation-wide survey with 134 HLLs of Korean indicated a high rate of HLLs' participation in church- or community-based events. Most learners indicated that fulfilling language requirements was their primary reason for taking Korean, followed by communicating with family members and friends.

Cho, Y.-M., & Chun, H. (2015). Integrating assessment in a college-level Korean heritage curriculum in the United States. *Bilingual Research, 61,* 163–189.

This study demonstrates the need to develop diagnostic tests tailored to linguistic characteristics of HLLs. Based on the examination of SAT II Korean, TOPIK, and placement tests of other institutions, the researchers suggest effective placement strategies for HLLs: (1) focusing more on production skills than receptive skills; (2) understanding their linguistic profiles and learning goals; (3) designing writing tasks more carefully in order to identify areas considered challenging for HLLs, such as orthographic proficiency, complex grammar structures, and discourse organization.

Choi, J., & Yi, Y. (2012). The use and role of pop culture in heritage language learning: A study of advanced learners of Korean. *Foreign Language Annals, 45*(1), 110–129.

This study suggests pop culture as a "point of access" (p. 116) to literacy practice for advanced-level HLLs. Study results show that the learners are actively engaged in a variety of literacy practices using popular media to re-establish and reinforce their sense of identity. Distinct from many existing studies on HL identity, the researchers frame the identity construction from the perspective of global citizens, rather than from that of Korean-Americans.

Huh, S., & Choi, Y. (2015). Lasting effects of the Korean community schools on American college students' Korean language proficiency, motivation, and attitudes. *Journal of Korean Language Education, 26*(3), 287–318.

In this survey study with 106 students enrolled in a Korean course at a large university, HLLs who had attended a Korean Community School (KCS) before college were found to be placed in significantly higher levels than those who did not. These learners also showed a more positive attitude toward studying Korean at the tertiary level and demonstrated stronger motivation to improve their Korean. The vast majority of HLLs who attended a KCS indicated that they were studying Korean to communicate better with their family.

Jee, M.-J. (2016). Exploring Korean heritage language learners' anxiety: "We are not afraid of Korean!" *Journal of Multilingual and Multicultural Development, 37*(1), 56–74.

This study reports a negative correlation between the level of anxiety and the achievement of 61 HLLs. Study results show that the learners had a higher level of anxiety in writing than in reading. Interestingly, the HLLs who identified themselves as Korean—i.e., had a stronger sense of identity as Korean—showed less anxiety, and, thus, received higher grades.

Kang, H.-S. (2010). Negative evidence and its explicitness and positioning in the learning of Korean as a heritage language. *The Modern Language Journal, 94*(4), 582–599.

In this experimental study, Kang explores the effectiveness of negative evidence, a type of corrective feedback, in learning the past-tense suffix. The researcher points out that HLLs' proficiency often declines, and their grammatical accuracy tends to stagnate as they reach adulthood. The statistical analyses showed that a reactive provision of negative evidence, immediately following an error, was more effective than a preemptive, proactive provision, and that explicit negative evidence was more effective than implicit negative feedback.

Kim, H.-Y. (2003). Heritage students' perspectives on language classes. *KLA, 8*, 315–326.

This study explores HLLs' perspectives on their Korean learning in college. The researcher conducted individual interviews of 20 students who had taken a Korean course at the researcher's institution. According to the researcher, "the recurring theme" was identity. Results show that the HLLs reaffirmed their Korean identity through taking a Korean class and that they especially enjoyed cultural contents and literacy practices in class. An interesting finding is that, while all students expressed desire to maintain and improve their HL, only one student was committed to passing down Korean to his/her own children, due to a lack of confidence in their spoken Korean. The researcher projected that "the Korean language will probably be lost among third-generation Korean-Americans" (p. 324).

Kim, J.-I. (2015). Issues of motivation and identity positioning: Two teachers' motivational practices for engaging immigrant children in learning heritage languages. *International Journal of Bilingual Education and Bilingualism, 20*(6), 638–651.

The researcher examined two Korean teachers' use of language in their Saturday Korean Schools. The analytical focus was placed on the teachers' positioning of themselves and their use of motivational talk. One teacher, who positioned herself as a "director," focused on asserting her authority as a teacher and improving her students' accuracy. In contrast, the other teacher, who positioned herself as a "supporter," focused more on encouraging her students, boosting learner autonomy, and making the learning process enjoyable.

Kim, M. (2013). The mental lexicon of low-proficiency Korean heritage learners. *Heritage Language Journal, 10*(1), 17–35.

This study explores HLLs' mental lexicon and provides empirical evidence for the lack of collocation-based associations by HLLs. Although HLLs typically have a larger vocabulary and more exposure to natural language use, the HLLs in this study did not show higher accuracy than non-heritage learners. However, the results do indicate HLLs' conceptual associations are stronger than those of non-heritage learners.

Lo, A. (2009). Lessons about respect and affect in a Korean heritage language school. *Linguistics and Education, 20*(3), 217–234.

This study illustrates children's language socialization into the practices of (dis)respect at a Korean-American heritage language school. The researcher investigated the teachers' meta-discourse about their students' language and behavior, and found that the teachers often made comments about their own affective state and stance (e.g., *kipwun, maum*) to frame the students' behavior as (dis)respectful. In addition, also through meta-discourse about their own feelings, they often conveyed ideologies about their students' identity as Korean-American, which was given priority over respecting students' feelings, the American norm.

Park, E., Song, S., & Shin, Y. (2016). To what extent do learners benefit from indirect written corrective feedback? A study targeting learners of different proficiency and heritage language status. *Language Teaching Research, 20*(6), 678–699.

This study provides empirical evidence that indirect corrective feedback (e.g., underlining erroneous parts of writing) can be effective in helping learners self-correct their errors, although only "treatable" ones. HLLs in the study were able to correct mostly their errors with particles, while non-heritage learners were also able to correct orthographic errors as well as particle errors. These findings suggest that HLLs, who are more exposed to oral language, tend to have more difficulty in acquiring orthographic accuracy than non-HLLs do.

Shin, J. (2009). Resource-sharing practices in a mixed Korean language classroom: Critical perspectives. *KLA*, *14*, 47–73.

It is widely acknowledged that two separate tracks are ideal to meet the different needs of HLLs and non-HLLs. However, due to insufficient enrollment and funding, this solution is not always tenable for most institutions. In response to the need to accommodate both learner groups in the same classroom, the researcher examines a prevalent approach to teaching a mixed class called "resource-sharing," in which HLLs and non-HLLs were paired in communicative activities. The results based on a semi-structured interview with 11 focal participants show that non-HLLs often felt marginalized and stressed working with HLLs due to a lack of cultural capital and "unhealthy" power dynamics, although they certainly benefited from their HLL partners' linguistic resources.

Shin, S., & Lee, J. (2013). Expanding capacity, opportunity, and desire to learn Korean as a heritage language. *Heritage Language Journal*, *10*(3), 357–366.

Concerned with advanced language attrition in the Korean American community, the researchers propose ways to help young HLLs develop and maintain their HL proficiency based on the Capacity development, Opportunity creation, and Desire (COD) framework. Such suggestions include: (1) increasing opportunities to learn Korean in a formal setting by promoting Korean community language schools; (2) providing adequate professional development for teachers; (3) developing appropriate curricula for HLLs; (4) including marginalized HLLs such as interracial children and adoptees; (5) using technology to address the literacy needs of transnational adolescents; (6) hiring Korean-speaking teachers for extra-curricular activities; (7) using Korean at home and involving HLLs in other Korean-speaking communities; (8) increasing opportunities to live and work in Korea; (9) exposing HLLs to Korean values and sentiments through popular culture; and (10) creating authentic purposes for using Korean and raising sociolinguistic awareness.

Shin, S., & Kim, S. (2000). The introduction of content-based language teaching to college-level Korean program for heritage learners. *The Korean Language in America*, *5*, 167–179.

This study suggests Content-Based Language Teaching (CBLT) as an effective pedagogical solution for addressing the needs of HLLs. The researchers advocate the efficacy and feasibility of CBLT in the heritage classroom. Typically, by the time HLLs start learning Korean in the classroom, they have already acquired extensive linguistic and cultural competence, compared with traditional, non-HLLs. Therefore, HLLs are usually able to handle the subject matter with relative ease and confidence. The researchers also argue that CBLT exposes HLLs to meaningful language use and eventually motivates them to make use of their Korean outside the classroom.

Sohn, S.-O., & Shin, S.-K. (2007). True beginners, false beginners, and fake beginners: Placement strategies for Korean heritage speakers. *Foreign Language Annals, 40*(3), 407–418.

This study was motivated by the researchers' observation that placing HLLs into an appropriate course level is often problematic due to their wide range of proficiency levels and skills. Placing them in a lower-level course may discourage non-HLL students because of HLLs' high level of oral/aural fluency. Placing HLLs into an upper-level course may also be problematic because HLLs tend to lack linguistic knowledge (e.g., grammar and spelling) and literacy skills. To address these placement issues, the researchers suggest several placement strategies for HLLs: (1) examining various profiles of HLLs, and, based on that, determining what the HLL can do best in spoken proficiency (i.e., establish the ceiling); (2) determining the HLL's literacy and cognitive ability pertinent to his/her academic potential as well as everyday functional ability; (3) adopting a "noncompensatory" approach in which the HLL is determined to meet the minimum requirement for the level; and (4) conducting a mandatory oral interview.

Ahn, S. (2018). "I realized I am Korean": Heritage language learning and identity development from study abroad experience. *Studies in Foreign Language Education, 32*(2), 27–53.

Bae, G. (2005). *Learning to be Korean: The process of identity negotiation and representation for Korean–American elementary school children at heritage language school and home* [Doctoral Dissertation]. The Pennsylvania State University, University Park, Pennsylvania.

Bae, J. (2006a). The evidence for equivalence of parallel test-forms for assessing narrative-task-based writing skills. *Korean Journal of Applied Linguistics, 22*, 189–212.

Bae, J. (2006b). Two-way immersion students' writing skills in Korean as a first and foreign language in the United States. *Bilingual Research, 31*, 55–96.

Bale, J. (2010). International comparative perspectives on heritage language education policy research. *Annual Review of Applied Linguistics, 30*, 42–65.

Byon, A.S. (2003). Chapter 4.

Cho, G. (2000). The role of heritage language in social interactions and relationships: Reflections from a language minority group. *Bilingual Research Journal, 24*(4), 369–384.

Cho, G., Cho, K., & Tse, L. (1997). Why ethnic minorities want to develop their heritage language: The case of Korean–Americans. *Language, Culture and Curriculum, 10*(2), 106–112.

Cho, H. (2014). "It's very complicated" Exploring heritage language identity with heritage language teachers in a teacher preparation program. *Language and Education, 28*(2), 181–195.

Cho, H. (2018). Korean–English bilingual sibling interactions and socialization. *Linguistics and Education, 45,* 31–39.

Cho, S. (2008). *Korean immigrants' social practice of heritage language acquisition and maintenance through technology* [Doctoral Dissertation]. The University of British Columbia, Vancouver, Canada.

Choe, H., & Park, Y. (2004). Parents' strategies for 11 maintenance in Korean graduate student families. *KLA, 9,* 259–272.

Choi, J. (2015). A heritage language learner's literacy practices in a Korean language course in a U.S. university: From a multiliteracies perspective. *Journal of Language and Literacy Education, 11*(2), 116–133.

Choi, J., & Yi, Y. (2012). Chapter 4.

Choi, J.-O. (2007). A longitudinal study of code switching. *Korean Journal of Applied Linguistics, 23*(1), 261–286.

Chung, E. (2018). Long-form negation in adult Korean heritage speakers. *Bilingual Research, 72,* 255–280.

Chung, J. (2012). *The relationship of heritage language/culture education with academic achievement: A study of the 1.5 and 2nd generation of Korean American high school students* [Doctoral Dissertation]. The University of Oregon, Eugene, Oregon.

Chung, M. (2019). *A teacher action research: Motivation of the participants for learning Korean as a heritage language using sheltered instruction in the United States context* [Doctoral Dissertation]. Texas A&M University, College Station, Texas.

Ee, J. (2018). Exploring Korean dual language immersion programs in the United States: Parents' reasons for enrolling their children. *International Journal of Bilingual Education, 21*(6), 690–709.

Finch, A. (2009). Community schools in the UK: Key issues and recommendations. *Journal of Korean Language Education, 20*(3), 205–234.

Fraschini, N. (2017). I thought that I don't qualify to call Korean my "national language" - Identity and authenticity in Korean-Australian heritage language learners. *Journal of Korean Language Education, 28,* 45–80.

Han, H. (2011). *"Am I Korean American?" Beliefs and practices of parents and children living in two languages and two cultures* [Doctoral Dissertation]. University of Illinois, Urbana-Champaign, Illinois.

Gatti, A., & O'Neill, T. (2017). Who are heritage writers? Language experiences and writing proficiency. *Foreign Language Annals, 50*(4), 734–753.

Gatti, A., & O'Neill, T. (2018). Writing proficiency profiles of heritage learners of Chinese, Korean, and Spanish. *Foreign Language Annals, 51*(4), 719–737.

Han, H. (2012). Early bilingual development in a Korean-American Community. *Bilingual Research, 50,* 269–294.

Higgins, C., & Stoker, K. (2011). Chapter 4.

Hong, J. (2006). Syntactic properties of Korean and the syntax-level profile of Korean heritage learners. *The Language and Culture, 2*(3), 1–13.

Hong, Y. (2005). Chapter 4.

Jee, M.-J. (2011). Perspectives on the learning of Korean and identity formation in Korean heritage learners. *Teaching Korean as a Foreign Language, 36,* 265–289.

Jee, M.-J. (2014). Heritage language learners' anxiety: Any changes over a year? *Korean Language Education Research, 49*(4), 109–107.

Jee, M.-J. (2015). A study of language learner motivation: Learners of Korean as a foreign language. *Journal of Korean Language Education, 26*(2), 213–238.

Jee, M.-J. (2016). Korean-American students' beliefs about language learning: The effect of perceived identity. *Journal of Korean Language Education, 27*(2), 275–302.

Jeon, M. (2005). *Language ideology, ethnicity, and biliteracy development: A Korean-American perspective* [Doctoral Dissertation]. The University of Pennsylvania, Philadelphia, Pennsylvania.

Jeon, M. (2007). Biliteracy development and continua of biliteracy. *Korean Journal of Applied Linguistics, 23*(1), 201–215.

Jeon, M. (2008a). Korean heritage language maintenance and language ideology. *Heritage Language Journal, 6*(2), 206–223.

Jeon, M. (2008b). Chapter 4.

Jeon, M. (2010). Korean language and ethnicity in the United States. *The Modern Language Journal, 94*(1), 43–55.

Jo, H.-Y. (2001). Chapter 4.

Joo, A., & Shin, S.-C. (2016). Characteristic features of English-L1 KHL learner orthographic errors. *Journal of Korean Language Education, 27*, 1–36.

Joo, H. (2005). *Biliteracy development: A multiple case study of Korean bilingual adolescents* [Doctoral Dissertation]. The Ohio State University, Columbus, Ohio.

Joo, H. (2008). The influences of biliteracy practices on identity construction. *Bilingual Research, 37*, 265–285.

Joo, H. (2009). Literacy practices and heritage language maintenance: The case of Korean-American immigrant adolescents. *Journal of Asian Pacific Communication, 19*(1), 76–99.

Kang, H.-S. (2010). Korean as heritage language in the U.S. university classroom. *Journal of Less Commonly Taught Languages, 8*, 141–167.

Kang, H.-S., & Kim, I.-S. (2012). Perceived and actual competence and ethnic identity in heritage language learning: A case of Korean-American College students. *International Journal of Bilingual Education and Bilingualism, 15*(3), 279–294.

Kang, P. (2013). *The effects of heritage language use and free voluntary reading in English upon the acquisition of academic English by Korean American students* [Doctoral Dissertation]. University of Southern California, Los Angeles, California.

Kang, S.-G. (2016). Early detection of English attrition in Korean-English bilingual children. *Journal of Language Sciences, 23*(3), 327–344.

Kim, A.-Y., Park, A., & Lust, B. (2016). Simultaneous vs. successive bilingualism among preschool-aged children: A study of four-year-old Korean–English bilinguals in the USA. *International Journal of Bilingual Education and Bilingualism, 21*(2), 164–178.

Kim, C., & Pyun, D. (2014). Heritage language literacy maintenance: A study of Korean-American heritage learners. *Language, Culture and Curriculum, 27*(3), 294–315.

Kim, E.-J. (2003). An analysis of particle errors by heritage and non-heritage learners of Korean. *KLA, 8*, 37–49.

Kim, E.-J. (2004). Korean-English bilinguals and heritage language maintenance. *KLA, 9*, 244–258.

Kim, H. (2017). Syntactic complexity in the writing of Korean heritage learners in the United States. *KLA, 21*(2), 186–217.

Kim, H.-S. (2001). Issues of heritage learners in Korean language classes. *KLA, 6*, 257–274.

Kim, H.-S. (2002). The language backgrounds, motivations, and attitudes of heritage learners in KFL classes at University of Hawai'i at Manoa. *KLA, 7*, 205–221.

Kim, H.-S. (2008). *Processing strategies and transfer of heritage and non-heritage learners of Korean* [Doctoral Dissertation]. University of Hawai'i at Manoa, Honolulu, Hawai'i.

Kim, H.-S., & Jee, M. (2017). Heritage language proficiency in relation to attitudes, motivation, and age at immigration: A case of Korean-Australians. *Language, Culture and Curriculum, 31*(5), 99–134.

Kim, H.-S.H. (2004). A pilot test on processing transfer and strategies of heritage and non-heritage learners of Korean. *KLA, 9*, 225–243.

Kim, H.-Y. (2005). Construction of language and culture in a content-based language class. *KLA, 10*, 50–70.

Kim, I. (2012). Phenomena of discourse marker use of bilingual children and implications for heritage language education. *KLA, 17*(1), 24–54.

Kim, J. (2008). *Negotiating multiple investments in languages and identities: The language socialization of generation 1.5. Korean-Canadian University Students* [Doctoral Dissertation]. The University of British Columbia, Vancouver, Canada.

Kim, J.-H. (2010). Binding interpretations of Korean core reflexives by Korean heritage speakers in US and in China. *Korean Journal of Applied Linguistics, 26*(1), 131–161.

Kim, J.-T. (2001). The degree of L1 interference among heritage and non-heritage learners of Korean: Do heritage students have advantages over non-heritage students? *KLA, 6*, 285–296.

Kim, K. (2014). *Unveiling linguistic competence by facilitating performance* [Doctoral Dissertation]. University of Hawai'i at Manoa, Honolulu, Hawai'i.

Kim, K.-R. (2001). The sociolinguistic constraints on code switching. *Bilingual Research, 19*, 112–135.

Kim, K.-R. (2003). The sociolinguistic constraints on Korean-English bilingual children's code switching behavior. *Bilingual Research, 22*, 140–162.

Kim, M. (2002). Writing as a facilitating methodology for mixed beginning classes. *KLA, 7*, 129–141.

Kim, S. (2013). When keeping up means falling behind: The dear price of stressing "correct" orthography in teaching Korean as a heritage language. *KLA, 18*, 71–91.

Kim, S., O'Grady, W., & Cho, S. (1995). The acquisition of case and word order in Korean. *Bilingual Research, 12*(1), 127–139.

Kim, S., & Sohn, S.-O. (2016). Service-learning, an integral part of heritage language education: A case study of an advanced-level Korean language class. *Heritage Language Journal, 13*(3), 354–381.

Kim, S.-J. (2015). Negative Polarity Items (NPIs) in heritage Korean maintenance and transfer. *KLA, 19*(1), 36–57.

Kim, S.-Y. (2013). *Errors in inflectional morphemes as an index of linguistic competence of Korean heritage language learners and American learners of Korean* [Doctoral Dissertation]. The University of Kansas, Lawrence, Kansas.

Kim, S.-Y. (2017). A situated perspective on bilingual development: Preschool Korean–English bilinguals' utilization of two languages and Korean honorifics. *International Journal of Bilingual Education and Bilingualism, 20*(1), 1–19.

Kim, S.-Y., & Lim, J. (2007). Errors and strategies observed in Korean heritage learners' L2 writing. *Foreign Languages Education, 14*(4), 93–112.

Kim, Y.-M. (1996). Crossing disciplinary boundaries in studying home language maintenance and re-learning. *Bilingual Research, 13*, 35–62.

Kwak, J., & Kim, J. (2007). Korean Heritage learners' self-assessment of writing activities in the student workbook. *Journal of Korean Language Education, 18*(2), 1–19.

Laleko, O., & Polinsky, M. (2013). Marking topic or marking case: A comparative investigation of heritage Japanese and heritage Korean. *Heritage Language Journal, 10*(2), 178–202.

Lee, C.-B. (2000). Two-track curriculum system for university Korean language programs. *KLA, 4,* 3–12.

Lee, D. (2001). L2 development through collaborative interaction. *Journal of Korean Language Education, 12*(1), 181–198.

Lee, D., & Lee, K.-O. (2002). Acquisition of Korean numeral classifiers by Korean/English bilingual children. *Journal of Korean Language Education, 13*(1), 265–278.

Lee, D.-J. (2001). Recent trends in foreign language teaching in the United States: The role of heritage learners. *KLA, 6,* 203–211.

Lee, E. (2014). *Speech production and perception of heritage speakers of Korean* [Doctoral Dissertation]. University of California, Los Angeles, Los Angeles, California.

Lee, E. (2018). L2 and heritage Korean tense morphology in discourse: Interplay between lexical and discursive meaning. *Heritage Language Journal, 15*(2), 173–202.

Lee, E., & Zaslansky, M. (2015). Chapter 1.

Lee, J. (2005). Through the learners' eyes: Reconceptualizing the heritage and non-heritage learner of the less commonly taught languages. *Foreign Language Annals, 38*(4), 554–563.

Lee, J., & Takashi, M. (2016). Korean parents' attitudes toward bilingual education in the U.S. *Journal of Korean Language Education, 27,* 79–97.

Lee, O.-S. (2017). A psycholinguistic measurement of language dominance in bilinguals. *Journal of Language Science, 24*(4), 207–223.

Lee, S., & Cho, H. (2017). Understanding the language learner from the imagined communities perspective: The case of Korean language learners in the U.S. *Journal of Korean Language Education, 28*(4), 367–402.

Lee, S., & Kim, H. (2002). Motivational orientation of students of Korean and its relationship to language achievement. *KLA, 7,* 189–203.

Lee, S.K., & Ahn, R. (2001). Language shift in bilingual students: A sociolinguistic survey of Korean-American College students. *KLA, 6,* 181–201.

Lee, T. (2014). Errors in the production of adult early and late bilinguals. *Journal of Less Commonly Taught Languages, 16,* 33–55.

Lee, T., & Rastogi, T. (2013). Variation among heritage speakers: Sequential vs. simultaneous bilinguals. *Journal of Less Commonly Taught Languages, 14,* 1–26.

Lee-Ellis, S. (2011). The elicited production of Korean relative clauses by heritage speakers. *Studies in Second Language Acquisition, 33*(1), 57–89.

Lee-Smith, A. (2019). Building a community of heritage language learners. *Journal of Korean Language Education, 30,* 1–44.

No, S.-H. (2011). *Language socialization in two languages, schoolings, and cultures: A descriptive qualitative case study of Korean immigrant children* [Doctoral Dissertation]. University of Iowa, Iowa City, Iowa.

Noji, F., & Yuen, S.-A. (2012). Developing content based curriculum: Aimed toward superior level of proficiency. *KLA, 17,* 93–108.

Oh, M.K. (2002). Three Asian scholars' bilingual view of bilingualism. *Bilingual Research, 21,* 260–284.

Pae, H., & Sevcik, R.-A. (2016). Child, home, and heritage language: The influence of home literacy activities on emergent reading skills in a sequential language. *Bilingual Research, 64*(64), 21–54.

Pak, H. (2005). *Language planning for biliteracy at a Korean American church school* [Doctoral Dissertation]. The Universiy of Pennsylvania, Philadelphia, Pennsylvania.

Park, C. (2007). *Maintaining Korean as a heritage language* [Doctoral Dissertation]. Arizona State University, Tempe, Arizona.

Park, E. (2008). Chapter 4.

Park, H.-Y. (2008). Linguistic capital and code-switching. *Bilingual Research, 36,* 137–166.

Park, H.-Y. (2009). Chapter 4.

Park, S. (2010). *The linguistic and cultural influence of Korean ethnic churches on heritage language and identity maintenance among Korean Canadian students in Quebec* [Doctoral Dissertation]. McGill University, Montreal, Canada.

Park, S. (2011). The role of ethnic religious community institutions in the intergenerational transmission of Korean among immigrant students in Montreal. *Language, Culture and Curriculum, 24*(2), 195–206.

Park, S., & Bae, S. (2013). Korean immigrant youth's individual trilingualism within the English-French bilingual framework of Canada. *Bilingual Research, 52,* 149–179.

Park, S., Lee, J., Kim, H., Joo, H., & Lee, D. (2003). Needs analysis of the Korean community (language/culture) schools in Hawaii. *KLA, 8,* 255–293.

Park, S., & Sarkar, M. (2007). Parents' attitudes toward heritage language maintenance for their children and their efforts to help their children maintain the heritage language: A case study of Korean-Canadian immigrants. *Language, Culture and Curriculum, 20*(3), 223–235.

Park-Johnson, S. (2017). Code mixing as a window into language dominance: Evidence from Korean heritage speakers. *Heritage Language Journal, 14*(1), 49–69.

Pyun, D., & Lee-Smith, A. (2011). Reducing Korean heritage language learners' orthographic errors: The contribution of online and in-class dictation and form-focused instruction. *Language, Culture and Curriculum, 24*(2), 141–158.

Ramsey, S. (1995). Children without a native language. *Journal of Korean Language Education, 6,* 59–66.

Richards, K. (2000). Teaching students with diverse backgrounds. *KLA, 4,* 65–76.

Ro, Y. (2010). *Navigating a bilingual/biliterate childhood: A longitudinal study of three second-generation young learners in the U.S.* [Doctoral Dissertation]. University of Illinois, Urbana-Champaign, Illinois.

Ro, Y., & Cheatham, G. (2009). Biliteracy and bilingual development in a second-generation Korean child: A case study. *Journal of Research in Childhood Education, 23*(3), 290–308.

Ryu, J. (2015). The basic research to build virtual Korean language schools. *Journal of Korean Language Education, 26*(1), 89–115.

Seo, Y. (2017). *Early bilingual development: Expanding our understanding of family language policy in heritage language maintenance* [Doctoral Dissertation]. University of Washington, Seattle, Washington.

Seong, G. (2006). Form and function of code-switching in Korean/English bilinguals' e-mail notes. *Bilingual Research, 30,* 245–273.

Shin, E. (2005). Chapter 1.

Shin, H. (2015). *Korean heritage school teachers' professional identity* [Doctoral Dissertation]. George Mason University, Fairfax, Virginia.

Shin, S. (2008). Korean heritage language education in the United States: The current state, opportunities, and possibilities. *Heritage Language Journal, 6*(2), 153–172.

Shin, S.-C. (2008). Language use and maintenance in Korean migrant children in Sydney. *Teaching Korean as a Foreign Language, 33,* 139–167.

Shin, S.-C., & Joo, A. (2015). Lexical errors in Korean-Australian heritage learners' compositions. *Journal of Korean Language Education, 26,* 129–162.

Shin, S.-C., & Jung, S.J. (2015). A critical look at research on heritage language development and maintenance of Korean. *Teaching Korean as a Foreign Language, 43*, 97–134.

Shin, S.-C., & Jung, S.J. (2018). Language maintenance and shift in the Korean community in Australia. *Language Facts and Perspectives, 45*, 251–279.

Shin, S.-C., Ko, S., & Rue, Y.-J. (2016). Heritage language learning: A needs analysis study on Korean-Australian tertiary students. *Journal of Korean Language Education, 27*(1), 111–155.

Shin, S.-Y. (2010). The functions of code-switching in a Korean Sunday School. *Heritage Language Journal, 7*(1), 91–116.

Shin, Y.-S. (2015). *Weaving their identities: A narrative inquiry into Korean heritage language learners* [Doctoral Dissertation]. University of Illinois at Urbana-Champaign, Champaign, Illinois.

So, Y., Sohn, S.-O., & Kim, J. (2018). Analysis of Korean heritage learners' writing across different discourse types. *Heritage Language Journal, 15*(3), 319–340.

Sohn, S.-O. (1995). The design of curriculum for teaching Korean as a heritage language. *KLA, 1*, 19–35.

Sohn, S.-O. (1997). Issues and concerns in teaching multi-level classes: Syllabus design for heritage and non-heritage learners. *KLA, 2*, 139–145.

Song, J. (2007). *Language ideologies and identity: Korean children's language socialization in a bilingual setting* [Doctoral Dissertation]. The Ohio State University, Columbus, Ohio.

Song, J. (2019a). Language socialization and code-switching: A case study of a Korean–English bilingual child in a Korean transnational family. *International Journal of Bilingual Education and Bilingualism, 22*(2), 91–106.

Song, J. (2019b). *Wuli* and stance in a Korean heritage language classroom: A language socialization perspective. *Linguistics and Education, 51*, 12–19.

Song, M., O'Grady, W., Cho, S., & Lee, M. (1997). The learning and teaching of Korean in community schools. *KLA, 2*, 111–127.

Suh, E. (2014). *Incomplete acquisition in the nominal domain of Korean by heritage language speakers* [Doctoral Dissertation]. University of Toronto, Toronto, Canada.

Wang, H.-S. (1995). The impact of family background on the acquisition of Korean honorifics. *KLA, 1*, 197–211.

Wang, H.-S., & Liu, C. (2014). Biracial Koreans and their approaches to Korean language learning. *Teaching Korean as a Foreign Language, 40*, 171–206.

Yang, J. (2003a). Motivational orientation of Korean learners and ethnic identity development of heritage learners. *KLA, 8*, 295–314.

Yang, J. (2003b). Chapter 1.

Yi, Y. (2005). *Immigrant students' out-of-school literacy practices: A qualitative study of Korean students' experiences* [Doctoral Dissertation]. The Ohio State University, Columbus, Ohio.

Yi, Y. (2008). Voluntary writing in the heritage language: A study of biliterate Korean-heritage adolescents in the U.S. *Heritage Language Journal, 6*(2), 224–245.

You, B.-K., & Liu, N. (2011). Stakeholder views on the roles, challenges, and future prospects of Korean and Chinese heritage language-community language schools in the Phoenix metropolitan area: A comparative study. *Heritage Language Journal, 8*(3), 359–384.

You, C. (2001). Heritage vs. non-heritage issues revisited. *KLA, 6*, 275–284.

You, S.-H. (1997). A remedial method of teaching Korean orthography. *KLA, 2*, 57–69.

Young, S. (2012). *Looking into bilingualism through the heritage speaker's mind* [Doctoral Dissertation]. The University of Maryland, College Park, Maryland.

Annotated bibliography for Chapter 6 Literacy and multiliteracies in Korean language learning and teaching

Byon, A. (2004). Understanding the reading process of beginning American KFL learners. *Journal of Korean Language Education, 15*(1), 259–280.

Through the Think-Aloud Protocols, the researcher found that beginning-level learners tended to adopt a bottom-up approach rather than a top-down approach in a reading task. The learners mostly relied on text-driven strategies through which they focused on interpreting word- and sentence-level meanings, although some learners utilized reader-driven strategies, such as recognizing features that hinder comprehension. The researcher argues for the pedagogical efficacy of the Think-Aloud Protocols based on their pedagogical value in helping learners acquire sociocultural and contextual knowledge required for the macro comprehension of the given text.

Choi, J. (2015). A heritage language learner's literacy practices in a Korean language course in a U.S. university: From a multiliteracies perspective. *Journal of Language and Literacy Education, 11*(2), 116–133. ·

This study demonstrates that adopting a framework of multiliteracies in an advanced heritage Korean class helped the learner acquire increased motivation and agency (e.g., selecting texts of her own interests and engaging in voluntary reading and writing). More importantly, multiliteracies practices incorporating multimodality helped the learner develop a biliteracy identity as a Korean-American speaker of Korean. According to the researcher, a particularly noteworthy finding was the learner's "transformation" by gaining a "new literate identity" (p. 126).

Gatti, A., & O'Neill, T. (2017). Who are heritage writers? Language experiences and writing proficiency. *Foreign Language Annals, 50*(4), 734–753.

This larger-scale study examines correlations between heritage Mandarin Chinese, Spanish, and Korean learners' scores on a Writing Proficiency Test (WPT) and their biographical factors. Factors that were positively related with proficiency level include age of arrival and the number of years of schooling in the target language country. When HLLs enroll in an upper-level course, they typically aspire to develop literacy skills required in various academic and professional contexts. The researchers, therefore, argue for the usefulness of a proficiency-based approach to teaching writing to HLLs to help them develop functional abilities at an advanced level and beyond.

Kang, Y.-S., & Pyun, D. (2013). Mediation strategies in L2 writing processes: A case study of two Korean language learners. *Language, Culture and Curriculum, 26*(1), 52–67.

This study addressed a paradigm shift from a product-oriented to a process-oriented approach in writing in foreign language education. The researchers examined "mediation" strategies used by two advanced learners enrolled in a fourth-year Korean class at a US university. Through semi-structured and informal interviews, Think-Aloud sessions, and Stimulated Recall sessions with the learners, the researchers found that the learners used various types of mediation strategies while composing: computer-mediated strategies (e.g., online dictionaries), community-mediated strategies (e.g., instant messenger), L2-mediated strategies (e.g., thinking in the target language), and self-mediated monitoring strategies (e.g., private speech). The researchers conclude that teachers should view writing as a dynamic socio-cognitive process and encourage learners to make use of available resources appropriate to their cultural and historical experiences.

Kim, C., & Pyun, D. (2014). Heritage language literacy maintenance: A study of Korean-American heritage learners. *Language, Culture and Curriculum, 27*(3), 294–315.

Literacy maintenance of HLL is one of the most pursued inquiries in the fields of foreign language education and bilingualism. This study set out to investigate factors affecting HL literacy competence. The researchers examined compositions of 56 HLLs of Korean in grades 4–12 and in undergraduate studies. Statistical analyses reveal that the overall frequency of Korean use and types of literacy practices are most significantly correlated with writing scores. The researchers conclude that "purposeful and focused" literacy practice "beyond daily verbal communication" is crucial to maintain and develop heritage literacy.

Kim, H.-Y. (2016). Socially engaged writing in the KFL class: A post-product, post-process approach. *Language Facts and Perspectives, 37,* 119–148.

This study is a valuable addition to the existing body of research on KFL literacy in that it addresses the recently emerging view of literacy as a social action, through which learners develop not only grammar and vocabulary, but critical thinking skills, meaningful self-presentation, and a sense of community. Kim examined third-year KFL students' development of writing skills over two semesters within the person/context approach to writing. The overall objective of the study is to explore whether content-based writing tasks are indeed beneficial for developing literacy. The participants were asked to write five to six commentaries in each semester after viewing movies on Korean culture, such as the cultural history of Korean food and South Korea's educational system. The students also posted their comments on their classmates' commentaries on the course website. Their film commentaries were analyzed utilizing T-Unit Length, T-Unit complexity ratio, and Word Variation–2, in order to investigate the participants' development of writing skills in fluency, grammatical complexity, and lexical diversity, respectively. Results show growth to some degree in all three areas by all but one participant.

Ko, K. (2011). Grammar versus content: KFL/ESL teachers' trends in feedback on college student writing. *KLA, 16,* 41–72.

This study compares ESL and KFL teachers' feedback on writing and finds a significant difference between the two groups of teachers. While ESL teachers focused on providing feedback on the global content in earlier drafts, KFL teachers focused on sentence-level local issues in all drafts. The researcher interprets the results as discrepancies in the professional training and teaching strategies of ESL and KFL teachers. For example, unlike the ESL teachers, most of the KFL teachers in the study taught a beginning-level class and employed a single-draft approach. In addition, the KFL teachers were less concerned with plagiarism and genre-appropriate styles. In the researcher's view, KFL teachers need to be informed of process-oriented approaches to teaching literacy.

Kwak, J., & Kim, J. (2007). Korean heritage learners' self-assessment of writing activities in the student workbook. *Journal of Korean Language Education, 18*(2), 1–19.

This study explores learners' evaluation of writing activities in the workbooks accompanying their required textbooks, *Integrated Korean I* and *II.* Sixty-five HLLs of Korean, who were enrolled in first-year Korean courses, participated in the study. Survey results show that learners viewed grammar-oriented writing activities (e.g., rewriting sentences with different sentence endings) as most useful. They also found context-dependent activities to be useful for vocabulary learning (e.g., answer the question based on one's real life). Interestingly, learners found writing activities given after reading a passage to be the least useful ones. The researchers suggest that teachers carefully balance grammar and vocabulary exercises and design reading activities that are connected to writing, in order to facilitate novice-level learners' literacy skills.

Pyun, D., & Lee-Smith, A. (2011). Reducing Korean heritage language learners' orthographic errors: The contribution of online and in-class dictation and form-focused instruction. *Language, Culture and Curriculum, 24*(2), 141–158.

As anachronistic as it may sound, this study grants orthographic accuracy a priority in literacy education for heritage learners. According to the researchers, in-class dictation and form-focused activities were effective in improving heritage learners' accuracy, as HLLs have mostly been exposed to spoken language prior to their formal learning of Korean. Their argument was based on the learners' improved scores on dictation tests (from the pre- to the post-test) and responses to an open-ended questionnaire. Most learners felt that these activities helped them improve their spelling and that they gained a sense of achievement.

Shin, S.-C., & Joo, A. (2015). Lexical errors in Korean-Australian heritage learners' compositions. *Journal of Korean Language Education, 26,* 129–162.

This study examines errors in vocabulary made by 69 Korean-Australian learners of Korean in grades 7–12. The researchers identify six types of lexical errors upon analyzing their compositions: simplification and redundancy, code-switching, semantic similarity (e.g., 애견동물for 애완동물 'pet'), idiomatic collocation, nonconventional register, and literal translation. Overall, errors with simplification and redundancy were the most frequent type of errors, followed by code-switching. The least frequent type of error was literal translation. It is unclear how these findings lead to better understanding heritage literacy development. However, the researchers argue that learners seemed to rely heavily on their previous language exposure at home (mostly spoken), which is limited to the personal domain.

Yi, Y. (2008). Voluntary writing in the heritage language: A study of biliterate Korean-heritage adolescents in the U.S. *Heritage Language Journal, 6*(2), 224–245.

The researcher explores the literacy practices of two adolescent learners of Korean through weekly interviews, face-to-face and online conversations, field notes, and the learners' autobiographies and writing samples. The analytic focus was placed on the learners' voluntary writing in Korean in their daily life. For both learners, a majority of their Korean writing consisted of instant messaging and online chatting. Online community and SNS postings also held a major place of their literacy practice. Given that the study was conducted more than a decade ago, these results underscore the need to incorporate digital modes of communication to help younger learners develop literacy skills and function effectively in today's globalized and digitalized world.

Bae, J. (1995). Preliminary results of the Korean literacy development of students in the Korean/English Two-Way Immersion Program (KETWIP). *KLA, 1*, 181–195.

Byon, A. (2004). Understanding the reading process of beginning American KFL learners. *Journal of Korean Language Education, 15*(1), 259–280.

Byon, A. (2005). Chapter 2.

Carreira, M., & Kagan, O. (2011). The results of the national heritage language survey: Implications for teaching, curriculum design, and professional development. *Foreign Language Annals, 44*(1), 40–64.

Choe, H., & Park, Y. (2004). Chapter 5.

Choi, J., & Yi, Y. (2012). Chapter 4.

Gatti, A., & O'Neill, T. (2017). Chapter 5.

Jeon, M. (2007). Chapter 5.

Kang, Y.-S., & Pyun, D. (2013). Mediation strategies in L2 writing processes: A case study of two Korean language learners. *Language, Culture and Curriculum, 26*(1), 52–67.

Kim, C., & Pyun, D. (2014). Chapter 5.

Kim, H.-Y. (2016). Socially engaged writing in the KFL class: A post-product, post-process approach. *Language Facts and Perspectives, 37*, 119–148.

Kwak, J., & Kim, J. (2007). Chapter 5.

Lee, J. (2011). Chapter 1.

Lee, S. (2002). Chapter 2.

Lee, S., & Mcvannel, M. (1999). Chapter 2.

Pae, H., & Seveik, R. (2016). Chapter 6.

Pak, H. (2005). Chapter 5.

Park, C. (2007). Chapter 5.

Park, E. (2008). Chapter 4.

Park, E.S., Song, S., & Shin, Y. (2016). To what extent do learners benefit from indirect written corrective feedback? A study targeting learners of different proficiency and heritage language status. *Language Teaching Research, 20*(6), 678–699.

Ro, Y., & Cheatham, G.A. (2009). Chapter 5.

Shin, S.-C. (2007). Types and patterns of English L1 students' misspellings in Korean. *Journal of Korean Language Education, 18*(3), 99–122.

Shin, S.-C., & Joo, A. (2015). Chapter 5.

Strauss, S. (1999). Using television commercials as aids for teaching language, grammar, and culture. *KLA, 3*, 235–252.

Yi, Y. (2008). Chapter 5.

You, S.-H. (1997). Chapter 5.

You, S.-H. (1999). Incorporating the internet resources into various levels of KFL classes. *KLA, 3*, 267–280.

Annotated bibliography for Chapter 7 Korean language assessment

Kim, Y. (2004). What has language proficiency got to do with accommodation in interviewer-interviewee interaction?: The case of Korean oral proficiency interview discourse. *Bilingual Research, 25*, 41–62.

This study takes a qualitative and microanalytic approach to analyze a native speaker interviewer's accommodation toward a non-native speaker interviewee's breakdown. Although the types of accommodation were limited compared to previous literature, the interviewer should differentiate in their use of accommodations depending on the interviewee's proficiency level: clarification request for high-proficiency interviewees, and grammatical and lexical simplification and question reformulation for lower-level.

Lee, Y. (2000). Designing a Korean language placement test. *KLA, 4*, 181–210.

This is the first article from a series of research studies on the developmental process of a web-based placement test. Lee identifies the purpose of test development and structures the test in this paper. Although the project itself was launched in the late 1990s, this study still provides practical information, as it deals with detailed information regarding item specifications, pretesting, item analysis, and selection process.

Lee, Y. G., Yuen, S., Kim, H., Ahn, C. S., Yoon, S., Baek, S. B., & Park, S. (2002). Guidelines for item-writing for the curriculum-based placement test: Development and application. *KLA, 7*, 247–260

The researchers explore the process of a web-based placement test development at a large state university. They suggest two extended sets of guidelines, one each for lower level and for advanced level, which may be used to write test items. The item writing process using this guideline is also described in detail.

Shin, S.-Y. (2016). Investigating the validity of KFL text difficulty as defined by the ILR reading scales. *Journal of Less Commonly Taught Languages, 18,* 159–174.

The study suggests that Korean text difficulty could be better evaluated using multiple indicators, rather than solely relying on the Interagency Language Roundtable (ILR) text difficulty hierarchy. Shin finds that neither KFL teachers nor test-takers perceive text difficulty as the same as the ILR scale. ILR emphasizes text type, while content and/or individual linguistic features seem to be more important to KFL teachers and test takers. The analysis also shows that the ILR text type and the actual test-takers' performance had no correlation. Shin also points out that text difficulty should be determined in the interaction with the readers.

Ahn, C. (2003). Three measures of interlanguage pragmatics in KFL learners. *KLA, 8,* 165–180.

Cho, S. (2004). Oral proficiency interview: Pros and cons. *KLA, 9,* 144–151.

Cho, Y.-M., & Chun, H. (2015). Integrating assessment in a college-level Korean heritage curriculum in the United States. *Bilingual Research, 61,* 163–189.

Choi, I. (2000). Revisited reliability on speaking portion of unit test at DLI: Rater reliability. *KLA, 5,* 225–229.

Fouser, R. (2010). Chapter 2.

Gatti, A., & O'Neill, T. (2017). Chapter 5.

Kang, H.-S., & Kim, I.-S. (2012). Chapter 5.

Kang, S., & Kim, M. (2000). Assessing levels of proficiency in Korean. *KLA, 4,* 211–222.

Kang, S., & Lim, B.-J. (2011). Chapter 2.

Kim, H. (2016). Comparing native and non-native rater assessments of Korean oral proficiency: A FACETS analysis. *Korean Language Education Research, 51*(5), 83–113.

Kim, M. (2000). Chapter 1.

Kim, Y., Tracy-Ventura, N., & Jung, Y. (2016). Chapter 1.

Kwak, J., & Kim, J. (2007). Chapter 5.

Kwon, Y., & Choi, J. (2017). Chapter 2.

Lee, D., Lee, Y., & Park, S. (2002). Web-based Korean language placement tests. *KLA, 7,* 261–273.

Lee, J. (2016). Research on Korean language placement test development: Based on selected English language placement tools. *Journal of Korean Language Education, 27,* 99–131.

Lee-Ellis, S. (2009). The development and validation of a Korean C-test using Rasch analysis. *Language Testing, 26*(2), 245–274.

Park, S. (2001). Exploring the possibilities of WBLT for operational testing purposes: Web-based Korean as a foreign language test. *KLA, 6,* 101–110.

Shin, S. (2014). Students' perceptions of assessment, feedback and categories. *Journal of Korean Language Education, 25*(4), 51–55.

Sohn, S.-O., & Shin, S. (2007). True beginners, false beginners, and fake beginners: Placement strategies for Korean heritage speakers. *Foreign Language Annals, 40*(3), 407–418.

Annotated bibliography for Chapter 8 KFL program building and professional development

Cho, H. (2014). "It's very complicated" exploring heritage language identity with heritage language teachers in a teacher preparation program. *Language and Education, 28*(2), 181–195.

Heritage language (HL) teachers are seldom discussed in HL education and teacher education, even when HL education focuses mainly on such issues as identity and literacy development. Cho examines HL teacher education practices and describes pre-service teachers' work in community-based HL schools. Research data were collected from five undergraduate students who participated in the *Careers in Language Education and Academic Renewal* (CLEAR) program in Hawaii over three semesters. Results indicate how a teacher preparation program enabled HL teachers to become more aware of the dynamic nature of HL teacher identity and changed their views of HL identity over time. This article calls for the reconceptualization of HL identity and offers several suggestions for diversity in HL teacher education.

Cho, Y.-M., Kang, S., Lee, H. S., Wang, H.-S., Kim, H.-Y., Kim, H.-S., & Suh, J. (2015). Overview. *KLA, 19*(2), 153–177.

Elaborating on the 5 Cs (Communication, Cultures, Connections, Comparisons, and Communities) in *Standards for Learning Korean* (2012), Cho et al. provide a comprehensive Standards-Based College Curriculum for Korean Language Education. Learning objectives and teaching materials for levels 1 through 6 as well as heritage level provide Korean language educators with a useful reference guideline for future curriculum design and assessment in the university setting.

Choi, E. (2016). The current status of Korean language education in the United States: Class offerings in K–16 schools and Korean community schools. *KLA, 20*(1), 29–52.

By analyzing the current Korean language course offerings in K–16 schools, Choi explores recent trends and changes in the field of Korean language education. Results show that the concentration of Korean enrollments in the Pacific and Northeast regions is mitigated with increased learning opportunities and accessibility to KFL courses in the other regions between 2006, 2010, and 2015. It is noteworthy that, along with Korean programs in regular schools, Korean community schools continue to fulfill their supplementary role by providing sustained learning. For more systematic KFL research and planning in the future, collaboration between the local communities and public school programs is suggested for standardized data collection on Korean course offerings.

Ee, J. (2018). Exploring Korean dual language immersion programs in the United States: Parents' reasons for enrolling their children. *International Journal of Bilingual Education and Bilingualism, 21*(6), 690–709.

With the expansion of dual language programs, Korean dual language immersion (KDLI) programs have been established among Korean American communities in the greater Los Angeles area since the early 1990s. Ee presents the various factors affecting parents' decisions to enroll their children in a KDLI program. Survey and interview data were collected from more than 450 parents in seven elementary-level KDLI programs in California. It was found that both Korean and non-Korean parents chose a KDLI program for bilingual abilities, better academic success, and enhanced integration abilities. However, differences between participant groups were identified: the primary attraction of a particular school to Korean parents was its offering of a KDLI program, while a school's diverse student body and safe neighborhood were major factors motivating non-Korean participants.

Kim, H.-S., & Lee, H.-S. (2010). Enhancing sociolinguistic competency through Korean on-line TV: Advanced level KFL curriculum. *KLA, 15,* 23–45.

This study focuses on an advanced-level KFL curriculum incorporating sociolinguistic and pragmatic elements. Kim et al. point out that pragmatic and sociolinguistic aspects (e.g., speech level, gender, and dialects) have rarely been explicitly incorporated in the KFL curriculum due to the focus on grammar and communication. An advanced-level content-based course was designed and introduced where online TV shows of various genres and readings on Korean sociolinguistics were utilized to enhance sociolinguistic competency. KFL learners' responses from questionnaires and interviews suggest that explicit sociolinguistic instruction should be provided to enhance their sociolinguistic competency.

Kim, S., & Sohn, S.-O. (2016). Service-learning, an integral part of heritage language education: A case study of an advanced-level Korean language class. *Heritage Language Journal, 13*(3), 354–381.

This study demonstrates how HLLs develop an increased awareness of sociocultural aspects of language use and academic-professional proficiency through service-learning in local communities (e.g., a Korean cultural center and a cardiology hospital). The researchers argue that engaging learners in civic service within the curriculum also enables the implementation of the 5 Cs, especially the fifth C, Communities, in meaningful ways. The learners also had an opportunity to reconnect with their heritage identity.

Ryu, J. (2015). The basic research to build virtual Korean language schools. *Journal of Korean Language Education, 26*(1), 89–115.

Ryu covers various topics in e-learning and focuses on the government supporting online Korean language education abroad since e-learning was first adopted into foreign language education. This paper points out several major problems, such as lack of budget and inter-organizational collaboration for overseas Korean online education. Ryu also envisions the possibility of an online education system for overseas Koreans and proposes virtual Korean language schools based on blended learning.

Wang, H.-S. (2014). Korean language teachers in higher education in North America: Profile, status, and more. *Journal of Less Commonly Taught Languages*, *16*, 147–187.

Although there has been considerable progress in KFL, little attention has been paid to Korean language teachers. Wang has been investigating Korean language teacher profiles, instructional duties, and job satisfaction over the years and assessed the current status of KFL educators. Data based on the survey questionnaires on personal profile, workload, salary, and others were analyzed. Results show that Korean language teachers seem satisfied with their job overall: more satisfied in their main instructional duties, but less so in non-instructional duties (e.g., workload, salary, etc.). Based on the findings, Wang proposes to investigate other teacher-related issues in the broad context of Korean language teaching.

Bae, J. (1995). Chapter 6.

Bae, J. (2006a). Chapter 5.

Bae, J. (2006b). Chapter 5.

Bale, J. (2010). Chapter 5.

Bey, C., & Stanchfield, G. (1997). Teacher training for college level: Proficiency-oriented instruction. *KLA*, *2*, 3–14.

Blank, L., & Blank, L. (1995). The high school Korean language curriculum guide. *KLA*, *1*, 13–17.

Boylan, P., & Kang, S. (1995). Syllabus design for the less commonly taught languages (Korean). *KLA*, *1*, 3–11.

Byon, A. (2001). Developing a business Korean course based on a systematic approach. *KLA*, *6*, 153–172.

Byon, A. (2002). A proposed syllabus for Korean 600 "Introduction to KFL pedagogy." *KLA*, *7*, 89–105.

Byon, A. (2008). Korean as a foreign language in the USA: The instructional settings. *Language, Culture and Curriculum*, *21*(3), 244–255.

Cheon, S. (2017). The design, implementation and evaluation of Korean K-12 teacher training workshops. *Journal of Less Commonly Taught Languages*, *21*, 145–165.

Cho, S. (2000). Teaching Korean in the US: Methodology, and institutional concerns. *KLA*, *4*, 77–93.

Cho, Y.-M. (2015). Introduction. *KLA*, *19*(2), 149–152.

Cho, Y.-M., & Chun, H. (2015). Chapter 7.

Cho, Y.-M., Kim, H.-Y., & Park, M.-J. (2015). Curriculum/curricular framework. *KLA*, *19*(2), 178–380.

Choi, A. (2001). Chapter 4.

Choi, H.-K. (2002). Chapter 3.

Chun, H., & Cho, Y.-M. (2018). Building a locally relevant curriculum for Korean language teachers. *KLA*, *22*(1), 46–26.

Chung, I., & Peterson, M. (2006). Korean as a world language. *KLA*, *11*, 1–16.

Crookes, G. (2012). Program theory and the University of Hawai'i Korean language flagship programs. *KLA*, *17*, 63–76.

Damron, J. (2009). An analysis of student evaluations of native and non-native Korean foreign language teachers. *Journal of Less Commonly Taught Languages*, *7*, 73–92.

Ee, J. (2017a). Two dimensions of parental involvement: What affects parental involvement in dual language immersion? *Bilingual Research Journal*, *6*(2), 173–178.

Ee, J. (2017b). Understanding parents' expectations and concerns for a dual-language program through the lens of community cultural wealth. *KLA*, *21*(2), 218–249.

Evon, G. (2000). The value of the Korean humanities in the American academic context. *KLA*, *5*, 191–197.

Fouser, R. J. (1997). Toward a new paradigm in Korean language teaching. *Journal of Korean Language Education*, *8*, 295–311.

Glisan, E., Swender, E., & Surface, E. (2013). Oral proficiency standards and foreign language teacher candidates: Current findings and future research directions. *Foreign Language Annals*, *46*(2), 264–289.

Ha, J. (2001). Chapter 1.

Jamieson, C. (1995). Start-up Korean. *KLA*, *1*, 93–104.

Jeong, H.-J. (2012). Needs analysis of Korean language programs. *KLA*, *17*, 49–62.

Jung, J.-H. (1997). Chapter 2.

Kang, S. (2012). Curricular design for content-based advanced north Korean dialect materials: Pedagogical principles and practical issues. *KLA*, *17*, 79–92.

Kang, S., & Lim, B.-J. (2011). Chapter 2.

Kim, C. (1999). Considerations on curriculum and teaching methodology for intermediate business Korean. *KLA*, *3*, 283–295.

Kim, C. (2015). A study on the level of mastery of advanced Korean language curricula in Korean language institutions. *Journal of Korean Language Education*, *26*, 163–187.

Kim, G.-S. (2000). Implementing cultural content in advanced Korean course. *KLA*, *5*, 117–121.

Kim, H.-Y. (2003). Heritage students' perspectives on language classes. *KLA*, *8*, 315–326.

Kim, K. K.-O. (2000). Chapter 4.

Kim, S. (2004). "Representing" Korea in the American University. *KLA*, *9*, 33–69.

Kim, S. (2017). A survey on postsecondary Korean language programs in the United States. *Journal of Less Commonly Taught Languages*, *21*, 99–126.

Kim, Y.-H. (1997). Chapter 4.

Koo, E.-H. (2000). Teaching the Korean language with music and songs: Theory and practice. *KLA*, *5*, 123–131.

Kwon, H. (1999). Overview of the Korean native language arts program for bilingual Korean students in New York City public high schools. *KLA*, *3*, 319–327.

Kwon, H. (2003). Standards based Korean language instruction in New York City public high Schools. *KLA*, *8*, 337–344.

Lee, C.-B. (2000). Chapter 5.

Lee, D.-E., & Lee, D.-E. (2008). A needs analysis for the articulation of the domestic and overseas Korean programs for American students. *Bilingual Research*, *38*, 341–367.

Lee, D.-J. (1996). Korean language education past and future. *Bilingual Research*, *7*, 69–103.

Lee, E. (2000). Korean language education in secondary schools. *KLA*, *5*, 25–28.

Lee, J., & Jeong, E. (2013). Korean-English dual language immersion: Perspectives of students, parents and teachers. *Language, Culture and Curriculum, 26*(1), 89–107.

Lee, S. (2000). A critical analysis of issues in secondary Korean education: A comparative study--1997 and 2000. *KLA, 5,* 29–40.

Lee, S. (2007). Language policy in a Korean-English two-way immersion setting. *Language, Culture and Curriculum, 20*(2), 109–125.

Lee, Y., Yuen, S., Kim, H., Ahn, C., Yoon, S., Baek, S., & Park, S. (2002). Guidelines for item-writing for the curriculum-based placement test: Development and application. *KLA, 7,* 247–260.

Lee, Y.-G. (2000). Chapter 2.

Lee, Y.-G., & Kim, Y. (2000). Needs assessment, goals and objective setting, and materials development for third- and fourth-level Korean courses at the University of Hawaii at Manoa: A systematic approach to program development. *KLA, 4,* 13–49.

Lim, B.-J. (2002). The use of the internet resources to teach business Korean. *KLA, 7,* 79–87.

Merril, C. (2000). Articulation K-8 (elementary and middle school): The Korean English dual language program. *KLA, 5,* 17–24.

Merrill, C. (2002). The future of Korean language education in the United States. *Teaching Korean as a Foreign Language, 27,* 301–340.

Noji, F., & Yuen, S.-A. (2012). Chapter 5.

Park, C. (1997). Issues and approaches in teaching the Korean performance tradition in the context of East Asian Studies. *KLA, 2,* 205–215.

Park, S., Lee, J., Kim, H., Joo, H., & Lee, D. (2003). Chapter 5.

Ra, C. (2017). Chapter 4.

Rhee, Y. (1995). Managing foreign language program in the department: DLI's case. *KLA, 1,* 37–40.

Roh, J. (2016). Chapter 2.

Sasse, W. (1996). Teaching Korean culture through Korean studies. *Bilingual Research, 7,* 331–360.

Shin, H. (2015). Chapter 5.

Shin, H., Haley, M., & Eqab, S. (2016). An examination of Korean heritage school teachers' perceptions on teaching and learning after an intensive summer professional development program. *Journal of Korean Language Education, 27*(1), 203–220.

Shin, H., & Wong, S. (2017). Formation of Korean heritage school teachers' transnational identity. *Journal of Less Commonly Taught Languages, 21,* 128–144.

Shin, S., & Kim, S. (2000). The Introduction of content-based language teaching to college-level Korean program for heritage learners. *KLA, 5,* 167–179.

Shin, S.-C. (2010). Strategic direction and tasks for the global expansion of Korean language education. *Journal of International Network for Korean Language and Culture, 7*(2), 93–119.

Shin, S.-C. (2011). Exploring the linkage between Korean language and Korean studies education: An Australian experience. *Teaching Korean as a Foreign Language, 36,* 113–137.

Shin, S.-C. (2012). Linking Australian secondary schools with tertiary language programs. *Teaching Korean as a Foreign Language, 37,* 195–222.

Shin, S.-C. (2016). Korean language education in Australian schools and universities: Current state, issues and challenges. *Journal of Korean Language Education, 27*(4), 57–102.

Shin, S.-C., & Baik, G. (2002). Learning to teach needs analysis for a KFL teacher training program. *Journal of Korean Language Education, 27,* 169–203.

Silva, D. (2007). Issues in Korean language teaching in the United States: Recent facts and figures. *KLA, 12,* 106–125.

Sim, S. (2018). An analysis of research trends in KFL education for overseas Koreans. *Korean Language Education Research, 53*(5), 139–157.

Sohn, H.-M. (2000). Curricular goals and content standards for K-16 Korean language learning. *KLA, 5,* 3–16.

Sohn, H.-M. (2012). Korean flagship: A new frontier for advanced language study. *KLA, 17,* 3–17.

Sohn, J. (1997). The foreign language teaching program. *Journal of Korean Language Education, 8,* 313–324.

Sohn, S.-O. (1995). Chapter 5.

Sohn, S.-O. (1997). Chapter 5.

Spagnoli, C. (1999). Chapter 4.

Stromberg, C. (1997). Breaking the mold: A non-heritage learner's experience in a multi-level Korean class. *KLA, 2,* 159–165.

Sung, K.-S. (1995). Some problems of Korean language education abroad. *Bilingual Research, 12*(1), 291–323.

Wang, H.-S. (2012). A proposal for advanced level Korean Curriculum. *KLA, 17,* 109–127.

Yeon, J. (1996). Chapter 2.

You, C. (2001). Chapter 5.

Yow, B. (2001). Korean language education in New York City Public Schools. *KLA, 6,* 215–221.

Index

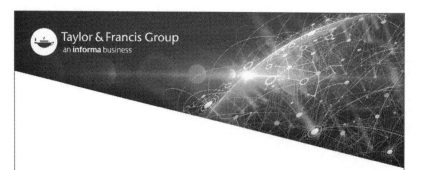

Made in the USA
Las Vegas, NV
26 January 2021